CAPITAL AND THE INTERNATIONAL

On the Dialectic of Value and Sovereignty

Andrew Davenport

BRISTOL
UNIVERSITY
PRESS

First published in Great Britain in 2026 by

Bristol University Press
University of Bristol
1-9 Old Park Hill
Bristol
BS2 8BB
UK
t: +44 (0)117 374 6645
e: bup-info@bristol.ac.uk

Details of international sales and distribution partners are available at bristoluniversitypress.co.uk

DOI: 10.51952/9781529259681

British Library Cataloguing in Publication Data
A catalogue record for this book is available from the British Library

ISBN 978-1-5292-5966-7 hardcover
ISBN 978-1-5292-5967-4 ePub
ISBN 978-1-5292-5968-1 ePDF

Cover design: Newgen
Front cover image: Unsplash/Steve Johnson
Bristol University Press uses environmentally responsible print partners.
Printed and bound in Great Britain by CPI Group (UK) Ltd, Croydon, CR0 4YY

FSC
www.fsc.org
MIX
Paper | Supporting responsible forestry
FSC® C013604

Bristol University Press' authorised representative in the European Union is:
Easy Access System Europe, Mustamäe tee 50, 10621 Tallinn, Estonia,
Email: gpsr.requests@easproject.com

To Laura,
in love and thanks

Contents

Acknowledgements

This book has been a long time in the making. During that time, however, it has been my great good fortune to have been a member of a department that continues to value, and so to provide space for, the kind of large-scale theoretical work that requires prolonged and patient immersion in difficult ideas. Accordingly, I would like to thank the Department of International Politics at Aberystwyth for affording me both the opportunity and the time to bring this book to completion. In particular, I would like to thank my friend, and colleague at Aberystwyth, Mustapha Pasha for his unstinting enthusiasm for the project right from the beginning. I would also like to thank Ellen Pearce and the team at Bristol University Press for their swift and professional shepherding of the book through the publication process. Above all, though, I am deeply grateful to my partner, Laura Considine, who lived, or endured, this book through all the long years, and whose love and support saw me through the most difficult times. The book is dedicated to her.

Introduction

In the 21st century, there is, for the first time in history, both a single global economic space, the capitalist world market, and a single global political space, the international states-system. Together, these two structures encircle the world, with nowhere permitted to remain outside and unintegrated. Just as the states that make up the international space have laid claim to every part of the territorial surface of the earth, so existence within them is to an ever increasing extent mediated by the market. Capital and the international thus constitute the two basic forms of life in the globalised world. It follows that if the modern world-system is to be comprehended as a whole, then the central question for theory is: *why* do these two structures exist together, in and through each other, encompassing the entire world? Or, to state the problem more fully, what is the *logical* connection between the fragmented and anarchic international states-system and the tendentially universalising capitalist world economy? Remarkably, however, this question, which is fundamental to the comprehension of the modern world-system, has received, as yet, no answer. Still more remarkably, in fact, it has hardly even been recognised as a question to be asked in the first place. What this striking absence signifies is that the point of intersection of the world market and the states-system, the dividing line where they both come together and are separated from each other, does not present itself straightforwardly as an object to theory but is instead hidden from it, forming a seemingly inconceivable limit. The logical relation between capital and the international marks a horizon of the modern world, therefore, that theory has been unable to reach and within which it remains enclosed.[1]

At one level, that this most basic of all theoretical questions about the modern world-system continues to be not merely unanswered but unasked is a consequence of the fragmentation of knowledge across different academic disciplines. Within this overall structure of division and totality,

1 In this sense, capital and the international should be understood together as, in Adorno's terms, two 'torn halves of an integral freedom, to which, however, they do not add up' (Adorno and Benjamin 1999, p 130).

the study of political life is split between Politics (or Political Science), for politics within borders, and International Relations (IR), for politics across borders. Correspondingly, the study of economic life is given over to the discipline of Economics and its multifarious subfields. As positive sciences, these disciplines take their object domains to be given, accepting them as already constituted fields of knowledge that have been bounded and separated off from each other. Once they are apprehended on this basis, however, the relation between these domains can then only be conceived in terms of their external interactions. It was in accordance with exactly this conception that International Political Economy (IPE) was established in the early 1970s as a subdiscipline to bridge the gap between IR and Economics. Assuming international politics and global economics to be intrinsically separate and distinct spheres, the basic interest of IPE has then always been in the essentially functional question of *how* these two spheres reciprocally influence and affect each other.[2] While IPE is centrally concerned with what happens at the boundary between IR and Economics, therefore, the borderline itself remains its unthought presupposition. Consequently, although the question of *why* capital and the international exist together, their logical connection, underlies the entire discourse of IPE, as its determining ground, it cannot be articulated within it.[3] Still less can it arise within IR and Economics, for each of whom the other can only appear as foreign territory, over the disciplinary boundary line. In this way, the structure of modern thought silences and renders unthinkable the borderlines that divide up the total space of knowledge into a multiplicity of discrete subject areas. Indeed, it is essential to the coherence of the modern scientific conception of knowledge that the boundaries through which it is constituted should remain unknown to it.

More deeply, however, this fragmentation of knowledge is itself a manifestation, or reflection, of the fragmentation of being in modernity. In the experiential structure of the modern subject, existence itself is divided into a series of bounded spheres, each of which is at once separate from all the others and also, somehow, interrelated with them, so that together they form a whole. Unlike in the pre-modern world, the parts of this whole are not ordered hierarchically: none of them stands above the others, entitled to rule, and none of them stands below, to be ruled. Rather, they are all equivalent to one another, at once both different and the same. Within this

[2] Or 'the interrelationship between public and private power in the allocation of scarce resources', as the leading textbook in IPE puts it (Ravenhill 2020, p 18). Correlative to its inherently functional orientation, because IPE is completely internal to the world of capital and the international, it can only address quantitative and distributional issues.

[3] In IPE, that is, capital and the international are brought together only externally, through a composite third term, rather than being mediated *in each other*.

structure, all of the parts are dependent upon the whole – they *are* only as parts of the whole – but the whole itself is nothing more than the being-together of the parts, their unity-in-separation. Or, put differently, none of the parts is equal to the whole – they are all limited and, precisely, *partial* – but the whole, in turn, has no being of its own beyond, or in addition to, the parts. The parts are thus immanent to the whole and the whole is immanent to the parts. This logic of division and totality, the simultaneous integration and disintegration of being, is what Giorgio Agamben has termed the *anarchy* of the modern world, its ungroundedness and lack of any final foundation.[4] When it is situated within this metaphysical context of the totalisation of being through its fragmentation, the relation between the economic space of the world market and the political space of the states-system ceases to be a functional question and becomes, instead, a metaphysical one. It is concerned not with how capital and the international work but, much more profoundly, with what they *are*.

If the problem of capital and the international is properly metaphysical, then it requires to be addressed in the fundamental terms of the being of the economic and the political, their constitution as such. Accordingly, the question of *why* the capitalist world market and the international states-system exist together, demands, in the first place, a change in the basic register of enquiry. Hitherto, studies of the modern world-system have been overwhelming cast in historicist and sociological terms. Such studies have typically sought to trace the historical formation of the modern states-system, on the hand, and the global economy, on the other, assigning causal efficacy in this dual process to whatever sociological factors they happen to give priority to. No matter what their other merits may be, however, these historical-sociological accounts are incapable of grasping the modern world-system as a whole. This is because, precisely in their commitment to history and sociology, as particular disciplines of modern knowledge, they are wholly internal to, and so entirely constrained by, the logic of division and totality. Consequently, they must assume politics and economics to be two given and inherently separate spheres that are related to each other only externally. The logic of the whole – the point where capital and the international come together – thus necessarily exceeds their scope. Instead, that logic can only be comprehended in the register of philosophical thought. For it is the very idea of philosophy to be, in contrast to the specialised sciences, a 'non-particularized pursuit'.[5] As Adorno put it: 'Philosophy seeks to think the unconditioned, to transcend positivity and the accepted existence of sciences – arbitrarily dedicated to separate objects, and which starkly isolate

4 Agamben 2019a.
5 Adorno 2005c.

matter and method – and to contrast the scientific domain with the unfettered truth.'[6] It is exactly the whole, or the unconditioned, therefore, that is the proper object of philosophical thought. More specifically, it is the exclusive object of philosophical thought in what was traditionally considered to be its highest and most exalted form, as speculative metaphysics.

When it is conceived in metaphysical terms, the logical relation between the world market and the states-system ultimately resolves itself into the logical relation between *value* and *sovereignty*. These are the foundational concepts of the economic and the political, respectively. As such, they sit at the centre of the economic and political problematics – that is, the basic theoretical scenarios of economic and political thought – which are constructed around them.[7] Value and sovereignty are thus both borderline concepts, through which economic and political space are constituted in the first place. Together, they mediate inside and outside, the economic and the non-economic, the political and the non-political. It is at the level of these two foundational concepts, therefore, that the existence of the economic and the political is to be, as it were, suspended so that their very being may be placed into question.

It follows that in order to grasp the conceptual relation between value and sovereignty, it is necessary to break open the economic and political problematics and to lay out their essential structural logics. Neither Economics nor IR, though, has ever been able to conceive of an enquiry of this sort. For its part, economic thought always presupposes the validity of its own problematic. Indeed, as the argument of the book will show, economic thought *must* presuppose this validity simply in order to be what it is – if it were able to bring its own problematic into question, it would immediately negate itself as, precisely, *economic* thought. The plausibility of the economic idea as such – that is, of the economic conception of existence – depends upon the economic problematic itself being accepted as an irreducible given and its structural logic remaining unexamined. Furthermore, because it is always already enclosed within its own constituted space, economic thought is necessarily incapable of thinking itself. It is thus unable to construct a coherent theory of value, as the concept that constitutes the economic in the first place. More precisely, the basic illogicality of economic thought is that if it is value that actually brings the economic as such into existence, then value cannot itself be accounted for on the assumption of the validity of the economic. The a priori self-enclosure of economic thought means

---

6 Adorno 1982, p 41.

7 For this reason, there can be no proper theory of capital that is not grounded on a coherent theory of value and no proper theory of the international that is not grounded on a coherent theory of sovereignty.

that the theoretical explication of the concept of value, and with it of the economic itself, cannot be achieved from within the disciplinary boundaries of Economics. Rather, this work of theory, essential for the comprehension of the modern world-system at the conceptual level, can only be done from outside the space of Economics altogether.[8]

Where economic thought presupposes the validity of the economic problematic and then largely confines itself to functional and quantitative questions, so IR has typically assumed the international space itself as given and then asked how politics within that space work. Whether the answer is framed in terms of balance of power, international society, liberal world order, hegemony, or empire – the conceptions of international order that have together dominated the discourse of IR – is thus really of only secondary importance, since they all ultimately rest upon the same foundational assumption. Even the more recent attempts in IR to conceive the international itself, though, continue to be defined by the boundary line. Both the historical-sociological idea of the international as a specific dimension of the general social world, for example, and its more philosophical rendition as a distinctive resolution of the problem of universal and particular, still assume the logic of division and totality.[9] Consequently, while the literature on sovereignty in IR has certainly shown that its inside/outside structure is considerably more complex and intractable than the discipline has generally recognised, it has not actually grasped that logic itself. Moreover, to the extent that the concept of sovereignty has been critiqued in IR, it has been without any corresponding enquiry into the concept of value. The work that has been done on sovereignty and the international has simply not touched the economic at all, as if it were forbidden to trespass upon alien ground.[10] As a result, value, one of the two foundational concepts of the

[8] Of all disciplines, it is in fact IR that forms a privileged site for the explication of the economic. Since the inside/outside division of sovereignty is virtually thematic in IR, as constitutive of its central object, it is the requirement to think capital and the international together that clearly exposes the corresponding inside/outside division of value that structures the economic problematic but which economic thought cannot comprehend. Precisely the demand to think the whole by bringing capital and the international together, therefore, is what takes economics beyond itself.

[9] Rosenberg 2016b; Walker 1993, 2010, 2016.

[10] Characteristic in this respect is the work of R.B.J. Walker, which, on one side, has provided extensive and influential analyses of sovereignty and the international in IR but, on the other, has left value and capital almost completely unaddressed. As a result, one of the two 'torn halves' of the modern world-system is effectively absent from Walker's thought altogether, at least at a theoretical level. Something similar is true also of Sergei Prozorov's ambitious 'void universalism' project (Prozorov 2014b and 2014c), which assumes without question that the concept of universality can be rethought with regard to 'world politics' in complete abstraction from global economics.

modern world-system, has no presence in IR. For all its professed critical intention, therefore, the literature on sovereignty and the international in fact continues to respect, and conform itself to, not only the immediate disciplinary boundary between Politics/IR and Economics but the deeper fragmentation of being of which that boundary is an expression

The consequence of the failure of both Politics/IR and Economics to think their foundational concepts in sufficient depth is that neither has been able to reach up to the highest level and grasp the modern world-system as a whole. Instead, like IPE, they both continue to take the capitalist world market and the international states-system in separation from each other and to understand them as only externally related. As a result, the fundamental reality of the being of the modern world-system, the coexistence of capital and the international as two universal structures, remains unexplained. Theory is thus trapped within a totalised global system whose basic form it does not comprehend. If it is the case, however, that the relation between the world market and the states-system is properly logical – that is, if capital and the international *must* exist together because they imply each other in their very concepts – then not only is it not possible to theorise value and sovereignty from within the logic of division and totality, but there can be no adequate exposition of either that is not at the same time the exposition of the other. To answer the metaphysical question of capital and the international, and to comprehend the modern world-system as a whole, therefore, it is necessary to grasp the division between the economic and the political by thinking value and sovereignty together and revealing their point of indifference. Such is the purpose of this book.

The argument of the book achieves this purpose, in significant part, by way of Marx. It is not, however, a Marxist argument. Rather, the book uses Marx as the vehicle for a much larger argument about the economic as such. More specifically, through its engagement with Marx the book develops an ontological critique of the economic. Over the last four decades, from the 1970s onwards, social and political theory have in general moved away from Marx and Marxism, taking their distance from a tradition that had come to seem in many respects outdated and turning their attention, instead, to other perceived forms of injustice and oppression. In repudiating Marx, however, what theory did not do was establish any new position of thought in relation to capital. Instead, the question of capital – of the thing itself rather than merely its manifestations – was pushed into the background and veiled in silence. The general turning away from Marx was thus, more deeply, a turning away from capital altogether as an object of theory. While it was perhaps experienced at the time as an act of liberation, opening up new areas of critical inquiry, in retrospect this abandonment of capital can be recognised really to be an admission of incapacity, an implicit acknowledgement that in the globalised world capital had moved entirely beyond the reach of theory – it was now simply too big, too overwhelming, and too difficult to think. In becoming the absolute reality, that is, so capital also became a theoretical mystery. The effect of this profound incapacitation of theory in relation to capital was to relegate Marx's thought to a shadowy and uncertain position. Although modern critical theorising has widely rejected Marx as irrelevant to its sensibilities and concerns, since it has been able to develop nothing else, whenever it finds itself confronted with the question of capital, even if only at an empirical level, it typically continues to have recourse to an essentially Marxist vocabulary and mode of analysis. Because there has been no sufficient reckoning with Marx, therefore, no thorough accounting of what was wrong in his idea of capital, theory has not actually moved beyond him at all. Instead, by simply turning its back on him rather than working through the problems of his thought, it continues to be trapped within the very same limits that Marx himself did not comprehend.[11] As a result, the completely capitalised world has no proper theory of capital. Indeed, it does not even have a coherent conception of what capital is.

Moreover, since it did not understand the meaning of the collapse of Marxism, the general turning away from Marx failed to see the radically new concept of capital that in fact emerges from it. What above all distinguishes Marx within the general field of economic theory is that he pushes the economic idea of existence further than any other thinker, driving it to an extreme. In Marx, the economic is not apprehended simply as one particular dimension of being among others but is instead invested with an immense metaphysical significance, as both the foundation of being and its ultimate truth. It is the very extremity of this vision that makes Marx exemplary. For, in elevating it into a metaphysics and philosophy of history, his thought constitutes the supreme expression of the economic experience of the modern subject. As such, it is the epitome of all economic thinking. At the same time, however, precisely by virtue of the singular intensity of his commitment to the economic idea, his fierce conviction of the essential truth of labour and production, the irresolvable contradictions of economic thought are exposed more clearly in Marx than anywhere else. Indeed, as modern Marxist theory has in effect shown, the economic problematic actually breaks apart altogether under the metaphysical weight that Marx places upon it. The real significance of Marx's thought, its truth content, thus does not lie in his doctrine of historical materialism, with its various propositions about modes of production, class struggle, revolution and so on, nor even in his theory of capital. Rather, it is that by forcing it to its

[11] To use Hegel's dialectical terminology, the repudiation of Marx was thus abstract rather than determinate negation (Hegel 2018, p 53/¶79; Hegel 2010, p 33). Hence, it could not move beyond what it negated.

limit, Marx causes the economic conception of the world, which is in every way fundamental to modernity, to collapse. The insistence on the absolute truth of the economic instead reveals its absolute falseness. It is in this sense that Marx is really the occasion for the argument rather than its object. The logical incoherence of the economic idea is worked out through an extensive engagement with Marx because he is its most zealous and devoted believer.[12]

This incoherence emerges from what is by far the most important development in the theorisation of capital in recent decades. Since its crisis in the 1970s, through exactly the same period in which theory in general turned away from Marx, there has taken place within the field of Marxist economic thought a prolonged debate over the basic nature and validity of Marx's conception of value. What is immediately striking about this debate is that in it the kinds of questions that once intensely preoccupied Marxist economics – questions such as: where does profit comes from? what counts as productive labour? how does exploitation work? what causes crises? and so on – have completely fallen away, tacitly recognised to be no longer pertinent or meaningful. They have been superseded, instead, by considerations of an entirely different order concerning the being and becoming of value, its mode of existence and logic of development.[13] Through these discussions, the concept of value has thus at last begun to be freed from the confines of the economic conception and opened out into its properly first-philosophical dimensions. However, because this debate has taken place only deep within the ghetto of Marxism, it has been doubly constrained. In the first place, the discussion has throughout remained enclosed within the imaginative horizon and discursive parameters of Marxist thought; and, secondly, since it has been conducted exclusively among experts in the specialised field of Marxist economic theory, it has gone unheard by anyone other than adepts. The effect of this twofold confinement is that, on one side, the participants themselves have not grasped the full significance of what they have done or perceived its far-reaching implications, and on the other, the immense importance of the modern Marxist debate on value for the understanding of capital has gone entirely unrecognised in the wider field of theory. For, by working through the problems in Marx's attempt to formulate the concept of value, this debate has in fact opened the way to nothing less than a revolution in the theorisation of capital, liberating it not just from Marx, at last, but from economic thought altogether.

[12] As Roberto Calasso puts it: 'No one has ever dreamed the dream of capital with such faith as Marx developed in his soul' (Calasso 2018, p 254).

[13] Hence the debate has been as much among philosophers and social theorists as economists.

The revolution that the value debate has initiated is the project of developing a properly dialectical theory of capital. By freeing the theorisation of value from the constraints of the economic idea, dialectical theory radically transforms the very concept of capital.[14] It is through working out this transformation that the book is then able to reconceive the relation between value and sovereignty. The ultimate purpose of the ontological critique of the economic, and the complete rethinking of the concept of capital that follows from it, therefore, is to transcend the division between economics and politics that is foundational to modern thought in order to comprehend the modern world-system as a whole. The book brings capital and the international together at a logical level by demonstrating that value and sovereignty are essentially dialectical in their basic structure: as borderline concepts, they are both marked by the fundamental metaphysical division that separates inside and outside.

Ever since Kant branded it a 'logic of illusion',[15] no term in the lexicon of theory has been so abused and misused as dialectic. In truth, however, dialectic is simply the metaphysical structure of modernity – that is, the logic of division and totality – fully worked out. As Kant understood it, the central fallacy of the metaphysical tradition, in the form in which he inherited it in the middle of the 18th century, was that it did not properly differentiate inside and outside.[16] The consequence of this failure to respect the boundary line, confusing the two sides and so allowing them to infringe upon each other, was that the history of metaphysics constituted, for Kant, nothing but a perpetual 'battlefield',[17] a scene of endless and futile controversies through which no scientific progress could ever be made. Accordingly, Kant's 'critical' solution to the basic problem of metaphysics, as he saw it, was to insist upon the division, clearly separating the material from the conceptual, or the faculty of sensibility from the faculty of the understanding. Through this rigorous marking out of the borderlines, which would confine pure reason within its proper limits once and for all, metaphysics was to be transformed into a science and its conflicts

---

14 Through exactly the same period, this development in Marxology has been paralleled by a general movement in Hegel scholarship away from, or at least beyond, the *Phenomenology of Spirit*, which, with its apparent social and historical themes, dominated 20th-century readings of Hegel, to the *Logic*, with its purely conceptual and metaphysical concerns. Given that the *Phenomenology* was conceived by Hegel as preparing the ground for the system of speculative metaphysics that is then fully set out in the *Logic*, this development represents a considerable deepening of the understanding of Hegel and dialectic, just as the revolution in value theory constitutes an enormous advance in the understanding of Marx and capital.

15 Kant 1999, p 384/B249.

16 Redding 2009, Chapters 3 to 6; de Boer 2022. This error is what Kant termed '*the metaphysical fallacy of subreption*' (Kant 2007, p 408 (emphasis in original))

17 Kant 1999, p 109/Bxv.

thereby resolved into a perpetual peace. The decisive advance that German Idealism, and above all Hegel, then accomplished, in the wake of Kant's strict inscription of the boundary line, was finally to surpass the oppositional structure of reflection, which Kant had pushed to its limit, altogether. In the movement from Kantian transcendentalism to Hegelian dialectic, the two sides of the line, inside and outside, were brought back together, and their identity demonstrated, *on the basis of the division itself.*[18] In this way, Hegel reestablished the validity of speculative metaphysics, or the thought of the whole, against Kant's critical prohibition. He did so, though, not by regressing behind Kant to a dogmatic pre-critical position but by having already passed through the purifying fire of Kantian critique and resolved it into dialectic.

Logically speaking, the division is at once a point of union and a point of separation – both one and two. It is thus inherently dialectical. More precisely, in Hegel's usage, *dialectic* is the division in its aspect of contradiction (one as two), whereas *speculation* is the division in its aspect of unity (two as one).[19] This fundamental metaphysical logic of simultaneous separation and identity, which follows from the division, is what Hegel termed the 'Concept'.[20] The overcoming of the externality and opposition of reflection in order to grasp the two sides of the division together in their unity is what gives speculative dialectic its distinctive immanent, interior, self-determining quality, as the autonomous development of the logic of division into totality.[21] Moreover, since the laws of thought that are laid down in formal logic, including the law of non-contradiction, are founded upon the separation of inside and outside, the thinking of the division itself cannot presuppose them. Instead, in its effort to comprehend the logic of the Concept in its fullest extent, Hegelian dialectic reaches back behind the laws of thinking to discover an older

---

18 With Hegel, therefore, philosophy became for the first time presuppositionless and without foundations; or, more precisely, Hegelian dialectic rests upon a negative foundation. It follows that, where dialectic seeks to grasp the logic of division as such, the dialectical critique not just of Kantian transcendentalism but of all non-dialectical forms of thought is that they are ultimately governed by the division as by a 'hidden overlord' (Agamben 1993, p 137), presupposing it as their given and unthought ground.

19 Hegel 1991, pp 128–33//§§81–2.

20 Bowman 2013, Chapter 1; Ng 2020. '*Begriff* [Concept] means the logical subject itself, logical thinking as it develops through its entire movement of self-comprehension. ... Far from being the static, neatly circumscribed thought-content which we call a "definition", the Concept is the movement of comprehension itself' (Hegel 1991, p 348). As such, the 'Concept' is the full metaphysical truth of the narrowly epistemological sense of the 'concept'.

21 'Speculation, not reflection, is the master key to Hegel's dialectic. Reflection is the companion of argument. Like argument, reflection operates at a distance from the object, forming it and judging its essence through an independent standpoint of thought. Speculation captures in thought the inner life of the object. To speculate is to follow in language the inner movement of consciousness, to relate the inner life of the object. Speculative thinking is mimetic thinking'

and more original mode of thought, one that is not based upon the fixed oppositional structure of reflection but rather precedes it. It is only through the movement of this more primordial mode of thought, a movement that is reconstructed in Hegel's *Logic*, that the formal laws of thinking are then properly grounded, and thereby justified, for the first time.[22] In going beyond Kant, and thinking thought through to its very end, therefore, Hegel at the same time leads it right back to its origin, rediscovering the archaic rationality of myth, which likewise is not governed by the laws of thought, at the heart of the most enlightened reason.

In his early Jena writings, as he sought to overcome the reflective fragmentation of knowledge into the multiplicity of positive sciences in order to comprehend the whole, Hegel makes the claim, which would lastingly shape his conception of the history of thought, that in all times and in all places there has only ever been one true philosophy – that reason, as such, is one. No matter what their apparent differences, all individual philosophies that are worthy of the name are to be understood as just so many moments, or aspects, of that universal *philosophia perennis*, the unfolding of which provides them with their truth content.[23] If this claim is to be granted, though, then it must surely hold good for Hegel's own philosophy as much as for any other. Seen in this perspective, which it itself establishes, Hegel's thought in fact marks a kind of threshold. For, by following the dialectical logic of division through to its construction of an all-encompassing totality, Hegel brought the traditional project of philosophy, as the complete conceptual determination of the world, to its culmination.[24] The ultimate effect of Hegel's rendition of dialectic was thus to leave thought poised on the dividing line itself, at the point of indistinction, where it can no longer be the inherited programme of philosophy, which has reached its end, but is not yet its actual transcendence.[25] Against this Hegelian background, each of the three thinkers with whom this book engages in detail – Marx, Adorno and Agamben – then seeks to carry philosophical thought across the metaphysical threshold at which Hegel reaches his limit, beyond dialectic. As such, all three can be comprehended in relation to one another as constituting, in their very different ways, moments in the working out of that one true philosophy.

(Verene 2009, p 3). It is this interior logical movement that Hegel attempts to capture with his conception of the 'speculative judgment' (Hegel 2018, p 39/¶61).

22 McNulty 2023. Hegel's dialectical *Logic*, which is at the same time metaphysics, is thus really the logic of logic.

23 Hegel 1977a; Hegel 1991, pp 37–8/§13; Hegel and Schelling 2000.

24 In this respect, as Donald Verene notes, 'Hegel is the end of something, and not the beginning' (Verene 2009, p 88).

25 This is no doubt why, after Hegel, the motivating impulse of so much of 19th- and 20th-century philosophy, whether continental or analytic, was somehow to surpass the project of metaphysics, or otherwise terminate it. It also explains the intense hostility to dialectic that was such a pronounced feature of philosophical thought generally in that period.

Through his attempt to recast dialectic in economic terms, Marx may be understood as a distinctive variant of the general tendency in modernity of the supplanting of metaphysics by science. In Marx's materialist conception, it is the evolution of the principle of production through the class struggle, not the self-development of the Concept, that is supposed to provide the master key to history. Historical materialism was thus the first, and surely the most influential, of all of the many attempts to demystify the dialectic by subordinating it to a putative 'real world' of human activity (or 'praxis') that would underlie it and from which it would derive: economy, politics, society, history, and so on. In the wake of the collapse of Marxism and the universalisation of capital, however, the effect of the revolution in value theory has been to negate this conception altogether. The fundamental achievement of the value debate is to have demonstrated that the theorisation of value must begin not with the supposed materialism of production but, on the contrary, with the actual conceptuality that arises in exchange. The necessary implication of this theoretical revolution is that there is, in fact, no material reality that stands behind the Concept as the solid ground from which it would derive as a secondary form. Rather, it is the Concept, which is presuppositionless and self-determining, that comes first. Understood in metaphysical terms, what this reversal in priority between production and exchange signifies is the inevitable reemergence of speculation from out of the incoherence and breakdown of reflection. In his famous analysis of so-called commodity fetishism in Volume I of *Capital*, Marx made great play of the metaphysical character of the commodity, claiming to have seen through the mystifying illusion of generalised exchange by resolving it into the plain socio-historical reality of human labour that is imagined to lie behind it.[26] As it turns out, however, metaphysics is not really social and historical at all; rather, society and history are really metaphysical.[27]

Although he never fully broke from Marxism, despite considerable doubts and reservations, in the most characteristic part of his thought Adorno did not adhere to the Marxist programme of reducing the dialectic to an emanation of the practical-material human world. Instead, in his effort to think dialectic beyond Hegel, Adorno sought to understand how it was that the Concept could emerge from out of pre-subjective nature, separating itself from the all-encompassing natural context and bringing into being the self-conscious subject.[28] As he conceived it, dialectic was thus constituted in the

---

26 Marx 1990, pp 163–77.

27 Through his conceptual *Aufhebung* of mysticism, by contrast, Hegel shows dialectic to be more rational than science (Hegel 1991, p 133/§82; Magee 2008a and 2008b).

28 In its central aspect, Adorno's thought thus took shape as a reworking of the Hegelian conception of the genesis of the dialectic, in which the Concept first exists in-itself within pre-subjective nature and then becomes for-itself in the human subject.

relation, or tension, between the Concept, as the medium of freedom, and what he termed 'myth'.[29] In this way, Adorno strove to think the dialectic itself dialectically, comprehending the Concept as simultaneously inside and outside nature, at once different and the same.[30] The basic intention of his 'negative' dialectic, therefore, was to resignify the line that separates the conceptuality of thought from the pre-conceptual world. Indeed, the whole of Adorno's thought could be summarised as a single, sustained protest against the pain of that division, which traps the human subject within nature precisely in liberating it from it. However, for all the subtlety and perceptiveness of his effort to release thought from its own self-enclosure by turning it away from the traditional primacy of identity and towards non-identity, Adorno was never able actually to grasp the line itself. Even though he recognised that 'the division which makes everything objects must itself become an object of thought, instead of guiding it',[31] in the end his thinking always remained defined by the boundary that separates subject from object, inside from outside. As a result, despite the eloquence of its protest, it could never be more than a kind of longing, without fulfilment.

It is surely for this reason that Agamben judges negative dialectics to be 'an absolutely non-messianic form of thought'.[32] Instead, for Agamben, with the completed globalisation of the world at the end of the 20th century, the essential matter of thought, or *die Sache selbst*, as Hegel would have put it, has become precisely the division itself. This metaphysical circumstance is clearly announced by Agamben in the early essay, 'Tradition of the Immemorial', where he makes the claim that 'the historico-social experience of our time is that of an *original partition*, an *Ur-teilung*'.[33] What this experience signifies is that thought has reached a kind of terminal point, at which the whole logic of history as the transmissibility of tradition – that is, the processual, self-developing logic of the dialectic – has finally come to an end. The accusation that Agamben levels against virtually the entirety of contemporary thought,

---

[29] Although it covers a wide semantic range, at its core 'myth' in Adorno means something like nature in its aspect of the unyielding and the eversame, as a closed context of blind self-preservation. As with much else in his thought, the term was borrowed, and adapted for his own purposes, by Adorno from Walter Benjamin.

[30] The continued entanglement of reason in myth, its as-yet unredeemed indebtedness to what it would escape, is why Adorno called dialectic 'the ontology of the false condition' (Adorno 2001b, 'The Antagonistic Whole').

[31] Adorno 2005d, p 134.

[32] Agamben 2005b, p 38.

[33] Agamben 1999h, p 112 (emphasis in original). The notion of an '*Ur-Teilung*, or *ursprüngliche Teilung*, an original, primordial, and primitive division of an original oneness and unity' (Ng 2020, p 169), which was of great importance in the formation of Hegel's conception of thought (Henrich 1997, Chapter 6), derives from Hölderlin (Hölderlin 2009; Henrich 1997, Chapter 4).

however, is that it is exactly the imperative demand to think this '*original partition*', now that it has at last been unconcealed and so can be thematised for itself, that it has above all refused. Rather than follow the movement of the dialectic, and try to carry thought beyond the Hegelian threshold by grasping the division as such, it insists upon maintaining the line, even at the zero point.[34] In his rejection of the 'imperfect nihilism' of contemporary philosophy,[35] which simply reinscribes the division and so leaves the project of metaphysics unfulfilled, Agamben's thought in fact shares something of the spirit of German Idealism, which, in pursuit of the Absolute, revolted against the resignation and boundary setting of Kantian critique.[36] Indeed, if in his time Hegel renewed the possibility of the speculative thought of the whole through the dialectical resolution of Kant's reflective divisions, so Agamben may be said to have done something similar for thinking in the 21st century with his conception of the messianic. At the culmination of the dialectic, speculation, which in Hegel took the form of the dialectical conjunction of opposites, in Agamben becomes messianism, or the thought of the division itself.

By working out the dialectic of value and sovereignty through these three theoretical engagements, the argument of the book transcends the boundary between politics and economics to grasp the modern world-system as a whole. In doing so, it finally attains the horizon of modernity within which theory has hitherto remained enclosed. What thought then encounters at that metaphysical boundary line is nothing other than its own foundational division – that is, the division of inside and outside as such. In the Hegelian conception of dialectic, the long odyssey of spirit comes to an end when thought returns to itself by closing tight upon the line, as completed identity in otherness. The Absolute, for Hegel, is thus absolute division.[37] This is the properly metaphysical meaning of the globalised world-system of capital and the international. It follows that the movement of the dialectic beyond the totality of value and sovereignty would be the messianic 'absolution' of the Absolute through its redemption from division.[38]

★★★

---

34 Agamben 1999f, p 134.

35 Agamben 1995, p 91. The implication of this sweeping accusation is that late 20th-century philosophy as a whole remains confined within the space delineated by Hegel. Precisely in its anti-dialecticism, therefore, what contemporary thought actually attests is, as Agamben elsewhere puts it, 'the supremacy of dialectic in our time' (Agamben 2007, p 39; cf., in this context, Maker 1994, Part 2).

36 Agamben 1999h, pp 113–15.

37 As Hegel thus says of the Absolute in the early *Differenzschrift*: 'being opposed and being one are both together in it' (Hegel 1977a, p 156).

38 Agamben 1991, pp 92–3.

As it proceeds through the sequence of its chapters, the argument of the book describes a circle. It begins, in Chapter 1, by setting out the fundamental contradiction that shapes the problematic of the international and determines its meaning in the philosophy of history. On the one hand, the completed international space of the modern world represents the culmination of the history of political being and thus of human self-determination. On the other, the modern international has been experienced most powerfully in IR by Realism not as a pacified space of freedom and reconciliation but as a closed system of guilt and necessity, which presents a permanent existential problem of survival. The central contradiction of international theory is thus that in the modern international the principle of freedom – sovereignty – has become the principle of entrapment. In this respect, the international, as the totalisation of political space, in fact forms a limit point of history altogether. The task of international theory is to comprehend that limit in order to transcend it.

Chapter 2 turns to the relation of the economic to the international space. It does so by focusing on Marxism, as the tradition of economic thinking for which the logical relation of capital and the international above all constitutes a problem. Since Marxism makes a claim to the whole precisely in the name of the economic, it cannot allow the political structure of the international simply to stand outside the economic idea, as two inherently separate and distinct spheres, in the way that orthodox economic and political thought typically do. Rather, it must try to resolve the international into the terms of Marxist theory by closing the gap between the economic and the political. In exploring the encounter of Marxism with the international, the chapter first sets out how Realism in IR has presented the specific problem of the fragmented structure of the international to Marxism. It then shows that the recent debate in Marxism over the status of the international in the context of Marxist thought has failed to resolve that problem. Beyond the specific limitations of Marxist thinking, however, what the failure of Marxism in relation to the international reveals is the general impossibility of grasping the inside/outside division of sovereignty on the basis of the economic problematic. If the logical relation of capital and the international is to be comprehended, therefore, it is the economic idea itself that must be interrogated.

Across its middle chapters, the book works through the economic problematic to an entirely new conception of capital. This part of the argument engages in detail with the modern Marxist debate on value. The achievement of this debate has been twofold: on the one hand, a positive work of construction, and on the other, a negative work of destruction. Hence, Chapters 3 and 4 go together, forming a pair. Chapter 3 surveys the positive side of the value debate, setting out its major themes. It shows how, in seeking to reposition the theory of capital after the crisis of Marxism in the 1970s, the value debate recognised Marx's theory as, at least in important part, a qualitative *critique* of political economy rather than a quantitative economics. It is these elements of qualitative critique that set Marx's theory apart from orthodox economics (or political economy). Rethinking Marx's method in *Capital*, the debate has then strongly emphasised its dialectical elements. In particular, it has elaborated the centrality to the theory of capital of the 'value form', the specific conceptuality of value that arises in the process of exchange. At the centre of the modern Marxist thinking about value, therefore, are the metaphysics of exchange. Chapter 4 then turns to the negative side of the value debate. In developing the dialectic of the value form, the debate has recognised that there are, at the same time, substantial elements of Marx's theory – essentially his 'materialism' of labour and production – that do not fit with a dialectical theory of capital. In tracing out this fundamental discontinuity, what the debate has in effect done, without fully realising it, is to break Marx's theory apart along its central metaphysical fracture between labour and exchange, or content and form. However, because it wishes to remain within Marxism, it is unable to resolve the contradiction that it has revealed. The logic of the value debate itself thus leads the theorisation of value and capital beyond the limits of Marxism.

At the centre of the book, Chapter 5 forms the hinge on which the argument as a whole turns. In exposing the fundamental fracture in Marx's theory, the debate on value has in fact split open the economic problematic itself. Accordingly, this chapter addresses the central unanswered question that arises from the debate: what is the relation between dialectic and the economic? In order to answer this question, it is necessary to establish both the meaning of the economic problematic as such and the specific position of dialectic in modern thought. To that end, the chapter steps out of the confines of Marxism and into the much wider context of the metaphysical structure of modernity. The argument of the chapter unfolds in four stages. First, it sketches the rise of the economic subject, the modern 'Individual', in the 17th and 18th centuries through a series of radical separations from older forms of being. Drawing upon Adorno, the chapter then develops the structural homology between the economic problematic and the problematic of epistemology, which evolved concurrently through this period as expressions of the experiential form of the modern Individual. Having established this homology, the chapter explores Adorno's dialectical analysis of the contradictions of epistemology that necessarily arise out of the basic dualistic structure of the epistemological problematic. Finally, it shows how, in the movement of philosophy from Kant to Hegel, the epistemological problematic, with its strict divisions of form/content, subject/object and inside/outside, resolved itself into dialectic and the speculative identity of opposites.

The dialectical reformulation of the concept of value necessitates, in turn, a radical transformation in the concept of capital. This is the theme of Chapters 6 and 7, which again go together and form a pair within the overall structure of the argument, the first undertaking a negative work of destruction and the second a positive work of construction. Chapter 6 sets out a new interpretation of Marx's enormously influential conception of capital, in light of the dialectical theory that the book has developed. The purpose of this reading of Marx is finally to clear the space for a new, fully dialectical, theory of capital. It shows that Marx's idea of capital constitutes a radicalisation of the experience of the modern, economic Individual. Indeed, the innermost ambition of Marx's thought is to make the Individual immediately identical to the whole. By absolutising the economic idea, however, Marx only succeeds in magnifying the insoluble contradictions of content and form that are intrinsic to economic thought as such. So far from being beyond capital, therefore, Marx's thinking is in fact completely internal to it. Chapter 7 then begins the work of developing a new dialectical concept of capital. If, as the value debate has shown, the theorisation of value must begin from exchange, then it follows that the concept of capital must also be developed from exchange. This is achieved through a reading of the first two chapters of *Dialectic of Enlightenment*, where, in particular through his celebrated discussion of the wanderings of Odysseus, Adorno sketches the origins of the dialectic in terms of the prehistory of exchange and the relation between identity and myth.

With the comprehensive rethinking of the concepts of value and capital having been completed, in Chapter 8 the argument is finally able to return, on this new foundation, to the question of sovereignty and the international. It does so by reading Giorgio Agamben's theory of sovereignty, developed from Carl Schmitt and Walter Benjamin, alongside Adorno's critical account of dialectic. The argument demonstrates that the structure of inclusive exclusion that Agamben terms the 'sovereign relation' is the same as the dialectical inside/outside structure of the concept, as analysed by Adorno. That is, sovereignty and identity go together. On this basis, the chapter then goes on to show that all of the major themes of Agamben's account of sovereignty – *Bann*, state of exception, potentiality, form of law, bare life – can be understood as figurations of the dialectic. It is through this dialectical reading of Agamben, therefore, that value and sovereignty are at last brought together at the ontological level in a unified theory.

The world-spanning systems of capital and the international represent the culmination of the dialectic of value and sovereignty. At its end, therefore, the dialectic returns to its beginning, coming back to the original division of inside and outside from which the whole process started. The Conclusion completes the argument of the book by showing that it is this contemporary metaphysical condition of the encounter with the original division that Agamben seeks to grasp through the central idea of his thought: the messianic. What this idea intends is nothing less than the final resolution of the dialectical logic of division and totality. Messianism is thus the authentic form of speculative thought at the end of the dialectic.

1

The Problematic of the International

The logic of political space

At the most elementary level, the international can be understood as a spatial configuration. More precisely, it is a configuration of political space: a particular mode of political existence, the modern sovereign state, goes along with a particular mode of spatial constitution and orientation, the international. Regarded historically, this spatial configuration emerged from the dissolution of the political organisation of medieval Europe over a long period of time, between approximately the 14th and 17th centuries, the 1648 Peace of Westphalia traditionally being cited, rightly or wrongly, as the moment in which the new territorial logic crystallised. So much is familiar in IR. However, while its exact causes continue to be a matter of debate, when looked at in a wider perspective, the transition from European feudalism to the modern states-system can be recognised as just one moment, albeit a decisive one, in a single, overarching and much more fundamental narrative. That narrative is the essentially conceptual story of the development of human political space as such in its relation to the world. If the properly metaphysical meaning of the problematic of the international is to be comprehended – that is, its meaning in the philosophy of history – then it is within this conceptual dimension that it requires to be situated.[1] The overall narrative of political being in its spatial aspect is made visible in the clearest and most easily apprehensible way in a historical atlas of the world.[2]

1 It may well be that the problematic of the international can in fact only be grasped in the register of the philosophy of history. Martin Wight, for one, thought so. His classic essay 'Why is there no international theory?' concludes with the observation that: 'It is tempting to answer the question with which this paper begins by saying that there is no international theory except the kind of rumination about human destiny to which we give the unsatisfactory name of philosophy of history' (Wight 1966b, p 33).

2 Overy 2015.

Taking the world as a whole and beginning as far back as the archaeological record is able to reach, the atlas traces the development of political space through the millennia and centuries, through the rise and fall of empires, the innumerable migrations, invasions and wars, from deepest prehistory up to the present day. At the highest level, therefore, what the historical atlas provides is a representation of the unfolding logic of political space that culminates in the modern international.

In the very earliest ages that the atlas tries to represent there is in fact almost nothing to represent. For the tens of thousands of years in which humans were not organised as anything more than small bands of hunter-gatherers the atlas struggles with the contradictory task of giving visual form to something that has no form. There is nothing that is fixed and objectified, no identifiable socio-political spaces, no boundary lines, and no distinction between inside and outside. Since hunter-gatherer groups, it seems, did not form polities, there was nothing that would constitute even a proto-international. The most that can be indicated in spatial terms, therefore, as humans slowly spread out from their origins in Africa, are just very generalised flows of movement, almost as abstract and indeterminate as nature itself. In the absence of anything definite to represent, the atlas indicates what can be said of human existence at that time largely by way of natural factors: what parts of the world were more or less habitable, where food supplies and other resources could be found, where the materials for certain tools were located, where pasturage and the domestication of animals first took place, and so on. Furthermore, since humans had not yet decisively separated themselves from the world that encompassed them, nothing really appears to happen. Where there was next to no determinacy, no political space and no self-identical subject, the world was without time and so without history. Such change as did take place is indicated less by intra-human events, therefore, than by the gradual and laborious development of capacities for controlling nature. Vastly the preponderant part of the overall span of human existence thus fills just a handful of empty and eventless pages. In these earliest epochs, when the division of humans from nature had hardly yet taken place, what the historical atlas attempts to depict is really neither historical nor political. For these distant ages there is in fact a basic contradiction in the logic of the atlas, in that the content – the primacy of nature over the undeveloped human subject – denies the form – abstract and discursive – in which the representation is cast.

An epochal advance is usually thought to have occurred with the beginning of agriculture and human settlement in the Neolithic revolution about 8000BC, although, as the historical atlas notes, the 'symbolic revolution' marked by the beginning of ritual may well have been 'of greater immediate significance than the economic changes' in the emergence of the first civilisations.[3] In any case, what eventually resulted from the transition to settlement and cultivation was the establishment, starting about 3500BC, of the city as a separate and distinct space marked off from surrounding nature. In this new interior space humans could begin to conceive of themselves as free, self-determining beings able to create their own socio-political existence. The emergence of urbanisation thus represented a step-change in the relation of humans both to the world and to each other, involving 'a complex division of labour; literacy and a literate class (usually the priesthood); monumental public buildings; political and religious hierarchies; a kingship descended from the gods; and ultimately empire, or the claim to universal rule'.[4] For a long time, though, these spaces of emergent universality, ranging for the most part across the southern belt of Eurasia and into northern Africa, are still not clearly representable by the atlas. General indications can be given but, beyond the concentration of the city, there is no definite boundary line, no sharp separation of inside and outside. Instead, they shade into each other through indistinct marchlands and expansive border zones, or simply dissolve into wild nature. While the city might form a more or less stable centre, therefore, the different political entities of the archaic world were only loosely coordinated internally, not yet bound together into a tightly integrated whole. Furthermore, they were still comparatively small and separate, together occupying only a tiny percentage of the total land mass of the globe. By far the greater proportion of the world continued to be unsettled and unknown, so that determinate political space remained very much the exception rather than the rule.

Through the era of the classical world, as myth gave way to abstract reason and monotheism supplanted the old pantheon of gods in several of the major civilisations, political space continued to develop both in scale and definition. Not only does the atlas record the existence of many more cities but the various imperial structures reach further in their extent and their boundaries are more clearly delineated. With this increase in the scale and determinacy of political space, the quality of time also changes, becoming weightier and more dense as it is increasingly filled with intra-human events. While the overall narrative is uneven and irregular, with established civilisations sometimes falling to 'barbarian' invasions or otherwise ceasing to exist, the overall dynamic of the progressive expansion of political space is clear. Correspondingly, as the outside was increasingly brought within, so something like an international space started to cohere:

---

3 Overy 2015, p 38.

4 Overy 2015, p 54.

> The earliest civilizations arose at a few scattered points in the vast and sparsely inhabited Eurasian landmass. Between 1000 BC and AD 500 the pattern began to change. Although America, Australasia and Africa south of the Sahara still stood outside the mainstream of world history, and were to stay so for a further thousand years, the civilizations of Europe and Asia now formed a continuous belt. By AD 100, when the classical era was at its height, a chain of empires extended from Rome via Parthia and the Kushana empire to China, constituting an unbroken zone of civilized life from the Atlantic to the Pacific.[5]

Right up to the advent of modernity, however, human political space did not come together across the globe to form a single system. Instead, the thousand years between the end of the classical period and the 16th century is referred to by the historical atlas as 'The World of Divided Regions'.[6] Although they each no doubt experienced themselves as universal and complete world-spaces, seen from the vantage point of globalised modernity, the civilisations that constituted the different regions remained limited and particular. This divided world of expansive imperial formations – not just across Eurasia but now including the Maya, Aztec and Inca empires in the Americas and the those of Ghana, Mali and Songhay in Africa, among others – was the final stage in the prehistory of the international. It was a space of enormous variation in levels of development, much of it still unbounded and unclaimed, a space in which there co-existed a great variety of political entities, differentiated both in their mode of organisation and their spiritual form, separate from each other but, across Eurasia at least, in close interaction.

The transition from the world of divided regions, in which inner unity and external connection were still comparatively loose, to the modern international came with the revolution in the form of political existence signified by the emergence of the sovereign state in early-modern Europe. As is now well-established, far from being a purely endogenous development, the transformation that took place in Europe was a result of the continent's deep and complex involvement with the world beyond its boundaries. Modernity was not the expression of a uniquely European spirit, therefore, but the product of world history as a whole. However, and with all due recognition of this wider context, it remains the case that, in terms of tracing the overall development of human political space, the most striking feature of global history since the 16th century is the iteration across the world of the form that was first established in Europe in the early-modern period. The

[5] Overy 2015, p 76.

[6] Overy 2015, pp 106–67.

ground for this global transformation was prepared by the construction of the vast European empires, a process of overseas conquest, extending to all continents, through which Europe's own internal revolution was crucially mediated. Moreover, the dissolution by empire of the many and varied pre-modern political forms was a protracted and intensely violent process, marked by the erasure of innumerable ways of life. It took four centuries of this almost incalculable upheaval for modernity to effect its radical reconstitution of political space, leaving the old 'divided world' behind forever. With the receding of the European empires in the second half of the 20th century, though, the modern order of global political space finally emerged on its proper scale, no longer a merely intra-European or Western affair, but now extending right across the globe.

The modern international is distinct in a number of ways from the forms of political space that preceded it. First, and most strikingly, it encompasses the entire world. Seen from the global perspective of modernity, even the largest pre-modern empires were restricted in their extent, able to occupy only a limited part of the Earth. The modern international, by contrast, has achieved a kind of conceptual break-through. With the generalisation of the state form, every part of the territorial surface of the globe has been claimed by political space, so that the boundaries go right up to each other.[7] For the first time in history, therefore, the world has been incorporated into a single, integral and all-embracing system of political organisation. The international is thus a totalising structure, universal in scope and leaving nowhere outside. In the same way that it claims the world exclusively for itself, so the international also permits just one form of political entity. Where pre-modern political space had, viewed globally, always been mixed, incorporating a wide variety of forms, from sprawling empires at one end, through independent city states, to small hunter-gatherer groups at the other, in the modern international there is only the state. In this respect, the work of modernity in creating the international space has been the imposition of uniformity, the compulsory adoption of the state form on pain of extinction. The rule in the modern international is 'no state, no status' – like can only recognise like. The universalisation of political space achieved in the international is thus matched by an equal process of homogenisation, the reduction of all possible forms of political being to just one. Correlatively, every mode of political authority other than the sovereignty of the modern state has been delegitimised: personal rule and dominion are finished, empires and emperors consigned to the past, and

7 Even that remote and inaccessible part of Antarctica that is not claimed by any state is still within the logic of the states-system as a whole in that it has been deliberately set apart by international agreement.

kings and queens reduced to titular figureheads. Whether it is called system or society, therefore, the fully achieved international is a space of complete uniformity and equivalence, every unit being, in essence, identical to every other. At the culmination of the long history of the development of political space, the political map of the contemporary world thus presents a perfect image of totality: the international.

Taken as a whole, the narrative that is laid out in the historical atlas describes a fundamental reversal. At the very beginnings, nature completely subsumed the human. Indeed, there was scarcely anything that could be described as human in distinction from nature, as the world was still entirely unpolitical. At the end, in the global political space of the modern international, humans have completely subsumed nature. Indeed, there is scarcely anything that can still be described as nature in distinction from the human, as the world has become entirely political. The narrative runs from simple hunter-gatherer pre-societies, which knew no division, through to modernity, in which division is absolute. Across its pages, the atlas traces the ever increasing distinctness and determinacy of political space, through the steadily intensifying sharpness of the separation of inside and outside, right up to the fixed and abstract form of the modern state. At each stage the interior of the political space itself is further integrated, so that in the end every part is bound together into a functional whole. This dynamic of internal unification goes along with external totalisation, so that in the modern international the entire world is drawn together into a single system – *the* international. Through the course of this double-sided process, the political subject progressively makes the world its own, tightening its grasp upon it ever more firmly: where the fluid bands of hunter-gatherers lived close to the land but did not possess it, the rigidified modern state has separated itself radically from the world but claims its territory as its exclusive property. As the atlas represents in the simplest terms, therefore, history as such is a movement from the universality of nature over humans to the universality of humans over nature, a development that originates in the scattered and diverse and concludes in the systematised and totalised. Where, at the start, the subject was barely a subject at all, having no firm identity in opposition to the world, at the end, in the modern international, when it has identified the world completely with itself, it has become absolute.

When it is considered in this way, the narrative that the historical atlas presents can be seen to have two contrasted but interrelated dimensions. At one level, the tale it tells is almost infinitely various and diverse. It is the grand historical story of the rise and fall of all of the different empires and civilisations across the world, of the innumerable wars, invasions, migrations and revolutions, and of the multitudinous other forms of interaction that make up human history. At another, deeper, level, though, the narrative is uniform and absolutely coherent. Beneath the numberless events of history, the historical atlas records the systematic expansion of human political being. In this dimension, the story is simple and linear, a movement from nowhere to everywhere and from nothing to everything. Viewed in retrospect, from the vantage point of its completion, this movement can also be seen to have been rigorously teleological: although development is uneven across different parts of the world, taken globally the narrative unfolds just the single story of the continual increase in the scale and determinacy of political existence. Furthermore, the working out of this dynamic is strictly directional and unilinear. At no stage, through the entirety of history, does the extent of global political space recede or take a step backwards, nor does it ever expand and contract, coming and going in waves. Rather, it simply expands, relentlessly and unstoppably. At this deeper level, therefore, what the historical atlas lays out across its pages is really the unfolding of a *logical* process. The narrative of the formation and expansion of political space is the process of the ever more complete spiritualisation of the world, in the Hegelian sense of *Geist*, its systematic absorption into the interiority of the human subject.[8] Furthermore, as the historical atlas again depicts very clearly, the logic of political space is initiated by and progresses through division. The subject takes the world into itself by separating itself ever further from the world – that is, it internalises by externalising. This inside/outside dynamic culminates in the totality of the modern international, which is at once absolute separation and absolute identity. The completed international space is to be understood, therefore, as a perfected logical form. The two levels of the narrative are interrelated in that the strictly logical process works itself out, as Hegel might have said, behind the back of or, perhaps more precisely, through the history of events: the singularity and necessity of logic is the truth of the diversity and contingency of history.[9] Unfolding completely immanently, entirely from within itself, the logic of political space is really the logic of self-determination, or the logic of sovereignty. The narrative that runs through the historical atlas, emerging with ever greater clarity from each

---

8 The narrative that the historical atlas presents is thus in a literal sense the process of dialectical *Erinnerung*, the subject's internalisation of the world which is at the same time its own inwardising, or going into itself, through the creation of its own interior space.

9 Hegel 2018, p 58/¶87. The logical process of the development of political space that is set out in the historical atlas in fact exemplifies the Hegelian 'cunning of reason': 'In external history we have right before our eyes what is particular, namely, drives and needs. We see these particular elements engaged in mutual destruction, headed for ruin, [whereas] the idea is what is universal, and in the struggle it is free from assault and is unscathed. This is what we may call the *cunning of reason*, since reason avails itself of these instruments and shines forth untouched or, rather, brings itself forth. Rational purpose (*Vernunft-Zweck*) realizes itself by means of the needs, passions, and the like of human beings; what is personal and private is quite insignificant over against what is universal; individuals are sacrificed and relinquished' (Hegel 2019, p 96 (emphases in original)).

successive page, is thus in the most general sense the story of the expanding freedom of the human subject. If the subject is unfree to the extent that it is subordinated to any power outside itself,[10] then every stage in the growth of political space, every new and more determinate form of political being that extends its dominion, signifies an increase in its sovereignty, until it has internalised the entire world and made itself absolute.

Schuldzusammenhang

It ought to follow from this logic that, as the final result of the subject's progressive liberation of itself from nature, the completed political space of the modern international would be experienced as a fully achieved state of human self-determination and reason. When the world has been wholly resolved into the interiority of the subject, universal freedom should finally be realised. As it has been most powerfully articulated within IR, however, the international is the very opposite of a space of universal freedom. Indeed, in the formative phase of its thematic elaboration, IR was established precisely on the definitive rejection of the idea of the international as a pacified, harmonious and rational space. This was the foundational judgement that was written into the history of the discipline as the outcome of the first 'Great Debate', Realism's defeat of Idealism.[11] In giving expression to the distinctive character of the international, Realism insisted that at the level of the whole human political existence does not open out into an unbounded space of universal freedom and harmony but instead forms a closed and inescapable condition, the defining imperatives of which are power, conflict and self-preservation. The rationality of political being that is achieved within the borders is abrogated on the outside. For Realism, the international thus constitutes what Walter Benjamin termed, in reference to the archaic world of myth, a *Schuldzusammenhang* or context of guilt.[12] In fact, most of the major themes of the Realist discourse – necessity, timelessness, stasis, equilibrium, repetition, enclosure, hubris and nemesis, guilt and punishment,

[10] 'The human being is essentially spirit, and spirit is essentially this: to be for oneself, to be free, setting oneself over against the natural, withdrawing oneself from immersion in nature, severing oneself from nature and only reconciling oneself with nature for the first time through this severance and on the basis of it' (Hegel 2007b, pp 525–6).

[11] In this respect, it is really irrelevant whether the first so-called Great Debate in IR actually happened or not, or whether it misrepresented the international thinking of the interwar period, as the revisionist historiography in the discipline has claimed (for a summary overview, see Schmidt 2013). Rather, what matters is the metaphysical experience of the international that has been articulated through IR right from its origins in the first Debate.

[12] The German word *Schuld* means both 'guilt' and 'debt'. Although it is usually translated as 'context of guilt', a *Schuldzusammenhang* is thus equally a context of debt or indebtedness.

tragedy – ultimately originate from the sphere of myth and the experience of eternal unfreedom that it reflects. Whether or not Realism is still the dominant theoretical position in IR, it was certainly pre-eminent in the decades when the discipline was in formation and lastingly established the terms in which the international would be thought. Indeed, such has been the importance of Realism in shaping the imaginary of IR that, as and when they have arisen, other theoretical approaches to the international have almost always found it necessary to justify themselves and prove their own validity by measuring themselves against it, continually struggling to break free of its spell. This persisting power of Realism – its status as a kind of theoretical *archē* in IR – ultimately derives from its vision of the international as a *Schuldzusammenhang*, or 'an order whose sole intrinsic concepts are misfortune and guilt, and within which there is no conceivable path of liberation'.[13]

Whether it is grounded in an *animus dominandi* within or the structure of anarchy without, the fundamental Realist perception is that in the international guilt cannot be avoided because it is incurred not through fault but a priori, by virtue of mere existence. Ever mindful of this inescapable guilt complex, Realism counsels prudence and the virtue of the lesser evil in negotiating the exigencies of international political life.[14] Survival is to be achieved through renunciation, the admission of defeat in advance, and the forswearing of any ambition to know the whole. Accordingly, against the overweening vainglory of rationalist social science, the modern revival of Classical Realism looks to Greek tragedy because 'by making us confront our limits and recognize that chaos lurks just beyond the fragile barriers we erect to keep it at bay, tragedy can help keep our conceptions of ourselves and our societies from becoming infused with hubris.'[15] It is self-defeating folly to believe that reason, a weak and fallible instrument, is capable of grasping the Absolute. Instead, humans should respect the limits that cannot be transcended and not imagine themselves to be the equals of the gods. To suppose oneself to be free within the unfree whole is culpable delusion.[16]

[13] Benjamin 2004b, p 203.

[14] Morgenthau 1965, pp 192 and 202.

[15] Lebow 2003, p 364.

[16] Herein perhaps lies the reason for Realism's discomfort with the notion of sovereignty, 'a bothersome concept' according to Kenneth Waltz, whose discussion is careful to remain strictly functional and non-conceptual: 'To say that a state is sovereign means that it decides for itself how it will cope with its internal and external problems,' but 'to say that states are sovereign is not to say they can do as they please, that they are free of others' influence, that they are able to get what they want. … The sovereignty of states has never entailed their insulation from the effects of other states' actions. To be sovereign and to be dependent are not contradictory conditions' (Waltz 1979, pp 95–6). Except that they are: sovereignty surely contains within its concept the idea of freedom, and freedom, in any

In the context of guilt, good intentions untempered by judicious appraisal of the objective constraints are always liable to be twisted by the cunning of fate into disastrous outcomes:

> Neville Chamberlain's politics of appeasement were, as far as we can judge, inspired by good motives; he was probably less motivated by considerations of personal power than were many other British prime ministers, and he sought to preserve peace and to assure the happiness of all concerned. Yet his policies helped to make the Second World War inevitable and to bring untold miseries to millions of people. Sir Winston Churchill's motives, on the other hand, were much less universal in scope and much more narrowly directed toward personal and national power, yet the foreign policies that sprang from these inferior motives were certainly superior in moral and political quality to those pursued by his predecessor.[17]

Catastrophe follows from the attempt to step outside the limits and think directly in terms of the whole. The pursuit of narrow self-interest is, instead, the surest guarantor of survival.[18] The skill of the successful statesman thus lies in constantly adapting himself to objective circumstances, renouncing happiness and fulfilment in favour of the cold-eyed, realistic calculation of the balance of forces.[19] Accommodating himself to a reality that cannot be meaningfully changed, he negates himself in order to preserve himself.

---

emphatic sense, is incompatible with a condition in which heteronomous circumstances necessarily impose unavoidable constraints. No attempt is made by Waltz to analyse the meaning of sovereignty or to examine why and how freedom (sovereignty) and necessity (the constraints of the international) exist together, indeed constitute each other. Similarly, Raymond Aron, at the conclusion of his discussion of the difficulties involved in defining sovereignty, observes in positivistic vein that 'personally, I should offer no objection to abandoning this concept, because of the ambiguities it sustains' (Aron 2009, p 743). It is, of course, precisely the ambiguities that make the concept indispensable.

17 Morgenthau 2006, p 6. As in myth, the logic of the international is that the context of immanence is never breached and that human intentionality always comes to naught: 'Time and again it has been the tragedy of Political Idealism to witness the fatal reversal whereby, as soon as the situation or condition under attack was replaced by something new, the laws of Political Realism turned the result into the opposite of the expected utopia' (Herz 1951, p 39).

18 'Wars undertaken on a narrow calculation of state interest are almost certain to be less damaging than wars inspired by a supposedly selfless idealism' (Waltz 2001, p 114).

19 In Morgenthau in particular, the figure of the statesman is invested with something of the pathos of the tragic hero, an existential Everyman, exemplary in his exceptionality, who raises himself above natural circumstances and yet remains trapped within them, caught in-between: 'the statesman is indeed the prototype of social man himself; for what the statesman experiences on his exalted plane is the common lot of all mankind. Suspended between his spiritual destiny which he cannot fulfil and his animal nature in

For Kenneth Waltz too, in his reformulation of Realism in structural terms, the subjective motives of political actors are largley irrelevant because in the international sphere they are overdetermined by the objective condition of anarchy. Indeed, the demands of the perennial circumstance of anarchy so completely nullify the individuality of the political entities involved that Waltz sees no difficulty, in fact a necessity, in reducing them to qualitative identity, taking into account only quantitative differences, variations in capability in the pursuit of survival.[20] The continual pressure exerted by the whole renders each alike as an identical empty 'unit', merely an executor of the higher laws governing its existence.[21] Like the timeless world of myth, in Realist thought the context of anarchy is immemorial and unchanging, impervious to any progress. History thus takes place within a fateful condition that is not itself historical. States and their leaders come and go, driven by their own ambitions and desires, but the whole remains always the same: 'While men and gods may attempt in their short span to assess their fates by a measure other than blind destiny, existence triumphs over them in the end.'[22] As Waltz emphasises again and again, the force of circumstances is such that, whether they wish it or not, in their international existence states are compelled endlessly to repeat the same few patterns of behaviour: war or peace, attack or defence, opposition or alliance.[23] Hence the 'dismaying persistence'[24] of the conflict-ridden condition of the international.[25] Not to

which he cannot remain, he is forever condemned to experience the contrast between the longings of his mind and his actual condition as his personal, eminently human tragedy' (Morgenthau 1965, p 221).

20 Waltz 1979, pp 93–7.

21 Thirty years before Waltz, John Herz was already writing that 'because of the security competition among the political units any new unit and its leaders have to adopt power as the basis of their politics', whether they want to or not (Herz 1951, p 25). In the subsequent generation John Mearsheimer repeats the thought: 'all great powers act according to the same logic regardless of their culture, political system, or who runs the government' (Mearsheimer 2014, p 18).

22 Adorno and Horkheimer 2002, p 11.

23 In its parsimonious, 'scientific' brevity (of an already short book, only the first six chapters really constitute the theory proper; the final three are largely extraneous), in its paradoxical combination of thinness and import, self-evidence and opacity (the theory explains both everything and nothing – 'Is structure … an empty concept? Pretty much so, and because it is it gains in elegance and power' (Waltz 1979, p 70)), and in the conflicts that interpretation of its meaning has aroused, *Theory of International Politics* has something of the quality of an oracular utterance.

24 Waltz 1979, p 66.

25 The real interest of *Theory of International Politics* is in trying to articulate the eternal eversameness of the international, its myth-character. For this reason, all of the many critiques that mistake it for a predictive theory, fault it as such and try to fill or supplement it with other variables and factors, do not improve on Waltz's work. Rather, the power and importance lie precisely in the emptiness.

understand or, worse, wilfully to contravene the logic of anarchy is to lay oneself open to destruction: 'the requirements are *imposed* by an automatic sanction: Departure from the rational model imperils the survival of the state.'[26] Just as with the mythic hero, failure to acknowledge the force of necessity, whether out of vanity, vaulting ambition or simple carelessness, leads inexorably to downfall. As Waltz laconically remarks: 'states are free to disregard the imperatives of power, but they must expect to pay a price for doing so'.[27]

The single principle of order in the condition of anarchy is the balance of power, 'the masterpiece of international politics'.[28] However, while it is central to all versions of Realism,[29] a precise statement of balance-of-power theory remained for a long time elusive.[30] Hans Morgenthau's analysis in *Politics among Nations* illustrates the difficulty involved. He is in no doubt about the necessity and importance in international politics of 'a configuration that is called the balance of power', chiding the presumptuous and moralistic misconception that 'men have a choice between politics and its necessary outgrowth, the balance of power, on the one hand, and a different, better kind of international relations, on the other'.[31] In his discussion, a sort of guide to policy options, he then presents an overview of the different patterns and structures and the methods available to the statesman. When he reaches his concluding 'Evaluation', though, he is confronted by a conundrum.[32] Although, in its classical configuration, among the states of Europe from approximately the 17th century onwards, the working of the balance of power prevented 'universal dominion by any one state', this liberty was won 'only at the price of warfare, which from 1648 to 1815 was virtually continuous and in the twentieth century has twice engulfed practically the whole world'.[33] Indeed, even the brief periods of peace 'were preceded by

26 Waltz 2001, p 201 (emphasis in original). As in Waltz's discussion of sovereignty, freedom is no such thing, amounting to an ever present dilemma of adaptation or doom: 'Pursuing a balance-of-power policy is still a matter of choice, but the alternatives are those of probable suicide on the one hand and the active playing of the power-politics game on the other' (Waltz 2001, p 205). Either way, there is no escape.

27 Waltz 2000, p 37.

28 Wight 1966b, p 21.

29 Waltz describes it as 'the main theoretical prop of those traditionally called realists' (Waltz 2008, p 137). Wight, perhaps only half-jokingly, observes that 'for those who believe in this deity, to propitiate it by periodical holocausts, which is called "maintaining the balance", is itself the fundamental principle of statecraft' (Wight 1991, p 164).

30 In his historical survey of usage of the term, for example, Martin Wight distinguished nine separate meanings (Wight 1966a).

31 Morgenthau 2006, p 179.

32 Morgenthau 2006, Chapter 14.

33 Morgenthau 2006, p 213.

the wholesale elimination of small states and were interspersed … by a great number of isolated acts of a similar nature.'[34] The order and stability of the balance, its timeless elegance, were thus the result of relentless conflict and destruction, the weakest being consumed in the struggle. Perplexed by the irrational means by which the rational outcome of equilibrium was achieved, Morgenthau concludes by expanding upon the three main weaknesses of the balance of power as the guiding principle for policy in international affairs: 'its uncertainty, its unreality, and its inadequacy'.[35] The central point of his critique is the virtual impossibility of correctly calculating, from among the innumerable variables, what policy would serve to maintain or correct the balance. No individual state, which in any case must be concerned always with its own self-preservation, can grasp the universal so as to formulate a course of action that would promote an equilibrium. In international politics subjective reason is forever inadequate to the objective whole.[36]

Waltz solves the explanatory difficulties that Morgenthau finds himself entangled in by removing all elements of foreign-policy consideration and reformulating balance-of-power theory in wholly objective terms.[37] Not only do subjective factors of state motivation not account for the creation and perpetuation of balances of power, but they vitiate the meaning of the theory. Sweeping away the assorted errors that result from attempting to ground the balance of power in 'internal' factors, Waltz is categorical: the theory must be one of outcomes rather than motives, of the results inevitably produced, often against their intentions, by the uncoordinated actions of states with diverse motivations. 'To contrive and maintain a balance may be the aim of one or more states, but then again it may not be. According to the theory, balances of power tend to form whether some or all states aim for universal domination.'[38] What Waltz sees is that the balance, the point

[34] Morgenthau 2006, p 213.

[35] Morgenthau 2006, p 214. See also Morgenthau's editorial comments on the balance of power in *Principles and Problems of International Politics*, where he likewise affirms that it is a 'misconception, not yet extinct, that a nation has a choice between a balance-of-power policy and some other kind of foreign policy … a nation which disregarded the requirements of the balance of power would either have to conquer the world or perish' and that 'the enormous number of wars known to history are a monument to its failure as an instrument of peace', a failure he attributes to subjective error, as 'either its principles were disregarded or, more frequently, a nation erred in comparing its strength with that of another' (Morgenthau and Thompson 1950, pp 103–4).

[36] In Hume's short text on the balance of power, pursuit of the balance is linked to the prudence of the wise statesman, who rejects the lures of overweening ambition and 'jealous emulation' in a policy of deliberate self-limitation (Morgenthau and Thompson 1950, pp 105–9).

[37] Waltz 1979, Chapter 6.

[38] Waltz 1979, p 119. Arnold Wolfers, in his earlier discussion, noted 'an almost irresistible pull towards equilibrium' (Wolfers 1965, p 124).

of indifference, comes about not despite the ambitions and strivings of the powers involved, but precisely *through* them. The final outcome of all the struggles and conflicts is stillness – the sum of the factors is ultimately always zero. In this way, the balance of power is revealed as a kind of universal law of non-contradiction, or equivalence, which is realised only as the quintessence of all contradictions. Through the cunning of the balance, what always was, the unchanging condition of anarchy, is continually reinstated.

Thus clarified, what the theory loses in immediate explanatory capacity, it gains as the minatory expression of fate: 'Realist theory predicts that balances disrupted will one day be restored. A limitation of the theory ... is that it cannot say when. ... Of necessity, realist theory is better at saying what will happen than in saying when it will happen. Theory cannot say when "tomorrow" will come.'[39] As with the fulfilment of a mythic prophecy, reversal of fortune is inevitable but not predictable. Vengeance, 'the mythical prototype of exchange' as Adorno called it,[40] may strike suddenly or hang over its victim for many generations, awaiting its moment. It is certain, though, that any power that exceeds its limits, and so offends against the logic of anarchy, will eventually pay the price and be humbled, as it is compelled to make reparation for its guilt: 'It is so ordained that one atones at once, another later; but even should one escape the doom threatened by the gods, it will surely come to pass one day, and innocents shall expiate his deed, whether his children or a later generation.'[41] With the restoration of the balance new powers will have

39 Waltz 2000, p 27.

40 Adorno 2005a, p 159.

41 Solon, Athenian statesmen and lawmaker, quoted in Horkheimer and Adorno 2002, p 5. Contemporaneously with Solon, and long before Thucydides, the single surviving fragment of the pre-Socratic philosopher Anaximander of Miletus, virtually the origin of Western philosophy, expresses the unvarying structure of giving and taking, assertion and retribution, that is inscribed in the logic of the balance of power: 'And the source of coming-to-be for existing things is that into which destruction, too, happens, "according to necessity; for they pay penalty and retribution to each other for their injustice according to the assessment of time."' (Kirk, Raven and Schofield 2007, p 118). Adorno, whose thought repeatedly recurred to the Anaximander fragment, comments: 'We might say that in its development hitherto history is constructed like a gigantic process involving the exchange of cause and effect. It is as if the principle of exchange were not only the determining factor in the countless myriad of actions that constitute the life of human beings, but as if the macro-structure, the macro-cosmic nature of history, were itself just one great exchange relationship in which penance follows the act of taking so that in this sense history never escapes from the bonds of *myth*. This was a presentiment, incidentally, that was not alien to the early philosophers. ... If you take the famous saying of Anaximander and also certain statements of Heraclitus, and look at them from the standpoint of the philosophy of history ... you will get something of a sudden insight into the exchange structure of history' (Adorno 2006, p 93 (emphasis in original)). Balance-of-power theory is the modern rationalisation of this mythic exchange structure, the prehistory of which

arisen and old ones declined, but through it all the principle of equivalence reigns supreme and unchanging.

The centrality of anarchy and the balance of power to the Realist vision explains the latter's essentially static-repetitive conception of history, in which movement takes place in the form of circularity or cyclicality, the story of the rise and fall of great powers – always the same archetypal tale, merely with different players.[42] Since nothing new, nothing qualitatively different, may ever come into being, time is ultimately issueless.[43] Statements to this effect from the Realist literature are well known and much cited: 'International politics is the realm of recurrence and repetition';[44] 'the texture of international politics remains highly constant, patterns recur, and events repeat themselves endlessly';[45] 'the behaviours of states, the patterns of their interactions, and the outcomes their interactions produced [have] been repeated again and again throughout the centuries despite profound changes in the internal composition of states';[46] 'the wealth of historic precedents which taught the eternal recurrence of strife and conflict among the units of international society';[47] and so on. For Realism, a science of international politics means resignation to the international *Schuldzusammenghang* as permanent and unalterable because it is only through acceptance of, and adaptation to, its repetition-structure that survival may be secured. Thus in Morgenthau's formulation: 'The realist parts company with other schools of thought before the all-important question of how the contemporary world is to be transformed. The realist is persuaded that this transformation can be achieved only through the

can be traced back beyond Thucydides to the very moment of transition, when myth became reason, in pre-Socratic thought.

42 An obvious example is Robert Gilpin's *War and Change in World Politics*, which thinks macro-history in terms of alternations of 'Growth and Expansion' (Gilpin 1981, Chapter 3) and 'Equilibrium and Decline' (Chapter 4): ancient history was 'The Cycle of Empires' (pp 110–15), the modern world 'The succession of hegemonies' (pp 144–5).

43 Waltz turned to structure in order to capture the texture of the international precisely because it is what ensures 'a common quality of outcomes even though the efforts of agents and agencies vary' (Waltz 1979, p 74). For him, bipolarity is the most stable form within anarchy (Waltz 1979, Chapter 8). More than merely a panglossian affirmation of the Cold War superpower stand-off, this is mythic dualism as scientific theory: 'Just as the constellation Gemini, like all other symbols of duality, refers to the inescapable cycle of nature … the scales (Libra) held by Zeus, which symbolize the justice of the entire patriarchal world, point back to mere nature' (Horkheimer and Adorno 2002, p 12). Scales are, of course, a classical image for the balance of power (Little 2007, pp 40–9).

44 Wight 1966b, p 26.

45 Waltz 1979, p 66.

46 Waltz 1993, p 45.

47 Herz 1951, p 75. In similar vein, see also Wolfers 1965, p 249.

workmanlike manipulation of the perennial forces that have shaped the past as they will the future.'[48] The question is indeed all important, but the Realist sentiment of disillusioned, grown-up responsibility provides no answer.[49] For it is precisely resigned submission to the 'perennial forces' and the endless patterns of repetition they produce that forecloses the possibility of any real transformation.[50]

> The principle of immanence, the explanation of every event as repetition, which enlightenment upholds against mythical imagination, is that of myth itself. The arid wisdom which acknowledges nothing new under the sun, because all the pieces in the meaningless game have been played out, all the great thoughts have been thought, all possible discoveries can be construed in advance, and human beings are defined by self-preservation through adaptation – this barren wisdom merely reproduces the fantastic doctrine it rejects: the sanction of fate which, through retribution, incessantly reinstates what always was. Whatever might be different is made the same. That is the verdict which critically sets the boundaries to possible experience.[51]

48 Morgenthau 2006, pp 12–13. E.H. Carr observes that 'realism tends to emphasize the irresistible strength of existing forces and the inevitable character of existing tendencies, and to insist that the highest wisdom lies in accepting, and adapting oneself to, these forces and these tendencies' (Carr 2001, p 10). In fear of the extremes, he and Herz plead unconvincingly, even despairingly, for a sensible blend of Realism and utopianism, a moderate middle way. Later, Morgenthau came to regard the development of nuclear weapons as having produced 'the only real revolution that has occurred in the structure of international relations since the beginning of history' (Morgenthau 1970, p 260). The elemental force of nuclear weapons, their monstrous destructive power, seemed to demand the move from an international order to a supranational one through the formation of a world government. For all its realism, though, this demand remained merely exhortatory, 'ought' rather than 'is', and thus un-Realist. No way out of the context of guilt could be envisaged, even as it threatened to destroy itself completely.

49 This sentiment is typical in Realism: compare Carr's characterisation of the supersession of utopianism by Realism as the development of mature science out of childish wishful thinking (Carr 2001, Chapter 1). In this 'bourgeois disillusionment', Adorno and Horkheimer perceive 'the external schema for the internalization of sacrifice' (Horkheimer and Adorno 2002, p 45). Rational science thus replicates age-old myth.

50 In IR, Realism is the expression of the dialectic of demythologisation: 'the more the illusion of magic vanishes, the more implacably repetition, in the guise of regularity, imprisons human beings in the cycle now objectified in the laws of nature, to which they believe they owe their security as free subjects' (Horkheimer and Adorno 2002, p 8).

51 Horkheimer and Adorno 2002, p 8.

International theory

The meaning of the problematic of the international within the philosophy of history lies in the contradiction between the logic of political space that is set out in the historical atlas and the Realist conception of the perennial condition of anarchy. On one side of this opposition, the international represents absolute freedom. As the foundational concept of the political, sovereignty signifies the formation of a space of human self-determination that is removed from and transcends the context of blind nature. In the beginning, when nature was sovereign and all-encompassing, there was no space of freedom and no political subject. Only with the drawing of the line, marking out the division between inside and outside, did the world start to become determinate, settled and knowable. Over millennia, as the subject gradually separated itself ever further from the natural context through increasingly objectified forms of interiority, political being inexorably extended its reach, bringing more and more of the world inside the boundaries. With the transition to modernity and the generalisation of the nation-state across the world, global political space finally came together as a whole, closing over completely to form the modern international. Seen in this perspective, the international represents the final outcome of the laborious, ages-long effort of humans to mediate the world to themselves and to become self-creating and self-determining beings. In that moment of fulfilment, the world disappears altogether into the subject: nowhere remains outside, nowhere is still *terra incognita*, nowhere is as yet unclaimed. Instead, through the universality of the international, the modern subject is completely at home in the world – wherever it looks it finds itself reflected back to itself, so that its identity is continually reaffirmed in everything it encounters. No longer recognising any external power to which it would be subordinate, it grounds itself upon itself as a self-authorising sovereign entity. The logic of political space thus culminates in the absolute freedom of the sovereign state, which encompasses the whole world in the form of the international.

And yet, when the resolution of the world into political space has been completed, what results is experienced most compellingly not as freedom and autonomy finally achieved, the immemorial history of strife and conflict at last brought to an end, but as an unchanging state of antagonism and struggle. In the Realist vision, the international is not, and cannot be, a rational and coherent whole. Rather, it forms a closed and self-divided condition, where insecurity is endemic and self-preservation the primary imperative. At the culmination of its historical evolution, therefore, sovereignty and political being do not issue in a reconciled humanity no longer at war with itself but instead come up short, constituting a seemingly inescapable context of guilt. Where once pre-political humans were caught within the endlessly repetitive cycles of nature, now fully political humans are entangled in the perpetual, cyclical struggle for power and survival within the international – a second state of nature, as Realism imagines it. In terms of the philosophy of history, the paradox of the international can thus be stated quite simply: through the form of the international the human subject has indeed attained the whole, but only in such a way that it cannot know itself as a whole. The development of the identity of the sovereign subject results in a totality that is anonymous and without identity; or, put differently, the totality of sovereignty is itself without sovereignty. This is the real meaning of 'anarchy', the central concept of IR theory. While any number of criticisms can and have been made of Realism as a theory of international politics, it is nevertheless correct in its fundamental perception of the nature of the international space: that the whole is, and always has been, divided and subjectless. The metaphysical core of the problematic of the international is thus formed of a dialectical *coincidentia oppositorum*, in that the international is both the fullest expression of human freedom and self-determination and a space of absolute unfreedom and enclosure, a perpetual *Schuldzusammenhang*. In the international, that is, the principle of freedom, sovereignty, has itself become, by a mythical reversal, the principle of entrapment. The task of international theory, is to comprehend this opposition speculatively by grasping the two sides, freedom and entrapment, together in their identity.

As it is, though, IR has continually reproduced this central contradiction without ever managing to bring it to consciousness and make it thematic. Indeed, the discipline was founded directly upon it, in the dispute between Realism and liberalism that formed the theoretical field during the First Debate and has then recurred again and again within it, marking its central fracture. Although typically framed in disciplinary narratives as an argument between distinct and diametrically opposed positions, this has always in fact been an internal struggle between the two sides of the modern international. The questions it revolves around all reflect the inextricable conjunction of freedom and entrapment, progress and repetition, that is deeply inscribed into the experience of the international. Can human political sociation at the level of the whole finally become pacified and self-aware or is it condemned forever to blindness and conflict? Is it possible for the modern principles of political reason to be extended from the bounded 'domestic' realm of the state to encompass the international or must global political space always remain fragmented and ungoverned? If the idea of modernity is 'one world', how can the whole and the parts of that world be reconciled with each other? The international is thus the site at which a fundamental schism within modernity's self-understanding is revealed, a division that the modern subject cannot heal from within itself because it is constituted through it. This double-sidedness is expressed in the Jekyll-and-Hyde, two-in-one character of liberalism and Realism in IR. On one side, the modern subject trusts in the universality of its reason to bring freedom and order to the whole; on the other, precisely in the fragmented universality of the international, its reason encounters a limit that it cannot comprehend.[52] As a defence mechanism against this split consciousness, where it runs up against its boundary line in the international the modern subject divides itself into two opposed positions, eternally locked in combat and unable to acknowledge their intimate kinship. The endlessly reiterated argument between Realism and liberalism is in fact the single but divided voice of the modern subject, which is at once limited and unlimited, universal and particular.

The split within the modern subject that is exposed in the international points back beyond the temporal boundary of modernity, far into the past. This is the meaning of what has often been framed in IR, notoriously, as Realism's 'timeless' wisdom, its continual perception of the old in the new. That timelessness is the guilt conscience of the modern world, its memory of an indebtedness that it continues to owe. The historical atlas strikingly evidences the decisive advance in political being that occurred with the advent of modernity. Although it required many centuries to be completed, the move from the restricted and still localised, pre-modern 'divided world' to the unrestricted, globalised world of modernity was the result of a conceptual revolution: a form of constraint that had hitherto held political space within its limits was forever surpassed, liberating it to become all-encompassing. And yet, in the same movement by which this epochal change came about, something else, something more fundamental, stayed the same. Although the great pre-modern political entities could form the idea of a cosmopolis, a universal empire or a one true church, in retrospect, seen from the perspective of modernity, their narrowness and restriction is clearly evident. For all the ambition towards universality, in the divided world there was not, and could not be, a global subject. In one respect, modernity leaves that condition behind, eliminating the diversity of political forms through the replication of the sovereign state across the world. However, this immense labour of reducing the diverse to the identical, or the many to the one, ultimately produces not the world in itself but, rather, the international. In the modern world, humanity does not constitute an integral whole but exists through the anarchic form of fragmented global political space. Division and conflict,

---

[52] In his lectures on Kant's *Critique of Pure Reason*, Adorno remarked on this deep structure of modern thought: 'What this expresses, of course, is a genuine social situation. On the one hand, the world with all the resources at its disposal is caught up in a constant process of rationalization: in the production process, in its shaping of individual human relations, in bourgeois society generally. It is permeated with science to a constantly increasing degree. At the same time, the irrationality of the whole, that is to say, the blindness of the forces at work, and with that the inability of the individual to determine his own life in accordance with reason, remains intact' (Adorno 2001a, p 64).

the age-old scourge of war, are not overcome, therefore, but instead recur in new and intensified forms, as Realism never tires of insisting. While the immense literature on modernity abundantly attests its radical novelty, the revolutionary transformation that it effected across so many dimensions, in the end the modern world has been unable to change the one thing that really matters. At the level of the whole, humanity has not yet opened its eyes and recognised itself but remains just the same as it always was: blind, divided and self-antagonistic. Now, as before, there is no global subject but only an international one.

The problem in the philosophy of history that the international brings into precise focus is thus why modernity represents at the same time both enormous upheaval and unchanging identity, revolution and continuity. Something persistent, something obscure and archaic, was carried over the historical borderline that separates the modern international from the pre-modern divided world. While sovereign political being underwent a far-reaching change of form, which enabled unlimited expansion and unification, in that very change it nevertheless remained essentially the same, as an inside set against an outside, a part shut off from the whole. For all its world-spanning extent, therefore, the international no more allows a genuine and undivided humanity than did the great empires that together made up the differentiated, restricted and uneven world before modernity. Through the reorganisation of political space that modernity effected, the world was simultaneously integrated and disintegrated, forcibly pulled together and equally forcibly pulled apart. As a result, despite this profound revolution in form, the global political space, considered as a whole, continues to be fragmented and conflict-ridden. The meaning of the international thus has to be grasped as both continuity and discontinuity, each existing within the other. This contradiction is again indirectly registered in IR through the foundational and endlessly recapitulated dispute between liberalism and Realism, the one always celebrating cooperation and harmony, the other perpetually lamenting division and conflict. Precisely through the form of its universalism, liberalism cannot help but incur the debts that Realism insists must remain forever unredeemed – the dark guilt conscience dwells within the bright cosmopolitan ideals. While modernity surely constituted a world-historical rupture, therefore, from the perspective of the international it can nevertheless be recognised as a kind of *Aufhebung*, a conceptual transformation that at once negates and preserves. It was a moment of advance within the unfolding logic of sovereignty: radical change that stays exactly the same.

In the international, modernity thus reaches its limit.[53] The metaphysical meaning of Realism in IR is that through the consciousness of its continued entanglement with the archaic, modernity is compelled to reckon the

[53] Near the dawn of modern international thinking, in his 'Idea for a Universal History with a Cosmopolitan Aim', Kant already conceived the international as a kind of metaphysical

insufficiency of its reason and acknowledge its debt. The limit of modernity, however, is also a limit of more than modernity. As is clear from the historical atlas, history and time as such are consequent upon the spatialisation of the world through division that founds sovereign political being.[54] The process of history is then the progressive resolution of the world into the interiority of the subject through successive shapes of sovereignty. However, when the logic of political space finally broke through the pre-modern restrictions and attained the form of the modern international, a limit point was reached that

horizon, which both invites the construction of a universal history and frustrates it. The problem that Kant struggled to resolve in that text is that the logic of separation and totalisation – what Kant called 'the *unsocial sociability* of humans' (Kant 2009, pp 111 (emphasis in original)) – through which history has progressed culminates in the international as a condition of subjectless anonymity. The contradiction in the relation of the political to the international is thus that the intentionality of political reason does not extend beyond the boundaries to encompass the totality itself; or, as Kant put it, that there is '*purposiveness* in the arrangement of nature in the parts and yet *purposelessness* in the whole' (Kant 2009, 115 (emphases in original)).

54 It follows from this that, as Realism in IR obscurely perceives, the condition of internationality as such is not historical. It thus cannot be comprehended by historicist thought. What is accessible to historicism, on the presupposition of the inside/outside division, are the various forms of international existence that have occurred through history (thus, for example, the English School's interest in tracing the development of 'international society' (Bull and Watson 1984; Watson 1992; Dunne and Reus-Smit 2017)). What is not accessible to it, however, is the presupposition itself – that is, the ground of sovereignty as such. Historicism thus assumes a division of form and content and is unable to grasp them in their dialectical unity. Indeed, as Constantin Fasolt has shown, the modern conception of history as the site of the self-creation of the human subject, rests precisely upon the sovereign division of inside and outside (Fasolt 2004). Historicism thus oversteps the bounds of its jurisdiction when its presumes to sit in judgement on the philosophy of history, which is essentially concerned with the unfolding of the logic of the division itself. Properly speaking, in fact, there is no historical origin of internationality as such, in the sense of a chronological moment that could be inscribed into a continuum of before and after. As Giorgio Agamben puts it: 'Such a concept of origins is useless to the human sciences whenever what is at issue is not an "object" presupposing the human already behind it, but is instead itself constitutive of the human. The origin of a "being" of this kind cannot be *historicized*, because it is itself *historicizing*, and itself founds the possibility of there being any "history"' (Agamben 2007, p 56 (emphases in original)). Instead, the condition of internationality, understood in this originary sense, reaches back behind historicism's conception of history to what Agamben terms 'ultra-history', the comprehension of which demands 'a new and more primary experience of time and history': 'What is described here as ultra-history is something that has not yet ceased to take place and which, exactly like the system of myth, guarantees the intelligibility of history and its synchronic coherence' (Agamben 2007, pp 165 and 167; cf. in this context Hegel's remarks on the indetermination of being and nothing from which dialectical logic proceeds: 'Thus the beginning of philosophy is the ever present and self-preserving foundation of all subsequent developments, remaining everywhere immanent in its further determinations' (Hegel 2010, p 49)).

is at once quantitative and qualitative. The expansion of political space always worked through the division of inside and outside, the subject continually testing the strength of its identity by measuring itself against the resistance of the world beyond the borderline. Each new shape of political being signified an advance in the subject's capacity to identify the world with itself, bringing it inside. However, with the completion of the international space, this process – which is nothing less than the historical process itself – encounters a seemingly absolute boundary. Put simply: there is nowhere left to go, nowhere left to incorporate that is not already inside. The world has been completely subsumed, such that it has ceased to exist as something substantive beyond the reach of the sovereign subject. If the historical atlas invites the understanding of history as the story of the human subject's extrication of itself from submergence in nature and its progressive internalisation of the world, then the modern international brings that narrative to a close. The limit of modernity is also the limit of history altogether. The international thus constitutes a metaphysical threshold, a point of simultaneous completion and incompletion. The inside/outside movement of sovereign self-determination has come to end, but it has not yet fulfilled itself by producing a self-determining global subject. Or, to put it differently, the borderlines remain in force but their logic has been suspended.[55]

---

[55] Agamben 1998, p 51. If the international forms the limit point of modernity, it also marks the limit of the Hegelian philosophy of history. Since the modern state constituted for Hegel the highest form of the ethical life of spirit, as the realisation of freedom and self-consciousness, he was never able to thematise the international as such. Consequently, as Angelica Nuzzo observes, when it reaches the metaphysical horizon of modernity in the international, and is confronted with a boundary that it cannot comprehend, the Hegelian vision becomes uncertain and opaque: 'As the state, itself the culmination of the sphere of ethical life, expands (or alienates itself) on the international scene in the confrontation of many states, Hegel discloses the horizon of world history and its periodization. … In this systematic position, however, history is properly – and problematically – a moment of tense transition rather than the reconciled (and conciliatory) culmination of the movement of objective spirit. The field of world history seems to represent an abrupt interruption – even a reversal – in the ascending structure of the progress of freedom from the level of "abstract right" though "morality" up to the different moments of "ethical life". Already in the confrontational relations between autonomous states (*Völkerrecht*) right loses its power of actuality, sinks back to the level of an ineffectual "ought", and is constantly undermined by contingency, while the anarchy of a renewed state of nature seems to propose, yet again, the resurgent condition of abstract right' (Nuzzo 2013, p 212). See also, in this context, Karin de Boer's argument that Hegel's philosophy of history, and the conception of dialectic that shapes it, is able to show how the contradictions of history resolve themselves into modernity but is not then able to resolve the contradictions of modernity itself (de Boer 2009 and de Boer 2010, Chapter 9). The movement of negation through which the logic history has unfolded itself into modernity no longer suffices to carry the human subject beyond modernity.

International theory is concerned with what happens to the political when it reaches this threshold. At the Greek origins of the Western tradition, the political space was canonically defined by Aristotle, in reference to the *polis*, as that which is most proper to humans, who are by nature political animals. The quality of being political was associated by Aristotle with a capacity to inhabit the intelligible and to distinguish the just from the unjust. It was what differentiated the human form of association from the herds and hives of animal groups, enabling something more than just self-preservation and brute subsistence: the pursuit of living well, or the good life.[56] From the beginning of its theorisation, the political was thus understood as denoting the freedom of the human subject, no longer subordinate to the blind power of nature. In the West, the *polis* marked a crucial turning point in the development of political being. A new level of objectivity was achieved, which brought with it a transformed sense of the freedom of the political subject and its ability to determine its communal existence. At the end of the long history of its development, though, Aristotle's perception of the liberatory quality of the political has turned into its opposite, a reversal that has been brought about through the unfolding of the immanent logic contained in the idea of sovereignty itself. From being the essential medium of freedom, the inside/outside division, upon which the principle of sovereignty was founded, has become a kind of block, which stands in the way of and prevents a further, and final, transition, one that is felt to be urgent and imperative but whose quality remains profoundly obscure. The problem of the political now, in the totalised world, is thus why sovereignty, as the medium of human self-determination and freedom, does not, in the end, produce a free global subject, but only a self-divided international one. The central question of international theory, therefore, is: why does the political produce the international?

When the problematic of the international is understood in these terms, the meaning of international theory changes. In one sense, the international is the expression of the ultimate triumph of sovereign subjectivity in its conquest of the world as a whole. In that very triumph, though, it also becomes, through a dialectical reversal, a fundamental critique of sovereignty. For it is precisely in the moment of its totalisation that the congenital deficit of political space is at last laid bare: the whole that the international forms is not yet the whole, not the world in-itself. In this way, the fragmented and subjectless character of the international points back to the originary guilt of sovereign political being. With the completion of the international space, the debt that the political subject incurred at its origin through separating itself from the world, a debt that has progressively accumulated through all of the developments of its form,

[56] Aristotle 1998, pp 2–5.

has finally come due. Accordingly, international theory cannot simply assume the division of domestic and international as given, concerning itself with what happens across borders in contrast to what happens within them. Rather, the line itself, the division of inside and outside through which sovereign political being first came into existence, becomes the object of theory. As international *relations*, however, IR theory is predicated on the division, which it has always presupposed as its given and unthought foundation. Confining itself to how relations between political entities work, or ought to work, in the international space, it is theory from within the logic of division and totality rather than theory of that logic itself. Although the contradiction of presence and absence that arises from the opposition of inside and outside virtually defines the entire theoretical field, because it takes the division for granted and assumes the normative validity of the inside space, the basic problem of the international presents itself to IR theory in terms that simply reproduce the contradiction: can the international be made more like the domestic? The persistent effort to think the outside in the terms of the inside thus simply follows the logic of division, which it does not understand. Ultimately, therefore, IR theory has always been political theory *in* the international, and not theory *of* the international – inside/outside theory, not theory of inside/outside. As a result, it has never been able to articulate the problematic of the international in its proper terms.

The relation of the international to the political is likewise misconstrued in the idea of a transition from the limited to the unlimited, the movement from the bounded space of the state to the wider field of the states-system or, more generally, 'global politics'. The crystallisation of the problematic of the international during the course of the 20th century does indeed mean a movement beyond the singular political entity, but not at all in the sense of a straightforward shift upward in levels, the architectonic role that Aristotle once awarded to Politics, as the most comprehensive science, now being assigned to International Relations.[57] To conceive of it in this way is to tie international theory to the historical logic of sovereignty as if this were still alive and continuing when the completion of the international space in fact signifies its final arrest and suspension. It is a perspective that remains within the movement of inside and outside that has reached its end point precisely in the international. As such, it fails to grasp the meaning of the international. Rather, if the international constitutes the negative totalisation of the positivity of the political, then the relation of international theory

[57] As Stanley Hoffmann proposed decades ago (Hoffmann 1959; see Linklater 2007 and Booth 2011a for more recent versions of the same idea). For a critique of the general linear imaginary in IR of a simple move upward in levels from 'international' to 'world', see Walker 2010.

to political theory is contradictory, or dialectical. International theory is concerned with what happens to the political at the metaphysical threshold where the logic of sovereignty has completed itself but without having achieved its essential idea. It is reflection on why absolute freedom is at the same time absolute entrapment. International theory neither contents itself with the received opposition of inside and outside, therefore, nor does it attempt, yet once more, to extend the rationality of the political from within, across the limits that constitute the fragmented international space. Rather, it aims to bring the tradition of political thought to its fulfilment by reaching all the way back to the origin in order to resolve the division that founds the order of sovereignty in the first place. In the international, the political thus turns against itself, through its own logic, so that it might finally realise its idea in the freedom of the whole.

2

The Economic and the International

The logic of economic space

Alongside the ever increasing extent of human political space, the historical atlas also charts another narrative, albeit one that, because of its fluid and indeterminate nature, is harder to represent visually. Almost as far back as it is able to reach, the atlas records evidence of what would come to be termed trade, or exchange, between human groups. As with political space, though, while it can be traced deep into prehistory, it took a long time for the form of exchange to establish itself firmly and then to develop. Just as, in the millennia between the Neolithic revolution and the period of the classical civilisations of the ancient world, it is only very gradually that it is possible to demarcate emergent human political space with any clarity, inside and outside not yet being firmly separated, so, in the same way, for much of this long span scarcely anything that could be identified as a definite trade route, a continuous and permanent line of exchange, can be discerned. Accordingly, only the vaguest and most general indications are provided by the atlas, often not much more than the sites at which archaeological discoveries have been made from which proto-exchange activities can be plausibly inferred. In the same way that the interior spaces themselves had still to cohere properly and become clearly differentiated from their surrounds, so the connections between them had not yet crystallised but remained comparatively formless, readily dissolving back into the enveloping embrace of nature.

Again as with the logic of political space, the beginning of urbanisation and the founding of the city marked a decisive step-change. The abstraction and interiority of the demarcated urban space was accompanied by an advance in modes of exchange relation, in particular the development of the money form. The earliest cities, established in the ancient Near East, constituted nodal points in an extensive network of trading routes stretching across the entire region. As the atlas notes, 'during the 3rd millennium BC goods were being traded between the Indus and the Mediterranean',[1] and by 1500BC these routes reached even further, on to mainland Greece and Southern India. In this period the cities became the political and cultural centres of the first empires, so that, where its origins had been just scattered points on the Eurasian landmass, by the height of the classical era human civilisation extended right across the continent, from the Atlantic to the Pacific. For as long as there was political stability within and between these more or less contiguous imperial spaces, lines of exchange that reached all the way from Britain to Japan were maintained, with the famous Silk Road, stretching between Iraq and China, at their centre. Furthermore, in this period of imperial expansion and through on to the end of the classical world, the flourishing overland routes of exchange were supplemented by the beginnings of an extensive maritime trade, not only in the Mediterranean but also in the Red Sea, Persian Gulf, Arabian Sea, the northern Indian Ocean and Bay of Bengal, and on as far as the South China Sea, generally at this stage still sticking close to the coastlines of Asia rather than venturing far out into the oceans, but nonetheless opening up a new, fluid medium of circulation, the sea.

The thousand years between the decline of the classical period and the European expansion of early modernity is named by the historical atlas 'The World of Divided Regions', an epoch characterised by the consolidation of political authority across a number of, sometimes vast, imperial spaces, their power often symbiotically linked with the elaboration and spread of the great world religions – the sultanates of India, Imperial Japan, the T'ang and Sung dynasties in China, the rise of the Muslim world and the Ottoman Empire. While hostility and war between these regions periodically disrupted what were by now well-established regularities of trade, it is difficult for the atlas to represent the way in which precisely those eruptions of conflict – the Germanic tribal migrations into Roman Europe, the spread of Islam across West and Central Asia and North Africa, the Crusades, the various invasions of the nomadic Mongol empire, and so forth – while causing severe dislocations of economic space in the short term, in the long run in fact served to promote further interconnection. As old centres of power declined and new ones arose, so pathways of trade shifted direction, accommodating themselves to and taking advantage of the opportunities that an altered geopolitical landscape presented. In any event, when the history is looked at as a whole, the character of the overall development is once again clear: across the period, the expanding reach and internal organisation of political space is precisely matched by the increasing extent, both in scope and density, of exchange relations. Indeed, by no later than 1250, the trading routes that

1 Overy 2015, p 55.

had long traversed Eurasia had extended down the coast of East Africa and connections had been created to the emerging states of the west of that continent, although the Americas, Australasia and much of southern Africa continued to remain outside this expanding economic space of exchange.[2]

Despite the substantial growth of exchange relations, however, in the world of divided regions geographical distance still entailed qualitative variation, the trading routes linking together market spaces that continued to be predominantly localised and uncoordinated. It was not yet possible for the many to be bound together into one and so for a unified and integrated economic space to be created. For all its extensive development, therefore, throughout the entire historical epoch stretching from the founding of the first cities right the way through to the complex and large-scale inter-societal carrying trade of the 13th and 14th centuries, exchange was always ultimately constrained by a conceptual limit. The moment of mediation in the exchange process, the M in C–M–C,[3] remained dependent upon the two poles of the transaction. It was alive when it was in motion, as it passed between one market space and another, but when it reached its destination, and the movement of circulation came to a halt, it lapsed. The quantitative limit to exchange was thus also, and more profoundly, a qualitative limit: it measured the capacity of the form of value to incorporate the world into itself and to transform it into economic objects. By the same token, for all that during this long historical sweep political space had expanded enormously from its origins in the ancient cities of the Near East up to the great civilisations of the 'World of Divided Regions', nevertheless, looked at as a whole it always remained in minority. As the historical atlas comments, on the eve of the epoch of European expansion 'the area occupied by the major civilizations … was relatively small. Over three-quarters of the world's surface was inhabited by either food gatherers or herdsmen … or by hand cultivators'.[4] Sovereign power and the political space it establishes, just as much as exchange value and the economic space it creates, thus continued still to be subordinate to, and exceptions from, the world around them.

Breaking through that constraint constituted the transition to modernity. Just as political space underwent a revolution, therefore, so did the form of exchange. Before, trade had been a more or less irregular connection between externally related and qualitatively divergent spaces, which were only loosely bound together by the networks of exchange. Now, as the world beyond

2 Overy 2015, pp 154–5.

3 That is, the money in commodity–money–commodity, Marx's schema for the simple exchange transaction.

4 Overy 2015, p 170. At the same time between perhaps two thirds and three quarters of the world's population was concentrated in the areas of the major Eurasian civilisations.

the borders rapidly contracted, until it disappeared altogether, so exchange was internalised, becoming an essential dimension of the being of modern states, the continual circulation of value their very lifeblood. In the early part of this transformation, Europe's centre of gravity shifted from its south, orientated to the Mediterranean, the Near East and the ancient overland routes across Asia, to its north-west, which looked out to the Atlantic Ocean and gained its wealth from the new triangular trade with West Africa and the eastern seaboard of the Americas. With constant, self-sustaining, exchange now intrinsic to the existence of modern polities, the maritime trade of the civilisations of the Mediterranean and southern Asia was dwarfed in scale and revolutionised in form by the opening up of all of the oceans of the globe, the resistance of the land finally being overcome as the fluid and uniform sea became the predominant medium of circulation. Viewed in retrospect, from the vantage of its completion, the *telos* of the whole process can be recognised as the formation of a single, integrated economic space coextensive with the world as a whole – a global economy. For pre-modernity it is possible for the historical atlas to indicate the major trade routes connecting the various different political spaces. For the modern world, though, no such representation is possible. Just as political space, through the singular form of the bounded nation-state, now claims the entire landmass of the Earth, so the globe as a whole has been subsumed to exchange: together, they are everywhere. If one side of what the atlas portrays, at the highest level of generality, is the continual process of the transformation of the world into political space, culminating in the modern international, then the other is its simultaneous and coextensive metamorphosis into economic space, which culminates in the capitalist world market.

The narrative of the historical atlas thus, in fact, traces the working out of two concurrent logics: a logic of political space and a logic of economic space. Again when seen in retrospect, this second logic is every bit as linear and teleological as the first, systematically unfolding itself, page after page, through all the manifold events of history. In fact, taking the process as a whole, it would be legitimate to speculate that these two fundamental logics have developed together at an interlocking rhythm and pace, undergoing homologous conceptual transformations at historical turning points in their inexorable movement of expansion. In any event, viewed at the very high level of abstraction that the historical atlas affords, it is evident that the formation of political and economic space took place simultaneously, and that the ultimate outcome of this dual process is, on the one hand, the international states-system and, on the other, the global capitalist economy – 'states and markets', the two basic structural forms of the modern world. Like the completed international space, therefore, the capitalist world market is really a logical form; or, perhaps more properly, it is the culminating point of a purely logical process. Further, these twin, concurrent logics work through a double movement of separation and totalisation: from wild nature to ordered political space, and from the rough materiality of the world to the smooth conceptuality of exchange. Indeed, it might be said that the historical process is nothing other than the continual unfolding of the logics of political and economic space, until everywhere has become sovereign territory and everything an object of value. In essence, what the historical atlas portrays, therefore, is just this two-sided logic, which reaches its endpoint only when the whole world has been internalised to the absolute subject. That subject, however, remains unconscious of itself as a whole: composed of an infinitude of economic actors concerned only with the pursuit of their own self-interest, the capitalist world market is just as anarchic and subjectless as the international states-system. The logic of economic space thus no more produces a self-aware global subject than does the logic of political space. Instead, together they form a totality that is anonymous and without identity.

If the formation of political and economic space culminates in the world-spanning system of capital and the international, then the logic of their development, initiated so many millennia ago, far back in prehistory, has finally come to an end. With everywhere having been incorporated into political space and everything having become a commodity, the movement has at last played itself out. At this threshold, therefore, when the process has been completed and so presents itself as a whole, it ought to be possible to look back and comprehend its inner meaning – that is, to understand what the two logics are and why they exist together. These questions have scarcely ever been asked, though, let alone answered. Virtually without exception, modern thought has instead remained this side of the metaphysical boundary line, within the logic of division and totality. Since the disciplines of modern thought – in this context, principally Politics and IR, Economics, Political Economy and IPE, History and Sociology – are premised upon the fragmentation of being, they standardly assume politics and economics to be two ontologically separate spheres of human existence, and so take the dividing line between them as given and unproblematic. The question of the logical, or conceptual, relation between capital and the international thus lies beyond their horizon – it is, quite literally, unthinkable to them – and so remains unaddressed. As a result, the totality of the modern world-system, and what might lie on the other side of it, escapes comprehension.

The one tradition of thought, however, that could not content itself with this assumption of two separate and discrete spheres that interact only externally was Marxism. This is because the fundamental claim of Marxism, central to its entire idea, was to have attained a position beyond the limits of capitalist modernity. From this position, it believed itself to have revealed the logic of history as a whole, to have shown capital to be only one 'mode of production' among others, and so to have opened the way to a radically new and unrestricted form of social being. Moreover, through its theory of history and its conception of capital, Marxism made this claim to the whole on the basis of the economic idea itself: in the Marxist vision, the fundamental necessity of the production and reproduction of material existence would ultimately overcome all division to produce a free humanity for the first time. What thus sets Marxism apart in this context is that, if it is to stay true to its indispensable messianic intention, it cannot accept the dividing line that separates the economic and the political from each other as simply given and irreducible. The theory that claims to be beyond the limits of capital cannot allow the international, as the political form of capitalist modernity, simply to stand outside the bounds of the economic idea. If Marxism is to sustain its claim to the whole, which is central to its very idea, then it must be able to account for the international from within its own theoretical terms. More than for any other tradition of theory, therefore, the conceptual relation between the logics of political and economic space represents a crucial *problem* for Marxism. Precisely through its extreme commitment to the economic idea, it is in Marxism's encounter with the international that the problem of the logical relation between capital and the international has made itself most powerfully felt. By the same token, it is also in this encounter, and in the failure of Marxist thought in the face of the international, that the impossibility of comprehending that relation from within the logic of the economic idea has been most clearly evidenced.

The second image

The tradition of Marxist thinking about international politics antedated the academic field of International Relations and, through much of the 20th century, developed separately from it. As, in the later decades of the century, it came into contact with IR, so the way in which it had come to think about the international sphere placed it in a contradictory position in relation to the mainstream of the discipline. Marxism could function quite straightforwardly as a radical opponent of liberalism, which typically sought to interpret international politics through its narrative of historical progress – the international space as a site for the pursuit of cosmopolitan aspirations; the spread of market relations and the increasing density of global linkages furthering the consolidation of international society; the violence of states being reined in by civil society actors and the embedding of ethical norms; the spread of democracy creating a zone of peace within which warfare had effectively been renounced; and so on. To all of this Marxism naturally felt itself in opposition. For it, capital was constituted through irreconcilable class division and was inherently exploitative. Just as one class ruled over another within capitalist states, so on the international stage those states competed against one another individually and exploited weaker countries collectively. The proclaimed universality of liberal values was thus merely a high-minded cover for the pursuit of power. So far from leading to pacification, therefore, the international politics of capital were in fact epitomised by domination and conflict. This rejection of liberal irenicism lent Marxism a certain affinity with liberalism's principal antagonist within IR, Realism.[5] The latter's refusal to accept that the globalisation of liberal principles could mitigate the conflictual character of the international matched both Marxism's urge to debunk liberal pretensions to universalism and its desire to reveal liberal internationalism as a project of domination led by the greatest capitalist power of them all, the USA. An association of convenience with Realism thus assisted Marxism in its efforts to represent itself, rather than liberalism, as the bearer of progress. In the struggle against liberalism, Realism could be considered, objectively, an ally of sorts.[6]

Against liberalism, Marxism always contested the content of international politics. It developed theories that tried to explain the politics of capital on a worldwide scale, the general claim being that they should be understood as imperialism, neo-colonialism and hegemony rather than as cosmopolitanism, international society and democratic peace. In any case, whatever the preferred terms, this was always an argument about how to understand the dynamics of international politics. What it never became was an argument about the international as such. Indeed, given the way in which Marxism conceived of itself, the international could not become a theoretical object for it in its own right. Liberalism acknowledged that its political status was founded on the inside space of the modern world, the bounded nation-state. That space having been constituted, liberal thought continually attempted to extrapolate internal relations across the boundary to the international sphere, struggling ever and again to negotiate its contradictions. In response, Marxism certainly opposed the liberal version of the political space, its mode of organising political power – the capitalist state was to be denounced as a class state. But, in the same way that it assumed the validity of the economic, Marxism did not contest the political itself, the essential quality of being political. Instead, while it sought to reformulate politics in terms of class rather than citizenship, hammering out its own rough

[5] This affinity goes back at least to E.H. Carr, for whom, in a notably coarse reading, Marxism in its most effective elements was just a species of Realism, a kind of sociology of knowledge whose utility lay in uncovering the economically interested, and thus relativistic, origins of all apparently disinterested, universalist claims (Carr 2001, pp 63–6).

[6] 'There will be issues on which Marxists and realists will find themselves on the same side—for example, in contesting exaggerated expectations of inter-state harmony after the end of Cold War and criticizing idealist conceptions of the international' (Callinicos 2007, p 543). Hence Marxism's enjoyment of Realism's 'sometimes splendid demolitions of liberal ideology' (Callinicos and Rosenberg 2008, p 96).

version through the rhetoric of party, struggle and revolution, it nevertheless continued to think of itself as engaged in political conflict over power in society. The dispute with liberalism was over which version of this political quality would ultimately win: liberal-capitalism or socialism/communism. Like liberalism, Marxism also extrapolated from its version of the political ground: against cosmopolitanism, it proposed 'socialist internationalism' – the same political form (state and international) but with a different content. Marxism thus understood itself to be an actor within the socio-political scene of modernity. It could assume that its proper task was to contest the content of international politics because it took for granted that it occupied the arena with liberalism, as the two principal antagonists in the central political struggle of the modern world. Of much greater consequence than the differences between the various Marxist theories of international politics, therefore, was the assumption that underpinned them all and gave them their sense: that Marxism existed *inside* the political space of modernity.

It is here that the limits of Marxism's affinity with Realism become evident. For it was the validity of exactly this foundational assumption that Realism effectively questioned. The argument with liberalism in IR was over the content of international politics, cooperation and harmony being countered by conflict and exploitation. The two protagonists could dispute because they took it that they shared centre stage. Realism situated itself elsewhere, though, and posed to Marxism another type of question altogether. Presenting the other side of the divided experience of modernity, Realism measured Marxism against its sense of the necessary limits of the political and its disillusioned appreciation of continued entanglement within the irrationality of the fragmented and conflict-ridden whole. In doing so, it reformulated the problem of capital and the international in radically different terms.

In a largely overlooked essay from 1981, Norberto Bobbio asked 'is there a Marxist theory of international relations and, if it exists, what is it?'. This question, he went on to suggest, could effectively be rephrased as 'is there a Marxist theory of war?', because war is 'the central question of all theories of international relations'.[7] The difficulty of finding a satisfactory answer derived in part, according to Bobbio, from Marx's neglect of the theme. Living in the age of revolutions, Marx was convinced that class conflict had superseded inter-state warfare as the dominant vector of historical change – the irresistible movement into the future that so enraptured him came from within society, through the class struggle, rather than from outside. It was thus

[7] Bobbio 1987, pp 198, 199, 207–8. Bobbio, a sympathetic liberal critic of Marxism, was of course a figure in political theory rather than IR, but the position he puts forward in this essay is clearly a Realist one in the IR sense.

to the Leninist theory of imperialism that one had to turn to find a Marxist theorisation of international political conflict. However, this theory, Bobbio argued, could not be regarded as satisfactory. First, its linking of imperialism to a stage of capitalism invited the simple objection that there had been many wars before the era of capital. Secondly, with the decline of inter-imperial rivalry after World War II, Marxist theory found itself having to bend and stretch the meaning of the term 'imperialism' to an implausible degree in order to encompass economic exploitation of the Third World, which did not necessarily involve war. Thirdly, Bobbio suggested that of all the conflicts that had taken place since 1945 only one could legitimately be regarded as falling under the catch-all rubric of imperialism.[8] The upshot of these shortcomings was that the obvious had to be acknowledged: that war, the quintessential issue of international politics, is a historically much wider and more varied phenomenon than the Marxist theory allowed for. Imperialism thus fell far short of being an adequate theory of international politics.

The primary task of such a theory, for Bobbio, was to grasp the generality of international conflict. War is a phenomenon of such centrality to the human experience that no reductionist understanding of it could be sufficient, and, in Bobbio's view, of the existing theories only one, the theory of power politics, had sufficient breadth to encompass the history of international conflict in all its variousness:

> The power theory of politics is not vulnerable to the criticisms which the earlier theories were open to, because it explains wars without any central reference to ideological, political or economic systems. Differences between such systems may serve to explain why such varied permutations of conflicts arise between states in the first place, but they do not explain why such conflicts are so often settled in that particular way of resolving disputes – one which is prolonged, violent and ruthless – known as war.[9]

What the theory of power politics recognises, precisely by virtue of a certain 'thinness', is that there is something about political entities *per se* that separates them from each other in such a way as to give rise to the continual possibility of conflict, and ultimately war, among them. Since the specific causes of war are so various, a unitary theory is surely impossible. Instead, Bobbio proposed that 'to explain the phenomenon of war it is vital to start by examining the objective conditions of international relations'[10] – that is,

---

[8] Bobbio 1987, pp 207–8.

[9] Bobbio 1987, p 210.

[10] Bobbio 1987, p 210.

the international space itself. It is in the structure of the international, the external environment created by the formation of interior political space, that the reason for the perenniality of war, its persistence through the ages, is to be found:

> What in the last analysis remains absolutely indisputable is that, if there are non-negotiable conflicts which as such lead to armed confrontation, this stems exclusively from the nature of the international system, which is a system in dynamic equilibrium … a system which is continually breaking down and reconstituting itself, whose principal agent of dissolution and reconstruction so far has been the use of force, the last resort of all political power.[11]

For the student of IR, Bobbio's conclusion has an obvious affinity with Kenneth Waltz's insistence on the importance of the 'third image' for the character of international politics. Where Bobbio asked whether Marxism had an adequate theory of the causes of war, however, Waltz looked at the problem from the other side, examining Marxist ideas about transcending international conflict. For Waltz, the interest of Marxism as a theoretical position in IR was as the most extreme representative of inside–out thought, or 'the fullest development of the second image'.[12] Marxism posited an ideal of socio-political organisation and then purported to extend it directly into the international space. This way of thinking was a consequence of its transposition of politics into class terms: in accordance with the primacy of production, the class division was considered to be the fundamental socio-political relation, and the state, as the site of politics, was held to be an apparatus of class domination. If capitalist society represented the extreme form of the class relation – polarised into the binary opposition of capital and labour – then the proletariat embodied the principle of an undivided, classless world. Although no very detailed consideration was given to the question within Marxism, the implication of this way of thinking appeared to be that with the communist revolution, states, as organisations of class rule, necessarily disappeared, which further implied that international relations went with them.[13] Marxism in its political thinking thus focused on what

[11] Bobbio 1987, p 212.

[12] Waltz 2001, p 125.

[13] Waltz quotes Engels' famous dictum that 'the government of persons is replaced by the administration of things and the direction of the processes of production. The state is not "abolished", *it withers away*' (Waltz 2001, pp 141–2. (emphasis in original)). There is an obvious ambiguity here: even if the state as instrument of class oppression were to 'wither away', does this mean that political communities somehow cease to exist? And if they do, what happens to their bounded quality?

it took to be the central division within society, class struggle as the motor of progressive universalisation, and assumed a harmony of interests among the international proletariat.

Waltz had little difficulty in detailing how this whole conception, always obscure in its logic, collapsed in the crisis that led up to the outbreak of World War I: as the screw tightened, the balance of power crumbled and war approached, so the international unity proclaimed by the various European working class parties inexorably broke apart and each ended up supporting its own national government. When it actually came to it, therefore, the universality of the proletariat proved to be an illusion. The body that could claim the allegiance of the workers in the ultimate and most exceptional circumstances, when their very being appeared to be at stake, was the state, not their class. Waltz traced two reactions to this trauma within Marxism. One was the Leninist turn to vanguardism – the forcible imposition of the purported universality of labour by means of centralised power. The other was the revisionist *rapprochement* with the state, 'as the embodiment of national unity and the instrument for the progress of the national proletariat'.[14] The former claimed to uphold the original vision of proletarian harmony but to achieve it made use of exactly the instrument of oppression and division that that vision thought itself to have surpassed, the state. The latter made its peace with the state and retreated into its own variant of the long-established liberal logic of second-image international thinking, that war was caused by bad states: capitalist states were bellicose but socialist states would promote peace. Either way, the particularity and closure of the sovereign state had conclusively re-emerged within the universalistic international thinking of Marxism. The contradiction contained in the very phrase 'international socialism' had torn Marxism apart.

While Bobbio's short text argues that Marxism lacks an adequate account of war, as the defining dynamic of international politics, Waltz's critique is situated within a wider set of reflections on the international space itself. His argument, both in *Man, the State, and War* and *Theory of International Politics*, deliberately diminishes the theoretical scope of Marxism. What Waltz charges is that when matched against the whole Marxism fails: it is only a second-image, reductionist, theory. It may be able to explain certain aspects of international politics, but it falls short of comprehending, let alone transcending, the divided global political space itself. Waltz's argument about the second and third images thus directly denies the central idea of Marxist thought. For the Marxist conception was of a diachronic movement towards universality and freedom: the historical unfolding of the logic of production, working itself out through class struggle, comes to its conclusion with the

[14] Waltz 2001, p 142.

transition from capitalism to communism. Realism, by contrast, perceives a persisting synchronic condition of political fragmentation and conflict that is resistant to transformation. The Marxist vision was based on the conviction that the diachronic, the historical force of economic development, would ultimately burst through and resolve the synchronic, the spatial fracturing. It was for this reason that when Marxism turned its attention to international politics it sought to frame it within the categories of its account of capital: the political and the international had to be construed in terms of the historical movement that capital and the logic of class history promised.

Against this, Waltz's argument amounted to a kind of outflanking manoeuvre. Where Marxism attempted to read international politics as an epiphenomenon of capital, Waltz argued the reverse, that the international relations of capital were just the modern form of interaction within the perennially fragmented global political space. Capital was certainly an important factor within contemporary international politics, but the international realm and the conflict that marks it were far older than the capitalist mode of production and so not reducible to it. Similarly, imperialism might have been given a distinctive inflexion in its capitalist form, but it was a general phenomenon, traceable far back into history, that tended to arise wherever there was a significant imbalance of power between political entities.[15] Waltz's account of the fate of international socialism was designed to show that as Marxism was increasingly forced to acknowledge the reality of the synchronic, the condition of internationality, so it was inevitably drawn back into the forms of the capitalist world that it purported to transcend. Marxist theory had been unable to show how the fractured global political space would be overcome with the transformation of production relations within society – the move from inside to outside, or from the bounded to the unbounded, failed. The meaning of Waltz's argument about the second and third images, reductionist and systemic theories, was thus that the synchronic in fact contains the diachronic within itself, not the other way around. The inside is held within the outside, so that all movement takes place within, and continually reproduces, stasis.[16] The effect was to enclose Marxism within the international *Schuldzusammenhang*.

As R.N. Berki clearly perceived, the implication of Waltz's second image argument was that 'the very existence of international relations poses a serious, and perhaps intractable, *problem* for Marxism'.[17] In his still unsurpassed article on Marxism and international relations, Berki notes that Marx's

15 Waltz 1979, Chapter 2.

16 Or, to put the point in more speculative terms, the temporal is ultimately contained within the spatial, spirit within nature.

17 Berki 1971, p 80 (emphasis in original).

thought contains at least two deficits regarding the international field and the overcoming of intersocietal conflict. First, Marx does not show:

> that there is an absolute coincidence between capitalism and the state, and second, [he does not] demonstrate that the *capitalist* state (with its *internally* antagonistic character) is the only possible form of political authority that still allows *external* diversity; hence the possibility of international conflict even in a hypothetical post-capitalist world.[18]

As both Bobbio and Waltz noted, Marx's reframing of the political in class terms rendered the external division all but invisible. Waltz's question – 'Is it capitalism or states that must be destroyed to get peace, or must both be abolished?'[19] – thus precisely identified the conceptual shortcoming in Marxist approaches to the international: does the disappearance of the state with the supersession of capital refer only to its internal character as instrument of class domination, or does it also extend to its external function of 'organizing and promoting the interests of a group of people distinguished by their permanent occupation of a certain geographical area'?[20] Marx did not consider this question and no coherent answer can be adduced from his thinking. Rather, two opposed conceptions can be discerned: on the one hand a vision of the complete unity of mankind, and on the other the postulation of 'non-antagonistic diversity along national lines'.[21] While the first of these appears to accord more closely with Marx's thought, Berki shows that in the actual history of Marxism it was the second that came to predominate. As a result, the ideal of the transcendence of division through proletarian unity was increasingly relegated to a merely rhetorical future and socialism came to be identified with nation and state. While this tendency was perhaps propelled by tactical considerations at times and might have demonstrated a certain pragmatism, nevertheless, Berki pointedly notes, the question is 'can Marxism *afford* this compromise?'[22]

The answer is no: resigned accommodation to an incorrigible reality contradicts the central idea and motive force of Marx's thought. To show this, Berki turns to the themes of 'alienation' and 'species-being' that shape Marx's early thinking. He notes that while it is clear in these texts that for Marx 'man's ultimate satisfaction is found only in a union with his fellow human beings', at no point is 'the *extent* of the collective unit' specified.[23]

[18] Berki 1971, p 84 (emphases in original).
[19] Berki 1971, p 84.
[20] Berki 1971, p 84.
[21] Berki 1971, p 86.
[22] Berki 1971, p 86 (emphasis in original).
[23] Berki 1971, p 94 (emphasis in original).

Berki plausibly argues that according to the logic of Marx's writings of the 1840s the collective unit can only be the world as a whole: if Marx's categories mean what they appear to mean, then it has to be acknowledged that all 'lesser entities – the state, the nation, the tribe, the family, and even the class – stand between "man" and the "species"'.[24] However the philosophical coherence of Marx's concepts is assessed, he was evidently thinking of the liberation of the whole through the transcendence of division. In an ingenious argument, Berki then correlates the idea of non-antagonistic national diversity with capitalist private property. In Marx, he suggests, private property ultimately denotes a contradictory relationship between the whole and the parts: through the modern division of labour, social production is organised as a totality, but the profit accrues to the owners of the means of production. Transposing this contradiction to the international sphere, in an age of all-round economic interdependence production is done on a global scale, but nation-states, as bounded entities claiming exclusive possession of a certain territory, remain the equivalent of private property owners within this universal space. On Berki's reading, the compromise of 'non-antagonistic national diversity' thus signalled the failure of Marxist thought in the face of the international and its regression back into the forms of the capitalist world. The proclamation by prominent Marxists of the day of the 'sovereignty' and 'equality' of socialist states was clear proof that, unable to comprehend the fragmented international space through its own concepts, Marxism had instead made itself at home within quintessentially modern-capitalist categories.

The Realist critique of Marxism changed the terms of the problem of capital and the international. In its dispute with liberalism, Marxism had always situated itself within the political–international space and contested its dynamics. Realism, however, was not interested in that debate. For it, 'cosmopolitanism versus imperialism' was little more than shadow boxing. The real issue lay elsewhere, in the form of the international itself. The Realist perception is that, for as long as it has been able to claim the status of sovereign political being, humanity has existed within a self-divided and antagonistic external political space. Further, it is in the very nature of bounded political being to preclude the reconciliation of the whole: the formation of the rational inside space, the ground of political subjectivity, necessarily has as its obverse the production of the irrational outside, where no global subject can exist. Whatever the different forms it has passed through in its historical development, order within has always been shadowed by disorder without. Realism put this fundamental problem in the philosophy of history to the tradition of Marxist international thought and judged its

---

24 Berki 1971, p 97.

response to be inadequate – merely 'second-image' thinking, incapable of grasping the anarchic character of the international. Indeed, it is through the very extremity of its second-image convictions that the deep uncertainty and ambivalence of Marxism in relation to the international becomes manifest. Both Waltz and Berki note the characteristic unmediated opposition. On one side there is an extravagant vision of a total, undivided whole, a conception of classless unity that purports to leap straight beyond the fractured international space, annulling the boundaries altogether. On the other, there is the basically illicit appropriation of capitalistic forms without explaining how, in their socialist or communist version, they would not be subject to exactly the same limitations of particularity and antagonism – internationalism without the international. This doubled placing, both within and beyond, is a consequence of how Marxism sought to resolve the contradictory structure of the modern subject: it wanted to wrest from liberal cosmopolitanism the progressivist aspect while at the same time refusing Realism's consciousness of limits. Put simply, it wanted the freedom without the unfreedom, the inside without the outside, the political without the international. The Realist critique of Marxism suggests the impossibility of that positioning.

Realism unanswered

From roughly the turn of the millennium, once they had been fully assimilated to the discipline, Marxists in IR began to try to get to grips with its central object, the international itself, and with Realism's formulation of it in particular. At the same time, in the new geopolitical environment of the post-Cold War world, Marxists outside IR were also rethinking their theories of international politics. In both cases, the basic issue was the same: whether, and how, the international itself could be comprehend within the theoretical discourse of Marxism. As the Marxists in IR were well aware, Marx himself provided no direct assistance in this respect. Not only were his writings on international politics merely occasional, but he had never perceived the international as an object in its own right, so how it might relate to his body of thought remained an open question. It was precisely this absence of received authority that has made the recent Marxist debate over the international so revealing of the limits not just of Marxism but ultimately of the economic idea itself. For in confronting the international, Marxism has been challenged to reckon its own theoretical resources: could it comprehend the international space so as to answer Realism's second-image accusation? In the event, however, the contemporary Marxist discussions have essentially repeated the two contradictory positions that both Waltz and Berki observed within traditional Marxist approaches to the international – either accommodation and remaining within or a merely gestural leap beyond. The principal effect of the debate has thus been to demonstrate the persisting inability of Marxism to mediate inside and outside, the limited and the unlimited, on the basis of its conception of capital, and so to grasp the fragmented space of the international.

Under the rubric of 'historical materialism', much of the mainstream of Marxism understands itself as a version of social theory, the aim of which is to identify the basic factors shaping society in order to reconstruct its developmental process. In all variants of Marxism, these factors are taken to be economic: the primacy of production and the class divided organisation of social labour. Given this social-theoretical framing, the international is then understood as a specific dimension of the general social field. For the greater part of recent Marxist work in IR, the problem of the international has thus presented itself as essentially one of incorporation – how to fit the international into historical materialism as part of a comprehensive theory of society and history. The guiding idea is that the account of social processes is to be made more complete through the thoroughgoing integration of the international dimension into the explanatory framework. This approach can be seen at work across the various subdivisions of current Marxist IR. Contemporary Neo-Gramscianism, for example, emphasises the international import of Gramsci's thought in its accounts of historical hegemonies and passive revolutions.[25] Postcolonial Marxism develops its anti-Eurocentric history of the 'Rise of the West' by explicitly foregrounding the international aspect of this long historical process.[26] And Marxist IPE understands phases in the historical interactions of the world market and geopolitics through an explicit recognition of the specificity of the international political space.[27] In all of these, the international is presented as a crucial additional factor: it is appreciation of the international context that permits a more complete reconstruction of the social and historical processes. The foremost representative of this approach in Marxist IR has been Justin Rosenberg, who in a lengthy series of articles over a number of years has elaborated the notions, first, of 'uneven and combined development' and, more recently, of 'multiplicity', in order to rectify the perceived deficit of social theory generally, and historical materialism in particular, in regard to the international.[28]

However, although it has no doubt made an important contribution to social theory, this approach misconstrues the significance of the Realist critique of Marxism. The meaning of the third image is that, by virtue of the boundary line, the ordered inside space necessarily generates the anarchic outside – the positive and the negative exist in and through each other. The

25 Morton 2007.

26 Anievas and Nişancıoğlu 2015.

27 ten Brink 2015.

28 See Rosenberg 2016a and 2016b for representative statements.

problem that Realism then poses is how to understand this contradictory unity, and the point of its critique of second-image thinking is that it is not possible to comprehend the whole solely from the inside. In the register of social theory, though, the international appears not as a problem of sovereignty, the formation of political subjectivity, and of inside and outside, but only as the particular dimension of inter-societal relations within the general historical process. In this way, it is ultimately reduced merely to a question of number: multiplicity. The properly metaphysical meaning of the international thus goes completely unrecognised in social-theory Marxism. For the problem of the international, the negative totalisation of political space, is in no way resolved, or even addressed, by the elaboration of the causal implications for historical development of the co-existence of multiple socio-political entities. Instead, it is a question precisely of the limits of the social, of the fragmented and unreconciled whole, of the perennial recurrence of conflict, and of the absence of a global subject. Since those limits cannot be grasped in the discourse of social theory, though, sociological and historicist Marxism can conceive the international only in inside terms. The relation of the political to the non-political, or the social to the non-social, disappears from view and what remains visible is just, once again, the interactions among socio-political entities, or between inside spaces. So far from actually comprehending Realism, therefore, Rosenberg simply transposes it into different terms – anarchy in the discourse of sociology.[29] Hence social theory Marxism remains very definitely international relations theory and never actually becomes a theory of the international. In fact, the real challenge of the international to social theory is not to incorporate societal multiplicity into the causal dynamics of the historical process but to explain why the social subject remains badly particularistic – that is, why there is no social subject at the level of the whole. In order to address that question, though, it would be necessary to perceive the limits of the social and so to recognise the inadequacy of social theory in the face of the international. In Rosenberg's work, however, it is not the mediation, and transformation, of social theory through the international that has been pursued but the integration of the international into social theory, its reduction to the terms of sociological thought. The premises of social theory may thus be strategically reconfigured, but its basic validity is not brought into question. On the contrary, the guiding assumption is that social theory, which is premised upon the inside/outside division, is all-encompassing and knows no limits. As a result, while he has undeniably done a great deal to establish it as a thematic within both Marxism and social theory generally,

[29] Davenport 2020.

Rosenberg's rendition of the international remains confined within the third image and does not answer Realism.

Although Rosenberg began from the problematic of modernity, the project of incorporating the international into the premises of social theory led to the notion of 'uneven and combined development' being elaborated far beyond the confines of the capitalist epoch, as a 'general abstraction' valid for the entirety of history.[30] Consequently, the specific question of the conceptual relation between capital and the international has not been addressed in his work.[31] That problem, though, had already been posed within Marxism by Fred Halliday, in the early 1990s. The Marxist paradigm, he noted, 'begs the question of why, if there is a world economy in which class interests operate transnationally, there is a need for states at all. What, in other words, is the specificity and effectivity of distinct states within a single economic totality?'[32] Over the following years, this question would make itself insistently felt within two central debates in Marxist IR: the revival of imperialism theory and the question of globalisation.

The so-called New Imperialism thinking of the early 2000s sought simultaneously to reaffirm the classical Marxist notion of imperialism and to update it for changed times. Part of this renewal was a questioning of the national-territorial assumptions of the classical thinkers and an attention, instead, to what David Harvey framed as a 'dialectic' between economic/capitalist and territorial/political logics of power – two logics that were intertwined but also often in contradiction with each other.[33] This no doubt added sophistication to the modern accounts of imperialism. Why, though, were there two logics? Why should capital, inherently global in its nature, exist through a fragmented territorial 'logic', the international? Harvey did not himself address the problem, simply assuming the territorial nature of capital. Others who joined the debate, though, did. In the influential view of Ellen Wood, for instance, positing two logics was a mistake that resulted from a failure to understand the nature of capital. In her view, the distinctiveness of the latter as a form of social power lay in the detachment of accumulation from personal, 'political', relations of domination and its transferral to impersonal, 'economic', processes mediated through the

[30] Rosenberg 2010.

[31] Indeed, it is not clear how it could arise within Rosenberg's developed conception: if the international as 'multiplicity' and 'uneven and combined development' is intrinsic to human social existence, then capital must, *a fortiori*, be international. Only the particular form through which a general transhistorical content appears could come into question – in effect, a concession to Waltz's placing of the diachronic within the synchronic.

[32] Halliday 1994, p 91.

[33] Harvey 2003. Although Harvey borrowed it from Giovanni Arrighi (Arrighi 1994, pp 33–4), the 'two logics' formulation in fact goes back at least to Chase-Dunn 1981.

market. A political/territorial logic of power could thus only be *pre*capitalist, as capitalist imperialism is economic and non-territorial.[34] In Wood's view, therefore, Harvey's assumption was theoretically unjustified: there is no territorial logic within the capitalist mode of surplus appropriation. However, having dismissed one half of Harvey's argument as conceptually underived, Wood still needed to explain the evident fact of the territorial reality of global capital, the states-system. This presented her with a difficulty: on the one hand, she was keen to emphasise the persistence of the bounded, territorial state as a means of resisting the universalising claims of liberal globalisation theory;[35] but on the other, having once expelled territoriality from the logic of capital, she could not easily reintroduce it. Caught in a theoretical dilemma of her own making, all that Wood could offer was an awkward compromise. Capital, she proposed, exists through many states for practical rather than conceptual reasons. Since it is beyond the capacity of any one state to project its power across the global economic space as a whole, the effective enforcement of capitalist social relations is ensured through the political fragmentation of the world.[36] The many states are thus the means through which capital pins down local populations and compels them to submit to market mechanisms. In short, 'global capital *needs* a fragmentation of political space'.[37]

The unsatisfactory nature of this solution, which amounted only to a 'soft functionalism',[38] was recognised by Alex Callinicos, who, allying himself with Harvey and the theory of imperialism, attempted a different approach to the problem.[39] Clearly feeling the need for a more conceptual solution, Callinicos tried to show 'how to solve the many states problem'[40] by turning to the pre-modern forms that Marx termed merchant's and usurer's capital, which, in the Marxist conception, had been absorbed into and transformed by capital proper. 'Why shouldn't the state system', he

---

34 Wood 2006.

35 See, for example, Wood 2003, Chapter 6.

36 'I should, perhaps, concede that the impossibility of a global state to match global capital is not something that can be grasped entirely on the theoretical plane. To a large extent, this proposition is a lower-level practical observation about the insurmountable difficulty of sustaining on a large geographical scale the close regulation and predictability capital needs' (Wood 2006, p 25).

37 Wood 2006, p 25 (emphasis in original). Wood thus strains to bring back together what she has first separated: 'the very essence of globalization is a global economy administered by a global system of multiple states' (Wood 2003, p 141). But this is clearly contradicted by her own argument, which denies any such essentiality to the political structure of the states-system.

38 Chibber 2005, p 157.

39 Callinicos 2007, 2009a, 2009b.

40 Callinicos 2009a.

asked, 'be conceived analogously, as a social form that develops prior to the dominance of capitalism but that is incorporated into and adapted to the capitalist mode?'[41] Doing so would, Callinicos claimed, be fully in accord with the method of *Capital*, which he understood as developing through the progressive incorporation of increasingly complex determinations not logically contained within those that preceded.[42] At the appropriate point in the exposition, the states-system could be introduced in this way and so regarded as '*a dimension of the capitalist mode of production*'.[43] Callinicos further proposed that a major reason why the many states remained separate even as capital was binding the world together could be found within the real-world workings of the global economy: the uneven and combined nature of accumulation created 'very powerful centrifugal forces that would strongly work to sustain the political demarcation of the world into territorial states'.[44]

Unfortunately, however, this line of thinking provided no real advance on Wood. First, Callinicos's analogy was entirely misconceived. Merchant's and usurer's capital were at least forms of capital, so it was possible to understand logically how they could be taken up into capital proper. But that this was not the case for the states-system was precisely the premise of the problem. Why it should be absorbed and extended within capital thus remained unexplained. Secondly, the 'non-deductive' introduction of the states-system established no necessary connection between capital and the many states. Indeed, on these grounds, there appeared to be no reason why any particular empirical determination could not be inserted into the theory, as it suited the needs of the argument, and then declared to be '*a dimension of the capitalist mode of production*'. Thirdly, Callinicos's economic explanation had no purchase on political fragmentation. The uneven and combined development of capital works at least as powerfully within states as it does between them, so it cannot constitute a sufficient explanation for why the global political form of capitalist modernity is a fragmented states-system – *economic* unevenness does not explain *political* division. So far from demonstrating how to solve the 'many states problem', therefore, what Callinicos and Wood really showed was that when the territorial existence of capital was no longer simply taken for granted, the Marxist theorists of imperialism were at a loss to account for it.

The revival of imperialism theory was in part a reaction to the high tide of globalisation in the 1990s. From a Marxist perspective, though, that moment

41 Callinicos 2009b, p 80.

42 This conception of the argumentative logic of *Capital* has been definitively refuted within contemporary Marxology (see Chapter 3).

43 Callinicos 2009b, p 83 (emphasis in original).

44 Callinicos 2009b, p 91.

could also be read in a very different way, as a fundamental transformation that rendered the old theories outdated. Thus William Robinson, for example, proposed that the movement in the late 20th century from a 'world economy to a global economy'[45] was the transition from nationally bounded economic spaces to an unbounded global capitalist whole, as a result of which capital could no longer be organised effectively through nation-states. In orthodox Marxist fashion, Robinson holds the state to be 'a moment of class power relations'.[46] While, for contingent historical reasons, this power had previously been organised on the scale of the nation-state, with the globalisation of capital, Robinson claims, those boundaries were being exceeded and a transnational capitalist class and state were coming into existence. The basic logic of the argument, therefore, is from the limited to the unlimited. In its actual exposition, however, Robinson's account in fact demonstrates considerable uncertainty about the status of bounded nation-states and the obvious empirical fact of their continued existence. Typical of the way in which he proceeds is thus that what he puts forward in one paragraph ('the nation-state is a historically specific form of world social organization in the process of becoming transcended by globalization'), he immediately retracts in the next ('National states may retain their form. They are not disappearing but will be around for a long time to come').[47] Throughout, the argument oscillates unstably between these two quite different positions: on the one hand, that nation-states are being remade in various ways by global capital, and, on the other, that they are actually being transcended by global capital. The first, uncontroversial and widely supported across the social sciences, is what the substance of Robinson's account in fact says. But he is driven towards the second by the terms of his theory of capital and state, in which the bounded and the unbounded are split apart and placed in opposition to each other. The history of capital is framed in the argument as a linear trajectory of spatial expansion, from the local to the global, the era of the nation-state being merely a passing stage in this process, while the class idea of the state extrudes nation and territory completely.[48] Theoretically constrained to the unlimited, Robinson is thus compelled, against all the evidence, to claim that the states-system is being superseded and that a transnational state is in formation. Meanwhile the limited – bounded political space – continually recurs within his account as an empirical reality but without receiving any adequate theoretical explanation.

---

45 Robinson 2004, p 9.

46 Robinson 2004, p 99.

47 Robinson 2004, pp 142–3.

48 'There is nothing in the historical-materialist conception of the state that *necessarily* ties it to territory or to nation-states' (Robinson 2004, p 97 (emphasis in original)).

Robinson offered a reading of globalisation in the terms of sociological Marxism. At much the same time, in *Empire*, Michael Hardt and Antonio Negri, put forward a Marxist philosophical interpretation (albeit a Marx now filtered through Foucault and Deleuze). Whatever the novelty of globalisation, though, the conception underlying Hardt and Negri's book is resolutely traditional. As far back as *Man, the State, and War*, Waltz had pointed out the characteristic idea of Marxist international thought: identifying a perfected form of social organisation and then purporting to extend it directly beyond the boundaries to the scale of the whole. Exactly this schema is repeated in *Empire*. According to Hardt and Negri, the early-modern humanist revolution threw off the old forms of theological bondage and unleashed humanity's constituent power, its productive potential and its capacity to make nature submit to its will: 'humans declared themselves masters of their own lives, producers of cities and history, and inventors of heavens'.[49] This was 'the primary event of modernity: the affirmation of the powers of *this* world, the discovery of the plane of immanence'.[50] It is in the radical immanence of the 'multitude', therefore, that humanity, for Hardt and Negri, finds its proper self. However, the liberatory revolution of immanence was immediately thwarted by the counter-revolution of transcendentalism, a project of limitation given its definitive formulation by Kant.[51] The cornerstone of the transcendental architecture was the sovereignty of the modern state, and so, by implication at least, the states-system. In this way, once again within Marxist accounts, the limited and the unlimited are severed from each other and posed in opposition: sovereignty and the transcendental are construed as a hierarchical imposition on the otherwise pristine and self-sufficient immanence of the multitude. The boundless constituent power of the multitude is ensnared in the machine of sovereignty and its limitless creativity is captured by the domination of capital – two forces, locked in opposition, that produce modernity as perpetual 'crisis'. In the imaginary of *Empire*, however, the multitude, like the revolutionary proletariat before it, cannot be repressed forever. Through its limitless productivity it compels the construction of a new, decentred form of imperial sovereignty spanning the whole world – Hardt and Negri's rendition of the moment of globalisation. Even this is insufficient, though, as the sovereignty of empire only prepares

---

49 Hardt and Negri 2000, p 70.

50 Hardt and Negri 2000, p 71 (emphasis in original).

51 Hardt and Negri 2000, pp 74–90. Hardt and Negri do not even attempt to explain why this counter-revolution should have been successful, indeed why it should have occurred at all, if the principle of radical freedom had already been discovered. Nor do they explain why the project of transcendentalism should have found expression in what is surely *the* fundamental, epoch-making philosophical text of modernity, Kant's *Critique of Pure Reason*, if it was merely counter-revolutionary and extrinsic to the reality of the multitude.

the way, in turn, for the final victory of the multitude and the resolution of the world into complete immanence.[52]

Just as in the orthodox Marxist narrative, the multitude is thus a total political subject projected to the scale of the whole. In realising its essence, it overthrows all structures of limitation, which are only ever extrinsic and inessential to its proper being. Rather than grasping the negativity of the limit, therefore, Hardt and Negri's affirmation of the positivity of radical immanence simply refuses it, turning its back on what it does not wish to see. Consequently, as R.B.J. Walker notes, the form problem of the international eludes them: 'the immanent critique of modernity does not automatically translate into an account of a politics that involves bringing the outside inside. One can no more move inside an inside/outside problem than move outside of it. In any case, such a move would involve a reversion to a notion of an inside separate from an outside'.[53] Like the traditional Marxists, Hardt and Negri want the inside without the outside, the political without the international. The same uncertainties that beset Robinson's sociological account thus recur within the philosophical discourse of *Empire*: what exactly is the status of the international within the process of capitalist globalisation? On the one hand, Hardt and Negri boldly proclaim that a new mode of 'imperial sovereignty' is coming into being, a networked sovereignty, without commanding centre, that is beyond the old form of international order. On the other, what the argument actually seems to delineate is a new kind of organisation of power *within* the international space: 'a "network power", a new form of sovereignty, emerged in the late 20th century and it included as its primary elements, or nodes, the dominant nation-states along with supranational institutions, major capitalist corporations, and other powers.'[54] As with Robinson, this latter claim has considerable plausibility, and in the less rhapsodic parts of their argument Hardt and Negri have some perceptive things to say about it. But again like Robinson, they clearly want to make the bolder, more ambitious claim. This is so for two reasons. First, it permits the separation of immanence and transcendence. If globalisation, as the progress towards immanence, was actually produced through nation-states and the inter-state system, then immanence would be generated through transcendence, fatally disrupting Hardt and Negri's simple binary schema. Secondly, it could not be allowed that globalisation, immanence and the multitude have as a condition of their existence the sovereign inside/outside

[52] 'Empire, despite its efforts, finds it impossible to construct a system of right adequate to the new reality of the globalization of social and economic relations. ... This impossibility is explained ... by the revolutionary nature of the multitude' (Hardt and Negri 2000, p 394).

[53] Walker 2002, p 344.

[54] Hardt and Negri 2006, p xii.

form that structures the modern order of transcendentalism and the division of international space, as that would put an insurmountable stumbling block in the way of the ultimate goal of the argument, the realisation of the undivided self-presence of the multitude. Accordingly, in order to maintain the projected outcome, globalisation must be separated from the international and counterposed to it rather than understood as produced by and working through the division of political space. Try as they might to escape it, therefore, in the affirmative visions of globalisation the positivity of the inside is continually haunted by the negativity of the outside.[55]

Where the imperialism theorists wanted to retain the international but could not account for its existence, the globalisers wanted to go beyond the international but could not account for its persistence. In both, the problem of capital and the international remained unresolved and the co-existence of the bounded and the unbounded unexplained. The most concerted attempt to address this issue, which crystallised as a puzzle within Marxist IR in the first decade of the new millennium,[56] was that of Hannes Lacher, and it is in the knots and tangles of his argument that all of the problems that Marxism has had in comprehending the international come together. Lacher's approach is shaped by the need to negotiate a series of contradictions that follow from Marxism's self-positioning in relation to the mainstream: on the one hand, he rejects globalisation as liberal ideology but retains it as both intrinsic to capital and the proper scale on which the universal, post-capitalist class should realise itself; on the other, he wants to assert the divided geopolitical space against liberal irenicism but, mindful of Realism, also to reject it as a timeless space of conflict. Since he is unable to resolve any of these contradictions, however, the argument is marked by continual confusion and instability.

In Lacher's preferred version of historical materialism, so-called Political Marxism, what is distinctive about capital is that it is an 'economic' form of accumulation, as opposed to the many precapitalist 'political' forms; that is, workers are forced to submit to the anonymous processes of the market rather than being subjected to personal subordination. Anxious to distance themselves from economism and structuralism, Political Marxists interpret the emergence of capital as a rearrangement of factors within the general

---

55 Reviewing the book from the perspective of IR, R.B.J. Walker soberly observed that, for all its excitement, the argument was greatly in need of 'a more sustained engagement with international relations as an expression of the problematic limits of modern politics' (Walker 2002, p 345). No such engagement would be forthcoming, though. Twenty years on, Hardt and Negri continued to proclaim 'revolutionary internationalism', declaring that 'the most powerful forces to contest and move beyond the rule of Empire will necessarily take the form of further internationalisms', without pausing to give any consideration to the concept of the international itself (Hardt and Negri 2019, p 76).

56 See *Cambridge Review of International Affairs* 2007 and Anievas 2010.

political field: capital is the result of a 'long process in which certain *political* powers were gradually transformed into *economic* powers and transferred to a separate sphere'.[57] The outcome of this differentiation of spheres was the emergence alongside the market of a 'purely political' state, an impersonal power structure that is separate from the economic system. In this conception, capital requires a political authority for functional reasons (primarily maintenance of property rights and enforcement of market dependence), and so the practical need for *a* state can be shown. But because the economic is detached from dependence on territory, the necessity of *many* states cannot: 'this logic of accumulation was not contained by political boundaries; as well as allowing commerce and trade to cross borders, capitalism makes possible the transnational organization of the extraction of surplus'.[58] As Lacher repeatedly emphasises, there is thus, for Political Marxism, no intrinsic connection between capital and the international.[59] In fact, not only is there no necessary connection, but the global development of capital should work to eliminate territorial division.

Although it is arrived at through a distinctive route, the conclusion here is a familiar one within recent Marxism – capital as such has no relation to bounded political space and there is therefore no *logical* connection between capital and the international. Working within the discipline of IR, however, Lacher is conscious of the obvious empirical reality of the international. His difficulty is thus how to account for the territorial structure of the international through a theory that excludes it a priori. It is precisely his determination to confront this problem head on, and not to accept a compromise in the manner of his mentor Wood, that makes his argument so revealing. The only way in which territory can be conceived within this version of historical materialism is as a corollary of 'political' accumulation: for reasons that remain unexplained, relations of personal rule apparently involve territory whereas impersonal relations do not.[60] The territorial nature of the modern state derives, for Lacher, from the era of European Absolutism, a form of personal rule that, according to Political Marxism, was non-capitalist and unmodern, since the state was the 'private property' of the sovereign.[61] Emerging apparently by accident out

[57] Lacher 2006, p 38, quoting Ellen Wood (emphases in original). Wood 1981 is the classic statement of this idea.

[58] Lacher 2006, p 97.

[59] See, for instance, Lacher 2006, pp 45, 59 and 119, among many examples throughout the book.

[60] Despite its title, Lacher's book contains no theory of territory, simply presuming it to be somehow a function of 'surplus extraction'.

[61] Lacher 2006, p 86. 'The absolutist states which principally formed the Westphalian system were not simply *relatively* but *absolutely* non-modern' (Lacher 2006, p 80 (emphases in original)). There is persistent instability in the argument here. At one moment, Absolutism is declared

of localised class struggles in the English countryside, capital was born into this pre-modern political structure. In response to the geopolitical pressure exerted by capitalist Britain, Absolutist continental Europe, organised in a precapitalist territorial way, was then forced through the transition to capitalist social relations in the 19th century.[62] Capital is, therefore, inherently non-territorial but came into existence within a territorial form that it has subsequently absorbed.

In this argument the international becomes a bizarre and unfathomable paradox. For Lacher, there is a strict distinction between economic and political accumulation: the former has nothing to do with territory; the latter is strongly territorial. Yet, as a matter of historical fact, 'economic accumulation' has continually reproduced territoriality within itself. Beyond simply asserting that capital internalised the states-system, Lacher cannot explain *why* this should be so – that is, why capital should have eliminated so many other pre-modern forms while perpetuating and extending just this one, which is apparently directly opposed to its own logic.[63] That the globalisation of capital has produced an international political space of some 200 precisely bounded states would seem to suggest that the borderlines are intrinsic to capital in some way, not that they are an unaccountably long-lived hangover of a precapitalist form. As it is, in Lacher's argument the capitalist state is radically schizophrenic: on its inside it is entirely modern and capitalistic but on its outside it is entirely non-modern and precapitalist. The inside and the outside of the same entity conform to completely different and antithetical logics. Given that Lacher so frequently insists upon the absolute incommensurability of capitalism and pre-capitalism, it is not clear how this could be so. Since he is unable to negotiate his own axiomatic separation of the bounded and the unbounded, Lacher is ultimately driven into an impasse. Capital, his theory tells him, ought to exist politically at the level of the undivided whole: 'the globalizing tendency of capital makes a corresponding process of political integration necessary. … Only a global state

to have been absolutely non-modern; at another, two forms of modernity are posited, an 'absolutist-bourgeois modernity' and a 'capitalist modernity' (p 102). If the first line of argument is followed, Absolutism as non-modern, then presumably modernity must be the age of capital? Yet halfway through the book Lacher announces that 'following the argument of the previous chapters, the equation of capitalism and modernity can no longer be maintained … there is no longer a direct substantive or even temporal nexus between capitalism and modernity' (p 101). This sort of confusion is typical of the book as a whole.

62 Lacher 2006, p 6.

63 The status of capital is in fact profoundly uncertain in Lacher's argument. On the one hand, he insists that capital is the defining category of the modern world and is radically different from everything that went before it; on the other, because so much has been evacuated from, and so becomes inexplicable through, his notion of capital, the master category turns out to be severely limited in its explanatory scope.

could secure the social and economic reproduction of transnational capital and thus fulfil the state function.'[64] However, this necessity is immediately gainsaid because it appears that the intrinsic dynamic of capitalist modernity towards deterritorialised globality will be thwarted, perhaps forever, by the inexplicable persistence of the precapitalist and pre-modern: 'It may be that territorial statehood, while not originating within capitalism, has become so entrenched that it is all but impossible to move towards a form of state that corresponds to capital's globalizing dynamic.'[65] In the end the two sides, the bounded and the unbounded, stand in stark opposition, entirely unmediated to each other, and Lacher is forced to recognise that the actual dynamic of the modern world flatly contradicts his theory and is incomprehensible through it. Why the supposedly precapitalist borders should not merely survive but actually proliferate so deep into the age of capital remains a mystery. Having received no sufficient theoretical explanation, boundedness and division then take their inevitable revenge, as Lacher is eventually forced to concede to exactly the Realism that he otherwise so scornfully reviles: 'The very fact of international anarchy … prevents the emergence of a state form adequate to capital's global existence'.[66]

From sovereignty to value

For most of the 20th century, mainstream international thought largely concerned itself with the big events of international politics – empire and decolonisation, World Wars and Cold War, globalisation and American unipolarity. Correlatively, Marxism concentrated on producing its own oppositional versions of the same themes – imperialism and inter-imperial rivalry, neo-colonialism and hegemony. It imagined itself as an active player within the dynamics of international politics, contesting them in the name of a radical alternative. However, at the end of the century, as the international space finally attained its properly universal scale and the presumed site of radical opposition was correspondingly eliminated, so the theoretical problem changed. It was no longer enough simply to contest the content of international politics; rather, the form itself had to be reckoned with. This was the challenge that Realism put to Marxism: could it comprehend the divided and unreconciled whole in such a way as to transcend it?

Surveying the various contributions to the recent Marxist debate on the international, the answer to that question is clearly negative. The principal achievements of Marxism in IR have been in its main discursive register of

[64] Lacher 2006, p 162.
[65] Lacher 2006, p 163.
[66] Lacher 2006, p 163.

historical sociology, which is limited to the causal reconstruction of historical processes and so is entirely oblivious to the metaphysical significance of the international, its meaning within the philosophy of history. While 'multiplicity' and 'uneven and combined development' have sought to translate IR into the terms of social theory, in doing so they nevertheless remain wholly within the problematic of the international as fragmented political space. Elsewhere, the record is one of complete failure. Both the modern-day proponents of imperialism theory and the enthusiasts for globalisation, as well as those who would position themselves somewhere between, have found it impossible, using whatever version of Marxism they prefer, to think the international itself in a theoretically coherent way. In every case, they have been unable to mediate the limited and the unlimited, and so to bring together bounded political space and unbounded economic space. The social-theory Marxists stay within the borders, while the globalisers leap straight beyond them. Others, the imperialism theorists and the Political Marxists, hedge: although they feel the resilience of the borderlines, because their theories tell them that capital ought to be limitless and all-encompassing they can only account for them with makeshift and ever more implausible explanations. The contemporary debate about the status of the international in Marxist theory has thus made no real advance beyond the traditional approaches to international politics within Marxism: while the classical theory of imperialism, World-Systems Theory and Neo-Gramscian conceptions of hegemony all, in their different ways, simply assumed the international space, in the end class and class struggle, 'social relations', 'uneven and combined development', and 'Empire' fare no better. In all of them, Marxism remains trapped by the line. What this fundamental theoretical failure makes clear is that Marxism has no theory of the inside/outside division that at once produces the bounded space of self-determination, on one side of the line, and the fragmented and anarchic space of the international, on the other. That is, Marxism has no theory of sovereignty. As a result, it is incapable of grasping the form problem of the international.

Marxism's failure to bring capital and the international together within the terms of Marxist thought in order to comprehend the modern world-system as a whole is not merely marginal or incidental to its ambitions as radical critique. Rather, it directly negates the central claim of Marxism, which is to have attained a position beyond the limits of capitalist modernity. The modern subject is at once open, inclusive and cosmopolitan, the proponent of 'humanity', and closed, exclusive and communitarian, the proponent of state and nation. The universality of the inside thus derives from exactly the boundary lines that at the same time render it particular, and it is around this contradiction that the entirety of IR has developed. That Marxism has been unable to resolve the contradiction is a consequence of the way in which it tried to position itself in relation to the mainstream. It sought to take from liberalism the positivity of the inside while denying Realism's negativity of the outside – that is, it tried to split inside and outside apart, perfecting the one and discarding the other. Rather than understanding the two sides of the modern subject, the limited and the unlimited, as necessarily conjoined, therefore, Marxism assumed that the limits were merely extrinsic and unnecessary. Accordingly, it imagined that it could simply cast them off, and so have the inside without the outside. This is what makes it, as Waltz perceived, the most extreme representative of second-image thinking. However, the general incomprehension of Marxism when confronted with the international reveals the falseness of this conception: the outside is either summarily reduced to the inside or it remains an unmediated externality. Marxism oscillates between these two poles, unable to bring them together and stabilise them in a coherent theory by grasping the line itself. In the split between Realism and liberalism, the modern subject exposes the metaphysical wound that it cannot heal. As its international thinking attests, that wound lacerates Marxism every bit as deeply.[67] Just as much as its antagonists, therefore, Marxism is trapped within the *Schuldzusammenhang* of the international.

The significance of its encounter with the international reaches far beyond the specific limitations of Marxism, though, right into the conceptual centre of the modern world. The divisions first between politics and economics and then, within the sphere of politics, between domestic and international are foundational to the experiential structure of the modern subject. If the coherence of that structure is to be maintained, then the logical relation

[67] The implication of its inability to comprehend the anarchic form of the international space is that Marxism's commitment to historicism, a commitment that is shared across 'critical' thinking generally, is misconceived and self-defeating. As the Realist critique of Marxist international thought demonstrates, it is only by grasping the essentially metaphysical problem of form – that is, the *logical* division of inside and outside that founds the order of sovereignty – that it is possible to go beyond the limits of the capitalist world. Since the metaphysics of inside/outside are integral to the modern conception of history, though, precisely its commitment to historicism prevents Marxism from ever comprehending the form problem of the international. As Giorgio Agamben has recognised, in its historical thinking, as in so many other respects, Marxism unquestioningly accepted the metaphysical inheritance of the very tradition that it purported to reject: 'Modern political thought has concentrated its attention on history, and has not elaborated a corresponding concept of time. Even historical materialism has until now neglected to elaborate a concept of time that compares with its concept of history. Because of this omission it has been unwittingly compelled to have recourse to a concept of time dominant in Western culture for centuries, and so to harbour, side by side, a revolutionary concept of history and a traditional experience of time' (Agamben 2007, p 99).

between the poles of these various binary oppositions, the point at which they both come together and are separated from each other, must remain silent and hidden. What was distinctive of Marxism within this general context was that through its claim to go beyond the limits of capitalist modernity, it purported to surpass these divisions. However, it did so only abstractly, in the Hegelian sense of the term, from one side of the line, on the basis of the economic idea. Indeed, it is precisely its absolutisation of the economic conception, its raising of it into a metaphysics and philosophy of history, that forces Marxism to try to account for sovereignty and the political in the 'materialist' terms of the economic. The deeper and more far-reaching implication of the inability of Marxism to grasp the inside/outside division of sovereignty, therefore, is that the totalised and fragmented space of the international cannot be understood from within the parameters of the economic idea. The borderlines that structure the international space are impossible to understand on the assumption, essential not just to Marxism but to modern thought as a whole, of the validity of the economic conception of existence. So long as the economic idea is taken for granted as a given and irreducible reality, capital and the international must remain separate from and external to each other, with the consequence that the world-system as a whole escapes comprehension. Precisely in its frustrated effort to overcome them, Marxism is thus in fact exemplary of the limits of modernity. This is the wider and more far-reaching significance of the failure of Marxism when confronted with the international. It follows that if the relation between capital and the international is actually to be grasped as a matter of theory, then the economic idea itself must be broken open and its metaphysical structure laid bare. In this way, the problematic of the international, and its central concept of sovereignty, leads directly into the problematic of the economic, and its central concept of value.

3

The Theory of Value: The Revolution in Value Theory

The value debate

In the 1970s, as the world-system of capital and the international accelerated towards completion, so Marxism, both as radical theory and as mass ideology, descended into terminal crisis.[1] While it had long been subjected to attack from outside, what was different this time was that, under the pressure of incipient globalisation and with social and political theory generally turning away from the Marxist paradigm, the internal coherence of Marxism itself splintered, the most damaging criticism in fact coming from within. A significant breach had already been opened in the previous decade by the Althusserian programme, which attempted to re-establish the purportedly scientific status of Marxism through rigorous structuralist readings of both historical materialism and the project of a critique of political economy.[2] Although it ran into the ground almost immediately, unravelling in tortuous 'self-critique', the brief vogue of Althusserianism had clearly signalled the deep uncertainty: old verities could no longer be believed in, so there was an urgent need for a root-and-branch reconsideration of Marxism, in particular regarding fundamental conceptual questions. Across the various national formations of Marxism this general crisis was articulated in distinctively different but overlapping registers: in Germany, largely philosophical;[3] in France and Italy, both political and economic;[4] in the Anglophone world,

1 Althusser 1978; Hoff 2017, Chapter 1.3.
2 Althusser 2005 and 2015.
3 For overviews of the major themes in the German debate, see Fineschi 2009 and Hoff 2017, Chapter 2.1.
4 For Italy, see *International Journal of Political Economy* 1997, *International Journal of Political Economy* 1998, Hoff 2017, Chapter 5.1, and Bellofiore and Wolf 2018. For France, see Hoff 2017, Chapter 5.2.

mainly economic.[5] Taking place in a fractious and polemical atmosphere, pervaded by a deep sense of disorientation, at their sharpest these debates reached right into the core of Marxism, for the question they ultimately revolved around, no matter what the register of discussion, was the status of the fundamental concept of Marx's theory of capital – value. As long as Marxism could be considered a more or less coherent whole, the 'labour theory of value', as it was generally known, was largely taken for granted, left to the specialist concerns of the Marxist economists and their technical debates about, for instance, the tendency of the rate of profit to fall. Once the superstructure of Marxism began to crumble, though, then the coherence of the base – the idea of value in Marx – was increasingly exposed to critical scrutiny. The concept that formed 'the *foundation* of [Marx's] attempt to understand capitalism',[6] thus became a problem. In fact, it became *the* problem, for if the foundation itself was insecure, then nothing solid and substantial could be built upon it.

The flash point for much of the controversy over the theory of value was the so-called transformation problem.[7] This was the place in the expositional architecture of *Capital* where the contradiction that appeared to exist in Marx's analysis between Volumes I and III was most intractably concentrated. The argument of the former, concerned with the production of capital, was elaborated by Marx in value terms, generally taken to mean quantities of labour expended in production, whereas that of the latter, dealing with the distribution of capital across the different branches of production and the formation of a general rate of profit, was concerned with prices of production and thus monetary quantities. The logical development of the argument across the three volumes thus seemed to necessitate a transition from one register, or level, to another: labour-value had to become, or be 'transformed' into, money-price. The reason this transformation was a problem was that Marx's explanation of it, sketched in Part 2 of Volume III, was generally recognised to be, at the least, incomplete:[8] following the presentation there, the movement from one level to another could not be successfully accomplished within the wider parameters of Marx's theorisation

---

5 Most of the major contributions to the Anglophone debate are collected in Elson 1979, Steedman et al 1981, Fine 1986 and Mohun 1994. See also Hoff 2017, Chapter 5.7 for a summary overview.

6 Elson 1979, p i (emphasis in original). In the words of one of the leading participants: 'The foundation upon which Marx holds the entire construction to be based must be laid bare and subjected to criticism' (Lippi 1979, p 96).

7 Marx 1991 and Marx 2017. See Fine and Harris 1976 for a survey contemporary to the debates in question. The most extensive recent treatment of the transformation problem is Moseley 2016.

8 See, for example, Meek 1967, pp 143–57 and Dobb 1973, pp 158–9.

of capital.[9] Although the issue of 'transformation' had been a subject of specialised debate for many decades,[10] in the 1970s it suddenly took on an altogether more urgent significance, as the main point of contention in the intense controversy over the validity of Marx's theory.[11] The proximate cause of this development was the mid-century work of the Italian economist Piero Sraffa. Although intended as a critique of neoclassical economics, when read from a Marxist perspective this appeared to demonstrate that both the rate of profit and prices of production could be accurately determined purely from '*physical* quantities of outputs and inputs', without any reference to 'values' as quantities of labour.[12] Sraffa's construction of a logically consistent system within the general surplus approach to economic analysis was thus read by the iconoclasts within Marxism as demonstrating that the economic problems that Marx had been unable to resolve could be settled without any reference to a labour theory of value. This meant that there was simply no need for a mysterious 'value' dimension – a quasi-metaphysical relic of classical political economy – which should accordingly be dispensed with if radical economic thinking was to make any progress.[13]

For the critics, the rejection of the labour theory of value was by no means a purely destructive operation of negation; on the contrary, it was intended to re-establish Marxist economics on coherent and defensible grounds. Nevertheless, the fact was that they were urging the abandonment of the central category of Marx's theorisation of capital. It did not take much to see that, all assurances aside, this was profoundly problematic. In what sense could Marxism still retain its essential substance if it willingly jettisoned its fundamental category? To do so was surely tantamount to an admission of defeat – no theoretical construction as elaborate as that of Marx could survive the uprooting of its foundation in that way. The problem that the

9 Specifically, while maintaining the two aggregate equalities Marx claimed to demonstrate: 'total gross price = total value, and total profit = total surplus value' (Moseley 2016, p xiii).

10 Böhm-Bawerk 1949. See Meek 1977, Chapter 5 for a summary of the literature.

11 Claudio Napoleoni, a leading protagonist in the Italian debates, went so far as to assert that 'the stance taken vis-a-vis the so-called transformation problem [is] the criterion of whether one positions oneself inside or outside Marxism' (cited in Reuten 1999, p 88).

12 Steedman et al 1981, p 15 (emphasis in original).

13 Steedman 1977 was the most forceful and influential statement of the general position, while Steedman 1981 and 1994 are summaries of the main points. Lippi 1979 and Hodgson 1982 further elaborated the post-Sraffian line of critique. A similar attitude of purging Marxism of antiquated theoretical commitments in order to bring it up to date and make it, or something like it, respectable and fit for the modern social sciences informed numerous other attacks on the theory of value from within Marxism in the English-speaking world at this time (see, variously, Cutler et al 1977a and 1977b, Hindess and Hirst 1977, Cohen 1978, Roemer 1981 and 1986, and Elster 1985 and 1986).

debates of the 1970s thus struggled with – the theoretical centre of the general crisis of Marxism – was that the value concept in Marx, which was meant to be the point of synthesis in his thought, where its various registers came together, had instead become the site of breakdown in the theory, as manifested in the transformation problem. It was the significance of the former aspect that the defenders of the theory of value were conscious of, the wider meaning of the concept in Marx and its purpose within his thinking. No matter how impotent they were in the face of the hard economic logic of numbers, they nevertheless understood that the value concept was intended to be more than simply an economic term – it was the social and historical concept that organised the theory of capital and gave it critical force. Through his idea of value, Marx attempted to combine a general theory of history and society and an 'economic' theory of capital. By understanding the value relations of commodities as a manifestation of social labour, it was supposed to be possible to grasp the distinctive form of organisation of production in capitalist society, and so to recognise capital as just one mode of production among others. In this way, Marx understood himself to have breached the absolutisation of capital, situating it within a larger narrative of successive forms of the organisation of social labour. It was in the concept of value, therefore, that the different dimensions of Marx's critical theory were supposed to find their unity, from the narrowly economic to the broadly speculative, linking the determination of prices at one end with the historical necessity of the mode of production at the other. If the value concept was discarded, then the radical, messianic ambition that was fundamental to Marxism went with it.

From the crisis of 1970s, there has unfolded within Marxism over the following decades a protracted process of the reconsideration of the concept of value and of the theory of capital constructed upon it.[14] The achievement of this line of research, known as value theory (or value-form theory), has been twofold, both constructive and destructive. Positively, in seeking to escape the theoretical dead-ends of the traditional reading and to find a

[14] The progenitor of this fundamental debate within Marxism can plausibly be regarded as having been Adorno: the *Neue Marx-Lektüre*, which is the most important and influential strand of the German discussions and stands at the centre of the debate, originated from Adorno's sociology seminars in Frankfurt in the early 1960s (Bellofiore and Riva 2015; Bellofiore and Riva 2018; Elbe 2018; Bonefeld and O'Kane 2022, Chapters 12 and 13; see also Backhaus 1980, pp 94–8 and Reichelt 1982). For a summary account of the 'new reading' of Marx from within Marxism, see Pitts 2018, Part I. The major English-language contribution to the value debate has come from the work of the International Symposium on Marxian Theory (Moseley 1993; Moseley and Campbell 1997; Arthur and Reuten 1998; Campbell and Reuten 2002; Bellofiore and Taylor 2004; Moseley 2005; Bellofiore and Fineschi 2009; Bellofiore, Starosta and Thomas 2014; Moseley and Smith 2015).

new position of critique, the modern thinking about value has rediscovered and substantially developed aspects of Marx's theory that orthodoxy had neglected. Specifically, it has focused upon the form dimensions and the elements of dialectical conceptual development to be found in Marx. Although advance in this direction has been halting, piecemeal and without any general consensus or synthetic overview, the effect, taken as a whole, has been to transform the understanding of value and reorientate the theorisation of capital in a fundamental way, drawing out and elaborating a perspective that was at most only half-visible in Marx. Negatively, while it began with the intention of recuperating Marx's theory, precisely through the conceptual rigour, theoretical precision and philological care that it has brought to the study of Marx's texts, modern Marxian value theory has increasingly become aware of, and so more and more exposed, the ambivalences and conceptual deficiencies that pervade Marx's understanding of value and that vitiate his presentations of it. Ironically, therefore, what started out as the defence of his theory of value has in fact became the most profound and far-reaching critique of Marx. For what it has definitively demonstrated is that there is no unitary concept of value to be found in his work. Instead, what Marx tried to compound by force in the mid-19th century was an amalgam of incompatible elements that could not be stabilised as a coherent concept. The primary achievement of the value debate in Marxism, therefore, has been to break Marx's theory of value apart and expose its central metaphysical fracture. In doing so, it has opened the way to an entirely new understanding of value and capital.

Repositioning the critique

The rethinking of value that was precipitated by the crisis of Marxism can be understood as, in the first place, the search for a new position of thought in relation to capital. This effort to reposition the critique began with the concerted rejection of the traditional Marxist idea of value. At its origins, the revolution in value theory was motivated by the conviction that there was more to Marx's theory of value than the orthodox interpretation recognised or than Marxism's critics allowed. In order to make visible what had been neglected, however, it was necessary to reshape the space of Marxism, establishing a distance from the defunct orthodoxy that would allow a productive re-reading of Marx. The central perception of this new direction of thought was that traditional Marxism had been rendered null by the development of capital because it shared the basic assumptions of mainstream economic theory. It had taken Marx's theory to be a critical political economy rather than a 'critique of political economy', as the subtitle of *Capital* stated. As a result, traditional Marxism was structurally identical to orthodox economic thought: in the same way that classical political economy had been a critique of unproductive feudal classes from the perspective of the bourgeois class, so Marxism was a critique of the exploitative bourgeois class from the perspective of the productivity of labour. The 'radical' idea of traditional Marxism was thus that the economy should be re-established on a proletarian basis, unleashing the productivity of labour to the benefit of the workers, who actually generated the wealth, rather than the capitalist class, who merely appropriated it. Consequently, critique was largely confined to issues of economic order and distributional equity.[15] In its initial phases, therefore, the rethinking of value sought to demonstrate that Marx's theory was misunderstood if it was straightforwardly assimilated to the discourse of economics, as a radical position within the field. If Marxism was to be rehabilitated as critical theory, it had to be differentiated from orthodox economic thought at a deeper level.[16]

The effort to re-read Marx in such a way as to locate a new theoretical position brought to the fore elements in his theory that articulated the qualitative character of the economic. This differentiated the new readings sharply from the traditional understanding, which was almost exclusively quantitative in nature. Having briefly disposed of the question of value through general considerations about production, labour and surplus, orthodox Marxism's attention was thereafter entirely given over to issues of price formation, the determination of the rate of profit and the allocation of the product.[17] Its criticisms of capital were then also conceived in quantitative terms of inequality and disproportion. Likewise, the Sraffian rejection of

15 As Maurice Dobb summarised the overall logic of the traditional conception, the concentration and centralisation of capital, along with the intensification of crises, would produce a 'growing acuteness of the struggle between Capital and Labour over the division of the product, until the working-producers should demand the expropriation of the capitalists and the vesting of capital in the community' (Dobb 1955, p 201).

16 Many of these limitations were incisively set out by Moishe Postone in his influential reinterpretation of Marx's critical theory, largely based upon a reading of the *Grundrisse* (Postone 2003). For all its merits, however, Postone's work manifests some of the intractable difficulties that the reinterpretation of Marx has had in dismissing the traditional reading while remaining within Marxism. His critique of traditional Marxism is both to the point, in that he identifies some of the profound limitations of the long-established ways of reading, and highly tendentious, to the extent that he presents these simply as misinterpretations of Marx. The situation in regard to Marx is in fact very much more complex than he recognises. As it is, his own interpretation is substantially misdirected in its understanding of value by its continued acceptance of some of the basic assumptions of the traditional framework (foremost, the primacy of labour and production, even if restricted (illogically) just to the epoch of capital).

17 Thus Maurice Dobb could state, apparently as straightforward fact, that 'Marx's primary concern had been with the distribution of income between classes' and that for understanding any economic system, capital included, 'a proper theory of income-distribution [is] the key to everything else' (Dobb 1955, p 194 and p 201).

the concept of value remained wholly on this quantitative ground. Once it had demonstrated that production prices and the rate of profit could not be determined through the labour theory of value, it could see no reason for retaining the value concept. Since quantitative questions were the only ones that it could conceive of asking, if Marx's value theory stood in the way of answering them, then it should be dispensed with. Correlatively, as it lacked a conceptual basis from which to pose anything other than quantitative problems, its conception of a post-value Marxist economics was wholly quantitative and distributional. With the totalisation of the capitalist world market in the late 20th century, however, quantitative critique within the space of the economic lost any meaning: there could be no quantitative economics that was qualitatively different from capital. In this circumstance, the qualitative nature of the quantitative became the real problem. The reconsideration of the value theory thus sought to break out of the confines of quantification in order to grasp dimensions of capital to which both the traditional reading and its Sraffian critique remained oblivious.

Traditional Marxism understood capital predominantly in class terms, as the power of the owners of the means of production over the wage-labourers. While this conception was undeniably important to Marx, the reconsideration of the value theory recognised that alongside it there was also in his work a different and more complex idea of the nature of capital. In Marx's analysis, capital forms itself as an objective, abstract reality that stands over and against all individuals, whatever their class. From the notion of 'alienation' in the early writings onwards, this idea of the objectivity of capital was a consistent theme within Marx's thinking, one that he repeatedly tried to work into the basic terms of the theory. Thus, in the *Grundrisse*, Marx's first attempt at an extended exposition of capital, it is asserted that, as a result of the 'objective dependency relations' that in capitalist society had replaced direct personal relations, 'individuals are now ruled by *abstractions*, whereas earlier they depended on one another'.[18] In this new condition of radical individuation, in which interdependence was increasingly mediated by the market, exchange relations based upon value attained an independence and objectivity that subsumed everyone, forming the autonomous, abstract totality that is referred to as 'the economy'. The perception of an abstract objectivity located in the totalisation produced by generalised exchange relations shifted the theoretical register, the class relation being demoted and set within a much larger structure of compulsion that arose from the process of exchange. Everybody in capitalist society is subordinated to the abstract, objective power of capital and has to conform to its demands – the economy leaves no one out. This all-encompassing

[18] Marx 1973, p 164 (emphasis in original).

objectivity of capital was to be developed, for Marx, from the concept of value:

> In Marx's analysis, social domination in capitalism does not, on its most fundamental level, consist in the domination of people by other people, but in the domination of people by abstract social structures that people themselves constitute. Marx sought to grasp this form of abstract, structural domination – which encompasses, and extends beyond, class domination – with his categories of the commodity and capital. … Within the framework of Marx's analysis, the form of social domination that characterizes capitalism is not ultimately a function of private property, of the ownership by the capitalists of the surplus product and the means of production; rather, it is grounded in the value form of wealth itself, a form of social wealth that confronts living labor (the workers) as a structurally alien and dominant power.[19]

Once this form of abstract domination had been clearly recognised, it was obviously inadequate to think of 'resistance' to capital in the standard intersubjective terms of class struggle, grounded in the affirmation of productive labour and the denunciation of its appropriation. The abstract totality of capital was a different order of phenomenon altogether, which could by no means be properly comprehended through the lens of class.[20]

The rethinking of value was thus drawn towards those aspects of Marx's theory that pointed towards the experience of capital as a closed context of abstract, law-like compulsion, in which 'the economy' has a life and movement of its own. This objectivity, however, is not an observable fact or thing 'out there' that can be apprehended empirically. Rather, it is an abstract objectivity, experienced as an ever more closely integrated conceptual web that spreads through the generalisation of commodity exchange. While orthodox economics routinely dismissed any notion of an abstract objectivity of value as 'metaphysical',[21] this objective-conceptual quality of value was increasingly recognised within the reframing of the value theory as central to Marx's critical achievement. For the rethinking of value, it was this theoretical interest, above all, that differentiated Marx from the field of classical political economy and established the distinctive nature of his theory. Marx's crucial perception was that the abstract-objective character of the economic space defined the whole field of political economy and yet entirely escaped the comprehension of the political economists. For all their vaunted rationality,

19 Postone 2003, p 30.
20 Bonefeld 2014, Chapter 3.
21 Backhaus 1992.

the economic domain remained completely opaque to them, in that they were unable to provide a properly conceptual account of its categories. Each of these bespoke the abstract objectivity of the economic experience, the life of capitalist society being everywhere, and to an ever increasing extent, mediated through 'value', 'price', 'interest', 'profit' and so on. Nevertheless, even though they structured capitalist experience as such, these categories were simply taken for granted by political economy, which unthinkingly confined itself to quantitative issues. Entirely enclosed within the world of equivalence, it could not conceive of interrogating the categories themselves and explaining what they are. As result, political economy was unable to recognise the boundaries of the economic space:

> [Marx's] central reproach against economic thought is that it assumes the 'ready made forms' as 'already really existing', that it presupposes the 'existence' (*Dasein*) of these forms; that it takes its concepts from 'everyday experience', reads them off the 'empirical world', that they are smuggled into the economic theory as if they 'fall out of the sky'.[22]

Across his economic texts, Marx repeatedly criticised economic thought for its failure to examine its own concepts. Assuming quantity as such, it never properly enquired into the qualitative nature of its quantities.[23] Further, since it was unable to experience anything beyond the economic space, it could not adequately ground the space itself. The aim of a 'critique of political economy' was thus to decode the abstract, purely quantitative objectivity of the economy. Where quantitative enquiry presumed an already formed and enclosed economic space, in which all factors had been reduced to identity

---

22 Backhaus 1992, p 21. Backhaus notes that for the economic subject to exist it is necessary that the boundaries of the economic space remain hermetically sealed, so that the categories of economics are experienced as ultimate givens, beyond the reach of thought: 'According to their theory [that of academic economics] the economic categories contain elements which are not available for rational analysis, that is to say, elements which are not mediated by the subject but possess an a priori character. This way of thinking was philosophically justified by Simmel's analysis of money, which claimed that abstract value, as is found above all in money *qua* value unit, constitutes an "originary phenomenon" and hence an *a priori* factor, which is a presupposition of all thinking' (Backhaus 1992, pp 60–61; see also Backhaus 2005).

23 'Mere quantitative considerations produce a vicious circularity of thought because the economist does not consider the underlying and unifying quality of the quantitative substance. ... Marx indicates that the bourgeois economist has always presupposed constituted forms (*konstituierte Formen*), that is, existing values in certain economic forms. Consequently, the economist is caught in a vicious circularity of thought because what needs to be defined is already presupposed in the definition' (Reichelt 1993, pp 71 and 74–5).

and thus made available to quantitative comparison, the rethinking of value attempted to go behind this assumption and investigate the qualitative problem of the formation of quantitative equivalence.

Dialectic

Recognising the categorial ambition of Marx's theory meant reconsidering his relation to the lineage of classical political economy, within which the idea of a labour theory of value had developed.[24] Traditional Marxism had generally placed Marx squarely in this line of descent: he was the proper inheritor of the economic thinking that began in the 17th century with Petty and Boisguilbert, flourished through the Physiocrats and Adam Smith in the 18th century, and, in David Ricardo, reached as far as it could go in its bourgeois form. For the orthodoxy that was the norm up until the 1970s, Marx had adopted the labour theory as it had been developed by his predecessors while, crucially, clarifying the nature of surplus value through an account of class exploitation and the commodification of labour.[25] This production-based idea of value as a quantity of 'embodied labour' foundered on the transformation problem, once it was shown that labour values could not be translated into prices of production. The critics who, in consequence, urged the abandonment of the theory of value had likewise assumed this interpretation of Marx's idea of value, not unreasonably given that it was standard within the Marxist tradition up to that point.[26]

Nevertheless, such an assumption opened an obvious line of defence of Marx's theory. This was to argue that the traditional reading of Marx's conception of value as effectively identical to that of Ricardo was mistaken. In unquestioningly adopting that same reading, the critics were also therefore in error. If it could be shown that they had attributed to Marx a conception of value that was not his own, then the force of their attack was weakened, and perhaps even deflected altogether: their critique might indeed apply to Ricardo, but not to Marx. At the early stages of the rethinking of value, this was a favoured strategy of many of those who wanted to resist the Sraffian attack.[27] Typically this defence took the form of an appeal to what Marx designated the 'dual character' of labour in capital; that is, the difference between the labour that produces use values, referred to as 'concrete labour', and the labour that produces exchange value, what in the Marxist terminology

[24] Milios, Dimoulis and Economakis 2002.

[25] Meek 1973 is the classic exposition of this traditional reading of Marx's value theory.

[26] Steedman 1977 and Lippi 1979.

[27] See, for example, Pilling 1972, Himmelweit and Mohun 1978, Pilling 1980, de Vroey 1981, Shaikh 1981, de Vroey 1982.

is known as 'abstract labour'. The claim was that both the traditional reading and the Sraffian critique overlooked the conceptual determination of labour that Marx tried to work out in his theory of value. It was precisely Marx's accusation against classical political economy that 'it failed to see that when it treated the difference between various types of labour in a *quantitative* sense, their *qualitative* unity was implied – that is their reduction to *abstract* labour'.[28] This notion of 'abstract labour', widely invoked in the literature, was intended to identify the form in which individual, 'concrete' labour becomes universal labour, or the qualitative becomes quantitative. 'Abstract labour' indicated the layer of social mediation that commodity-producing labour passed through in becoming value. If Marx's concept of value was assimilated to that of Ricardo, exactly the undifferentiated, conceptually indeterminate notion of 'labour' that Marx uncovered in classical political economy and subjected to criticism was falsely attributed to him. The reply to the critics was thus that rather than simply being 'labour' as such, 'Marx's "value" is the product of abstract labour',[29] the notion of 'abstract labour' indicating the recognition in Marx of a conceptual quality to value that classical political economy could not see.

The inability to perceive the difference between Marx's concept of labour and that of Ricardo was taken to be symptomatic of a deeper and more pervasive deficiency in traditional interpretations of Marx. This was a failure to understand the nature of the concepts that Marx had developed and, more generally, his idea of theory. The reconsideration of value evolved from the intuition that there were important aspects of Marx's theory that went unrecognised by orthodoxy. Indeed, what it understood increasingly clearly was that in its conceptually strongest elements Marx's theory did not at all fit with the notions of theory prevalent in economics and social science. In this way, Marx was further differentiated from the mainstream: from Böhm-Bawerk onwards, orthodox economics typically insisted that Marx should be made to conform to standards of theory that were not his own, professing incomprehension of his concepts otherwise.[30] This demand was by no means restricted to those approaching Marx with hostile intent, though. Just as they took his questions to be essentially economistic, so Marx's partisans all too often assumed that he worked with, or at least should be interpreted through, the procedures of mainstream economic science. These assumptions necessarily obscured precisely the elements in Marx's theory that the rethinking of value was concerned to identify and develop.

---

28 Pilling 1980, pp 48–9 (emphases in original).

29 Himmelweit and Mohun 1978, p 73. See also Milios, Dimoulis and Economakis 2002, Chapter 2.

30 Backhaus 1992, pp 54–6.

An important theme that emerged within the controversies of the 1970s and received concerted attention thereafter was thus the vexed question of Marx's *method*.[31] As with the transformation problem, this had its antecedents in Marxology. The difficulty of determining Marx's method with any certainty was traceable back to Marx himself, for nowhere in his voluminous writings could there be found any sustained consideration of issues of method and epistemology. In particular, there was a complete absence of methodological ground-laying in relation to the theory of capital.[32] Instead, all that Marx provided by way of guidance in this respect were a few scattered remarks in marginalia. Although often cited, taken together these *obiter dicta* amounted to little more than a series of cryptic and inconclusive hints that served only to deepen the confusion.[33] This absence of self-reflection in Marx, the lack of methodological and epistemological explicitness, opened the door wide to interpretation of his work through a variety of mutually incompatible modes of thought and notions of theory.[34] In this situation, questions concerning the method of the mature economic analyses could not be answered straightforwardly by reference to what Marx had intended. Rather they had to be approached through the logic of the work itself and determined in relation to what its internal coherence required.

---

[31] Moseley 1993 and Moseley and Campbell 1997.

[32] Symptomatic of the grave theoretical deficit this absence has caused within Marxism is the massive burden of overinterpretation that has been heaped upon the single text in Marx's oeuvre that could plausibly be read as something like an epistemological statement, the 1857 'Introduction' to the *Grundrisse*. What is surely most striking about this brief text, however, is its extremely rudimentary nature – just a few sketchy remarks about moving from the concrete to the abstract and then back again – by comparison with the extent, intensity and depth of reflection on the epistemological problematic that is to be found in Marx's predecessors in German Idealism. In any case, too seldom is it acknowledged by those who would endow it with enormous importance that the 'Introduction' is unfinished and was abandoned.

[33] The most celebrated of these is the 'Postface' to the second edition of Volume I of *Capital*. There Marx acknowledges the issue – 'That the method employed in *Capital* has been little understood is shown by the various mutually contradictory conceptions that have been formed about it' – but does nothing to resolve it, preferring instead to recycle the polemical rhetoric of his youth about the 'mystified' nature of the Hegelian dialectic, whose 'rational kernel' he claims to have discovered but does not actually explain (Marx 1990, pp 99 and 103).

[34] Why Marx was apparently incapable of methodological and epistemological self-clarification, continually avoiding them despite their obvious importance for the intellectual task of a theory of capital, and why, despite repeatedly promising to, he never managed to state plainly what he understood the 'rational kernel' of the dialectic actually to be, are questions that have not been thoroughly explored within Marxology. Plausible speculations, relating this absence to the basic contradictions within Marx's theoretical mind, can be found in Reichelt 1995.

The crisis of Marxism in the 1970s decisively invalidated the two principal interpretations of Marx's method that had guided the traditional readings. The first of these was the so-called logical-historical method, the authority of which derived from Engels. In his 1859 review of Marx's *Contribution to a Critique of Political Economy*, Engels stated that the task of theory was to clarify the evolutionary movement of history 'from the simplest to the more complex relations', and that the method of conceptual development in Marx was 'nothing but the historical method, only stripped of its historical form and interfering contingencies'.[35] In this conception, logic is effectively subordinated to history, the theoretical exposition being no more than a simplified tracing out of the process of historical evolution. Engels and those who followed him thus imagined that Marx's theory was concerned with 'the development of the broad system of commodity production up to and including the stage of capitalist production'.[36] The opening sections of *Capital* were understood as representing a society of 'simple commodity production', in which the direct producers were in possession of their own means of production and commodities were exchanged at their 'values', that is, amounts of labour time embodied in them. What Marx then demonstrated was how these simple value relations were modified when capitalist relations of production supervened on them. In the rethinking of value, this whole conception was dismissed as entirely mistaken. In the first place, Marx never used the term 'simple commodity production', which was editorially inserted by Engels into Marx's text.[37] Nor did he ever refer to the capitalist commodity as a derived or secondary form of the commodity. Furthermore, the historical conception could not work theoretically: only where all inputs are value-formed and production as a whole is for the purpose of valorisation can such a thing as a 'law of value' be said to hold. In fact, the notion of 'simple commodity production' revealed how far traditional Marxism was suffused with economism, as it read history through an economic rationality that only fully crystallised with capital.[38] Finally, the opening sections of Volume I of *Capital* did not depict a putative stage of simple commodity production *before* capital but rather the sphere of simple circulation *within* capital. While large parts of Marx's text certainly dealt with historical material, the method of the theoretical argument was not one of historical development; rather,

[35] Marx and Engels 1980, p 475.

[36] Meek 1973, p 152.

[37] Arthur 2004b, p 35.

[38] In 'simple commodity production', the 'argument for an historical existence of the "law of value" rests on a mythological conception of a preceding kind of production in which the bourgeois economic rationality of the striving for maximisation of profit by capital is projected back onto a situation in which such a rationality surely had no grounds for existence' (Eldred and Hanlon 1981, p 54).

the whole argument presupposed fully developed capital. Fundamental to the rethinking of value was thus a decisive reversal of priority between logic and history, breaking with the strongly historicist readings of *Capital* that had been virtually ubiquitous within Marxism.[39]

Where the Marxist tradition had not directly subordinated logic to history, its alternative idea of Marx's method was one of 'successive approximations'.[40] By this it was understood that Marx had initially sought, by abstracting from the real world, the simplest starting point for his system, which he found in the exchange relation and its quantitative aspect of exchange value. He then progressively introduced layers of complexity into the theory, each of which enabled him to move, step by step, closer to the reality of capital as it actually existed in the world, identifying general tendencies and laws along the way. The method of *Capital* was thus a series of consciously artificial constructions by the theorist, which taken in succession traced out a movement from the abstract to the concrete. The closer the level of approximation to reality within this sequence of models, the more definite the statement that could be made. The rethinking of value from the 1970s also rejected this reading of Marx's method. Value, as Marx understood it, was not established in its most general sense at the outset of the analysis and then progressively modified and made more 'realistic' as layers of complexity were introduced. Rather, it underwent fundamental conceptual redetermination at each stage of its development.[41] The failure of the traditional readings to grasp this mode of conceptual transformation resulted from the inadequacy of their understanding of abstraction, which they regarded as a subjective procedure of the theorist. According to Ronald Meek, for example, the use by Marx of 'general abstractions' derived from the materialist conception of history did not 'differ appreciably from that adopted by any responsible social scientist in arriving at and testing a hypothesis',[42] while for Paul Sweezy the primary difficulty of the method of successive approximations was in determining how far the researcher should abstract from reality.[43] In both, Marx's theory was assimilated to orthodox social science. The inadequacy of such a conception, however, was that it remains entirely external to its object. The

---

39 For critiques of the 'logical-historical' method in particular and historicising readings of *Capital* in general, see Arthur 1997, 1998 and 2004 (Chapter 2), and Heinrich 2012, pp 30–32. The emphasis in value theory on the logical rather than historical nature of the categories of Marx's theory is concisely stated in Robles-Báez 1997.

40 Sweezy 1946, pp 11–20 is the classic statement of this position.

41 Arthur 2004b, pp 22–3.

42 Meek 1973, p 148.

43 'The legitimate purpose of abstraction in social science is never to get away from the real world but rather to isolate certain aspects of the real world for intensive investigation' (Sweezy 1946, p 18).

stages or levels are posited arbitrarily, by decision of the theorist, and then compared with each other. Consequently, as Chris Arthur points out, 'there is no genuine development ... no immanent dynamic in the presentation; the shift from one "level of analysis" to another is due to a decision to add a further determination, e.g. "let money be invented", "let labour-power be a commodity"'.[44] What the new readings of Marx realised was that the conceptual development of value in *Capital* was neither a sequence of models assembled by the social-scientific researcher nor a simplified reconstruction of a historical process but, rather, a *logical* development, the movement of which was motivated from *within* the concept of value itself. The method of capital therefore had to be one that reflected the inner life and dynamic of the concept – the idea that value has of itself, in its process of self-determination.

The failure of the orthodox readings, based as they were on economistic and scientistic assumptions in relation to method and epistemology, opened the way to a reconsideration of the dialectical elements of Marx, which had been generally ignored or misrepresented precisely because they did not accord with the logic of positivist social science. The emphasis placed upon dialectic in modern value theory inevitably brought with it renewed attention to the influence of Hegel on Marx.[45] Within the Marxist tradition, the relation between Marx and Hegel had typically been construed in one of two registers: either triumphalism – the narrative of the 'materialism' of the societal labour process supplanting the 'idealism' of philosophical thought and of Marx thereby setting Hegel 'back on his feet' – or exorcism – the story of Marx progressively liberating himself from 'mystified' Hegelian encumbrances in order to become properly scientific. In both, there was a clear assumption of superiority: Hegel was at best a stepping-stone towards

---

44 Arthur 2004b, p 26.

45 How to understand the Hegelian-dialectical aspect of Marx's method had been a significant theme of the early reception of *Capital* within the European socialist and communist movements (see Day and Gaido 2017 for a comprehensive survey). With the advent of the general crisis of Marxism in the 1970s, however, the point of this long-standing controversy was very substantially sharpened. From its beginning, the modern German debate, above all, has been concerned with the question of dialectic in Marx (Backhaus 1980). In the Anglophone world, early contributions that recognised the importance of the Hegelian legacy for Marx's theory of value include Arthur 1979, Banaji 1979, Pilling 1980, Eldred and Hanlon 1981, Eldred, Hanlon, Kleiber and Roth 1982, Eldred, Hanlon, Kleiber and Roth 1983, Arthur 1986, Murray 1988, Winfield 1991 (originally 1976), Eldred 2015 (originally 1984), and Sekine 2021a and 2021b (originally 1984 and 1986, respectively). Since then, Hegel has become a standard, although not universally accepted, reference point for debates in value theory. See Burns and Fraser 2000 and Moseley and Smith 2015 for survey collections on the relation between the two thinkers. On the renewed emphasis on dialectic in the interpretation of Marx, see Albritton and Simoulidis 2003.

Marx, who had decisively overcome him. Following the collapse of Marxism and the disintegration of its theoretical coherence, however, this assumption was all but reversed. Now Marxian value theory looked to Hegel, as the foremost exponent of dialectical thought, to try to clarify what was obscure or mystified in Marx.[46]

Although his pronouncements on the subject were coy and ambiguous, it had always been recognised that Marx was in some sense a dialectical thinker. But for as long as Marxism appeared to have substance and reality, the question of dialectic in Marx was usually construed in historical terms: communism as the transcendence of capitalism. The dismissal of socialism and communism by capital at the end of the 20th century, and the consequent invalidation of the Marxist idea of the dialectic of history, rendered that conception obsolete. As a result, the question of Marx and dialectic could be recast in different terms. Within value theory the importance of Hegel for Marx was now established at the logical-categorial level and addressed to the problem of the construction and exposition of dialectical concepts. Moreover, re-reading Marx's theory of value in dialectical terms promised an escape from the dead-end of traditional Marxism, as dialectic involved an entirely different conceptual logic from social science. In dialectic, it is not the researcher who, employing a predetermined method that is brought to the object of inquiry from outside, constructs the concepts through which the object is classified and ordered.[47] Rather, reflection upon the object reveals it as being mediated, or conceptual, in-itself. This conceptuality is objective and 'real'.[48] It is not the nominalist creation of the theorist, applied to the object from without

---

46 The most important recent work on the development of Marx's thought in relation to Hegel is that of Roberto Finelli (2016). His interpretation is premised upon an explicit rejection of the standard Marxist version of the Marx–Hegel relation, according to which 'the transition from Hegel's idealism to Marx's materialism could not, and should not, mean anything but the result, following a linear progression, of a theory of becoming, initially confined to an abstract level of Idea and Spirit, and then finally found in the real activity of human beings and of their relations, in a historically concrete horizon' (Finelli 2016, p xi). Against this hackneyed narrative of Marx's materialism setting Hegel's idealism the right way up, Finelli's thesis is instead of 'a permanent and structural subordination' (Finelli 2016, p xi) of Marx to Hegel, a thesis persuasively substantiated by his demonstration of the crudeness of Marx's anthropological paradigm in comparison to the power and complexity of Hegel's theory of subjectivity.

47 '[Dialectic] is not an inductive method generalising from perceived instances a hypothetical law of the phenomena, to be further tested in experience; it is not a hypothetico-deductive system in which an axiom is made the basis of a sequence of inferences that formally follow from it, the result being, as it is said, already "contained" in the premises; it is not a transcendental argument for the conditions of possibility of a form of experience taken as established' (Arthur 2004b, p 83).

48 The increasing recognition within contemporary Marxism of the objective conceptuality of capital has given rise to a discussion, following the pioneering work of Alfred Sohn-Rethel

in order to fit it seamlessly into a classificatory framework, but is intrinsic to it as a universal *in re*. Accordingly, the task of the observing theorist is not to construct the object through a series of subjectively contrived hypotheses or models, but simply to follow the logic of the immanent conceptuality of the object as it unfolds itself.[49] Dialectical exposition, therefore, 'is the logical development of a system of categories, or forms of being, from the most elementary and indeterminate to the richest and most concrete.'[50]

The publication in 1973 of the English translation of the *Grundrisse*, a more obviously dialectical text than *Capital*, no doubt provided the impetus for the guiding idea of value theory as it developed from the 1970s.[51] This was that Marx understood capital as an objective totality formed by the self-development of value, as its most elementary category. For this new perspective on Marx, the interpretative challenge was both to grasp the nature of value and its structuring role within all of the other categories of the theory of capital, and also to perceive how Marx attempted to articulate the internal relationships of the various categories such that they progressively build themselves up into an ever more concretely determined totality. Because the system of capital is not an observable object but an abstract-conceptual *Zusammenhang*, the interlocking network of categories, in which they are all mutually determining, has to be reconstructed in

---

(1978), of the notion of 'real abstraction' (see, for instance, Oliva, Oliva and Novara 2020; on conceptual realism in Hegelian dialectic, see Stern 2008).

49 As both Hegel and Adorno insisted, it is thus inaccurate to refer to dialectic as a 'method' because method means a universal mode of knowledge developed in abstraction from the object and externally applied to it (Adorno 2001b, 'Substantiality and method'). The dialectical critique of method as such is that it is extrinsic and arbitrary, so that there is no guarantee that the object actually accords with the method that is imposed upon it; in fact, method only reveals what it already prescribes (Adorno 1982, pp 11–14). As it was developed from Descartes onwards, method is thus characteristic of what Hegel termed the philosophy of reflection, which assumes a strict division of subject and object. Dialectic, by contrast, understands itself as the logic of being itself: 'So soon as we settle into the idea that dialectic is a special kind of tool to be applied to anything whatever outside it, we are no longer in dialectic. Dialectic could not be a method or an instrument, but is, instead, an experience' (Jarvis 2010, p 161). This conception of dialectic as grasping the inner life of things, their animating principle, and not merely their dead externality, is announced by Hegel in the Preface to the *Phenomenology of Spirit*. For an extended reading of the Preface as a text on philosophical method, see Davis 2023. More generally, on dialectic and method in Hegel, see Maker 1982, Winfield 1990 and Houlgate 2022, Chapter 4.

50 Arthur 2004b, p 83. For discussion of the difference between analytical method and dialectical theory in the work of Smith, Hegel and Marx, see Finelli 1989.

51 The original text was published in East Germany in 1953 and in West Germany in 1967. Rosdolsky 1989 is the pioneering work on interpretation of the *Grundrisse*. For contemporary discussion of the position of the *Grundrisse* in Marx's economic work as a whole, see Bellofiore, Starosta and Thomas 2014. On the importance of Hegel's *Logic* for the *Grundrisse*, see Meaney 2002.

thought. From this, there results the expositional problem that the particular nature of dialectical concepts poses. In a dialectical argument, no concept is meaningful outside its place within the system; each constitutes a 'moment' of the totality and attains its proper determinacy only once the system has been fully unfolded. The progress of the dialectic is thus not a linear movement in which a concept is established and defined in its discrete autonomy as a starting point, the argument then proceeding, inductively or deductively, to subsequent concepts posited by the theorist. Rather, 'in a dialectical argument the meanings of concepts undergo shifts because the significance of any element in the total picture cannot be concretely defined at the outset'.[52] At every stage of the advance of the dialectical exposition the significance of each concept is redetermined. No concept is complete and closed off at any particular point in the exposition but each one is continually in development until the totality has been entirely elaborated. This is what is meant by dialectical concepts being fluid and in motion rather than positivistically fixed.[53]

In addition, the logic of dialectic moves simultaneously forward and backward: the exposition of the system in its full determinacy is also the grounding, and justification, of the initial categories in their completed actuality. Value is the most fundamental category of capital but it realises itself properly only when the system is exhibited in its full extent, as a whole. The abstract starting point is universal in-itself but this universality must make itself actual: it must become for-itself, so that it knows itself as universal, autonomous and self-determining. That is, in Hegelian terms, it must recognise itself fully in its other, so that the circle of identity is complete. The logic of dialectical development is that at every stage the Concept, in Hegel's strong metaphysical sense, reflects upon itself, becomes aware of the persisting insufficiency of the unfolding of its immanent contradictions, and so repeatedly redetermines itself, achieving ever more universal forms. This movement proceeds until such point as the Concept is able to 'posit the presupposition':[54] that is, when what was originally given to it from outside is produced by it from within itself, so that the Concept is grounded upon itself and is entirely self-determining. The development of the dialectic is thus motivated from within the Concept itself as it seeks to make actual its intrinsic universality. It was this conception of dialectical construction that was taken up by modern value theory. If the central concepts of Marx's theory were supposed to be dialectical in nature, then the task of reinterpretation was to read Marx's mature economic texts through the logic of dialectic.

52 Arthur 2004b, p 25.

53 On the movement of dialectical conceptual development, see Houlgate 2006, pp 42–53.

54 Bellofiore and Finelli 1998, pp 48–51; Finelli 2016, pp 7–14.

Hegel was the reference point for this new reading because, above all in his *Logic*, it was Hegel who had demonstrated the construction of a dialectical totality. Accordingly, this became the guiding thread for much of modern Marxian value theory as it attempted to work through the obscurities of Marx's exposition of value. The theory of capital was to be interpreted as a 'systematic dialectic': beginning with the elementary concept of value, the exposition should rigorously follow the immanent logic of dialectical development.[55]

The value form

What value theory thus rediscovered in Marx, by way of Hegel, was Marx's own partial rediscovery in his mature work of the logic of Hegelian form determination that he had long ago discarded with his turn to historical materialism. On the new reading, it was the recovery of the notion of dialectical *Formbestimmung* that enabled Marx to theorise modern society:

> according to the articulation and dualism of two worlds: 'world 1', as the sphere of appearance and visibility, animated by concrete things and individuals, and 'world 2', which is the sphere of essence and invisibility, animated only by the abstraction of a merely quantitative wealth which, precisely because it is mere quantity, cannot have any other purpose than becoming its own quantitative accumulation.[56]

At its core, the programme of the revolution in value theory over the last 40 years has been the progressive working out of this dialectical dualism of essence and appearance as it is formulated within Marx's theoretical construction, trying to establish both how it is grounded and elaborated there and what its implications are. If *Capital* was to be reinterpreted as the exposition of a logic of form determination, then it was first necessary to clarify the theorisation of value as essence, because it was only on that basis that a dialectical development could proceed. In the section on the

---

[55] On 'systematic dialectic' in Marxian value theory, see Reuten and Williams 1989, Smith 1990, 1998, 1999 and 2002, Reuten 2000 and 2019, and Arthur 2004b. Although dialectical value theory is at one on the importance of Hegel for understanding Marx's theory of capital, there is no general agreement on exactly how this should be construed – whether, for instance, a homology should be thought to exist between the categories of Hegelian logic and those of the theory of capital. For discussion of some of the points at issue, see Arthur 2003, Smith 2003, Arthur 2004b, Arthur 2005b and Murray 2005. The fullest exposition of the homology thesis is Arthur 2022. See also Levine 1978 and 1981 and Sekine 2021a and 2021b for large-scale reconstructions of the system of capital that take inspiration from Hegel and dialectic.

[56] Finelli 2016, p 77.

fetish-character of the commodity, Marx had strikingly characterised the commodity as '*ein sinnlich übersinnliches Ding*', a 'sensuous supersensuous thing', an object that combines in a contradictory way the immediate and the mediated, the concretely singular and the abstractly universal.[57] The *übersinnliches* quality of the capitalist object is its dialectical essence character and it was this dimension of the commodity that value theory focused upon and set out to clarify. What exactly is the 'supersensuous' nature of the commodity in Marx's conception? How does it arise and how, in the course of the exposition, is it further determined and developed? In addressing itself to these questions, value theory decisively shifted the focal point of interpretative controversy. The debates of the 1970s had largely been concerned with the breakdown of the traditional 'embodied labour' value concept on the transformation problem and thus with the issues addressed in Volume III of *Capital*, price determination and the formation of the rate of profit. The rethinking of the concept of value, by contrast, returned right to the beginning, to Chapter 1 of Volume I, obsessively working through the presentation and analysis of the commodity that Marx undertook there in order to reground the concept of value.

The exposition of a systematic dialectical theory of capital required the establishment of an objective concept of value, one that contained within itself its own dynamic of development.[58] Value theory found this objective conceptuality in Section 3 of Chapter 1, entitled by Marx, 'The Value Form, or Exchange Value'. This section had been almost entirely ignored by the traditional readings, which, committed to analytical and empiricist methods, were generally put off by its apparent dialectical-conceptual nature, preferring to derive their understanding of value from the reassuringly more straightforward Sections 1 and 2. Ronald Meek, for instance, after an extensive discussion of the first two sections over fifteen pages, allows a mere one paragraph for Section 3, in which he moves quickly to close off any curiosity the reader might have: 'There is no need for us to follow Marx's rather complex analysis of the "elementary", "expanded" and "money"

[57] As has been widely recognised in the English-language value theory discussions, the translation of this phrase in the standard Penguin edition as 'a thing which transcends sensuousness' (Marx 1990, p 163) dilutes the force of Marx's stark juxtaposition.

[58] Given the importance of the initiation of the dialectical development, there has been considerable debate within value theory about the adequacy, from a dialectical point of view, of the opening of *Capital*, almost all contributions finding fault with it in one way or another (see, for example, Winfield 2016, pp 13–30). On the general problem of the starting point for dialectical exposition, see Arthur 2004b, pp 24–33 and Maker 1990. The most authoritative statement is, of course, Hegel's, given in the section 'With what must the beginning of science be made?' at the start of the *Logic* (Hegel 2010, pp 45–55).

forms of value in any detail'.[59] It was, however, precisely this analysis of the forms of value that value theory concentrated upon as it endeavoured to reshape the understanding of Marx's ideas of value and of capital. For the new dialectical reading of Marx, the neglect of this section by mainstream economics and orthodox Marxism alike demonstrated both their conceptual incapacity and their inability to understand the nature of Marx's theory:

> The arguments discredited by Böhm-Bawerk as 'dialectical hocus-pocus' or by Schumpeter as 'philosophical' can be found above all in the theory of the value-*form*. Insofar as this is presented at all, it is either incomprehensible or rather expounded without comment. The lack of comprehension on the part of the interpreters is all the more astounding since Marx, Engels and Lenin have repeatedly referred to the eminent significance of the value-form analysis. In the foreword to *Capital* Marx energetically warns against neglecting the theory of the value-form.[60]

Where the dialectic of the value form was ignored, Marx's theory was directly assimilated to the classical labour theory of value and its conceptually undetermined notion of 'embodied labour'. This was the procedure of both traditional Marxism and the Sraffian critics of the theory of value, and so their neglect and incomprehension of the value form was central to the defence of Marx's theory.[61] Indeed, it was specifically through the determination and exposition of the form of value that Marx, by his own account, purported to differentiate his theory of value from that of classical political economy.[62]

59 Meek 1973, p 173. That this dismissive attitude to the exposition of the form of value is still prevalent within influential interpretations of Marx can be seen from David Harvey's treatment of Section 3, which opens with a statement hardly contrived to interest the reader in Marx's efforts at dialectical form determination: 'This section incorporates, in my view, a lot of boring material that can all too easily mask the significance of the argument being made. Marx sometimes puts on … an accountant's hat, and the result is a form of exposition that can be tedious in the extreme. … The wood-for-the-trees problem, which often arises in Marx's writing, is at its worst here' (Harvey 2010, p 30).

60 Backhaus 1980, p 99 (emphasis in original). Backhaus' article, composed in the mid-1960s, published in German in 1969 and translated into English in 1980, stands at the origin of modern value theory and is probably the single most influential text within it. The title – 'On the Dialectics of the Value-Form' – already announces the break from orthodox Marxism.

61 For example, Eldred and Hanlon 1981, p 55 and Eldred, Hanlon, Kleiber and Roth 1982, p 173.

62 Marx 1990, p 174: 'Even its best representatives, Adam Smith and Ricardo, treat the form of value as something of indifference, something external to the nature of the commodity itself.'

The qualitative distinction between Marxian and classical value theory, and so the critical positioning of the former in relation to the latter, was thus recognised in value theory as being located above all in the question of form.

The section on the form of value concerns the logical genesis of 'abstract value-objectivity'.[63] The analysis of the value form is intended as the explication of the 'doubling' of the commodity into sensuous material being on the one hand, and supersensuous ideal being on the other. In the simple form of value, polarised between the relative and equivalent forms, the identity of the two commodities, linen and coat, is implied but has not assumed a separate, objective form of its own. As it exists within this 'embryonic form',[64] the universality of value is still tied to, or trapped within, the particularity of its material integument. Since it does not yet exist for itself, it is altogether insufficient as an expression of value.[65] However, because the specificity of the commodity in the position of equivalent is in fact already 'a matter of complete indifference'[66] – in principle, any commodity could be the equivalent – the simple form of value conceptually passes over into the 'Total or Expanded Form of Value'. Here the indifference of the material form of the equivalent is explicitly recognised and so the network of exchanges and identifications is revealed as being inherently unlimited – a potentially infinite number of value equivalents can be posited. Nevertheless, this is still, in Hegel's terms, a bad infinity, nothing but 'a motley mosaic of disparate and unconnected expressions of value' lacking systematic unity and conceptual coherence.[67] On one side, 'the relative form of value of each commodity is an endless series of expressions of value which are all different from the relative form of value of every other commodity', and on the other, 'since the natural form of each specific kind of commodity is one particular equivalent form amongst innumerable other equivalent forms, the only equivalent forms which exist are limited ones, and each of them excludes all the others'.[68] This inadequacy is resolved in the 'General Form of Value'. Here the bad-infinite sequence of the expanded form of value is reversed: one commodity is set apart from all others, as the universal equivalent form. However, this remains deficient to the extent that the commodity that stands in the position of equivalent is simply one use value

---

63 Backhaus 1980, p 104. For treatments of Marx's development of the form of value, see Robles-Báez 1997 and Arthur 2004a.

64 Marx 1990, p 154.

65 'As merely implicit, value is a vanishing semblance. To be really of the essence it must become posited for itself; it must gain actuality in its further developed forms of appearance' (Arthur 2004b, p 95).

66 Marx 1990, p 154.

67 Marx 1990, p 156. On 'bad infinity', see Hegel 2010, pp 191–8.

68 Marx 1990, p 156–7.

among others – the abstract form of value has not yet properly lifted itself out of the material and acquired autonomy. In Marx's exposition of the form of value, this last deficiency is overcome with the transition to the money form. It is in money that the adequate form of value as identity-in-otherness is attained: all commodities are now identical to and exchangeable for one another because they are all identical to and exchangeable for money. With its achievement of the money form, the ideal conceptuality of value finds its proper objective being. In money, abstract value exists for itself in complete separation from the materiality of the object world, which it engrosses as the universal concept.[69]

The centrality of form in modern value theory accounts for the enormous importance placed upon money in the new readings generally, whatever their other differences of interpretation.[70] Neither orthodox economics nor traditional Marxism could make anything of the form dimensions of Marx's theory, which were not comprehensible from within their theoretical boundaries. Consequently, they could only take the object to be inherently economic. Where the 'supersensuous' essence character of the commodity was not theoretically grasped, the object was assumed to be exchangeable as such, by virtue of being either a product of labour or an item of subjective utility. The form of value was thereby dissolved into the material existence of the object so that the world appeared simply to *be* economic in itself. Indeed, it is characteristic of economic thought generally that it naively assumes the forms of capital because the identity of the commodity, its value form, is invisible to it. It therefore conceives of the value of the object as being constituted without reference to money: 'Both the labor theory of value of classical political economy and the theory of marginal utility of neoclassical economics are pre-monetary theories of value.'[71] Where capital

[69] The emergence of money is thus a *logical* necessity, implicit in the concept of value: 'it is important to notice that the whole argument is driven *conceptually*: for the concept of value to be meaningful, money is required. There is no trace in Marx's presentation of a quasi-causal story about commodity exchangers having as a result of the structure of their situation a tendency to invent money' (Arthur 2004b, p 71 (emphasis in original)).

[70] The necessity of money to the concept of value has been central to modern value theory from the beginning (Arthur 2005a and Arthur 2006). Indeed, drawing attention to the monetary dimension of Marx's value theory was one of the primary contributions of Backhaus' ground-breaking article: 'Innumerable authors ignore the claim of the labour theory of value to derive money as money and thus inaugurate a specific theory of money' (Backhaus 1980, p 102). For recent debate on Marx's theory of money, see Moseley 2005.

[71] Heinrich 2012, p 64. Helmut Reichelt comments at length on the 'categorical unconsciousness [that] continues to shape economic science', marking it as pre-monetary: 'Its theoretical endeavour rests on unreflected presuppositions. With its opaque naturalization of the commodity to a sheerly sensuous thing (from fixed capital to machinery and means of production) and its conception of money as a mere "given", economic thought renders the appearance of simple circulation a theoretical absolute.

is not understood as arising out of the development of the value-form, up to the point of its self-valorisation, the economic problematic as a whole is naturalised as a pre-conceptual process of the production and distribution of 'goods'. The positivism that results can only regard Marx's dialectical form theory as occultly metaphysical and thus reprehensibly unscientific. This is the origin of the irrationality of classical political economy that Marx excoriated it for, that it treated the categories of economics as if they had just 'dropped from the sky' and was unable to explain their genesis. By contrast, the new thinking about value understood, more or less clearly, that the importance of the value form, and in particular the money form, was that it dispelled this naturalistic illusion.

In its opposition to economic naturalism, modern value theory has generally held that Marx should be interpreted as intending a monetary theory of value.[72] For orthodox economics, money is a superficial and merely detachable layer that veils the 'real economy'. Its function is to provide a convenient *numeraire*, an external measure of value for objects that are, by assumption, pre-constituted as values, and so to facilitate exchange by overcoming the problems associated with barter. The abstraction of money is thus secondary to a primary material reality of production. Through its focus on dialectical form determination, modern value theory has effectively reversed this order. What it has shown is that value does not naturalistically pre-exist money, which is then merely a convenient instrument. Rather, money '*constitutes* the value dimension' as such.[73] Only through the conceptuality of money, as the general equivalent form, does the economic space come into existence – that is, only through money is there a value dimension at all. Money does not therefore link together a posteriori and in a merely external way a pre-existing world of objects that

The categorical-unconscious positing and discovery of the money-form as an *uno-actu* process (in Hegel's words: the money-form is posited as presupposed) manifests itself theoretically in the form of an unbridgeable gap that is typical of two-world theory where the many commodities, which are one-sidedly perceived as sensuous things, stand in an external relation to their unity, that is money. Characteristically, economic theory calls sensuous things goods, and money is "externally taken from the empirical world". As Marx argues, this is the way in which economics deals with its categories as a whole. That is, economic theory is, as it were, condemned to construct equilibrium relations between externally related quantities. ... Economic theory can only be a theory of quantities. It has to presuppose value as a macro-economic category and is no longer able to understand value as a form of social practice. Its conception of value is underhanded' (Reichelt 2005, p 61).

72 'The value theory is thus simultaneously a critique of all pre-monetary (subjective or objective) value theories which implicitly or explicitly lie at the foundation of classical and modern economic theories' (Eldred and Hanlon, 1981, pp 87–8).

73 Arthur 2005c, p 116 (emphasis in original).

is economic in-itself, but is instead qualitatively indispensable. It creates the economic space of equivalence and quantity and hence is an a priori of commodity exchange. It follows that in a monetary theory of value the value of the commodity does not inhere in the individual object as a property that is merely symbolised, or represented, by money but attains actuality only when the commodity is posited in relation to all other commodities through the general equivalent:

> [The] money form does not *represent* the presupposed 'value' of commodities; rather it *presents* it to them as their universal moment. Money is not a *re*-presentation of something given in commodities, but the only way of making value *present* ... it *is* the actuality of value. Once value is thus presented explicitly 'for itself' ... in money, it posits the commodities as values 'in themselves'.[74]

What modern value theory has understood is that there is a reciprocal relationship between the universal form of money and the multitude of particular commodities. The one exists only through the many, unity arising through difference; but the many require the one, without which they have no identity. The absurdity of economic thought, by contrast, is that in it commodities have value but without any value form. Their 'supersensuous' quality, which is posited only through their reflection into the general equivalent, is imputed to them directly. The general exchangeability of the economic object – its universality – is presumed rather than being recognised as requiring explanation. Consequently, there is no proper theoretical mediation in either traditional Marxism or mainstream economic thought of commodities and money, which can only be externally related to each other.[75] Pre-monetary theories collapse the conceptuality of value into the natural body of the object such that there is no difference between the object as material entity and the object as economic being. As a result, precisely in its materialistic naturalism, economic theory is always already enclosed within, and so can have no proper awareness of, the conceptual space of economic quantification and equivalence. It is only through a monetary theory of value, therefore, in which the conceptual necessity of money to commodity exchange is shown, that the question can actually be posed of the constitution of the economic space as such. Where the value of the commodity is formed by its relation to the general equivalent, and not merely represented by money, the economic character of the object is not identical

74 Arthur 2005c, p 114 (emphases in original).

75 This was one of Marx's specific criticisms of Ricardo's theory of value (Backhaus 1980, p 105).

to its material being, and so it becomes possible to ask how it becomes an economic object at all. A monetary theory that fully recognises the conceptuality of value thus dispels the apparent immediacy of the economic and so opens the possibility of far-reaching form critique. The commodity is no longer naturalistically assumed to be economic in itself; instead, it is recognised as having become economic through the conceptuality of value.

The value form is an exchange form. Accordingly, as it has developed in conceptual depth and critical force, the reworking of the concept of value by way of the value form and money has, with increasing conviction and emphasis, come to accord theoretical priority to exchange. If the determinacy of the form of value was to be properly established in opposition to economic naturalism, then the concept of value had to be derived, in the first place, from analysis of the exchange process.[76] Since traditional Marxism had largely ignored the value form, it had also neglected exchange, which appeared to it as something secondary to production and unremarkable in itself, merely giving indirect expression to what had already been determined in the labour process. The initial break from traditional Marxism had intimated a reassessment of the significance of exchange for the theory of value through the appeal to the notion of 'abstract labour'. Although without much theoretical clarity, this defence of Marx's theory recognised that the universal character of the commodity was inseparable from the equivalence that is continually effected in market exchange and that the exchange process was therefore essential to the concept of value.[77] However, in its recent and more advanced developments, value theory has moved considerably beyond the general perception that an equalisation somehow happens in exchange and has begun to look in detail at the inner conceptual determinations of the exchange process. In the section on the fetish-character of the commodity, Marx had remarked in satirical vein on the 'metaphysical subtleties'[78] of the commodity, and as value theory has begun to elaborate the objective conceptuality of the system of capital, so it has also come to recognise the true significance of this reference, which in fact reaches far beyond Marx's merely polemical intention. For what modern value theory has finally begun to discover is that at the conceptual centre of the theory of value are the metaphysics of exchange.

As Chris Arthur observes, 'the founding moment of the idea of capital is that there is a realm of ideality set up by the exchange of commodities.'[79]

---

[76] 'In value form theory it is the development of the forms of exchange that is seen as the prime determinant of the capitalist economy rather than the content regulated by it' (Arthur 2004b, p 11).

[77] See, for example, Himmelweit and Mohun 1978, pp 72–8.

[78] Marx 1990, p 163.

[79] Arthur 2016, p 66.

Since it is in the exchange process that this 'realm of ideality', arises, the theorisation of value must begin with the analysis of exchange. When two objects are posited as equivalent to each other in the moment of exchange, their materiality is displaced or set aside. This is not an abstracting from the specificity of individual use values to the general concept of utility but rather a negation of the material being of the exchanged objects altogether. In Arthur's words: 'an objective transcendental negation is brought about in the exchange of commodities through a total absenting of all the bodily characteristics of the goods exchanged'.[80] What takes place in exchange is thus an ontological negation – an '*infinitely negative judgement*' is rendered upon the objects that take on the commodity form.[81] As the complete negation of the materiality of the objects submitted to exchange, the commodity form posits itself as a '*pure form*'.[82] Entirely empty and void in itself, it does not express, or manifest, any content that might exist within the exchanging objects prior to the exchange and that would thus be given *to* the exchange process from outside. Rather, it arises only *in* the exchange. The pure form of value is posited through the ontological negation of the objects involved, and as a consequence of this negation it has an actuality of its own. The absolute negation of the material world exists as a positivity: the value form is what '*is* not-use-value'.[83] Although as an empty, pure form it is itself just an absence, sheer negation, in the process of exchange the absence is itself posited as present. Exchange is thus the presencing, or the making-present, of an absence. This presence-of-absence is what Arthur terms a 'Being-of-Exchange',[84] the abstract-conceptual subject of the dialectical exposition of value. The entire unfolding logic of value, which reaches its culmination in the capitalist world market, thus follows from an original division, a fundamental metaphysical fracture, that occurs in exchange: the 'primordial *separation* between use [better: content] and exchange [better: form]' stands at 'the origin of the systematic dialectical *development* of exchange determinations themselves'.[85]

In this way, the exchange process establishes the simultaneous opposition and interpenetration of two worlds: on the one hand, the 'sensuous' world

---

80 Arthur 2016, p 67.

81 Arthur 2016, p 67.

82 Arthur 2016, p 68.

83 Arthur 2016 (emphasis in original). The term 'use value' here is inaccurate. It is the pre-identical aspect of the thing that is negated in the objective ideality of the exchange process, not its use value – the two are very far from being synonymous. Indeed, part of what is inadequate in Marx's conception of value is that he understands it as an abstraction from use value (Taylor 2004, p 101).

84 Arthur 2016, p 71.

85 Arthur 2016, p 72 (emphases in original).

of the commodity as material thing, and on the other, opposite it and ultimately encompassing it in its entirety, the 'supersensuous' world of the commodity as ideal thing, the instantiation as a presence of the pure, contentless form of value. The complete absenting of materiality in the activity of exchange produces an empty nothing. However, as present and determinate, this nothing also has being – the abstraction that arises in exchange is *actual*, or *real*, as Nothing. The dialectic of the value form is then the dynamic movement of this Being-of-Nothing as it unfolds itself in its intrinsic universality:

> This Nothing is the *beginning* of the dialectic of the self-positing nothingness, because, as an immediacy, this Nothing has itself Being … but of course is equally Nothing, hence … it yields the Being-of-Nothing, namely *Nothingness*. … Both being *and nothing* are founding moments of *the value-form*.[86]

The determinateness of this Nothingness that is the essence of the commodity as supersensuous being is then its Being-for-another. This is its quality of exchangeability or capacity to be exchanged, through which it is identical to all other objects of the commodity world.[87] The being of the commodity, therefore, its essence and its self-identity, exists only by virtue of its relation with other commodities. The commodity 'refers to *itself* in its other',[88] proving its actuality as a Being-of-exchange in the relation to the many others. The unification of the manifold of commodities in the abstract sphere of ideality that is the economic space thus requires the positing of the Being-of-Exchange for itself as money: 'together, determined as "one One", so to speak, *by money*, they constitute a totality'.[89] Accordingly, it is in money, which is intrinsically totality, that value achieves actuality as absolute abstraction, the presence of absence or the being of Nothing.

The pure form of negation that arises in exchange is, in its absolute emptiness, universal, capable in principle of encompassing everything within its logic of form determination. However, although exchange produces a 'real' abstraction, an objective conceptuality, this Nothingness of the Being-of-Exchange can only maintain its existence by passing through successive exchanges. As soon as the exchange process is concluded and the object falls out of it, then the abstraction of exchange vanishes and the object reverts to

86 Arthur 2016, p 78 (emphases in original).
87 Arthur 2016, p 81.
88 Arthur 2016, pp 81–2 (emphasis in original).
89 Arthur 2016, p 84. (emphasis in original). For more extensive discussion of the dialectic of presence and absence, Being and Nothing, that is set in motion by exchange, see Arthur 2022, Chapter 5 and pp 71–81.

its merely material form.[90] Value must therefore be value-in-motion. Just in order to sustain itself and to maintain its ideal existence against the material world, the value form has to be constantly in process, always moving through a continuous, unbroken series of exchanges. The entire abstract sphere of 'the economy' thus depends on the freedom of value to pass through its various forms without resistance. It follows that for the proper theorisation of value 'conceptions that are premised on the idea of being as stasis fail':[91]

> The dualism of two moments that mutually presuppose each other can neither be defined statically nor in terms of its substance, but only as movement. Only when value is developed as value in movement, can the unity of its forms be conceptualized, as it is the case with Hegel's conception of law: 'The law is what remains in disappearance'.[92]

Value as pure exchange form can achieve perpetual motion, definitively establishing its autonomy and independence in relation to the material, only when it becomes self-sustaining. For value to make actual its intrinsic universality, it must ground itself upon itself, so that it generates itself from itself. The value abstraction thus drives towards a condition in which exchange is universal and systematic. This can only happen when the sequence of exchanges bends back upon itself so that the two ends link up and form a closed circuit.[93] Only when every step in the circuit is value-formed can value pass seamlessly through each one and become entirely self-determining and self-referential as capital.

In attaining the form of capital, value achieves its concept. What was universal in-itself becomes universal for-itself, and the circle of identity is completed. Value continually mediates itself with itself, comparing itself against itself quantitatively in the process of valorisation. The movement of value as capital, as it endlessly repeats its innumerable circuits, is what Marx referred to, using a term drawn from the sphere of myth, as the metamorphoses of value through its different forms: money capital, commodity capital, productive capital, and so on.[94] In Hegelian terms, value

90 'Money is really value for itself only when functioning as the aim of the capital circuit. A fixed sum is always a collapse to use value … apart from circulation it is just a metal dump' (Arthur 2004b, p 146).

91 Reichelt 2005, p 33.

92 Reichelt 2005, p 39. The phrase Reichelt quotes is from Hans-Georg Gadamer (Gadamer 1976, p 42).

93 For value theory, what in part differentiates Marx's conception from orthodox economics is that capital is not thought in terms of a set of static equilibrium relations between externally related variables but as a dynamic process unified by the endless self-movement of value.

94 Marx 1992, Part 1.

as capital is a 'genuine infinite':[95] its other has become simply a medium of its own identity, so that through its movement it always returns to itself.[96] As long as its dialectical development was still incomplete so that value had not yet achieved full autonomy, the world retained a substantiality of its own that was beyond the reach of the exchange abstraction and so not yet incorporated into the economic space of equivalence. When value becomes capital, though, the pure form has internalised the world altogether, so that what was once an externality in which value risked losing itself has been posited by capital from out of itself as simply the bearer of the self-perpetuating, endlessly self-renewing process of exchange. In the infinitude of capital, therefore, the limitless self-involvement of identity through its ceaseless mediation in its other, the world has become completely immanent to value.

95 Hegel 1991, pp 149–50/§94.

96 'Money functions as capital only when it is *perpetually* thrown into circulation, and it is in this sense that the movement of capital is inherently limitless' (Taylor 2004, p 104 (emphasis in original)).

4

The Theory of Value: From Labour to Exchange

Marx and naturalism

Emerging from the crisis of Marxism in the 1970s, modern value theory has above all taken up the form elements in Marx account of capital that had been neglected by the orthodox tradition. Indeed, it was precisely the collapse of traditional Marxism that liberated this aspect of Marx's thought from obscurity and ushered it into the limelight. Through its focus on the dialectic of the value form and the metaphysics of exchange, value theory has brought about in the subsequent decades what is effectively a revolution in the understanding of the foundational concept of economic thought. That is its positive, constructive achievement. The other side of its work, however, has been its negative labour of critique. For, in its rejection of the crude aconceptuality of Marxist orthodoxy, value theory could not help but become conscious of the inconsistencies and obscurities in Marx's attempts to formulate the basic concepts of his theory. Although it strongly emphasised the form aspects of his thought, it had to recognise that the theory as a whole was very far from being consistently form-determined and dialectical in its elaboration. Indeed, the more closely it has looked, the more it has put its finger on precisely the points where Marx fails to articulate the logic of form in a consistent way, and where, as a result, he remains mired in conceptual indeterminacy and a theoretically deficient naturalism. These failings are not incidental but follow a consistent pattern: they point towards a fundamental incoherence in Marx's conception of value, the conflictual presence of opposed elements that work against each other.

In seeking to rescue the critique from the decay of traditional Marxism, value theory returned to the very beginning of *Capital*, Part 1 of Volume I, with the intention of rearticulating the grounding concepts.[1] However, from

[1] Heinrich 2021.

the outset it was compelled to acknowledge that what it found there was a considerable degree of theoretical ambivalence. The logic of form was by no means clearly stated by Marx at the start but was mixed with, and largely obscured by, other elements whose conceptual status and relation to the dialectic of form were far from clear. The ambiguity in Marx's exposition of value in the opening chapter was recognised, and thematised as an interpretative problem, right at the beginning of the value theory revolution, in Hans-Georg Backhaus' ground-breaking article on the dialectic of the value form. Although his purpose was to effect a breach with economistic and positivist readings of Marx, Backhaus conceded that 'the deficient appraisal of the value-form analysis' to be found in traditional readings was 'not to be attributed solely to a certain blindness to the problem on the part of the interpreters' but that the fault lay just as much with Marx himself.[2] For even in the most developed versions of the opening of the theory of capital, Marx failed to establish in an adequate way the relation between the different dimensions of the commodity that he purported to identify. Specifically, Backhaus drew attention to a lack of mediation between the two halves of the opening chapter. In Sections 1 and 2, Marx first establishes the 'two factors of the commodity', use value and value, positing labour as the substance of value, and then proceeds to the so-called dual character of the labour contained in the commodity, 'concrete' labour and 'abstract' labour. In Sections 3 and 4, he then turns to the development of the value form and, on that basis, presents his famous account of the fetish-character of the commodity. Hence, the order of exposition in the analysis of the commodity in the opening chapter is one in which the labour 'substance' of exchange value is established separately from and before the form determination through which it supposedly appears. As a whole, Chapter 1 is thus structured around a theoretical division of content and form, a sundering that results in a logical hiatus between the second and third sections. At the origin of modern value theory, Backhaus was the first to state plainly that, from the point of view of a consistent form theory, this expositional procedure is extremely problematic:

> The analysis of the essence independently of its form of appearance leads to the situation that Marx turns back to the analysis of the form of appearance, quite without mediations, without demonstration of an inner necessity. … The defective mediation of substance and form of value is already expressed in the fact that in the development of value a gap can be shown. The transition from the second to the third section of the first chapter is no longer sensible as a *necessary* transition.

[2] Backhaus 1980, p 99.

> What strikes the reader, therefore, is the apparently easily understood theory of value-substance and the double-character of labour, which is unfolded in the first two sections. The third section, however, the theory of the value-form, is mostly understood only as an additional proof or as a 'dialectical' ornament of what was plainly already derived in the first two sections.[3]

The integrity of Marx's exposition of value thus breaks down almost immediately, in the very first chapter: there is a clearly discernible theoretical gap between the opening treatment of the 'substance' of value and the rendition of the value form that follows. In consequence, the conceptual form problematic is not clearly established at the outset as the governing logic of the theory of value as a whole. Instead of a single, systematic dialectical development of the value form, two distinct lines of thought are present, content and form, such that, without explanation or mediation, the analysis of the commodity suddenly shifts register in the middle of the opening chapter. How the two lines of thought, corresponding to the two halves of Chapter 1, relate to each other is thus unclear in Marx's text. Given this obscurity, it is little wonder that Marxist orthodoxy preferred to concentrate on the 'easily understood' Sections 1 and 2, which straightforwardly associate value with labour and so connect the theory of value with other Marxist doctrines concerning labour, production, social relations, the proletariat and revolution, and to set aside Section 3 as merely subsidiary, if not actually otiose. The traditional neglect and incomprehension of the whole value-form problematic could thus, for Backhaus, be traced back to the argumentative difficulties that Marx was never able to resolve in any of his many attempts to expound his notion of value and that continued to vitiate even the most authoritative version. As Backhaus summarises the basic deficiency: 'the mode of presentation in *Capital* in no way makes clear the expository (erkenntnisleitende) motive of Marx's value-form analysis'.[4]

The meaning of the value-form interpretation initiated by Backhaus is that it is solely through the form dimensions of his theory that Marx moves beyond the field of classical political economy, and that therefore the critical content of the theory of capital lies exclusively in the form problematic. As, since the 1970s, this primary demand of form interpretation has gradually become clearer, so value theory has, step by step, identified the places in the exposition of value where Marx fails to meet it. Obvious instances could be found in Marx's efforts to specify the nature of 'abstract' labour as part of his analysis of the 'dual character' of labour in capital, the crucial argument

3 Backhaus 1980, p 101.

4 Backhaus 1980, p 101.

that is intended to associate value with labour. In Section 2, where this 'abstract' labour is introduced, Marx repeatedly resorts to characterisations of the generality of labour in terms of a naturalistic physicalism:

> Tailoring and weaving ... are both a productive expenditure of human brains, muscles, nerves, hands etc., and in this sense both human labour. They are merely two different forms of the expenditure of human labour-power. ... the value of a commodity represents human labour pure and simple, the expenditure of human labour in general ... It is the expenditure of simple labour-power, i.e. of the ordinary labour-power possessed in his bodily organism by every ordinary man.[5]

Asserted entirely outside any logic of form determination, these physiological statements of 'abstract' labour evacuate the notion of 'all social and historical elements',[6] turning it into a kind of ontological constant that would seem to apply transhistorically, across all forms of social production. This naturalism of a supposedly universal labour authorised the 'crudest understanding'[7] of value, which, ignorant of all form elements, identified it directly with labour expended in production and thereby 'embodied' in the product. Accompanying these aconceptual, naturalistic statements of 'abstract' labour in Marx's argument is a substantialist idea of value that is also clearly discernible in the opening sections of *Capital* – value conceived of as a kind of substance that is produced by labour and that inheres in commodities by virtue of the expenditure of human labour power on them in their production. At numerous points in these crucial initial pages, Marx states emphatically that labour is the 'value-forming substance' and that an object 'has value only because abstract human labour is objectified or materialized in it'.[8] The value-character of the commodity, Marx's argument here says plainly, is its existence as an objectification of the general social substance that supposedly is human labour. From the idea that value is a substance existing in the commodity as a result of the productive expenditure of the labour power possessed by the 'ordinary man' it is, in truth, difficult *not* to arrive at some kind of 'embodied labour' conception of value, that is, the sort of Ricardian, pre-monetary understanding of value that was standard

5 Marx 1990, pp 134–5.
6 Rubin 1973, p 132.
7 Eldred and Hanlon 1981, p 40.
8 Marx 1990, p 129. Marx states directly that, as values, commodities 'are merely congealed quantities of homogenous human labour, i.e. human labour expended without regard to the form of its expenditure. ... human labour-power has been expended to produce them, human labour is accumulated in them. As crystals of this social substance, which is common to them all, they are values' (Marx 1990, p 128).

in traditional Marxism and which value theory since the 1970s has above all rejected.[9] This substantialist and physicalist conception of value is, in the sequence of Marx's argument, explicitly not attained through the value form but is altogether in place by the end of Section 2, before the question of exchange forms is even encountered. It has to be acknowledged, therefore, that the traditional interpretation in terms of a pre-value-form 'embodied labour', which modern value theory has striven to break free from, in fact finds very considerable warrant in Marx's texts – at the outset, in the first two sections of the opening chapter, no less – and so cannot be dismissed simply as a misreading.[10] On the contrary, the orthodox understanding was built upon elements that are clearly present in Marx's idea of value.

That Marx appears to have had in mind an 'abstract-labour embodied' theory of value, which is arrived at before the value form is introduced and therefore before commodities enter the process of exchange, meant that the status of the concepts in the opening sections of Chapter 1 became problematic from a form-theory point of view. For the general concepts that are supposed to ground the theory of value in the first two sections do not meet the standards of dialectical form determination. Instead, in order to make his arguments about the substance of value and the dual character of labour, Marx adopts a procedure of formal, reductive abstraction – value as abstraction from use-value, the simple setting aside or disregarding of use-value, as in the notorious 'third thing' argument by which Marx posits the commonality of being products of human labour as the basis on which exchange of commodities takes place.[11] Likewise, at crucial points Marx develops his account of value-as-labour by way of simplifying assumptions, purporting to justify this as necessary merely for the sake of ease of exposition.[12] Because they are arrived at completely outside the value form, these concepts, fundamental to the argument that is meant to connect value and labour in the opening sections, are in no way dialectical in nature.[13] Rather, they are static, analytical abstractions that are incompatible with the

[9] Geert Reuten plausibly proposes that Marx's conception is of an 'abstract-labor *embodied* theory of value' and that therefore the use of the term 'substance' is itself substantive in his theory and not merely metaphoric (Reuten 1993, p 99 (emphasis in original)).

[10] Eldred and Hanlon 1981, p 24; Eldred, Hanlon, Kleiber and Roth 1983, p 87.

[11] As with numerous other controversies over Marx's theory of value, the 'third thing' argument has been an issue of contention since Böhm-Bawerk in the late 19th century (Böhm-Bawerk 1949, pp 64–80; see also Furner 2004 and Murray 2006).

[12] 'In the interests of simplification, we shall henceforth view every form of labour-power directly as simply labour-power; by this we shall simply be saving ourselves the trouble of making the reduction' (Marx 1990, p 135). On these deficiencies in Marx's mode of argument generally, see Reuten 1993, pp 96–8 and Taylor 2004, pp 95–9.

[13] 'Abstract labour is not posited as universal labor in contradiction with particular labor. … Rather, the particular labor appears to be abstracted from' (Reuten 1993, p 97).

inherently dynamic form concept of value as capital.[14] Such abstractions are not 'real' abstractions, produced by an objective process of exchange, but are instead the product of the subjective abstracting work of the theorist. They are not the self-determining universals of dialectic, which encompass the singular within themselves and express its life, but formal-analytical generalities, arrived at by abstraction from the singular. Indeed, the whole argument of Sections 1 and 2 of *Capital*, in which Marx claims to demonstrate that labour is the substance of value and that the labour embodied in the commodity is 'abstract' labour, is derived merely by way of apparent mental generalisations, without any reference to, or mediation through, exchange and the value form. The objective concept of value, central to value-form theory, cannot be adequately determined in this way, which is why value theory has generally found fault with these aspects of Marx's argument in the opening sections.[15] The result of the undialectical mode of abstraction that underpins Marx's postulation of a labour substance in his theory of value is the hiatus in the exposition in Chapter 1 noted by Backhaus: 'the essence is defined, in contrast to the form of appearance, in a formal, logical way as the universal, typical and principal. The mediation of essence and appearance can only be construed as a pseudo-dialectical movement of pseudo-dialectical contradiction.'[16]

The duality of a naturalistic-physicalist notion of value substance existing alongside but not integrated with an objective-conceptual theory of the value form is further deepened in Chapter 1 by the ambiguities in Marx's account of the determination of the magnitude of value and its measure. In a value-form theory, the economic space of value is constituted through money because commodities have a value character only by virtue of their relation to the general equivalent. As the existing incarnation of absolute identity and absolute value, therefore, '*money is pure quantity*':[17]

> Within itself money shows only quantitative differentiations. It is something qualitative which exists as pure quantity, thus qualitative quantity or *quantum*. ... not only does money serve as the medium in which commodities express their value qualitatively, but definite units

---

[14] Reichelt 2005, p 39.

[15] Heinrich 2009, pp 90–2. This is, in effect, Marxism's very belated discovery of a fundamental principle of Kant's reformulation of metaphysics and then of German Idealism: that the intelligible is not to be conceived on the model of, or as in continuity with, the sensible, as a substance, substrate or thing. Rather, it is to be thought purely as *concept*.

[16] Backhaus 1980, p 101.

[17] Taylor 2004, p 103 (emphasis in original).

> of the commodity express also their value quantitatively in a definite amount of money. ... Money serves as the *measure of magnitude of value.*[18]

Value is a phenomenon of systematic exchange relations to which money is essential, and the magnitude of value and its measure must therefore be found within the nexus of those relations. So, just as for a form theory value necessarily requires money in order to have actuality, the magnitude of value can be measured only in money, which is a purely quantitative dimension. The value magnitude of any commodity must therefore be the money amount for which it exchanges.[19] In Chapter 1, however, Marx develops a quite different idea of the magnitude of value. His primary concern there is to secure the link between value and labour that is central to his conception of capital as a 'mode of production'. The necessity of establishing the argumentative primacy of the labour basis compels Marx to consider value-as-labour 'independently of its form of appearance'.[20] If value is to be understood as a form of labour, even if 'abstract' labour, then it follows that the real measure of value and its magnitude is the dimension in which labour can be measured: time. Accordingly, Marx follows his argument about the substance of value with a series of statements about the magnitude of value all of which are cast in temporal terms. Quite plainly, at this point in the argument, the magnitude of value is to be determined through the duration of labour time.[21] Once again, this aspect of Marx's value concept is in place before the logic of the value form is arrived at in the exposition, and therefore before the introduction of money as constitutive of the space of value. There are thus two different, and incongruent, accounts of the crucial question of the measurement of the magnitude of value at the very opening of *Capital*: on the one hand, explicit assertions, in accordance with the argument concerning the substance of value and the dual character of labour, that value is to be measured by reference to labour time; and on the other, following the line of the value-form idea and the necessity of monetary exchange, an implicit logical argument that value quantities must be measured in monetary quantities. From the evidence of Marx's text, it is clear that he was committed to the former. Precisely this commitment,

---

18 Eldred and Hanlon 1981, p 35 (emphases in original).

19 By the same token, the measure of the valorisation of value in capital is also an exclusively monetary one, the comparison of money against itself (M–M') at two points in the circuit of capital (M–C–P–C–M') (Taylor 2004, pp 106–10).

20 Marx 1990, p 128.

21 'How, then, is the magnitude of this value to be measured? By means of the quantity of the "value-forming substance", the labour, contained in the article. This quantity is measured by its duration, and the labour-time is itself measured on the particular scale of hours, days etc' (Marx 1990, p 129).

though, places at the foundation of the theory a damaging disjunction between the form of value and the magnitude of value – a further dimension of the split between the two halves of Chapter 1. In fact, Marx's desire to derive the magnitude of value from the labour substance essentially takes him back to the pre-form, pre-monetary, classical problematic, in which, exactly as he complained of in relation to Ricardo, there is a 'lack of conceptual connection between magnitude of value [i.e. labour time] and exchange-value (price)'.[22] The attempt to establish the magnitude of value outside the value form problematic and in terms of 'socially necessary labour time' then leads Marx into a series of conceptual thickets and confusions regarding the equalisation of different forms of labour, which all derive from the impossibility of determining the generality of value through labour without reference to exchange, the value form and money, problems that he attempts to resolve by means of further illicit assumptions of presentation and spurious procedures of reduction.[23]

These fundamental deficiencies in the articulation of the concept of value in Chapter 1 do not just exist where Marx attempts to determine value outside the value form – they also affect his construction of the value-form problematic itself, and with it his concept of money.[24] Marx's criticism of the inability of the classical political economists to explain the necessity of money to the functioning of the capitalist economy turned on his view that they failed to appreciate the implications of the private, dissociated structure of labour in capital. Because they assumed commodity relations, they did not ask '*why labour and the measurement of labour must take on a value-form*'.[25] That is, they did not see the value form of labour, the connection of labour and money, as a problem. It was in order to solve this 'riddle' that Marx developed his analysis of the value form, beginning from the comparison, in the simple form of value, of the 'relative' and 'equivalent' forms and moving from there up to the general equivalent.[26] This analysis is designed

22 Eldred and Hanlon 1981, p 37.

23 Eldred and Hanlon 1981, pp 37–40. Criticism of Marx's arguments in this context about skilled and unskilled labour, which follow from his introduction of the idea of 'simple labour' as a quasi-universal concept of labour, once again go back to Böhm-Bawerk (1949, pp 80–90). The most detailed treatment of the false arguments in which Marx entangles himself through trying to reduce all forms of labour to 'simple labour' is Bidet 2009, Chapter 2. Cf. also in this context the conceptual confusions that result from Marx's attempt to determine the value of labour power by reference to the naturalistic and physicalist notion of 'subsistence' taken from the classical tradition (Levine 1998b, pp 20–2).

24 The following draws on the analysis in Taylor 2004.

25 Taylor 2004, p 91 (emphasis in original).

26 Taylor (2004) refers in particular to Marx's exposition of the forms of value in the Appendix to the first edition of *Capital* (see Marx 1976).

to demonstrate the necessary link between value and labour – the bringing together of concrete-private labour and abstract-social labour – in a 'body of value', the commodity that functions as equivalent: 'the nexus for the unity of the two is the material "body" of a commodity serving as "equivalent value-form"'.[27] The outcome of Marx's rendition of the dialectic of the value form is the emergence of the general equivalent as a money *commodity*, that is, a product of labour, instantiated in the material shape of gold. The money commodity is thus supposed to combine content (as embodiment of an amount of concrete labour) and form (the same concrete labour counting directly as general labour, the immediate expression of socially validated labour time). In this argument, commodity money is 'the only immediate expression of value and the only true measure of *the social value of the labour time expended on all other commodities*'.[28]

Through his development of the value form, it thus appears at first sight that Marx succeeds where classical political economy fell short by demonstrating the necessity of money to the existence of a system of capitalist production relations, thereby linking together labour and money, content and form. However, as Nicola Taylor demonstrates, this is not in fact so, because the whole argument for commodity money, money conceived of as a 'body of value' that expresses a labour content contained within it, continues to rely upon an 'embodied labour' conception of value, which in turn rests entirely upon the undialectical abstractions and simplifying assumptions of Sections 1 and 2. The crucial connection between value and labour is still posited outside the value form itself – the labour exists directly in the commodity, 'embodied in it', and is then represented through the forms of value. Marx's development of the value form as commodity money thus does not resolve what Taylor identifies as the 'core problem' of the opening chapter of *Capital*, which is 'the indeterminate character of abstract labour and socially necessary labour time as *pre-monetary* categories'.[29] Rather, the form problematic in Marx's exposition remains tied to that conceptually weak and theoretically unsatisfactory basis. This is why, almost in the same breath in which he derives the necessity of money to commodity exchange, Marx denies that this is actually the case, without being aware of any contradiction, and asserts that the identity and equivalence of commodities really exist outside money and the value form altogether, in labour as such:

> It is not money that renders the commodities commensurable. Quite the contrary. Because all commodities, as values, are objectified human

[27] Taylor 2004, p 91.
[28] Taylor 2004, p 94 (emphasis in original).
[29] Taylor 2004, p 99 (emphasis in original).

> labour, and therefore in themselves commensurable, their values can be communally measured in one and the same specific commodity, and this commodity can be converted into the common measure of their values, that is into money. Money as a measure of value is the necessary form of appearance of the measure of value which is immanent in commodities, namely labour time.[30]

Here, money is not understood as constituting the value space but only as indirectly representing a pre-existing universal, quasi-material, content that is given merely through the expenditure of labour.[31] Even in what value form theory has taken to be the strongest part of his account of value in Chapter 1, therefore, Marx fails to establish the concept in a satisfactory way – the value form is not given its proper autonomy and determinacy but is instead subordinated to a crudely naturalistic and conceptually indeterminate problematic of embodied labour, labour substance and 'socially necessary labour time', the theoretical status of which is never adequately established.

A divided theory

Modern value theory has shown that it is only in the elements of form determination that Marx's theory goes beyond orthodox economics. At the same time, in radically reconceiving the theorisation of value, it has also conclusively demonstrated that at no point in his long studies of political economy did Marx manage to present a consistently worked out form theory. Even in the crucial text of the opening chapter of *Capital*, where the central categories are to be established and the direction of the theoretical enquiry set, there are profound theoretical inconsistencies and damaging failures of concept formation. For this reason, it has come to be acknowledged within the field of Marxian value theory that the reading of Marx cannot simply be regarded as exposition because there is no unitary theory there to be exposited – the argument is ineliminably confused. Instead, a value-form interpretation of Marx has to be, at the least, a 'reconstruction': that is, it is necessary in the first place to determine what in Marx's texts constitutes form theory and then to sift out the pre-form elements.[32] So much has

30 Marx 1990, p 188.

31 The debate over Marx's theory of money continues to be divided on the issue of commodity money (compare, for example, Williams 2000 and Germer 2005). The controversy arises from the confusions in Marx's concept of value: while commodity money is certainly no part of a value-form theory of capital, it is a necessity within the logic of Marx's theory, precisely because the latter is only partially value-formed.

32 This was first recognised by Backhaus in the 1970s (Backhaus 1980, p 98 (note 13); Bellofiore and Redolfi Riva, 2018, pp 389–91). See also Arthur 2004b, p 5; Reichelt

been demonstrated by modern research. However, although, at its best, value theory has evidenced in precise detail the theoretical ambivalences and inconsistencies in Marx's idea of value, it has not thought through the general logic of this theoretical failure, or the coherence of the incoherence. As a result, the constructive and destructive sides of value theory are inadequately mediated to each other. There is positive reconstruction of the categorial logic of the value form and negative critique of specific places in Marx's exposition where that dialectical logic falters or is insufficiently worked out, but the relation between these two is not made clear. The operative assumption, more or less explicitly stated, is that a form logic is the dominant framework of Marx's theory, in opposition to traditional Marxism, while the critical judgement on Marx himself is limited to pointing out in a merely ad hoc way the various conceptual shortcomings that, regrettably, continue to mar the argument. In the absence of a concerted overview of the theoretical failures in Marx, therefore, the value theory literature as a whole remains in a state of confusion on fundamental questions: it is not clear to what extent Marx was in fact, self-consciously, a form thinker and thus what the status of dialectic was within his concept of value, nor has it been adequately explained why, if there is a governing logic of form determination, there are nevertheless numerous undialectical elements within the statement of the fundamental concepts of his theory, and what, in turn, the meaning of this admixture is. Through its detailed philological and conceptual work, the research on value has made plain that there are incompatible logics within Marx's attempt to formulate a theory. However, it itself continues to be defined by that contradiction and has not yet mastered it.

The significance of the clashing logics at work in Marx has been most nearly determined in relation to the theorisation of, once again, money. Fundamentally, there are two opposed and antithetical approaches to the logical status of money within economic theory:[33] either production determines exchange, so that 'a set of production conditions underlies the logical structure of exchange relations' and money is 'excluded as a *determinant* of commodity exchange';[34] or 'monetary abstraction does not arise substantially in production but in the practical relation of commodity exchange', which means that 'money is a necessary condition for the

2005, p 52. Chris Arthur's major statement of systematic dialectic is explicitly conceived not as an exposition of Marx but as a reconstruction of the conceptual logic of capital by way of Marx and Hegel (Arthur 2022). In truth, what this general turn to 'reconstruction' indicates is that the value debate is not really about the interpretation of Marx at all. Rather, it signifies the gradual emergence from the ruins of Marxism of an entirely new concept of capital.

33 Taylor 2004. In making her argument, Taylor draws upon Levine 1983.

34 Taylor 2004, p 90 (emphasis in original).

existence of the (capitalist) value-form of exchange'.[35] The question for the theorisation of money is thus: does it go from production to money or from money to production? Marx's theory is ambivalent because he attempts, in a particular way, to combine these opposed logics, which results in the unsatisfactory theorisation of commodity money. More widely, the two different approaches to the question of money reflect two opposed conceptions of the logical direction of theory construction in general: does the movement go from content to form or from form to content? Again, both of these conceptions can be found uneasily combined in Marx. It is in the encounter with this fundamental theoretical question of the mediation of content and form that contemporary value theory reaches its limit. The reason it is unable to decide the question in a consistent and satisfactory way is that the ambivalence is essential to its self-identity as, precisely, *Marxist* theory, because Marx's own attempt to negotiate this issue – to use classical political economy and Hegelian dialectic against each other – was itself profoundly confused and contradictory. The theory of capital was constructed directly on this fault line, which generates the instability that runs all the way through it, right into the formulation of its central concept of value. In pointing out the deficiencies in the attempted statement of the value concept in Chapter 1, modern value theory was in fact just making this deep fracture visible. But it did not thereby manage to raise the brokenness at the base of Marx's theory to critical consciousness. This failure of theoretical perception demonstrates that the contradiction cannot be properly thematised and resolved from within the space of Marxism because it is, in truth, constitutive of it. The split both defines Marxism, making it what it is, and brings it to theoretical ruin.

The various ambivalences between production and exchange in Marx are ultimately symptoms of the basic theoretical duality that structures his entire idea of value and capital. What four decades of work on Marx's theorisation of value have made plain, without ever being able to state it directly, is that the fundamental deficiency, from which all of its specific problems derive, is that it attempts to combine two essentially different and incompatible paradigms. On the one hand, there is a general social and historical theory that accords centrality to labour and production as the irreducible material-economic ground of human life – a conception that is deeply rooted in modern thought as such and that was given doctrinal form in Marxism as so-called historical materialism; and on the other, there is a logical exchange theory, in which value is thought as a 'real' abstraction that arises in the process of exchange and objectifies itself in the formation of money as the general equivalent – the value form. The first of these was

[35] Taylor 2004, p 88.

emphasised by traditional Marxism to the almost total exclusion of the form-theory dimension, while the second has been the central concern of modern value theory. Just as these two readings of Marx – traditional and modern, historical and logical – effectively exclude each other, so it has become obvious from detailed scrutiny of the texts that Marx was never able to fit the two paradigms together to produce a consistent, unitary theory of value.

The split within Marxism over the nature of value thus really reflects a split within Marx himself. This is the logic of theoretical failure that is inscribed into the analysis of capital at the very beginning, in Chapter 1: Marx is unable to combine in a conceptually satisfactory manner the abstract generality of the value form with labour as the content, or substance, of value. They simply will not cohere, and the only way in which he can force them together is through recourse to undialectical, analytical abstractions, which cannot found a dialectical form theory, and the theoretical sleight-of-hand of simplifying assumptions. Reliance upon these subaltern and illegitimate procedures then leads to the hiatus in the exposition between Sections 2 and 3. The larger import of the various detailed criticisms that have been made of the theorisation in Chapter 1 is thus that there is in fact a double theory of value there – both a labour and labour time theory and a value-form and monetary theory – and that at no point do these actually come together to produce a stable and coherent concept. This duality in the theory was, in fact, the real meaning of the transformation problem, around which traditional, economistic Marxism collapsed in the 1970s. Effectively, what the Sraffian critics said was that there is no transition from a 'materialist' value space, conceived in terms of 'embodied labour' and measured through 'socially necessary labour time', to an 'idealist' monetary space of prices of production. At the culmination of the theory, 'inner' and 'outer', or form and content, the unity of which was never satisfactorily established at the start, finally come apart from each other altogether – capital cannot be thought as a movement from a naturalistic core of labour expenditure to a surface sphere of prices as forms of appearance.[36] Modern value theory sought to rescue Marx's construction from this breakdown but, in doing so, it could not help but rediscover at the very opening of the theorisation, in the various opaque and dubious formulations of Chapter 1, precisely the same failing: that there is no satisfactory conceptual mediation of the

[36] Beyond the transformation problem, the fundamental split between labour and exchange could also be discerned shaping debate elsewhere in Marxism at the time, for example in the controversy over world-systems theory and its allegedly 'neo-Smithian' conception of economic development (Brenner 1977). However, just as with value theory, since both sides of the debate remained committed to the basic economistic premises of Marxism, the underlying schism between production and exchange could not be made thematic and thereby opened out into its full theoretical dimensions.

division between labour and production on the one hand, and exchange and money on the other. They are in fact as far apart from each other at the beginning as at the end. The positive achievement of Marxian value theory thus turns out to be, in a larger sense, self-defeating. For the effort of recuperating Marx's concept of value finds itself, often unwittingly and *contre coeur*, tearing it apart much more thoroughly than any of its critics ever did, clearly exposing the basic incoherence that vitiates the construction right from the beginning.[37]

Because it wishes to remain Marxism, the whole of modern value theory is caught within the tension between the two irreconcilable paradigms in Marx. Instead of acknowledging the contradiction explicitly, though, and thematising it as an object of theoretical reflection, value theory typically represses awareness of it and tries to hold the two sides together. Only this concern not to rupture the field of Marxism entirely can explain the enormous importance accorded within modern value theory to the notion of 'abstract labour'. This term, in fact only passingly used by Marx himself, played a leading role in the debates of the 1970 and 1980s, as the aconceptuality of traditional Marxism was discredited and it was increasingly realised that the requirement of differentiating Marx from Ricardianism

[37] It is probable that in the attempt to force together essentially contradictory paradigms can be found the answer to a long-standing question prominent especially within the German debates on value: 'why did Marx conceal his dialectical method?' (Reichelt 1995; see also Reichelt 2005 and 2007). Close comparison of the various drafts of the theorisation of capital demonstrates that Marx progressively reduced dialectical-Hegelian terminology and modes of conceptual exposition, without ever eliminating them entirely. In the same way that he tried to combine Hegelian philosophy and classical political economy, so Marx's conception of capital was simultaneously dialectical and undialectical. The attenuation of the dialectical-philosophical elements in the successive drafts of *Capital* and the various ways in which the two paradigms, labour and production and dialectical value form, continually interfere with and contradict each other throughout the analysis have been documented in detail by Jacques Bidet (Bidet 2009). In the spirit of Althusserian-structuralist Marxism, Bidet interprets this as Marx moving, hesitantly and without full self-consciousness, away from the philosophical legacy, characterised as an 'epistemological support–obstacle', towards a properly scientific theorisation, although without in the end being able to achieve the complete break that would have allowed a consistently articulated theory. While Bidet may perhaps be right concerning Marx's self-understanding, it is equally possible to read all of the evidence that he adduces directly the other way around: as demonstrating how the labour and production paradigm, and its accompanying idea of science, confuses and vitiates the development of a properly dialectical, form-determined theory of capital. Seen in this perspective, Bidet's argument in fact consistently undoes itself, precisely demonstrating exactly what it denies. (For a critique of the conclusions Bidet draws from his analysis, see Reichelt 1993. The dialogue of the deaf between structuralism and value-form theory that results from their shared commitment to Marxism can be observed in Bidet 2005 and Arthur 2005b.)

could only be met through the elaboration of the form elements.[38] Since then, it has never been far from the centre of discussions concerning Marx's theory of value and considerable energy continues to be expended on controversies over its meaning.[39] The notion of 'abstract labour' results from the attempt to give due recognition to the form-conceptual nature of value while still remaining within the Marxist production paradigm: when the universal social substance of labour is mediated by exchange, its properly material reality is spirited away and 'concrete' human activity is transmuted into 'abstract' labour. It is labour in this 'abstract' form that then constitutes the substance of value. In this way, the notion of 'abstract labour' appears to allow the conjoining of the two different paradigms in Marx: labour remains the ground, but when it is subsumed to the value form it becomes 'abstract' labour, the historically specific form of social labour under capitalist relations of production. However, this appearance is illusory – the contradiction is not in fact resolved but merely displaced. Examination of the debates over 'abstract labour' shows that they are themselves hopelessly divided over whether it arises in production or in exchange; that is, whether it is the labour/production or the exchange/money paradigm that structures the concept and determines labour as 'abstract'.[40] The concept that was supposed to bring the two paradigms together is thus itself riven by the fundamental incompatibility. In truth, the notion of 'abstract labour' is not a reality of capital at all; rather, it marks the site of an unhealable wound in Marx's theory, indicative of what is simply false in his conception of value. Although it is required in order to try to conceal the split between the two paradigms, in its very wording it plainly bespeaks the fracture: it is the unstable meeting point of opposites, where value theory tries to combine content and form. The necessary failure of this effort is what accounts for the scholasticism and sophistry of so much of the debate.

At a detailed textual level, value theory has effectively demonstrated the shortcomings in the articulation of basic concepts in the opening sections of

38 The modern discussion of 'abstract labour' dates back to the work of Lucio Colletti in the 1960s, who identified it as the point at which the break with traditional positivistic readings of Marx should be located (Colletti 1972, pp 45–108, esp. pp 76–92).

39 The most extensive treatment of 'abstract labour' from within value theory is Murray 2000a and Murray 2000b.

40 For different renditions of the former position, see De Angelis 1995 and Kicillof and Starosta 2007; for the latter, see Arthur 2004b, Chapter 3, Bonefeld 2010 and Bonefeld 2014, Chapter 6. While the production centred notion is theoretically indefensible, reliant upon either a brute naturalism of labour or a crude dogmatics of class struggle, it does have a kind of truth content in that it correctly senses that there is something deeply problematic, from a Marxist perspective, in the exchange conception, which, when consistently pursued, pulls away from central Marxist doctrines about labour and 'materialism' to an extent that its proponents do not acknowledge.

Capital. The wedge that it has driven into the duality in Marx's idea of value in fact goes much deeper, though. For in its basic theoretical logic, the entire programme of the development of a value-form theory of capital radically contradicts the labour and production paradigm. The idea of historical materialism is that production is the ground of human existence and that labour is therefore the essential human and social element. For Marxism as a labour-and-production theory, labour is thus the real subject of capitalist society. The transhistorical truth of labour exists within the historical untruth of capital – all of the powers of capital are really the powers of social labour in alienated form. The political task, set by the materialist philosophy of history, is then for labour to realise itself by throwing off its false representation as capital. Within this conception, a theory of capital must show that labour, as the universal subject, is sublimated into an abstract-conceptual form as value – exactly what Marx tries and fails to do in Chapter 1. In the same way that it has moved from history to logic, ever since the collapse of labourism in the 1970s the inner trajectory of the reconstruction of value theory has been the transferral of subjectivity from labour to capital. That is, as it has developed the logic of the value form, so it has more and more insisted that it is value itself that has autonomy and is determinative. Value is the active principle of universality, incorporating into itself everything that it encounters in its drive to make itself the whole. Ceaselessly dynamic and in constant motion, it continually passes through its various forms in the endless circuits of capital. When value grounds itself upon itself as capital, the sovereignty of money becomes absolute: 'In M–C–M', money *initiates* – rather than merely *mediates* – a drive towards the limitless expansion of abstract wealth. … value is posited as the *subject* of a movement through time.'[41] The value form is the abstract-universal subject that comprehends within itself and binds together every moment of the never-ending process of capital. The capital-form is thus 'the *unity of value as subject*'.[42] It follows that in a properly value-formed theory of capital, labour, like everything else, is merely a predicate of the self-determination of the value form: 'value is the *subject* of a process to which labour is *subjugated*'.[43]

The traditional Marxist idea, in which labour is the subject and capital its deformation, must be articulated theoretically as a movement from content to form: labour as universal ground is embodied within a historically specific form of appearance that misrepresents it. The theoretical failings of Chapter 1 demonstrate the impossibility of that movement – there is no passage from the material ground of labour to the conceptuality of exchange and value.

---

41 Taylor 2004, p 105 (emphases in original).

42 Taylor 2004, p 105 (emphasis in original).

43 Taylor 2004, p 112 (emphases in original).

What value theory has begun to reconstruct, instead, is the opposite movement, from value as subject to the material world as content. Labour is not represented in value, therefore; rather, value produces labour.

> So far from labour embodying itself in commodities and thereby constituting them as values, the value form embodies itself in production, subordinates its purposes to value creation, and realises itself in the product, posited as nothing but its own othering, when it successfully gains control of the labour process.[44]

Capital cannot be understood by starting from labour because it is a form of existence not of labour but of value. It is thus not, as traditional Marxism would have it, that the innate productivity and creative power of labour, as the general social subject, is appropriated by capital as an external force (or by capitalists as a ruling class). Rather, labour can only be productive as part of capital because it can exist only in and through capital. Labour is a function of capital, not the other way around. The reality of capital is therefore drastically falsified when it is construed in terms of the alienated powers of labour. It is capital that is productive because production is nothing but abstract value's continual affirmation of itself as subject through the process of its self-valorisation. The productive power of society is the productive power of capital.[45]

If value is the active and determining subject, it follows that for the form paradigm to be fully worked out all elements of the theorisation of capital must be derived from the logic of exchange. However, precisely this imperative confronts Marxist value theory with an insuperable difficulty. Because Marx's theory of capital is not fully value-formed and has at its base two conflicting paradigms, value theory is unable to comply with its own primary theoretical demand. This incapacity is evident in the way in which, even where it claims to recognise the centrality of form determination, value theory still ultimately tries to frame the analysis of value through general propositions about labour and production that are not themselves grounded in the form paradigm. In the early contributions to value theory that were attempting to clear a new path, such inconsistency could perhaps be explained by the difficulty of breaking with deeply entrenched habits of thought.[46] However, despite the subsequent

---

44 Arthur 2004b, p 170. Confined within the boundaries of Marxism, this formulation still does not go nearly far enough, though: as with the correlative idea of the 'subjugation' of labour, it continues to assume a primary material world of productive activity that is, as it were, colonised by value as by something external and alien.

45 Napoleoni 1991. See also Arthur 2004b, pp 46–52.

46 At no point, for example, does Backhaus' pioneering article question the general Marxian framework of 'social labour' as proper to the understanding of value. Similarly, the Konstanz-Sydney school, inspired by Backhaus and the most far-reaching of early

advances in its understanding of form determination, value theory has not yet become aware of the incongruity of its concept of value with the entire labour and production framework. Instead, it still seeks to situate the value form within this general context. Geert Reuten and Michael Williams, for example, attempt to ground their systematic dialectical exposition of value and capital with the following representative statement:

> the starting point of the presentation of bourgeois society … is a transhistorical account of the material existence of human being: human procreation is existent in sociation and requires the creation and social allocation of useful objects. This creation and social allocation of useful objects is a naturally necessary condition for human existence.[47]

The basis for theoretical comprehension of value and capital here is its determination by a supposedly natural and eternal requirement of labour in the creation of utilities. The securing of 'material existence' must be socially organised, and the distinctiveness of capitalist society is that it fulfils this necessity by dissociating units of production from each other and production from consumption. Value is then introduced as the solution to this problem of social co-ordination: 'it is argued that value provides the particular bourgeois form of association'.[48] However, referring the concept of value back to general economistic propositions of this sort is completely illegitimate within a form theory of value. The framework of analysis – the social organisation of material production – is not mediated through the value form problematic but is simply presupposed, by definitional fiat, as antecedent to it. Since no attempt is made to justify or, in a Kantian sense, prove the priority of this underived naturalism, its theoretical status is not properly established: it is in no way evident why value, as the self-determining subject of capitalist society, should be subordinated to these arbitrary and dogmatic assumptions. There is in fact nothing in the concept of the value form itself that specifies it as a mode of association of dissociated labour or the solution to a general problem of social co-ordination. The value

---

Anglophone value-form theory, throughout assumed without question that value is a mode of organisation of social labour, a historically specific solution to a general societal necessity (Eldred and Hanlon 1981; Eldred, Hanlon, Kleiber and Roth 1982; Eldred, Hanlon, Kleiber and Roth 1983).

47 Reuten and Williams 1989, p 53.

48 Reuten and Williams 1989, p 53. Thirty years later, in his updated exposition of the systematic-dialectical totality of capital, Reuten once more placed at the foundation of his enquiry exactly the same dogmatic and unexamined presupposition, that capital is to be understood as a type of 'sociation', a historically specific form of a general, transhistorical requirement of the production of objects of utility for purposes of self-preservation (Reuten 2019, pp 31–40; likewise, cf. Arthur 2022, pp 9–18 and Murray 2017).

form is simply an exchange form, through which one thing is posited as equivalent to another. As such, it has no necessary connection with and cannot be derived from a supposedly transhistorical problematic of labour and social production. Indeed, as value theory has itself made clear, within a form theory of value, production must come after the exchange form and not before it, so that production is determined by value, not the other way around. Capitalist production can be derived from the conceptual logic of value; value cannot be derived from a general logic of production.[49]

That Marxian value theory has not been able to escape such confusions is a result of its failure to perceive the departure from basic doctrines of Marxism that its own insistence upon form theorisation implies. Any labour theory of value – and it can hardly be doubted that Marx understood value as a mode of existence of labour – must show that ultimately labour is the 'stuff' of exchange, that in circulation it is labours in some form (whether 'embodied' or 'abstract') that are being exchanged. Form must be referred back to content, value resolved into labour. This is why Marx begins his account of the commodity with labour considerations *before* coming to the value form: he has to establish that labour sits at the base of the entire theorisation.[50] The movement of a labour theory of value is thus always from content to form: from a general problematic of social labour and production to the specific instance of capital, understood as one historical system among others of the organisation of labour. When the direction of theory is reversed, though, the whole framing that supports a labour theory becomes untenable. Analysis of the value form per se, unprejudiced by any extraneous assumptions about labour, production, class, social relations, 'materialism', the 'living individual', the 'metabolism with nature' and so on, plainly shows that it has nothing to do with labour. The value form is an exchange form, an empty, contentless abstraction – *pure form*. Labour cannot be found 'in' exchange. Instead, the perspective that modern value theory has opened is upon exchange as a profoundly metaphysical process, in which an objective conceptuality, whose real meaning has barely begun to be understood, comes into being. This conceptuality is in no way reducible to, or comprehensible as, labour, in any shape or form. Value theory thus

49 What is really at issue here is the metaphysical significance of exchange (on which, see Chapter 7). When the exchange form is properly developed for itself, without being encumbered with any preconceptions, it completely explodes the economistic context within which not just Marxism but economic thought generally has always assumed that it should be located.

50 When read from a form-theory perspective, it becomes clear that the argument of the opening sections of *Capital* is in fact highly tendentious: the whole economistic framework of labour and production is simply assumed from the outset, rather than being theoretically justified, so that when Marx identifies labour as the 'substance' of exchange he is really just discovering in the commodity what he has already presupposed there.

destroys the simplistic, pre-theoretical idea, fundamental to Marxism, that exchange is, in one way or another, exchange of labours. Nothing can be found 'in' exchange, and that Nothing is value.

Once the theoretical primacy of exchange and the value form is recognised, there can be no return to any notion of labour as a general social substance. Although this is the evident sense of a consistently pursued theorisation of the value form, Marxian value theory cannot acknowledge as much because of the consequences that would be entailed for the wider coherence of Marxism. Even its best representatives, who have pushed the logic of form furthest within the limits of Marxism, thus in the end give way to the need to refer the form problematic in some way back to labour.[51] Doing so, however, contradicts the logic of form. A 'materialist', labour theory of value must accord a special status to labour as such, prior to exchange, so that the generality of exchange can then be 'fixed' to labour. Hence, it must try to move from labour to value. Once theory goes in the opposite direction and starts from exchange, then labour necessarily loses any privileged standing. Within a dialectical theory, to pick out labour as somehow of special significance is not merely arbitrary and dogmatic but violates the unfolding of the immanent logic of form.[52] The urge to reconnect the form theorisation to labour results from a reluctance to

[51] This sort of relapse mars such otherwise outstanding contributions as Taylor 2004 and Reichelt 2005.

[52] Chris Arthur tries to bring labour and value together within a dialectical form theory by arguing that labour has a privileged status because workers resist: 'capital finds that it is confronted with a special difficulty: the residual "subjectivity" of the worker poses unique problems for capital because it gives rise to a definite recalcitrance to being "exploited" which the other factors do not possess. … This is why, for a theory grounded on the *social form* of the economy, labour is to be correlated with value' (Arthur 2004b, pp 54–5 (emphasis in original)). The idea that workers manifest a recalcitrance to exploitation where other 'factors of production' do not is a crude anthropocentrism, unable to hear what Walter Benjamin termed the 'muteness' of nature, in its subjection to science, as resistance to the abstractness of form (Benjamin 2004c, pp 72–3). The formation of humans as 'labour' is really just one moment of the spiritualisation of the world as a whole through the Concept. In typical Marxist fashion, Arthur also absurdly overstates labour's resistance to capital. Consider the matter in its proper perspective: in 1800, 2% of the world's population lived in cities; by 2008, more than 50% did. In just 200 years, therefore, capital has effected a transformation in the conditions of human existence – separating people from the land, decanting them into cities, and absorbing them into the market – that was completely unimaginable in the previous 200,000. The truth is that capital has internalised the whole world to itself with breath-taking rapidity and ease, a process to which so-called resistance has been utterly irrelevant. Finally, even if it were the case that labour had to be compelled to accept capital's ends, this would in no way establish any *conceptual* connection between value and labour – that value somehow *is* labour, which is what Marx clearly thought and what any labour theory requires (the falseness of the argument is, in fact, obliquely confessed in the imprecise and evasive expression that labour is to be 'correlated' with value).

break with general Marxist dogma about labour and production, which is itself posited entirely outside the form problematic. However, when it is accepted that the theorisation of value has to begin with exchange and follow the progressive autonomisation of value until it grounds itself on itself as capital,[53] then the link with labour is definitively severed. In fact, even that is not quite correct – the link is not severed because, as the critique of Chapter 1 of *Capital* made plain, it was never actually established in the first place. Just as there is no theoretical passage from labour to value, so there is no way back from the value form to labour as its ontological ground. The two sides of Marx's theory of value have been irreparably broken apart.

53 Reichelt 1995 and 2005.

5

The Economic and Dialectic

Taken as a whole, the achievement of the value debate in Marxism since the 1970s has been profoundly contradictory. On the one hand, through its development of the value form and the metaphysics of exchange, it has set the theorisation of value on a radically new path, initiating a decisive break not just with traditional Marxism but with economic thought generally. On the other, precisely by virtue of its emphasis on form, it has split Marx's theory apart, right down the middle. The further the exchange paradigm has been elaborated in its proper autonomy, the clearer it has become that it cannot be subordinated to the economistic labour-and-production paradigm as the encompassing explanatory context. However, since Marxian value theory is unable to acknowledge the consequences of what it has done and still remain Marxism, it cannot resolve this contradiction. For all its positive reconstruction of the value concept, therefore, the Marxist debate in fact leaves the theorisation of value in a larger state of confusion. For while it has conclusively demonstrated that the theory must begin with exchange and the value form, it has not been able to show how the logic of dialectical form determination then relates to the wider economic 'ground' of labour and production – the two sides of the economic problematic, content and form, have simply fallen apart from each other.[1] Just as in the field of IR Marxism has been unable to grasp the inside/outside division that founds the international space, so it turns out that in its home domain of economic theory it has been unable to think the corresponding inside/outside division, the split between the material world and the exchange abstraction, that founds the economic space. Not only does Marxism have

[1] This unmediated schism reveals the basic shortcoming of modern Marxian value theory, which is that while it has definitively established the priority of logic over history in the theorisation of capital, it has not fully recognised the implications of this reversal. That is, it has not understood what a properly logical – or dialectical – theory of capital would actually be.

no adequate theory of sovereignty, therefore, but it has no coherent theory of value either.

The central question that arises out of the value debate is thus: what is the relation between the materiality of labour and production, on the one hand, and the conceptuality of exchange and value, on the other? Or, put more simply, what is the relation between the economic and dialectic? In order to answer that question, it is necessary to step beyond the confines of Marxism, out into the encompassing context of the metaphysics of modernity. For the problem that the contemporary value debate ultimately revolves around leads directly into the decisive turning point in modern philosophy, which opened the way to its highest achievement. This was the moment of German Idealism, when, in the transition from Kant to Hegel, the basic dualist paradigm of modern thought, which found its quintessential expression in the epistemological problematic, was finally resolved altogether into dialectic. In that brief moment, which came to an end with the death of Hegel, the metaphysical structure of modernity was worked out to its fullest extent.[2] It is only within this much larger philosophical perspective, therefore, that it is possible to understand, first, the meaning of the economic problematic as such, and then the specific position and significance of dialectic within modern thought.

Formation of the economic subject

In a classic work from the mid-1970s, the social anthropologist Louis Dumont sought to reconstruct the emergence of the economic category, as the dominant 'ideology' of the modern world, and to outline its essential lineaments.[3] For Dumont, a society governed by economic imperatives constituted a profound breach with traditional, holistic forms of community and signalled the emergence of a new shape of subjectivity.[4] From this premise of a world-historical rupture, he traced the immediate prehistory of the economic idea through the successive stages of its formation, as it was worked out in theoretical terms by a handful of exemplary authors (notably, Quesnay, Locke and Mandeville), each of whose partial contributions helped to pave

---

2 Of the moment in German philosophy that witnessed the transition from Kantian transcendentalism to Hegelian speculative dialectic, Dieter Henrich states: 'Chronologically speaking, the two decades at the end of the eighteenth century are a vanishingly small span of time … Yet the consciousness of mankind and the thoughts of philosophers made more progress in these decades than it had during many decades of stagnation. … Anyone at the present time seeking to contribute to the understanding of the foundations of modernity can find the best orientation by beginning here' (Henrich 1997, p 71).

3 Dumont 1977.

4 By 'traditional' and 'holistic', Dumont meant a society that values 'in the first place, order: the conformity of every element to its role in society' (Dumont 1977, p 4).

the way for the first great, synthetic statement of the modern economic conception, Adam Smith's *Wealth of Nations*. What Dumont's account is concerned to make evident is that the economic conception of existence emerged in Europe in the 17th and 18th centuries through a coherent series of separations from older, long-established ways of being. Only through these deeply inscribed divisions was it was possible for such a thing as a distinct economic dimension to come into being as the central sphere of modern life, orientating the activities, values and sense of self of modern subjects. As it is reconstructed in Dumont's argument, the subject became the *economic* subject once it had divested itself of modes of relation that were no longer felt to be valid and that had therefore ceased to be able to claim objectivity, authority and truth. For the economic conception to cohere in-and-for itself thus required the delegitimation of inherited forms of universality wherever they might serve to restrict the movement of value through its circuit as it became capital. Accordingly, politics, morality and religion were all reformulated around the central imperative of the freedom of value.

Beneath the various dimensions of the formation of the economic subject that Dumont surveys, are two themes, in particular, that he identifies as essential to the economic idea. The first of these is the primacy of 'the Individual'. By this term, Dumont does not intend 'the *empirical* subject of speech, thought, and will, the indivisible sample of mankind as found in all societies' but rather 'the independent, autonomous, and thus (essentially) non-social *moral* being as found primarily in our modern ideology of man and society'.[5] Where in traditional societies the whole was acknowledged to take precedence over the individuals it comprised, in economic society the Individual is conceived of as being anterior to society as such.[6] The economic subject experiences itself as an originary being, therefore, outside the system of mediation and ontologically prior to it. The system must then be constructed as a secondary formation from a multitude of such Individuals as its ground. The Individual is thus the 'elementary form' of economic society, its irreducible basic unit.[7] In Cartesian terms, this cell form is clear and distinct: separate and sharply bounded, autonomous and self-determining, beholden to nothing outside itself. No longer locatable within a hierarchy or given meaning by its position within a social order,

5 Dumont 1977, p 8 (emphases in original). As Adorno put it, the Individual is thus not simply 'the biological individual being' but 'that which is first constituted as a unity by the self-reflection, the Hegelian "self-consciousness"' (Adorno 2001b, 'Freedom and Organized Society'). In Hegel's terms, the Individual is an essentially conceptual entity as the dialectical unity, or syllogistic conclusion, of the universal and the particular. As such, the Individual is a figure of totality.

6 On the centrality of the figure of the Individual to classical political economy, see Iacono 2020.

7 Marx 1990, p 125.

the economic Individual is a universal equivalent form: 'every man is, in principle, an embodiment of humanity at large, and as such he is equal to every other man, and free'.[8] In the figure of the modern Individual the macrocosm and the microcosm are thus unified at the extremes: humanity as a whole, without exception, and the single, isolated unit, wholly self-enclosed and exceptional. The abstract Individual, who is the logical subject of economic modernity, carries humanity within itself as its abstract essence.

The second defining idea of the economic, consequent upon this absolute priority accorded to the Individual, is a further form of metaphysical reversal: 'The birth of economics actually implies a shift in primacy ... from the relations between men to the relations between men and nature or rather between *man* (in the singular) and things'.[9] The radically individualised, pre-social economic subject feels itself to be in relation not in the first place with other persons, but rather with nature as such, as it appears to present itself directly, outside and before any context of mediation.[10] In the experience of the economic subject, therefore, inside and outside have exchanged positions. What is most proper to this subject is its existence within a limitless world of material objects, before and outside society, through which it feels its autonomy and freedom to be confirmed. Objective value is located in the relation to things and the legitimacy of the sphere of mediation, as a derivative structure, is entirely dependent on the extent to which it facilitates the independence of the Individual, which exists in the first place in the immediate relation to nature – the social structure ought not to come between the Individual and its primary relation to things. Accordingly, within the economic mode of being, the experience of objectivity is itself thoroughly individualised.[11] As Dumont reads it, this reversal of priority between relations to people and relations to things was the ultimate sense of Locke's reorientation of the political ('subordination goes overboard and with it the link it maintained between relationships among men and relations between men and inferior creatures'[12]) and of Mandeville's promotion of the unfettered

---

8 Dumont 1977, p 4.

9 Dumont 1977, p 105 (emphasis in original).

10 It is this conception of a primary relation to nature that underlies the attempt by classical thought to ground its account of economic life on the notion of 'subsistence', as a kind of natural-material minimum requisite for the maintenance of bare life. From this irreducible minimum there then arise the various needs and wants the satisfaction of which ultimately results in the production of the 'surplus' that, in this conception, constitutes the secondary sphere of mediation (Levine 1977, Chapter 1; Levine 1998b, pp 8–29).

11 'The point to be borne in mind is that the stress on things, the mastery over things, is throughout a property of the individual, not of the society as a whole' (Dumont 1977, p 105).

12 Dumont 1977, p 48.

pursuit of self-interest ('the satisfaction of the individual's material needs is the only reason why men live in society'[13]). Together with the primacy of the Individual, the priority of the relation to objects forms the core of the economic idea, the necessary mode of being of the economic subject. Dumont thus concludes that, 'the rise of economics, i.e., the shift in value from one kind of relation to the other, and the full accession of the modern Individual … are solidary aspects of one and the same phenomenon.'[14]

In the economic conception, the world is encountered by the Individual in the first place as a purely material environment, and only on that foundation can a space of relations among persons then arise. The sphere of mediation is thus secondary, and functional, to a primary materiality. From this structure of experience there follows the fundamental assumption of all economic thought: that the world in itself, in its immediate material being, just *is* economic. What is meant by 'economic' here is that it is a natural and irreducible requirement of human existence to engage in the production and consumption of material goods for the purpose of self-preservation. That is the base condition of life. To be sure, humans may also be political, cultural, artistic, religious, warlike and a thousand other things. None of that is denied. But at bottom, beneath all forms of mediation, they have to be economic. In order to be anything more than nature, therefore, they must in the first place be nature – they must meet the eternal and inescapable necessity of getting their living by securing their material reproduction, fulfilling the primary imperative of sheer physical survival. The instrumental relationship to nature thus comes first: self-preservation demands economy. So thoroughly does this assumption of the fundamentally material-economic character of being shape the modern mind that it tends to appear to it as utterly self-evident and conclusive, scarcely even open to argument. What could be more obvious, more incontrovertible, than that humans must eat and drink, must have clothing and shelter, before they can even conceive of the higher things in life? Everybody, every society, surely has to satisfy those necessities just in order to be. Material imperatives are 'hard' and irreducible. The highest and most elevated is thus always to be referred back to the lowest and most basic, as its unsurpassable ground.

The formation of the modern economic subject reached completion at the moment in which it became possible for economic thought to produce a unified vision of human existence entirely from within the parameters of its

13 Dumont 1977, p 67.

14 Dumont 1977, p 106. Cf. David Levine's comment on the logic of neoclassical economic theory: 'The simplifying assumptions of the theory are designed, first, to construct the relation of the isolated individual to the world of objects, and subsequently, to build up a conception of the whole on this basis' (Levine 1977, p 185).

own experiential space – that is, when the economic had become the new metaphysics. The arrival of that world-historical moment was definitively announced in the opening sentence of the *Wealth of Nations*:

> The annual labour of every nation is the fund which originally supplies it with all necessaries and conveniences of life which it annually consumes, and which consists always either in the immediate produce of that labour, or in what is purchased with that produce from other nations.[15]

Here, in eminently prosaic and down-to-earth terms, the economic subject finds its authentic voice. The implicit logic of this statement is that in order to understand the life of society (society as such – 'every nation'), it is both possible and necessary to set aside all political, religious, moral and symbolic factors and to conceive of it as a strictly material process of the production, distribution and consumption of the 'necessaries and conveniences of life'. All non-economic dimensions of life can thus be seen past as ultimately inessential, merely superstructural. Indeed, they must be so bracketed if the truly economic essence of society is to be clearly perceived. For what lies beneath them, and in the vision of the economic subject is recognised as the primary and determining ground of society, is a natural-material condition of labour on nature for purposes of self-preservation. The life of society has thus come to be defined by and understood through what is outside it, the 'metabolism' with nature. Its mode of organisation is to be thought of not as set apart from nature, a divinely ordained order sanctified by tradition, but as a more or less effective response to the naked and perennial necessity of securing material existence. The socio-cultural world derives from this fundamental ontology of the modern subject. If the relation to things has priority over relations between people, then this natural and pre-social requirement also has, for the economic experience, normative force. For it is by reference to the economic demand that the proper organisation of society should be determined. There are, precisely, *principles* of political economy that must be understood and followed if society is to become wealthy to the greatest degree possible. The system of mediation, that which is more than nature, is thus to be judged according to how effectively it fulfils the requirement of nature: the good form of society is that which is economically most productive. Providentially, the society in which the wealth of nations is most abundant is also that which happens to afford the greatest individual freedom. However, the economic is not limited to any particular form of society because it is a general and inescapable necessity of

[15] A. Smith 1999, p 104.

existence. In the material terms of economic thought, all individuals and all societies are ultimately the same: because it is rooted in the natural demand of survival, human existence is irreducibly economic. For the economic subject, therefore, the material is the universal.

Economics–epistemology

The basic structure of the economic problematic is the radical separation of content and form. On one side, there is a non-conceptual materiality; on the other, a conceptual sphere of mediation. Between them lies an absolute division. It follows that the fundamental problem of economic thought is how to fit the two sides of its problematic, content and form, together in a coherent way. Before any of the specific questions of economics can arise, therefore, it is necessary to account for the constitution of the economic space in the first place. This is the function of the concept of value, which is a borderline concept precisely in that it mediates the division between the material world and the conceptual sphere. As Louis Dumont's analysis demonstrated, the modern economic conception came into being through an epochal transformation in the mode of relation of subject and object. The logic of this new relationship of inside and outside was developed by modern thought most profoundly not in its economic theorising, though, where it has only ever been naively assumed, but in its philosophical thinking. More specifically, between Descartes and Hegel it was the newly emergent epistemological problematic that constituted the central site at which the metaphysical form of the modern subject was worked out.

The economic and epistemological problematics were historically coeval and are structurally homologous.[16] Just as the economic conception arose out of the breakdown of a holistic social order, so, correlatively, the premise of modern epistemology was the collapse of the received objective world. With the disintegration of traditional sources of authority, inherited forms of knowledge were likewise invalidated. The characteristic project of epistemology in its early pioneering days was thus the dissolution of the pre-modern metaphysics of an objective structure of being, disqualifying it as, in Kant's term, unproven.[17] For the new epistemological subject, there was no longer an encompassing order of the world within which the subject was placed and from which it derived its meaning, no 'Great Chain

[16] The *Critique of Pure Reason* and the *Wealth of Nations*, as the defining statements in which the modern epistemological and economic problematics crystallised, were of course almost exactly contemporaneous, being published only five years apart.

[17] Kant 1999, pp 358–9/B303. Kant's is, of course, the definitive, epoch-making statement of the supplanting of pre-modern metaphysics, and ontology in particular, by the modern project of epistemology.

of Being' that linked one gradation to another, each in its natural place. All such claims to authority and truth were held to be arbitrary and to rest only on outmoded dogma. A primary intention of the earliest texts in which the modern subject wrestled itself free from the old ontology, therefore, was to overthrow the power of inherited objectivity. Descartes' project of radical doubt disqualified received authority entirely because it provided no certain foundation for knowledge and truth.[18] Likewise, Hobbes poured scorn on the credulous 'Schoolmen' for their metaphysical delusions and 'insignificant speech'.[19] The collapse of pre-modern ontology, and the meaning it once guaranteed, in turn provoked a crisis of objectivity that was repeatedly expressed as a crisis of knowledge: how could dreams be distinguished from waking rational thoughts? What if the world were merely an illusion spun by a malevolent deceiver? On what basis was real knowledge differentiated from rapturous enthusiasm? Beset by anxiety at his inability to find indubitable grounds of truth anywhere outside himself, Descartes' action in response was exemplary for the modern subject: radical separation and self-enclosure, the withdrawal of the self into itself, and its immersion in its own interiority as the only irrefutable source of certainty and validity.[20] From the ruins of the old metaphysics, therefore, the self-determining individual, prior to and outside society, emerged as the standard of reason.

What took shape in the epistemological and economic problematics was thus the experience of a kind of loss, or abandonment, of the world. In both, the object is held at a distance so that it no longer impinges upon the unity and integrity of the subject as a self-determining being. Correlatively, the subject reshapes itself in relation to this diminished substance, denuding itself of its residual world-ness so that it is not determined in any way from outside itself. This is the significance of the constitutive condition of the economic and epistemological problematics, the strict separation of subject and object.

18 Descartes 1985, pp 111–51.

19 Hobbes 2008b, p 10.

20 The emblematic figure of capitalist modernity in this respect is Robinson Crusoe, the absolutely isolated individual, drastically cut off in a pre-social condition of complete self-sufficiency, producing himself from out of himself. Decades before Defoe, though, Descartes had already made isolation and strict enclosure within one's borders the conditions of the freedom of the modern subject: first, in order to begin the process of reordering thought ('I stayed all day shut up alone in a stove-heated room, where I was completely free to converse with myself about my own thoughts'); then as his mode of life, when he settled in the Netherlands ('this desire made me resolve to move away from any place where I might have acquaintances and retire to this country [where] I have been able to lead a life as solitary and withdrawn as if I were in the most remote desert') (Descartes 1985, pp 116 and 126). The sought-after separation and isolation were found by Descartes in what was the most urbanised and commercially developed society in early-modern Europe.

Just as with economics, therefore, the central problem of modern philosophy is how to mediate form and content, concept and object, in a coherent way.[21] In Descartes, at the inauguration of modern epistemology, this separation was articulated as the duality of two substances, *res cogitans* and *res extensa*; in Kant, at the culmination of its classical phase, as the strict division between sensibility and understanding, which sits at the base of the argumentative structure of the *Critique of Pure Reason*. Between the subject, as *cogitans*, and the world, as *cogitatum*, there is inscribed a deep and inviolable boundary line, upon which the autonomy of the modern subject is founded. There is no longer to be any methexis with the world, which is instead reduced to mere 'content', appearing to exist in complete separation from the subject, as a kind of primary materiality. By the same token, the economic subject ceases to be a part of, or within, the world as an encompassing context of meaning, encountering it instead as a given material objectivity that exists solely for the purpose of satisfying the subject's now limitless needs and desires. What the subject knows of the world, from which it is drastically separated, is only what it can make of it. In the same way that the world is divested of any likeness to the subject, so the mind becomes an entirely empty point of abstraction, a *tabula rasa* as Locke proposed,[22] with no substantial affinity to the material world from which it has separated itself. A cognitive subject from which all materiality has been removed thus confronts a bare materiality from which all meaning has been drained.

The radical division of content and form that founds the economic and epistemological problematics also accounts for the peculiarities of their structure. In the first place, the scenario in each is entirely decontextualised. Separation from the world and withdrawal into interiority mean that the subject exists in a kind of nowhere. This indeterminate no-place is, in some way, there but it has no life or specificity of its own; rather, it just *is*, as a given materiality. Severed from any constitutive relation to anything outside itself and enclosed within its own sharply drawn boundaries, the subject likewise becomes entirely contentless, merely the abstract Individual. Existing prior to any context of mediation, it is equally disqualified and bare. The subject's relation to the state of nature within which it finds itself is then a paradoxical combination of proximity and distance, or inclusion and

---

21 As Hegel puts it in the introductory remarks on modern philosophy in his lectures on the history of philosophy: 'With the reflection of its being-within-itself, thinking at this stage arises essentially as something subjective in such a way that it has an antithesis in [outwardly] subsistent being. The exclusive concern is then to reconcile this opposition, to conceive the reconciliation at its ultimate extreme, to grasp the most abstract and ultimate cleavage of being and thinking. From this point onward, all philosophy concerns itself with this unity' (Hegel 2009, p 85).

22 Locke 2004, p 109.

exclusion. On the one hand, the original condition is all-encompassing: there is nothing above or below, nothing outside or beyond, just Individuals in nature. To this extent, subject and object are in continuity with each other, existing on the same base level. Just as the subject is a given entity outside society, so the object is a kind of ultimate and irreducible datum, the world simply as it is before any distorting mediation. However, in the actual experience of it, this material stuff turns out to be entirely insubstantial, all but immaterial. As soon as concrete experience has to be accounted for, the subject is revealed to be cut off from the world within which it is placed, encountering it only in extreme externality, at its borderline. In epistemology, the object does not pass into the subject in any substantive way, nor is the subject reciprocally involved with it. Instead, what is 'out there' transmits the blind data of sensation or intuition, which then have to be synthesised by the subject's conceptual capacity.[23] Correlatively, the subject is a closed and self-subsistent unit whose contact with the world happens only at the very edge of its being. As such, not only does the subject not *know* what is given to it, but there is nothing really there to be known in the first place:[24]

> Whatever is to be synthesized is so lacking in qualities that it is infinitely malleable by the forms of consciousness. The absence of qualities, the indeterminate nature of the material of knowledge, confers on it a kind of plasticity … that allows us to synthesize these givens without their placing any obstacles in our path. This means that our minds can manipulate them at will. They do not need to have any particular taste; it is enough if there is something to bite on. … As long as I have something between my teeth, my sovereign will can do with it whatever it pleases.[25]

In this respect, through its more insistent inquiry into the logic of modern experience, epistemology makes evident something that remains only implicit in economic theory. Although the subject's primary relation is to the world of material things, that materiality is in fact next to nothing. It

23 'You have reason, the faculty of intuition, man as a *tabula rasa*, who finds himself bombarded with sense impressions, without really knowing where they come from' (Adorno 2001a, p 50).

24 In classical epistemology, the object as the cause of sensations is completely external: 'it is contingent … the chaotic sensory manifold over which I have no control, but to which my knowledge refers. Moreover, it does not refer to it in the sense that we know the sensory. The fact is that we do not know the sensory; it is something that we *possess*, it is *given* to us. But it is opaque, blind and impenetrable' (Adorno 2001a, p 43 (emphases in original)).

25 Adorno 2001a, p 98.

is the necessary substratum of knowledge but it has no specific quality of its own that would inhibit what the subject can make from it. In economic theory, which is premised upon an irreducible material necessity, nothing is or can be said about the actual materiality of the world within which the economic subject is placed and that it labours upon. The economic substance is as decontextualised and emptied out as the economic subject. It is not experienced as anything other than the meaningless raw material of the subject's productive activity. In economic thought, therefore, the world in its non-conceptual original condition is entirely open and available, there to be appropriated: it provides no resistance to the economic Individual. While the primary materiality is the necessary ground of the subject's activity, it must not actually *be* anything.

The economic problematic is predicated on the primacy of the Individual, posited as a self-enclosed and irreducible unit in immediate relation to things. A mass of such discrete Individuals, existing in the original condition, then form the secondary context of mediation by choosing to exchange the products of their labour with one another. It follows that the explanatory logic of economic theory is that the whole of economic life should ultimately derive from the actions of Individuals, either their specific labour or their particular preferences. It is essential to the idea of economic thought, therefore, that the Individual not be lost within the whole; rather, it must always be possible to decompose the whole into its constitutive elementary units so as to reveal the Individual as its ultimate ground and truth. Accordingly, the direction of theory is from content to form and from Individual to whole. In the same way, the epistemological problematic in its classical form is strictly individualised. The knowing subject is a separate and isolated individual consciousness that, rather than being situated within any wider context of intellection, is just 'there'. This thinking consciousness is posited as confronting the given, external thing-world: it receives data externally from sensations and then processes them through its cognitive faculty in order to produce items of knowledge. The totality of knowledge should thus be composed from and traceable back to individual acts of cognitive labour on specific sensations or impressions.

Through this primacy of the Individual, epistemology and economics are, in a twofold sense, structures of immanence. First, in them, precisely as a result of being radically externalised, the objective world becomes internal to consciousness. Without meaning or form in itself, just the chaotic sensory manifold as Kant thought of it, the object has to be constituted as a knowable entity entirely through the subject's activity of cognitive labour on the primary materiality. Secondly, there is no longer any 'outside'. With nothing ontologically prior to isolated individuals in their immediate relation to nature, existence becomes wholly intramundane: only the flat, undifferentiated plane of natural equality, a state of original equivalence. Since transcendence, as something more than the subject, has been disintegrated, any sense the world can have that would reach further than natural givenness can only be produced by subjective intentionality. However, everything that is constructed by human artifice is always referable back to the irreducibly economic character of the original condition, so that it can really be no more than a variation on nature. Within this immanent condition of original individuality, the modern subject is free to create itself and its world. The price it pays for this freedom, though, is that its existence becomes merely tautologous because it can never experience anything substantial outside or beyond itself. Imprisoned within the bounds of its subjectivity, it is condemned to be its own meaning.[26]

The sense of the structure of experience encoded in the economic and epistemological problematics is thus a simultaneous liberation and restriction of the subject. On the one hand, the shackles of external authority are thrown off and the substantiality of the world altogether dissolved, so that objectivity becomes an achievement of the subject, which produces it through its activity. On the other, precisely in its liberation from authority, the subject is tied to the object far more strictly than before. Throughout the process of its formation, what the modern subject above all fought against was what it regarded as irresponsible speculation, the reckless positing of a multitude of a priori metaphysical entities. Paradoxically, this contempt for the extravagance of metaphysical thought, its lack of restraint, derived from the perception that it curtailed the sovereignty of the subject. The claims of pre-modern metaphysics were vain and deluded because in them the world remained to an extent in-itself and unmastered.[27] Fundamental to the overthrow of the old metaphysics, therefore, was the restriction of the subject for the sake of the freedom of the subject. The project of epistemology intended to determine, once and for all, the boundaries that would guarantee the universality of the sovereign Individual. Once established, those limits were not to be transgressed. In epistemology, therefore, thought was constrained to the world. It could not simply be spun out of itself but had to be validated through empirical experience: concepts were to be fulfilled by intuitions, just as value was to pass by way of things. Furthermore, for thinking to be meaningful, it had to take the shape stipulated by epistemology – to experience the object in any more substantive manner was forbidden. Correlatively, if the circuit of value was not to be disrupted, the object could be nothing more than a thing of exchange. The material world was thus established as the legal source of

[26] Adorno 2001b ('Peephole Metaphysics').

[27] In Hegel's terms, the older metaphysics was finite – that is, it was still governed by the reflective division of inside and outside – and so was not properly free (Hegel 1991, pp 65–76, §§26–36).

knowledge for modern subjectivity, but on condition that it be apprehended only in the most restricted, almost nugatory, way.[28]

Through the drastic division of content and form, the world falls apart into inner and outer. Radically separated from the knowing subject, it shrinks, on one side, into a kind of hard core, a non-conceptual materiality. The subject then exists on the surface of this rigidified thing-world: while it can manipulate the given matter to an almost unlimited degree, it cannot reach into it and actually know it. Through the division, therefore, the world is simultaneously opened and closed. With the unleashing of the economic process and the scientific understanding of the world that accompanies it, nature falls silent, reduced to a bare materiality that no longer speaks to the subject or exists for it as anything other than the passive and inert substratum of intentional, purposive action. Likewise, the world ceases to constitute a meaningful context of life but instead appears as an alien and indifferent environment that presents a permanent, existential problem of survival – economics. In the modern experience this inner core is in one sense primary since, as unmediated content, it is imagined ultimately to exist in itself, without any subjective addition: the world just *is* economic and the subject must accept that natural-material demand. At the same time, however, the achievement of intelligibility is transferred entirely into the subject. The radical division of content and form thus produces a situation of reciprocal nullification: the content, the inner world, can only be known through the form, but the form should only represent the given content.[29] In its modern, epistemological form therefore, knowledge becomes merely phenomenal, just the secondary, imperfect representation of the primary

---

[28] Hobbes: 'Originally all conceptions proceed from the actions of the thing itself, whereof it is the conception. Now when the action is present, the conception it produceth is called SENSE, and the thing by whose action the same is produced is called the OBJECT of sense' (Hobbes 2008a, pp 22–3); Hume: 'The impressions of reflexion are only antecedent to their correspondent ideas; but posterior to those of sensation, and deriv'd from them' (Hume 1985, p 55); Kant: 'There is no doubt whatever that all our cognition begins with experience; for how else should the cognitive faculty be awakened into experience if not through objects that stimulate our senses and in part themselves produce representations, in part bring the activity of our understanding into motion to compare these, to connect or separate them, and thus to work up the raw material of sensible impressions into a cognition of objects that is called experience?' (Kant 1999, p 136/B1). In the Introduction to his *Logic*, Hegel summarised this general conception: 'Turned against reason, this understanding behaves in the manner of *ordinary common sense*, giving credence to the latter's view that truth rests on sensuous reality, that thoughts are *only* thoughts, that is, that only sense perception gives filling and reality to them' (Hegel 2010, p 25, emphases in original).

[29] In both epistemology and economics, the two poles – the categorial forms and the material to be formed – are thus reduced to empty abstraction. Hence Adorno's joke that in Kant 'adding nothing to nothing produces something' (cited in Jarvis 1998, p 162).

materiality, the more or less faint impression or image of what was received through sensation. Truth is then confined to the correspondence of thought to a given objectivity: the concept should not add anything to or distort what is presented to consciousness but should be purified of all subjective factors that might interfere with transparent representation. In the parallel terms of economics, things can only be experienced and have objective validity insofar as they assume the commodity form and enter into the process of the self-valorisation of value, which should be as free and undistorted as possible. For the modern Individual, who is the logical subject of epistemology and economics, the inner world, the primary relation to things, is at once the necessary foundation of all knowledge and forever unknowable as it is in itself, whereas the outer world, the actual lived context of mediation, is secondary and, in a profound sense, unreal.

Contradictions of epistemology

Epistemology became the central site of modern metaphysics because the experiential structure of the modern subject, as it immediately appears to that subject, takes an epistemological form. Accordingly, Adorno understood epistemology not simply as one particular field of philosophical inquiry among others but rather as a kind of riddle requiring interpretation. If the epistemological problematic were to be deciphered, then the modern subject itself would be broken open. In his metacritique of epistemology, which stretches right across his *oeuvre*, Adorno thus sought to expose the contradictions that continually recur in the attempts to construct a coherent theory of knowledge on the presuppositions of epistemology.[30] His critique focused in particular on the sharp separations through which the epistemological problematic is structured: form and content, sensibility and understanding, concept and object, the a priori and the a posteriori. Because these divisions

[30] As with the other main themes of his thinking, the critique of epistemology is not condensed into a single text by Adorno but is instead woven through his writings. The most important sources include his study of Husserl (Adorno 1982), the 1959 Lectures on Kant's *Critique of Pure Reason* (Adorno 2001a) and *Negative Dialectics* (Adorno 2001b). Moreover, Adorno's dialectical critique of epistemology was substantially and openly indebted to Hegel, and in particular to Hegel's complex and multifaceted critique of Kant. The literature on Hegel's relation to Kant is, of course, vast. For concise overviews of the nature of Hegel's critique, particularly as it relates to epistemology and metaphysics, see Sedgwick 2006; de Boer 2010, Chapter 2; and Houlgate 2022, Chapter 2. On the general development of German Idealism between Kant and Hegel, see Beiser 2002, Henrich 2003 and Förster 2012; on Hegel's intellectual formation and the significance of Kant's critical philosophy in his development of dialectic, see the classic studies of H.S. Harris (Harris 1972 and 1983); and for recent book-length studies of Hegel's critique of Kant, see Bristow 2012, Sedgwick 2012 and Bowman 2013.

are all necessary to its formation, the epistemological subject is compelled to try to establish its account of knowledge through them. However, what Adorno aimed at showing was that the two sides of the various binaries cannot be maintained in separation from each other, with the result that epistemology, in its exposition, consistently negates itself. In this way, the epistemological problematic in fact pointed beyond itself, to its transcendence in dialectic.[31]

In his reading of epistemology, Adorno was principally concerned to demonstrate that the radical division of content and form that is constitutive of the epistemological problematic cannot be articulated coherently: no content can be specified to the exclusion of form and, likewise, the determination of the form always implies content. While the modern, epistemological subject's conception of itself necessitates the separation of the a priori and the a posteriori, in the theoretical constructions that should establish the coherence of its self-understanding it is unable actually to hold them apart. From one side, this argument was made by Adorno by way of a critique of the two categories through which the non-conceptual material appears within the framework of epistemology: 'sensation' and 'the given'. These categories sit at the base of the epistemological hierarchy: in them, the modern theory of knowledge tries to determine how what is not proper to the subject nevertheless comes within the space of subjective immanence. What Adorno recognised was that, because within epistemology they must be fitted to the demand of immanence to consciousness, these categories in fact falsify what they purport to designate. That is, 'sensation' is really somatic existence shaped to the intentionality of the cognising subject.[32] Through being categorised as sensation, that which is discontinuous with the self-enclosed intellective capacity of the subject is made continuous with it: the material is fitted to the conceptual. What in epistemological analysis is supposed to be pre-categorial is thus in fact already mediated, already a category of the mind: 'Sensation, the crux of all epistemology, is reinterpreted by this latter into a fact of consciousness'.[33] Within epistemology, sensation

[31] For an incisive analysis of the parallel contradictions of economic theory, which all ultimately result from the impossibility of making the economic problematic cohere on its own terms, see Levine 1977. The logic of Levine's Hegelian critique could be aptly characterised as 'economic concepts in dialectic' (cf. Adorno 1982, Chapter 3): at every stage non-dialectical systems necessarily generate contradictions that they cannot resolve, thereby revealing the dialectic in spite of themselves. Their truth thus lies solely in their disintegration: 'dialectic discloses each image as script. It teaches us to read from its features the admission of falseness which cancels its power and hands it over to truth' (Horkheimer and Adorno 2002, p 18). On the contradictions and incoherencies of neoclassical economic theory, in particular, see also Orléan 2014.

[32] 'The role played by sensation can be characterized as that of *indicating a state of the subject*' (O'Connor 2005, p 87 (emphasis in original)).

[33] Adorno 2001b ('Transition to Materialism').

is sensory experience emptied out in order to accord with the purity of the cognitive subject and the primacy of its form-giving power.[34] So far from being the material of the world as it is in-itself, before any subjective-categorial activity, therefore, it is entirely a category of the constitutive subject. As sensation, the object is already pre-formed.

The supposedly pre-conceptual status of sensation is thus really a consequence of its pre-conceptualisation.[35] The original condition, in which the material seems merely to be presented to the subject is already thoroughly mediated, shaped to the primacy of subjectivity. Exactly the same is true, on Adorno's reading, of the concept of the given, the stuff that the subject encounters in the immediacy of intuition. Although it functions in epistemological analysis as the non-conceptual material that the subject works on in categorial synthesis, it is in fact also a category of subjectivity and so already conceptual:

> The given is in its impoverished and blind form not objectivity, but rather merely the borderline value which the subject, after it confiscated the concrete object, has not completely mastered in its own magic circle. … The naked sensible datum, divested of its determinations, is the product of that process of abstraction, to which the Kantian subjective epistemology contrasted it; the purer the datum from its forms, the more threadbare, 'abstract' it becomes. The residuum of the object as the given, which remains after the abstraction of subjective additions is a deception of prima philosophia.[36]

Within epistemology, whatever is specified as pre-subjective and pre-categorial is in fact thoroughly saturated by constitutive subjectivity. The supposedly primary and immediate turns out to be mediated and therefore not primary; or, what is outside the circle of consciousness is really entirely within it and determined through it. In sensation and the given, the subject thus misrecognises its own activity: it takes to be an originary objectivity

---

[34] 'Sensation … is completely diluted of full reality through the reduction to subjective immanence. If it were true that material reality extends into so-called "consciousness" only as sensation and "sense-certainty", then all the more would objectivity be turned into a categorical performance of the subject' (Adorno 1982, p 156).

[35] This is in fact a condition of transcendental idealism. As Henry Allison observes, the implication of the Transcendental Aesthetic is that 'the very possibility of discursive cognition requires that the data be presented by sensibility in a manner suitable for conceptualization' (Allison 2004, p 14).

[36] Adorno 2001b ('Object not a Given'). In epistemology the 'given' functions as 'the boundary line where idealist philosophy both *needs and disavows* the reality of an external world' (Gordon 2016, p 73 (emphasis in original)).

what, as a bare 'something', has in fact been reduced to an abstract residue by the transferral of all cognitive activity to the rational subject.[37] The materiality upon which the structure of subjective intention is to be erected is so abstract and insubstantial because it has already been completely filtered by subjectivity.

The a priori character of the a posteriori was taken by Adorno to be objectively admitted within what he regarded as the most far-reaching statement of the modern epistemological problematic, Kant's *Critique of Pure Reason*. In Kant, the data given by sensation are grasped first through the forms of intuition, space and time, and then constructed into the phenomenal object by the categories of the understanding. In order to get at pure immediacy within the theory, the primary material unmediated by the subject, it is therefore necessary to apply a 'process of subtraction',[38] removing all of the subjective factors with which Kant's theory concerns itself in order to reveal what is outside the subject and simply presented to it. When this subtraction is carried out, however, it becomes apparent that no substantive pre-conceptual material can actually be attained. All that is left is 'something entirely amorphous', in effect nothing:

> It might be supposed … that there must be some *quality* – it is terribly difficult to find an appropriate word here – that is, there must be something that falls outside this generalizing mechanism with its all-inclusive abstractions. There must be something to represent what is given in nature, something that has not been shaped in advance, and which could then be described as a pure given. … if you then set out in search of properties that can be ascribed to this given, something that can be found in our consciousness quite without any input from us, you will regularly discover that all such properties have already been defined by Kant as *categories*. 'Quality' appears in the 'system of principles' and the idea that everything that exists has qualities is one of the principles of pure reason; it is a synthetic *a priori* judgement. It is, in other words, something that is generated by the mechanism of subjectivity, quite in the spirit of Kant. So what we are left with finally, if I may sum it up like this, is the concrete pole of Kantian philosophy, the point at which the processing mechanism, the conceptual machinery, the process of abstraction of the subject, has the least impact of all. This means that whatever is to be found on what we might term the outer skin of the subject and should therefore be closest to the absolute thing-in-itself,

37 'The given as the result of abstraction becomes discernible through its abstractness as itself just something produced' (Adorno 1982, p 140).

38 Adorno 2001a, p 123.

> this *ens concretissimum*, turns out to be completely abstract, as abstract in its way as the most abstract, most general concept of all, the pure 'I think'.[39]

The process of subtraction, peeling away the layers of subjectivity in order to expose a primary materiality not already mediated by consciousness, ends up with something that is really nothing. What Kant's philosophy thus demonstrates is that although the epistemological problematic is premised upon a pre-categorial matter that is encountered by the subject as given, no immediacy separated from the subject and simply confronting it, no primary materiality, can in fact be determined – the sheerly given is already formed by consciousness. In its apparent pre-subjective givenness, it is wholly subjective. When it follows its own logic to the extreme, epistemology thus reveals the untruth of its own founding division, that there is no content in the absence of form. The immediate is already, precisely in its very immediacy, completely mediated.[40]

Just as Adorno sought to show the form within the content of cognition, so, likewise, he sought to show the content within the form. The hypostatisation of form, its treatment as something a priori, towards which epistemology immanently inclined as the complement of the hypostatisation of the given as a posteriori, is both incoherent and illegitimate because it is not possible to conceive of form as such without reference to content. In relation to Kant, this argument was made by Adorno in part through consideration of the philosophical problem of constitution, and the relation between the *constituens* and the *constitutum* within epistemology. The entire burden of the first *Critique* is that the object requires the subject in order to be known, that the subject constitutes the object from the amorphous and chaotic material of the sensory manifold through its categorial activity. While the matter of sensation underlies cognition, within the epistemological problematic form must ultimately have precedence because without form there is no world at all. Content is determined by form but form must be, in a sense, pristine – it cannot be determined in any way by content because then it would lose its a priori status and be reduced to the level of the contingently empirical, which would destroy its validity. The necessity and universality of knowledge would then collapse into a lawless relativism. Within Kantian epistemology, that there is an objectively knowable world follows from the

---

39 Adorno 2001a, pp 123–4 (emphases in original).

40 Adorno 2001a, p 124. Indeed, on Adorno's reading, the whole 'content' side of Kantian epistemology is in fact a function of its formal dimension. Although the architecture of the system requires that form follows on content, in fact it is the other way around: the Transcendental Aesthetic implies the Transcendental Logic (Adorno 2001a, pp 222–34; Adorno 1982, pp 145–7).

formative power of the transcendental subject: the *constitutum* requires the *constituens* if it is to be anything at all. For Adorno, however, within its own argumentation epistemology unwittingly confesses that in questions of constitution, form cannot be radically divided from content as it would like. Form must in fact be involved with content in a way that reaches beyond and behind its intentional power of construction. Thus, for example, when Kant straightforwardly and unreflectively speaks of objects being given to 'us', the seemingly innocuous usage already concedes the dependence of form on what, strictly speaking, is supposed to be constituted by it in the first place, empirical subjects. Likewise, the supreme principle of form in transcendental idealism, the synthetic unity of apperception, is unthinkable without the material subject. The generality of the 'I think' requires the particularity of the empirical 'I':

> If you completely detach this 'I think', that is, the pure transcendental subject, from the actual 'I', then not only does all talk of an 'I' lose all its meaning but it also becomes impossible to imagine what Kant means by 'context of consciousness' or 'synthesis' or 'memory' or 'reproduction'. All these categories that we encounter in Kant would lose their entire meaning. If you separate the *constituens* – that is, the pure consciousness through which the actual world comes into being – from the *constitutum* – that is, the world in its broadest sense – then the former, the *constituens*, cannot even be imagined without the *constitutum* being imagined simultaneously.[41]

Although the critique of pre-modern metaphysics forbade the hypostatisation of the categories of the subject, by not working through the reciprocity of *constituens* and *constitutum* Kant, so Adorno alleged, in fact violated his own stricture in his positing of the transcendental.[42] Just as the material of cognition was cut off from the subject as knower, so within epistemology the empirical subject, as object, was increasingly cut off from itself as cognitive being in the form of the transcendental subject.[43] The abstract and

---

41 Adorno 2001a, p 147. See also Adorno 1982, pp 141–5 and Adorno 1993, pp 14–15: 'In the "uns" [us] that Kant, in his introspective naiveté, continues to use unreflectively, he acknowledges the relationship—and not only in their application but in their origin—of the categorical forms to something existing, namely human beings, that arise in turn from the interplay of the forms with sensory material.'

42 Adorno 2001a, p 147 and pp 217–18.

43 At this point, the two sides of the Kantian problematic meet in their extreme separation: just as the chaotic sensory manifold is given to the subject from below, through the unknowable thing-in-itself, so Kant admits, in the second version of the transcendental deduction of the categories, that the categorial forms of the transcendental subject are likewise underivable and simply given to the subject from above (Kant 1999, p 254/B146). The

impersonal transcendental subject works on an equally abstract materiality, with the empirical 'I' as their mere intermediary. A similar argument was made by Adorno in his criticism of the logical absolutism to which Husserl was driven in his desire to surpass subjective epistemology and to affirm the objectivity and truth of reason. While Adorno agreed with Husserl's critique of the psychological grounding of logical laws, he rejected the resultant hypostatisation of logic as pure being in-itself.[44] The central point of Adorno's lengthy critique was that the logical stands in need of the non-logical for its very existence to be possible. While it is true that validity is not to be reduced to genesis (Adorno's rejection of the sociology of knowledge), nonetheless logic cannot be coherently thought as purely ideal being but must ultimately refer back to the non-logical for its meaning to be sustained: 'the sense of logic itself demands facticity. Otherwise it could not be grounded rationally. Its ideality is not a pure in-itself, but rather must always be for another, if it is to be anything at all'.[45] Although logic does indeed constitute an objectivity that transcends the limited and contingent empirical individual, nevertheless it cannot be completely split apart from the thinking subject. The pure ideality of logic *is* only for thinking beings: 'without the possibility of thinking, to which the concept of the subject is immanent, logical absolutism would be senseless'.[46] Form implies content not merely as the

uncriticised dogmatism of these two poles – the thing-in-itself and the 'metaphysical deduction of the categories' – would become a key point of attack in the critique of the transcendental structure within post-Kantian German Idealism.

44 Adorno 1982, pp 41–88. The referent here is formal logic, which constructs the laws of thought in complete separation from the material of thought, not dialectical logic, which includes its opposite within itself, in the identity of form and content (Winfield 1990).

45 Adorno 1982, p 78.

46 Adorno 1982, p 72. More fully: 'The fact that every single object may be ignored, since formal logic applies to all, does signify that in the highest universality of the category "object in general", specific differences disappear altogether. What does not disappear, however, is the relationship of the propositions of logic to an "object in general". They hold only "for" objects. Logic can apply only to propositions; only propositions can be true or false. The law of non-contradiction, for example, could not be expressed without reference to the concept of contradictorily opposing propositions. But the concept of such propositions necessarily involves some content, not only because of the facticity of their proper execution, i.e. factual subjective judging, but also because of the material elements which underlie even the most abstract proposition, however mediated it may be, if it is going to mean anything at all, i.e. be a proposition. Thus the talk of logic as in-itself is strictly not permissible. Its very possibility depends on existents, the propositions, with all that this existence involves, just as conversely the propositions depend on logic which they must satisfy in order to be true. Formal logic is functional and not ideal being' (Adorno 1982, pp 66–7). (Cf., in this context, Agamben's observation that mathematics cannot be completely formalised as purely ideal being because it necessarily relies upon signification, and thus upon the negative foundation of metaphysics, which is the original division of content and form, subject and world (Agamben 1991, p 98).)

necessary material by which the constitutive function of the categories is fulfilled but, more profoundly, in its very concept *as form*.[47]

For Adorno, the epistemological problematic as such expresses a contradiction that goes to the very heart of the metaphysics of modernity. On one hand, the epistemological conception of knowledge expresses the modern subject's drive towards the 'seamless reduction to subjective immanence'.[48] Within the form of existence whose sense is codified in epistemology, the object as an intelligible, knowable entity must be held within the frame of the subject's intentional reason – outside that focus it becomes blurred and unstable, disintegrating into chaotic meaninglessness. On the other, however, exactly the seamless reduction to subjective immanence is dependent upon and therefore contains within itself the strict separation of subject and object, or inside and outside. In its doctrine of subjective constitution, epistemology intends the internalisation of the object to the subject, but its sphere of immanence, within which the subject is able to assert its priority, is premised upon the deeply incised borderline that divides subject from object. Even as the epistemological subject aims to produce the world complete, from out of itself, therefore, it is nevertheless forbidden to annul the line that, by separating it definitively from the world, constitutes it as the sovereign subject. As Adorno interpreted it, this contradictory demand of inclusive exclusion cannot be made good within the structure of the epistemological problematic:

> Mastering such aporia is the perennial effort of epistemologies, though none will succeed. Every one of them stands under Anaximander's curse, whose philosophy of being was one of the earliest but practically prophesied the coming destiny of them all.[49]

Each of the concepts of epistemology attempts to unify subject and object in identity by incorporating the object into the jurisdiction of consciousness. In doing so, however, they must always reinscribe the division between subject and object, form and content, upon which modern epistemology is based. It is for this reason that Adorno repeatedly described epistemologies, indeed what he thought of as subject-centred philosophies generally, as debt systems: 'The metacritique of epistemology requires constructive reflection upon its structure as one of guilt and punishment (*Schuld und Strafe*), necessary error and futile correction.'[50] Epistemological systems as such are trapped

---

47 'The *conditions of possibility* of transcendental forms are the very elements that are said to be constituted by those forms' (Adorno 2001a, p 162 (emphasis in original)).

48 Adorno 1982, p 26.

49 Adorno 1982, p 25.

50 Adorno 1982, p 25. For Adorno, all philosophies constructed on the principle of subjective immanence, whether they explicitly acknowledged it or not, formed debt systems in this

within a mythical cycle of repetition from which they can never escape. The more completely they succeed in incorporating the world into themselves, the more deeply they are divided from it. The redemption of the debt through the reconciliation of the two sides of the division is thereby endlessly postponed. As the modality through which the modern subject attempts to understand the contradictory, inside/outside, relation between itself and the world, epistemology thus forms a *Schuldzusammenhang*, or context of guilt.

Epistemology–dialectic

In his reading of epistemology, Adorno focused so intently on the unsustainability of the various separations upon which it is based because what concerned him above all was the way in which the working out of the metaphysical structure of the modern subject through the epistemological problematic led to the latter immanently surpassing itself as it became dialectic. In the *Critique of Pure Reason*, Kant set out the definitive statement of the form of modern subjectivity as it had crystallised within its epistemological self-understanding. In so doing, he drove to an extreme the various divisions upon which the modern, epistemological-economic, subject is based, construing them in the strictest possible fashion.[51] The sphere of the subject – form – was rigidly separated from the pre-conceptual material – content – so that the constitution of an objectively valid world through the law-like activity of the transcendental subject should be possible. Further, the Kantian account of the reason of the modern, sovereign subject demanded not only the divisions of form and content, sensibility and understanding, a priori and a posteriori, but also the inscribing of absolute boundary lines, staking out once and for all the borders that marked the limits of the theoretical reason of the modern subject. Transgressing those boundaries could only lead reason into self-destructive contradiction, the metaphysical antinomies from which it was the purpose of critique to rescue it. Hence the architectonic division of the first *Critique* into a positive and a negative side, the 'Transcendental Logic' and the 'Transcendental Dialectic'. In this way Kant brought the epistemological problematic, which had been in development for 150 years, to a culmination, paradoxically attempting to rescue objectivity through the very subject that had dissolved it.

This achievement, however, came at the cost of restricting knowledge to subjective constitution and placing the mysterious 'thing-in-itself' beyond

way; thus Kant (Adorno 2001a, pp 218–20), Husserl (Adorno 1982, p 26), Heidegger (Adorno 2001b, 'Lack as Gain'), and ultimately even Hegel (Adorno 1993, p 147).

[51] As Agamben puts it, 'In the history of Western philosophy, Kant represents the moment in which the break between the thing and thought is revealed as irreparable' (Agamben 2025, p 95). It is in that moment that existence becomes entirely economic.

the bounds of knowledge altogether, so leaving an unknowable 'real' world behind the phenomenal world of mere appearances. For Adorno, this was where the crucial transition point in modern thought was situated, in the radical recasting of the Kantian problematic, culminating in Hegelian dialectic, that was effected by German Idealism.[52] The post-Kantian thinkers enthusiastically accepted the critique of dogmatic metaphysics. What they rejected, however, was the one-sidedness of the Kantian system, its commitment to subjective construction, and the consequent limits that Kant placed upon reason through his confinement of thought to reflection and finitude. They rebelled against the resignation, or defeatism, of Kant's account of reason, which effectively ruled the great metaphysical questions out of court, prohibiting knowledge of the Absolute and thereby denying the fulfilment of the deepest impulse of reason.[53] As it was conceived within German Idealism, dialectic derived directly from Kantian epistemology in that it sought to fulfil the logic of transcendental idealism by taking it beyond itself. Where Kant assumed the principle of reflection, what the critical revision of subjective idealism, above all in Hegel, came to understand through reflection on reflection was that the strict separations upon which the Kantian system was constructed could not be maintained.[54] In his lectures on dialectic, Adorno summarised the decisive perception that propelled the movement of thought from Kant to Hegel:

> On the one side, in Kant, we have something like the form of knowledge or cognition, on the other side we have the content; the content somehow happens to reach knowledge from outside;

[52] The movement from Ricardo, in whom classical political economy reached its culmination, to Marx can be understood as a failed, distorted and truncated, parallel to this crucial transition in modern thought – the moment when economics might have come to self-consciousness as dialectic but did not. Seen in this perspective, the modern revolution in value theory can be recognised as the long-delayed working out of what went wrong in that second, abortive transition.

[53] In his early *Differenzschrift*, Hegel thus that states: 'The intellect, as the capacity to set limits, erects a building and places it between man and the Absolute, linking everything that man thinks worthy and holy to this building, fortifying it through all the powers of nature and talent and expanding it *ad infinitum*. The entire totality of limitations is to be found in it, but not the Absolute itself' (Hegel 1977a, p 89). The German Idealists regarded Kant's philosophy as the most thoroughly worked out expression of the *Reflexionskultur* of the understanding that characterises modernity, in which thought is taken to be merely a 'reflection' of a being that is wholly external and the Absolute is consequently unattainable.

[54] Adorno 2017, pp 64–5. On the movement of reflection from the empiricism of ordinary consciousness, through transcendental idealism to speculative dialectic, see Hyppolite 1997, Part 2, Chapter 2. On the distinction between reflection and speculation, see Hegel 1977a, pp 85–118; see also Verene 2007, Chapter 1.

> the content itself ... is actually withdrawn from reflection. [Hegel's critique is that] this whole separation ... has something rigid about it. On the one side I presuppose that there are certain forms, and on the other side I presuppose there are material contents, and I decree somewhat arbitrarily that these forms are only meant to be valid for these contents, but not valid in themselves. But, in reflecting upon these forms, I already turn the forms themselves into content, as it were, and thereby show that this distinction of form and content ... cannot possibly be conceived as an absolute distinction, and likewise, in turn, the supposed contents – i.e. the data of sensation – cannot possibly be given to me independently of my consciousness, independently of the identity of thought.[55]

By virtue of his more insistent examination of their own sense, Hegel mobilised and made active the rigid oppositions posited by modern thought. He revealed that it is not possible to hold form and content, or the two sides of any of the other dichotomies, apart in the way that is necessary within the epistemological problematic and that Kant most emphatically demanded.[56] Each side always already implies the other and cannot be conceived without it – its determination requires its opposite. The decisive advance of post-Kantian thought was thus that it developed the dynamic movement latent within what were construed in epistemology as static polarities.[57] In doing

55 Adorno 2017, p 66.

56 Hence, in his analysis of Kant, the young Hegel focused above all on those points in the system of transcendental idealism where an indifference of the divisions, an absolute identity of subject and object, was necessarily implied – that is, where Kant was effectively forced to admit the reality of the 'intellectual intuition' that he was otherwise so concerned to deny. This early fascination with intellectual intuition, as the speculative unity of thought and being, their necessary inseparability, became in the mature Hegel the rehabilitation, against Kant, of the ontological proof of God, that is, the idea of a necessary identity of concept and existence, or of a conceptual structure that is self-predicating (Harrelson 2009; Hodgson 2011; Moss 2022, Chapter 3; McNulty 2023, Chapter 2).

57 'For Hegel's idealism, reason becomes a critical reason in a sense that criticizes Kant once again, a negative reason that both preserves static elements and sets them in motion. The poles that Kant opposed to one another—form and content, nature and spirit, theory and praxis, freedom and necessity, the thing in itself and the phenomenon—are all permeated through and through by reflection in such a way that none of these determinations are left standing as ultimate' (Adorno 19993, p 8). In his discussion of continental idealism between Leibniz and Nietzsche, Paul Redding proposes that across the course of Kant's career, from the early pre-critical writings, through the Copernican turn and into the late *Opus postumum*, there is a clearly discernible overall trajectory towards the kind of positions that would only be explicitly articulated after him by the German Idealists (Redding 2009). Correlatively, Karin de Boer notes that the three *Critiques*, and especially the first, were conceived by Kant as preparatory works, intended to lay the ground for a comprehensive restatement of metaphysics (de Boer, 2022). In the event, however, Kant

so, it raised the epistemological problematic out of itself and transformed its sense.

Dialectic thus developed straight out of the high point of epistemological reflection in modern philosophy. It did not abstractly oppose itself to epistemology, as an alternative way of thinking, which would simply set aside or dismiss the claims of the epistemological experience, asserting itself by fiat to be beyond the subject–object distinction, but instead justified itself as the unfolding of the intrinsic logic of the problematic of reflection – that is, of the division itself.[58] This was why Adorno described Hegel as 'a Kant come into his own' and why his interpretation of Kant emphasised that the dialectic already existed objectively within the Kantian system, waiting to be drawn out, so that the transition from one to the other was properly immanent.[59] In this respect, the moment in which epistemology became dialectic was, on Adorno's reading, the moment in which the modern subject finally attained to an authentic consciousness of its own metaphysical structure. That subject initially became aware of itself in its separation and freedom from pre-modern modes of objectivity in the form of epistemology. Through the process of reflection on the contradictions of the epistemological problematic, though, it eventually discovered its intrinsically dialectical meaning. Dialectic thus did not annul the divisions constitutive of the epistemological problematic; rather, it preserved them and transcended them at the same time, liberating them from their narrowness and restriction. The realisation that the divisions could not be accepted just as they presented themselves but that each side always implied the other within itself transformed the meaning of the

was never able to work out the complete metaphysical system that he intended, a system that, de Boer suggests, 'may well have resembled Hegel's *Logic* much more closely than the *Critique* itself' (de Boer 2010, p 217). Seen in this light, Kant emerges as a transitional figure, who forms the crucial hinge between, in Hegel's terms, the pre-modern divided world of reflection and the totalised modern world of the Concept.

58 Hegel 'attacks epistemology by showing that the forms that epistemology considers to constitute knowledge depend as much on the content of knowledge as vice versa. … In order to demonstrate that, however, Hegel himself makes use of a more consistent epistemology. If epistemology, the doctrine of the contingency and impenetrability of content and the indispensability of forms, dug the trench between matter and form, Hegel extends epistemology until it becomes obvious that it is not its place to dig trenches, that in setting limits, consciousness necessarily transcends what it limits' (Adorno 1993, p 66).

59 Adorno 1993, p 6. 'Dialectic must, in an eminent sense, be regarded as Kantian philosophy which has come to self-consciousness and self-understanding' (Adorno 2017, p 14). As Hegel himself acknowledged, 'the Kantian philosophy … constitutes the foundation and the starting point of the new German philosophy' (Hegel 2010, p. 40). But where, as he complained, 'Kantian philosophy remains entirely within the antithesis', dialectic sought to grasp the division itself: 'the sole Idea that has reality and true objectivity for philosophy, is the absolute suspendedness of the antithesis' (Hegel 1977b, pp 67 and 68).

dividing lines that constituted the epistemological subject. Kant had already conceded that the antinomies of reason that he treated negatively in the Transcendental Dialectic were nevertheless a necessary part of reason and inalienable to it: reason could not help but transcend its boundaries, even if as a result it became entangled in contradictions, because to reach for the Absolute, the unconditioned, was intrinsic to reason itself.[60] Hegel took the step of accepting what was implied in Kant but that the latter still tried to guard against, that the dividing lines were not simply restrictions placed upon thought but were the very medium of its freedom. In doing so, he moved definitively beyond Kant by working out the logic of the latter's own construction:

> Hegel no longer accepts the tried Kantian opposition between sensibility and understanding, between thought and experience, in the way this is … insisted upon by Kant, for Hegel says that I basically cannot know how I can then arrive at something like sensibility at all, that there is nothing sensuous which is not itself mediated by the understanding, and vice versa, and therefore that this whole rigid separation between sensibility and understanding – upon which the Kantian doctrine of antinomies is based and which can in a sense protect me from contradictions – cannot ultimately be sustained at all. And that is precisely because there simply is no sensibility without understanding and no understanding without sensibility.[61]

The transition to dialectic came through the realisation that if each side contained the other, then the dividing line could not be taken merely as the marker of separation but was also the medium of identity. Indeed, it was precisely by being separated that the two sides were made identical in the first place.[62] The law of non-contradiction thus unfolded itself into the necessity of contradiction.[63] In this way, Hegel reversed the meaning of Kant's Transcendental Dialectic: if dialectic was inherent to reason, as Kant admitted, then it could not simply be error but must, in fact, be essential to thought. The logic of illusion was really, therefore, the logic of truth. Through this embrace of the intrinsically antinomic structure of reason – antinomy as 'the explicit form of truth'[64] – Hegel passed beyond the limits

---

60 On Kant's understanding of the necessity of metaphysics, see Willaschek 2018.

61 Adorno 2017, p 59.

62 On Hegel's development of Kantian dichotomy into identity, see Sedgwick 2012.

63 Moss 2022.

64 Hegel 1977a, p 108.

of the epistemological problematic to the dialectical logics of contradiction and speculation.[65]

In this way, dialectic reconceived the opposition of inside and outside that is foundational to consciousness as such. It opened out what was closed in upon itself in epistemology; or, more exactly, it showed that the strict closure was at the same time absolute openness. Viewed from the heights of speculative dialectic, epistemology was revealed as merely 'the subjective philosophy of reflection', the limited viewpoint of the understanding, which, in simply assuming the boundaries, could only posit a static polarity of subject and object: an individual cognising subject externally confronting a given object world, the real nature of which it cannot know and which it can thus only categorise and classify through its subjective conceptual activity. Within dialectic, this ultimately positivistic notion of an abstract subject simply registering a given objectivity became the dynamic, self-moving logical process of the Concept, through which subject and object are reciprocally brought into being in their simultaneous identity and opposition.[66] What had been construed by epistemology as a rigid antithesis between subject and object was thus set in motion in dialectic through the recognition of the dividing line not simply as fixity and separation but as the motor of a restless, unstoppable process of identification through division that is motivated from within its own immanent logic.[67] This is the movement from the understanding to reason, in the sense in which Hegel took over and adapted those terms from Kant.[68] Likewise, post-Kantian Idealism transformed the meaning of the limits that Kant had placed upon reason through its recognition that the very assertion by reason of its ability to set

---

65 Paul Redding argues that Kant's transcendental idealism is, in fact, double-sided or Janus-faced. One side, what Redding calls 'weak' transcendental idealism, looks back and effects a break with the past through the critique of pre-modern metaphysics, a work of boundary setting, intended definitively to separate inside and outside, that is articulated in epistemological terms. The other side, however, what Redding terms 'strong' transcendental idealism, looks forward and recasts the entire project of metaphysics, precisely on the basis of that separation, as reason's exclusive and unlimited concern with its own products (Redding 2009, pp 46–7). It is this 'strong' version of the Kantian critique of metaphysics that the German Idealists took up and developed.

66 Speculation is thus the logic of division fully worked out, in which the Absolute is in fact attained precisely through the movement of its Kantian prohibition: 'Hegel does not return to the prior dogmatism; he extends transcendental logic into speculative logic. The categories become the very categories of the Absolute' (Hyppolite 1997, p 58).

67 In Adorno's understanding, 'this transition from the antithesis between subject and object that prevailed in philosophy from Descartes to Kant to a dynamic relationship between subject and object is the decisive step taken by philosophy in that period' (Adorno 2001a, p 164).

68 Hegel 1991, pp 125–33/§§79–82.

limits upon itself must mean that it was at the same time beyond them: the positing of the limit necessarily implies its transcendence. In other words, if it was not already involved with the Absolute, right from the beginning, reason would not be able to determine itself as limited and finite: 'if our reason, in reflecting upon cognitive reason as such, did not possess within itself the power to judge with regard to the unconditional and with regard to what is absolutely binding upon us, then it could not possibly pass those negative judgements which are indeed presented in the transcendental dialectic'.[69] What the self-reflection of epistemology in its transition to dialectic thus demonstrated was that the unlimited is attained precisely through limitation. Epistemology saw only the side of limitation and criticised pre-modern metaphysics on that basis. Dialectic, by contrast, fused the two sides, the limited and the unlimited, together.

With the transcendence of epistemology into dialectic, the working out of the logic of modern subjectivity completed a process of reversal. In his analysis of its formation, Louis Dumont showed that the new economic subject rested on two fundamental presuppositions: first, the ontological primacy of the bounded and self-sufficient Individual in relation to the context of mediation; and secondly, a kind of materialism in the primacy of the relation to objects over relations to persons. Through the development of the epistemological problematic, both of these presuppositions were overturned, in that they were shown to resolve themselves into their opposites. In the first place, reflection on the cognising subject and the possibility of objective knowledge made evident that individual cognition was in fact dependent upon a universal, trans-subjective subject. This was central to Kant's identification of the transcendental sphere, and was then reformulated by Hegel as the logico-historical development of spirit.[70] At the core of the isolated Individual of epistemology there was thus discovered a universality that had to be acknowledged as the real *constituens*: the truth of

69 Adorno 2017, p 63; see also Hegel 1991, pp 105–6/§60.

70 Here, again, dialectic simply elaborated what was latent in and unrecognised by reflection philosophy. The Kantian critique was already built upon a distinction between the subject that engages in direct knowledge and the subject that critiques knowledge. Hegel then made the splitting of the concept of the subject between the empirical subject and the absolute subject thematic: 'consciousness as object, as something to be grasped philosophically, becomes the finite, limited and fallible thing it had already tended to be conceived as in Kant, who because of this finiteness forbade consciousness to wander off into intelligible worlds. … Conversely, the consciousness that grasps the finiteness of consciousness, the contemplating subjectivity that "posits" the contemplated subject, also thereby posits itself as infinite and—or so is Hegel's intention—when his philosophy is fully elaborated, proves itself in its infiniteness to be absolute spirit, to which nothing is external and in which the difference between subject and object disappears' (Adorno 1993, pp 71–2).

the subjective construction of objectivity was really the objective Concept. The empirical subject came to be understood as merely the bearer of this absolute subject, which worked through it. In this way, the limited and finite Individual was shown to be at the same time unlimited and universal spirit, each of which implied the other. A new objective, and indeed absolute, order of being was thereby discovered *within* self-enclosed subjectivity. Secondly, the materialism of the primacy of the relation to things became the idealism of constitutive subjectivity and the limitless productive activity of spirit. That the modern subject experienced itself in immediate relation to things was a result of its having thrown off the weight of pre-modern ontology, along with the structure of authority that supported it, and so liberated itself. For the modern subject in its rational autonomy, the world of objects appeared as immediately given, while mediation was secondary and derivative. In Kant, epistemology came to the realisation that the problematic of the subject encountering and cognising a given objectivity was insufficient: not only could no immediacy subtracted from mediation be identified, but without the categories and the transcendental subject there was no objectivity at all, other than the unknowable thing-in-itself, and so objectivity had to be understood as a function of subjectivity. The object as it was known was a creation of the subject, a perception again fully worked out by Hegel.[71] When its logic was unfolded, therefore, the anti-metaphysical positivism of the registering of a given objectivity was transformed into the speculative metaphysics of absolute idealism.[72]

The inner history of modern epistemology in its classical phase between Descartes and Hegel is the narrative of its self-transcendence.[73] Epistemology, like economics, was founded on a series of divisions and separations by which the modern subject came to understand itself as free and self-determining. However, as the inside/outside structure of experience encoded in the epistemological problematic was gradually worked out, so philosophy eventually came to comprehend the logic of division itself: form and

---

71 'Kant's successors no longer regard the concept of experience as one of mere material, as something that comes to the subject from outside. For very weighty reasons these philosophers believed that the contents of experience itself were to be inferred from the mind. It follows fairly compellingly that this must give a new twist to the concept of the speculative. According to this way of thinking, it means that reason is *everything* and that it therefore contains the element of the material in itself' (Adorno 2001a, p 49 (emphasis in original)).

72 Positivism is thus not simply the extreme opposite of dialectic but a moment within it (Adorno 2017, p 3).

73 For a reconstruction of that history, which demonstrates the irreducible incoherence of the epistemological problematic as such and so the necessary failure of the general project of epistemology as an account of knowledge, see Maker 1994, Chapter 11.

content, sensibility and understanding, the finite and the infinite, each always contained the other. The radical separation of form and content thus became the absolute identity of thought and being. Through that perception the epistemological problematic was resolved into dialectic. It was revealed as dialectic unaware of itself, the necessarily limited, one-sided and abstract (in the Hegelian sense) form in which the modern Individual must comprehend itself and its world if it is to maintain its self-understanding as an autonomous, free and self-determining subject. As the cognitive standpoint of the modern subject, epistemology expressed the conviction that the consciousness of the bounded Individual must be the ground of truth, although it could neither establish that ground adequately nor develop a coherent account of knowledge on its basis. The critique of epistemology demonstrates that the standpoint of the sovereign Individual is in fact internal to the dialectic, its immediate mode of appearance: content implies form, the limited implies the unlimited, the finite Individual implies universal spirit. From the perspective attained in post-Kantian idealism, epistemology could be recognised as dialectic distorted and truncated for the sake of the primacy of the Individual. This is the necessity of the epistemological-economic paradigm of the modern subject as well as its falseness. Dialectic is its truth.

6

The Concept of Capital: Marx and the Modern Subject

Economic thought assumes that the two sides of its problematic, content and form, must be related to each other as primary to secondary. Value, as the concept that connects them together, is thus imagined to arise on one side of the line, then somehow to pass across the division, in order to be represented on the other side through the conceptual forms of exchange. It is on this basis that capital is understood to be an economic phenomenon, one mode among others through which the primary material reality may be mediated. By breaking Marx's theory apart along its central metaphysical fracture between content and form, the revolution in value theory destroys this conception, which is the very foundation of the economic idea itself.[1] Once it is shown that the theorisation of value must begin from exchange, then it can no longer be grounded in the supposed primary materiality. That is, inner and outer cannot be made continuous in the way that economic theory must assume – there is no passage, or transition, across the division. This fundamental theoretical discontinuity is resolved when the economic problematic is situated within the wider context of the metaphysics of modernity. What became clear through the development of the epistemological problematic between Descartes and Hegel was that no coherent account of thought can be given on the assumption of a radical division of content and form: once they are taken in separation, it is impossible to fit the two sides together again, from either direction. Instead, the material and the conceptual have to be understood as being mediated in each other exactly in their separation – that is, they must be understood

1 It is thus immaterial whether what is supposed to be represented in exchange is labour, utility or anything else. Rather, what is at issue in the concept of value is the basic structure of the economic problematic as such – that is, the fundamental coherence and validity of economic thought at all.

as existing in what Hegel termed an original identity. This is the logical necessity of dialectic.[2] Translating across into the parallel field of economic thought, this means that value does not arise on one side of the line, in order then to be represented on the other. Rather, it mediates content and form in their reciprocal opposition-and-identity. Value does not, therefore, pass *across* the division; rather, it is located *in* the division. In dialectic, the division is thus no longer a silent and passive line but itself becomes active, generating both sides, the material and the conceptual, simultaneously in the dynamic unfolding of its logic.

The reformulation of the economic problematic as dialectical radically changes the meaning of capital. Put simply: if the relation between the material ground of labour and production and the conceptual forms of exchange is dialectical, and not representational, then capital is not an economic phenomenon. Even more radically, it means that there is actually no such thing as the economic, as a primary and irreducible material world of labour and production, at all. Rather, the economic is a phenomenon of capital – the objective materiality of the world is always already entirely mediated by value. That is, the material and the conceptual, thought and being, exist in an original identity. It follows from the revolution in value theory, therefore, that the concept of capital itself must be completely rethought. This work of reconceptualisation proceeds here in two stages. First, a work of destruction. The dialectical theorisation of value places Marx in an entirely new perspective, revealing both the real meaning of his enormously influential conception of capital and its radical falsity. The resolution of the economic problematic into dialectic thus makes it possible for the theorisation of capital finally to settle accounts with Marx once and for all. For if Marx's thought is the supreme expression of the economic experience of the modern subject, then it is by working through the problems in his basic idea of capital, and demonstrating its fundamental incoherence, that theory may at last move beyond him altogether to a new, and much more far-reaching, conception of capital. Secondly, a work of construction. The modern Marxist debate has definitively demonstrated that the theorisation

[2] In Hegel's *Logic* the categories are thus at once forms of thought and forms of being, always simultaneously inside and outside. Hence, for Hegel, logic is at the same time metaphysics and ontology (Houlgate 2022). The original identity of thought and being, precisely *in their division*, is the central speculative idea by which Hegel moved beyond the reflective problematic of epistemology, which he encountered in its most developed form in Kant and Fichte, and resolved its contradictions into dialectic. In his early text *Faith and Knowledge*, Hegel thus characteristically asserts that: 'This Idea of the absolute identity of thought and being is the very one which the ontological proof and all true philosophy recognize as the sole and primary Idea as well as the only true and philosophical one' (Hegel 1977b, p 94; see also Hegel 1977a, pp 155–63).

of value must begin from exchange. It follows from this that the concept of capital itself must also be developed from the metaphysics of exchange. Exchange was arguably the central obsession of Adorno's thought, and the account he sketched in *Dialectic of Enlightenment* of the origins of the dialectic in terms of the prehistory of exchange can be read as providing the founding elements of a new, and properly dialectical, concept of capital.

Emancipating the Individual

In the lengthy treatment of Marx with which his study of the 'genesis and triumph of economic ideology' ends, Louis Dumont begins with a deliberate reversal of orthodoxy. Because of his association with communism, Marx is usually assumed to be what Dumont terms a 'holist' thinker, that is, one who emphasises the collective, social dimension of human existence above all else and so emphatically repudiates liberal individualism. This, Dumont argues, is a serious misapprehension. Comprehending the logic of Marx's thought within the context of the formation of the economic experience in fact unequivocally demonstrates the opposite: that its central, animating figure throughout is the modern subject, precisely the Individual. Indeed, it could not be otherwise – the economic conception as such is inseparable from the figure of the Individual, and so, to the extent that Marx is an economic thinker, he cannot but be an Individualist. However, that Marx's thought, in its deepest convictions, was expressive of a commitment to the Individual was so from the outset, long before he consciously arrived at the economic as its determining theme. In his discussion of the young Marx's relation to Hegel, Roberto Finelli notes Marx's 'divinisation' of the human subject, his avowal of 'freedom' as the intrinsic essence of the human being.[3] Likewise, Dumont draws attention to Marx's adoption of the quintessential liberal-modern demand of 'emancipation'. Characteristic of Marx is that he appropriates this leading motif of modern subjectivity for himself and then attempts to drive it beyond what he takes to be its 'bourgeois' limits. Thus, in discussing Marx's impassioned declarations in his *Critique of Hegel's Philosophy of Right*, Dumont comments:

> It should be noted that what is in question is not essentially the reform of society or the deliverance of one class from oppression. The class with 'radical chains' is only the precondition of absolute emancipation for all men or, rather, of the emancipation of Man as an abstract being, of Man, that is, as a self-sufficient being and the incarnation of the highest value – as an Individual in the perfect modern sense of the

[3] Finelli 2016, pp 115–17.

> term. Moreover, the person who takes the vow obviously does so as an Individual in the same sense, as an independent being whose paramount value is precisely the Individual—man rid of his chains, purged of any dependence.[4]

Analysing the early writings, Dumont shows that their consistent guiding idea is radical emancipation, the liberation of the modern subject from all forms of restriction. The perspective of 'Man', the Individual to be emancipated, is always correlated with the immanent principle of being ('democracy', 'species-being', etc), and anything that is experienced as beyond, outside or separate from 'Man' is denounced as a limitation on the intrinsic freedom and universality of the subject, which must therefore be removed. Such is his yearning for the absolute emancipation of the Individual that Marx simply has no time for, or indeed any real interest in, the complex efforts of, for instance, Hegel or Rousseau to mediate the modern Individual and the socio-political whole. Instead, because it appears as something abstract that transcends the subject, the whole is summarily damned as insufficiently universal and so as a false and restrictive form.[5] In the *1844 Manuscripts* and the *German Ideology*, this motive force of Marx's thinking realises its elective affinity with the economic: the properly universal 'characteristic of the human genus' for Marx is production, 'free, conscious action on nature'.[6] Dumont demonstrates that once he has arrived at the economic as the immanent principle, Marx's guiding assumption is that all social forms must be comprehended as manifestations of this irreducible ground, which itself can be resolved into just one category, production, conceived of in terms of Individuals labouring on nature. No matter how complex the capitalist economy may be, its principle of explanation must always, in the end, be the productive activity of Individuals. When the Individual is recognised as the determining figure of all of Marx's thought, the deep accord that exists between the would-be radical and the orthodox classical thinkers whom he spurned becomes clear:

> The theorist of revolution, on the one hand, and economics as he found it, on the other, have first of all as their common ground the *individual subject*. … This valuation of man as an individual is at the root of the labor theory of value in Marx as in Smith and Ricardo; actually it explains that Marx accepts Ricardo's presuppositions or framework. The labor theory of value presupposes that production is severed

[4] Dumont 1977, p 118.
[5] Dumont 1977, pp 119–25.
[6] Dumont 1977, p 152.

> from exchange, distribution, etc., as the essence of economics, or of wealth. ... This corresponds to the search for the essence of economic phenomena in one substance (wealth, production, labor), ideologically in keeping with the individualist valuation and which we are at liberty to consider as the expression of a primacy of the relations with nature as against the relations between men. ... But the main point is that production, that is, the human relation to nature as paramount, is *of the individual*. Please note: this is true universally, so much so that, without knowing it, Marx is working within a kind of natural law concept of man as transcending all particular social constitutions and stages of production. Contrary to all appearances we have not left behind the '18th century individual'.[7]

The meaning of Marx's commitment to the modern Individual becomes fully evident, however, only when it is lifted out of Dumont's sociological framing and comprehended philosophically. Modern thought as a whole exists in the tension between, on the one hand an apparently non-conceptual material reality and, on the other, the subjective conceptual forms through which the primary materiality is supposedly represented. This is the structure of reflection philosophy – the epistemological and economic problematics – whose logical subject is the Individual. The ambivalence of liberal thought is that, even if they are imagined as only secondary and passive, merely mirroring the object so as to distort it as little as possible, the conceptual forms are nevertheless always present and therefore *de facto* necessary. Just as classical epistemology assumes the existence of the mind and its conceptual capacity by means of which the non-conceptual materiality can be cognised, so classical political economy assumes the economic forms through which the primary activity of individual labour and production is mediated. The concept is supposed to be merely a reflection of the givenness of the object, but the object can only be known through the concept.

From the very beginning, in the contrast posited in his dissertation of a given, non-conceptual 'world' and a separate and self-enclosed 'philosophy', Marx's thought, too, is situated within this modern structure of experience. However, what distinguishes him in this context is that, rather than simply accepting the division between form and content, he proposes to resolve it. Like Kant and post-Kantian philosophy, Marx wants an objectivity, a universality, that will raise the individual subjects out of the anarchic subjectivism into which modern society has disintegrated and that will bind them together into an ideal whole.[8] For Marx, this universality lies in the

7 Dumont 1977, p 167 (emphases in original).

8 Beiser 2002.

primary relation to things – that is, in what is immediate to the modern subject as Individual. The experience that his thinking bespeaks with unparalleled intensity is that it is in this relation to things that the subject is free, autonomous and sovereign. When it is able simply to give itself over, without let or hindrance, to material-economic activity, the Individual is fully emancipated and self-determining, not subordinated to any kind of authority, anything external to it that would limit it. In Marx's mind, therefore, the primary relation to things, the completely immanent condition in which the subject directly experiences its inherent universality, is truth. Correlatively, whatever appears to obstruct that immediacy, to interpose itself between the Individual and its object, becomes for him falsehood, a necessarily illegitimate limitation of the subject that 'alienates' the latter's intrinsic universality into an external and abstract form. This is the sense of the basic pattern of Marx's thought that worked itself out in developing variations through the early writings – democracy against monarchy, human emancipation against political emancipation, species-being against private property – until it finally found its authentic economic expression: labour, production and the proletariat as the universal ground of being.[9]

Marx thus purported to surpass the constitutive modern binary of a non-conceptual materiality and conceptual forms by splitting them apart altogether, setting them in opposition, and reducing the latter to the former. In doing so, he pushed to its conclusion a logic of disjunction and differential valuation between content and form that was already central to the structure of thought in classical political economy:

> In the first instance, classical political economy relates the form to its content as the accidental and inessential to the necessary. The implication of this is that the content is susceptible to conceptualization independently of its form, therefore of taking on different forms. Labor may or may not be division of labor, in either case it remains labor. Exchange-value is the form taken by the division of or the distribution of social labor in capitalist society which division may be effected through different formal arrangements in different forms of society. In capitalist society the distribution of the net product between the three classes takes place through the market, yet it is possible for such a

[9] In his analysis of the basic structure of Marx's thought, Helmut Reichelt notes that throughout his writings, from the early dissertation onwards, 'Marx identifies himself with the consciousness of a "super subject", whether humanity [*Gattungswesen*] or the working class; in any case, a "super individual" [*Überindividuellen*] who as carrier of a completely transparent knowledge, not only possesses absolute knowledge but also exists as a "universal" [*Allgemeines*] which is free from the limitations of the individual' (Reichelt 1995, p 55).

> distribution to be conceived independently of the market form and of the exchange of commodities, as a simple and immediate distribution of wealth. As a result, the three classes and their relation do not involve the market mechanism as an essential distinguishing feature. Social classes are themselves determinate in natural terms and independently of exchange. In each case, by implication, what is real is the natural, physical substance of the relations of capitalist production.[10]

Even if the forms are always present, for modern thought it is the material content, the productive relation to nature, that is really 'real'.[11] The objective non-conceptual world is constant and essential; the subjective conceptual forms are variable and extrinsic. The content is therefore conceived of as existing separately from the form through which it happens to be manifested; it is a material substratum behind the concepts through which it is represented. Classical thought, Adam Smith in particular, typically claimed to base the scientific nature of its understanding of political economy on this mode of argument, distinguishing what was manifested on the surface of society from its ultimate ground in nature. 'Explanation' thus meant reduction of appearances to a fixed external principle. Marx, in turn, tried to surpass the limits of classical political economy by adopting exactly the same explanatory procedure:

> Marx takes up this manner of criticism, turning it upon classical analysis itself. Where Smith criticizes the popular conception Marx criticizes Smith and upon the identical basis – the lack of ability to perceive anything beyond or beneath the surface forms of bourgeois economy, an inability to see those as *forms*.[12]

Once again, Marx does not in any way break from the structure of classical thought. What he does is appropriate it for himself and then attempt to force it beyond itself. He wants to make real a potentiality that appears to be there in the classical problematic but not to be followed out in it – to make unlimited what still exists only in a limited way in the 'bourgeois'

10 Levine 1977, p 157.

11 As Hegel puts it in the Introduction to his *Logic*, for ordinary consciousness: 'the object is complete and finished all by itself and, for its actuality, can fully dispense with thought; thought, for its part, is something deficient and in need of a material in order to complete itself, and also, as a pliable indeterminate form, must adapt itself to its matter. Truth is the agreement of thought with the subject matter, and in order to produce this agreement – for it is not there on its own account – thought is expected to be subservient and responsive to the subject matter' (Hegel 2010, p 24).

12 Levine 1977, p 155 (emphasis in original).

world.[13] Accordingly, Marx radicalises the division in reflection philosophy between an essential content and an inessential form by completely severing the two sides from each other: where for classical thought the forms are in principle variable and inessential, for Marx they must be so in actuality. The material ground constitutes a quasi-ontological content, or 'essence', while the various structures of separation or 'alienation' are just so many transitory and extraneous forms. These forms are not merely imperfect but deceptive, false appearances that must be destroyed if the essence is to be realised in its true universality. This absolutely undialectical way of thinking the relation of content and form is entirely typical of Marx's thought, recurring again and again throughout his work.

Two worlds

The organising idea of Marx's theorisation of capital is the two-world logic that he adopts from classical political economy: a primary world of production and a secondary world of exchange. As always, Marx accepts this characteristically modern mode of thought but wants to go beyond what he imagines to be its restricted capitalist form. Where classical theory was unable to bring its two worlds together in a coherent way, Marx posits a strong differentiation: the inner world is essence, universality and freedom, the outer world alienation, limitation and unfreedom. The fundamental idea that shapes Marx's concept of capital is thus that the entire sphere of exchange is to be understood as nothing more than a distorted manifestation of the true reality behind or beneath it, that of production.[14] In this way, Marx's theorisation of capital is developed wholly in accordance with the

[13] Marx's thought is thus dogmatic in the specific Hegelian sense (Hegel 2000, p 335; Hegel 1991, pp 69–70/§32) that it takes one of the finite determinations of reflection, in this case the economic, and purports to make it absolute by raising it to the level of the whole. This one-sided approach cannot help but intensify, rather than suspend, the contradiction with its opposite, the political.

[14] This is the significance of Giovanni Caravale's observation that Marx holds to a much more emphatic conception of a labour theory of value than is to be found in Ricardo and classical thought: 'In Ricardo the role of the labour theory ... is an analytical one: that of making it possible to identify a rule of exchange between commodities on the basis of which the inverse relation between diminishing returns in agriculture and the rate of profit could be brought to light without ambiguities. ... In Marx, on the other hand, the labour theory of value performs the much more vital role of supplying the foundation of the crucial theoretical concepts on which his whole theory is based (*c*, *v*, *s*) and of "revealing" the essence of capitalism behind the "facts"' (Caravale 1991, p 195). On Marx's attempt to surpass the ambiguities of classical thought by establishing a 'homogenous economic space' on the basis of 'embodied labour', pre-existing the market, see Bidet 2009, pp 12–14.

structure of thought that was established in his early writings: immanent, material ground alienated into false, abstract form. Even before any of its specific categories are developed, therefore, the theory is conceived on this basic model.

As Marx imagines it, every society can be understood, in the first place, simply as an indeterminate mass of productive activity. If this amorphous quantity of labour is to be effectively regulated in relation to the sum total of social need, then the overall labouring capacity must be distributed in a rational way among the various branches of production. In principle, there are different ways in which this organisation of the transhistorical necessity of labour and production can be effected, different possible forms of the underlying content.[15] What is crucial for Marx is that these secondary forms must always find their ultimate logic not within themselves but externally, in the primary material ground – the forces of production determine the relations of production. The necessary articulation of social labour is then a function of class, defined in terms of the relation to the means of production. In capitalist society, the class division of the relations of production is characterised by the enforced separation of labour from the means of production and the private ownership of the productive capacity of society by the capitalist class. These class relations fragment the underlying universality of social labour so that its reconstitution as a whole can happen only indirectly and unconsciously, through exchange. Essential to Marx's conception, therefore, is that the central phenomenon of capitalist society, market exchange, does not explain itself. It is in fact only secondary, just an effect of a historically specific set of relations of production. The market

[15] This conception is most succinctly summarised in Marx's famous letter of 11 July 1868 to Dr Kugelmann: 'Every child knows that any nation that stopped working, not for a year, but let us say, just for a few weeks, would perish. And every child knows, too, that the amounts of products corresponding to the differing amounts of needs demand differing and quantitatively determined amounts of society's aggregate labour. It is SELF-EVIDENT that this *necessity* of the *distribution* of social labour in specific proportions is certainly not abolished by the *specific form* of social production; it can only change *its form of manifestation*. Natural laws cannot be abolished at all. The only thing that can change, under historically differing conditions, is the *form* in which those laws assert themselves. And the form in which the proportional distribution of labour asserts itself in a state of society in which the interconnection of social labour expresses itself as the *private exchange* of the individual products of labour, is precisely the *exchange value* of these products' (Marx and Engels 1988, p 68 (emphases in original)). The basic idea here is that of essential content and inessential form: the necessity of the distribution of social labour is common to all societies, and thus unchangeable; all that changes is the way in which this necessity is fulfilled. The task of theory, then, is to reduce the appearances to the essence: 'where science comes in is to show *how* the law of value asserts itself' (Marx and Engels 1988, p 68 (emphasis in original)). This letter is from the year after the publication of the first edition of Volume I of *Capital*, and so can be taken to express Marx's mature conception.

thus results from the organisation of the productive base and is entirely subordinate to the primary world of labour, with no independence of its own. In this way, Marx attempts to root exchange in production, the secondary relations among persons in the primary relation to things. The exchange relation, and with it the value form, is really a production relation appearing in a different, and deceptive, guise. It is an expression of a deeper logic of production, which is itself external to exchange.

In Marx's understanding, classical political economy had already gone a considerable distance in reducing the outer world to the inner by revealing labour to be the universal substance of commodity exchange. The crucial limitation of classical thought, though, was that because it took capitalist relations of production at face value, it was unable to perceive the form as mere form, and thus as inessential:

> Political economy has indeed analysed value and its magnitude, however incompletely, and has uncovered the content concealed within these forms. But it has never once asked the question why this content has assumed that particular form, that is to say, why labour is expressed in value, and why the measurement of labour by its duration is expressed in the magnitude of the value of the product.[16]

Classical thought could not understand the specific value *form* of labour because, as the authentic expression of bourgeois consciousness, it naturalised the class relation. By contrast, the decisive critical accomplishment of the analysis in *Capital* was considered by Marx to be its demonstration that value, the central concept of capital, is merely a transient historical form of a universal labour content. *Capital* is thus conceived on the idea that form and content can be completely separated from each other. Furthermore, this separation is supposed to open up the critical perspective beyond the capitalist mode of production that was necessarily hidden from bourgeois economics: once value is recognised as a false, alienated form of an intrinsic labour content, then that primary material ground can be rescued from its estrangement and freed to exist in its own right, undistorted and immediate. It is in this way that Marx purports to subordinate the dialectic to an encompassing economic, labour-and-production framework: the dialectic of value does indeed result from the generalisation of exchange, but that is itself, in Marx's conception, merely the expression of the underlying relations of production. Inserting the dialectic into the economic conception in a

16 Marx 1990, pp 173–4. As Helmut Reichelt notes, 'this formulation implies that the content, which appears in this form, can also be conceived in separation from its form of appearance' (Reichelt 2005, p 41).

subsidiary position allows Marx to assume that the entire, infinitely ramified, conceptual life of value can, in the end, simply be dismissed by reference to the economistic philosophy of history. The 'value form of labour' is as transitory as the social relations of production that give rise to it. At a certain stage, those relations will no longer serve to develop the forces of production and will instead become fetters upon them. They will then be overthrown by the 'Revolution', allowing the universality of labour finally to emerge from beneath the deceptive veil of value, in the form of the communist *Gesamtarbeiter*.

If the basic character of Marx's theory is to be grasped, it is essential to see that its fixed intention, before anything else, is to demonstrate that the relations between persons are always in fact just alienated forms of the relation to things. At every stage, Marx is determined to show that the movement of theory is always from the inner world to the outer, from production to the market. While no other economic thinker has ever gone so far in developing an objective-dialectical theory of value through the forms of exchange, therefore, equally none has ever insisted so emphatically on exactly the opposite conception: that the entire sphere of exchange must be regarded as simply an illusion, a kind of enchantment or hallucination ('magic and necromancy'[17]) that captivates the credulous bourgeois mind but which can easily be dispelled by reference to the rational materialism of production.[18] What is completely anathema to Marx is that the conceptual forms of capital should be allowed any independence or validity in themselves. To him, they are nothing more than a gigantic web of misperception thrown over the scientific truth of production, in which the freedom and security of the conscious-intentional Individual are grounded. For all that the market appears to be self-animated and to have an uncontrollable life of its own, Marx's conviction is that it can ultimately be revealed to be nothing more than a phantasmagorical expression of the productive base. Marx's notion of economic science, which governs his concept of capital, is thus to demonstrate as a matter of theory that the outer world, what appears on the surface as the movement of the forms of capital in exchange and circulation, is in fact wholly driven by and entirely referable back to the inner world of labour and production: the market results from a historically specific set of relations of production; exchange is exchange of labours; value is a mystified form of labour; money is a commodity; profit and

17 Marx 1990, p 169.

18 No doubt Marx was only able to venture as far as he did in elaborating the dialectic of value because his general economistic theory provided him with the reassurance that, as against the self-evident material reality of Individual production, it was really all just metaphysical hocus-pocus.

interest are forms of 'surplus value'; value is produced in the labour process and merely circulated on the market; accumulation is the appropriation by capitalists of value that is produced by workers; the equalisation of the profit rate is the distribution of labours expended in production; market prices are transformed manifestations of value quantities already determined in production; and so on. It is absolutely fundamental to Marx's idea of capital – what it is, how it works, what its historical meaning and fate are – that the system of exchange should be resolved without remainder into the general economic problematic codified in historical materialism. It must be shown to be a 'mode of production', a historically transient form of the immanent, universal ground of labour. The theory must at every point lead back from exchange, as a secondary and dependent form, to production as primary and originary.

At the deepest level, it is exactly this conception, the very core of Marx's idea of capital, that has been invalidated by the modern theorisation of value. The single most important conclusion definitively established by the revolution in value theory is that the conceptualisation of value must begin not with production but with exchange. This perception is, in fact, the foundation of the entire development of value theory since the 1970s: the rejection of traditional, positivistic Marxism was premised precisely upon the recognition of the conceptual indeterminacy of the orthodox production paradigm and the decisive theoretical importance of the forms of exchange. The first principle of a properly dialectical theory, from which all else follows, is thus that value originates in exchange, without any reference to labour and production. In this way, a fundamental reversal has been effected in the direction of theory, negating Marx's conception at its root: exchange and the market cannot be subordinated to production but must come first. Further, not only has value theory demonstrated that exchange is the primary category, but it has also shown that production follows theoretically from exchange, not the other way around. Production is not assumed at the start but arises as a result of the movement of value in the exchange process, within the elaboration of the form dialectic. Only when value, in seeking to actualise its intrinsic universality, succeeds in grounding itself upon itself, as capital, does production become an apparently primary and self-standing category at all. That is, production is entirely a category of exchange – it only has any conceptual determinacy when it is precisely situated within the circuit of value. Capital, as the self-movement of value, posits production as a moment within its own process. In light of the dialectical theorisation of value, therefore, to assert production as a general category anterior to capital is illegitimate. Although it appears as absolutely self-evident to the modern mind, the supposed necessity of material production, as a primary and irreducible reality, is in fact merely dogmatic and without any properly theoretical justification. As Hegel understood, the dialectic must begin with no presuppositions. That is, nothing can be posited outside the context of mediation; everything must pass through the form of value. The collapse of traditional Marxism was, at a theoretical level, a consequence of the impossibility of adequately explaining exchange and the market from a dogmatically assumed primacy of production. What the theorisation of value that emerged out of that collapse has shown is that it is the opposite movement of theory that is actually correct: production is an effect of exchange, not its ground.

Once it is accepted that value must be theorised from exchange, then it follows that the universal conceptuality of capital can in no way be understood as secondary and dependent, merely a distorted reflection of the material reality of production that is, as it were, given outside and behind. The limitless movement of value through its endlessly multiplying and interlocking circuits is not derivative of a materiality that is external and prior but, on the contrary, has an absolute independence and motive force of its own. Capital is value as sovereign: free, self-determining and autonomous. Correlatively, just as value theory has shown that the conceptualisation of value must begin with exchange rather than production, so it has recognised that it is not labour that is the subject of capitalist society, as traditional Marxism assumed, but value. Value is the active, moving principle of capital, the agential force. The system is formed by the dialectic of Being and Nothing that comes into existence with, and unfolds through, exchange, and the ceaseless movement of value expresses the immanent drive of the objective abstraction to universalise itself. Within the process of self-valorising value, therefore, labour and production have theoretical standing solely as bearers of the abstract value form. By the same token, it is capital, not labour, that is the productive power. It makes no theoretical sense to think of capital in terms of a pre-conceptual labour process the products of which are subsequently put onto the market, and therefore of a movement from a primary, naturalistic sphere of production to a secondary, conceptual sphere of exchange. Production is a moment within the circuit of value and can only be coherently theorised as entirely value formed. The notion that labour, as the creative essence of the human being, produces wealth that is then appropriated by capitalists provides no basis for coherent theory.[19] Instead, the modern theorisation of value has evolved, in its entirety, from the recognition that value is not a substance produced by labour.[20] Indeed, value is not 'produced' at all – it is not something made, which can then be appropriated, or 'accumulated', but a universal form of

[19] So far from being the greatest strength of his thought (as, for example, Scott Meikle (1985) claims), Marx's attempt to combine the Aristotelian–Hegelian tradition with political economy by recasting the notion of essence in 'materialist' terms is thus in fact its primary fallacy, generating irresolvable confusions and contradictions.

[20] There is thus no such thing as the 'subsumption', either 'formal' or 'real', of labour to capital.

validity that brings into being a world of compulsory labour and production. It follows that within a dialectical form theory money cannot be, as Marx supposes, a commodity. That is, production does not precede circulation. There is no general, primary condition of goods being produced and then subsequently exchanged, in a more or less primitive way, out of which process money arises as a universally accepted medium of exchange. Money is not 'set apart' or 'excluded' as one commodity among others, in order to articulate or organise *post facto* a pre-monetary sphere of production. As value theory has gone a considerable distance in demonstrating, the role and meaning of money are completely the reverse of this conception. So far from being derived from a pre-monetary ground of productive activity, money constitutes the conceptual value sphere within which material production becomes a determinate category in the first place. Money is not itself produced, therefore, but is the necessary condition of production.[21] It does not passively represent an underlying non-conceptual, material logic of labour expenditure but is itself the active and dynamic force, determining the world in accordance with the self-reproduction of capital.

In the two-world conception that Marx takes over from classical political economy, theoretical explanation is premised upon a general idea of external determination: the capitalist economy, which exists only in the conceptual forms of value, is to be accounted for by reference to an extrinsic and already given material ground of Individual labour.[22] The theory thus imagines that the reality of capital is not located within the marketplace at all but is to be found somewhere else, somewhere external, in a wholly indeterminate pre-market, pre-monetary, pre-exchange condition, the presumed naturalistic state of direct labour on nature. Accordingly, within the two-world logic, moving from inner to outer, prices are 'the socially contingent form of a conceptually primordial productive act',[23] conceived in terms of labour-value.

[21] Or, as David Levine puts it, money does not *have* value; rather, it *is* value (Levine 1983, p 26). Indeed, money is *absolute* value (Arthur 2022, pp 117–19).

[22] 'Methodologically, determination is identified by classical political economy with reduction to an independently fixed condition. It is this independence which allows the material relations to exert a causal, therefore determining influence over the social relations of exchange. The characteristic project of classical economics is that of establishing the consistency of the substantively economic relations of exchange and distribution with the theoretically primordial relations of the material reproduction of the species' (Levine 1978, pp 2–3). It is precisely this methodological commitment that dialectic, above all, rejects: 'The hallmark of the [dialectical] system's character is the strict immanency of its genesis and development, its freedom from external determination in the constitution of its categories. And as Hegel acknowledges, a claim to such autonomy and immanence can only be supported insofar as the system has in, in some sense, a beginning which is itself devoid of external determination, to wit, a presuppositionless beginning' (Maker 1990, p 28).

[23] Levine 1978, p 5.

The fundamental quantities of the economy are established without reference to any process of mediation and of the interaction of the units of capital, so that profit is taken to be a form of the 'surplus-value' that is already 'fully determined in magnitude by the immediate relation of the owners of the conditions of production to the direct producers'.[24] Once the set of values has been given through labour, the purpose of theory is then to show that the secondary world of exchange corresponds at all points to the primary world of production, that is, that 'prices and profits are fully determined as transformations of value and of the rate of surplus-value'.[25] Throughout, the guiding assumption is that the purpose of theory is to reduce the conceptual to the material, to resolve the constituted space of capital back into a naturalistically conceived condition of production outside and anterior to it. However, the logic of two worlds, in which the 'outer' world of the exchange process is merely an extrinsic reflection of the 'inner' world of material labour and all essential determinations are removed from the former and located in the latter, drastically stunts and distorts the theorisation of capital:

> The full determination of value and surplus-value within the immediate production process leaves for the analysis of circulation, competition, price formation and accumulation only the task of reconciling the 'apparent' and therefore superficial, forms with an already fully developed essence. This idea has the most profound implications for the conception of economic life. It excludes any substantive market determination of capitalist expansion by making the constitution of capital in the form of a system of interacting particular units inessential to the deduction of the laws of economic development. In all respects the conception of the economy as a living totality, determined within its own process of self-development, dissipates into a wholly abstract conception of the immediate production process viewed as a material interchange.[26]

---

24 Levine 1978, p 5.

25 Levine 1978, p 5.

26 Levine 1978, pp 5–6. Levine comes closer to recognising this fundamental inadequacy of Marx's theory – that the basic conception radically falsifies the very nature of capital – than any other commentator. Cf. his concluding remarks on the fallaciousness of Marx's argument for commodity money: 'For Marx, the commodity-money idea expresses the way in which the multiplication of need and growth of social wealth are made subordinate to a process of material circulation governed by allocative principles involving the distribution of labor and surplus-labor. In the end, Marx fails to overcome the classical theory of money because he fails to fully incorporate the dynamic, developmental quality of market relations into his conception of modern economy' (Levine 1983, pp 28–9). That is, Marx drastically misunderstands the form of freedom in capital, and thus also the form of unfreedom.

The two-world idea upon which the economic problematic is based, the assumption that 'the system of capital as a whole is the redetermination of what is already determined', denies the specific conceptuality of value and so precludes the proper comprehension of the reality of capital as an infinitely flexible, infinitely complex, self-moving process.[27] Although it does not think of itself in this way, the project of modern value theory, the development of a dialectical concept of capital, can only be properly understood as the concerted effort to liberate theory from the profound misrecognition of the nature of capital that governs Marx's conception. The theoretical structure of capital – the categories of value and profit, the dynamics of competition and accumulation, and the dialectics of universal and particular, abstract and concrete, through which the self-development of the system works – cannot be coherently comprehended on the assumption that capital is in all essentials determined wholly outside itself, in a putative natural-material space anterior to exchange. Rather, only when the two-world, reflection logic that is the foundation of Marx's theory is entirely abandoned, and capital is understood not as the deceptive appearance of a pre-given condition of production but as itself autonomous, self-determining and self-moving – that is, as dialectical – can a coherent theoretical account begin to be developed.[28]

A delirium of capital

Marx's concept of capital is, in essence, a radicalisation of the classical problematic. Consequently, in trying to make real the inner logic of the classical mode of explanation by compelling it beyond its merely 'bourgeois' limits, Marx substantially increases the demands on theory that classical thought was itself already unable to satisfy. For the drastic separation of form

---

[27] Levine 1998a, p 25.

[28] As David Levine correctly perceives, it was Marx's profoundly confused attempt to combine dialectic with political economy that prevented him from developing any coherent conception of method: 'The presumption has been that Marx employed his own distinctive method, a presumption fuelled by Marx's claims about his work, in particular his claim to have put Hegel on his head. … I question this presumption. I argue that, rather than having his own method, Marx combined two methods, each the antithesis of the other. The first method is associated with the political economy of Marx's period, the second with German philosophy, especially that of Hegel. … The method associated with political economy seeks to understand economic relations as manifestations of external determination, particularly in nature. The method associated with Hegel seeks to understand economic relations within a larger whole or system that gives them an internal (in this sense systematic) determination. More broadly, then, the two streams, whose confluence some imagine Marx to be, actually flow in opposite directions. One finds determination in externally given presuppositions, the other in a system developed without such presuppositions' (Levine 1998a, pp 16–17).

and content to hold, Marx has to substantiate the content, the transhistorical, pre-conceptual ground of labour and production, as conceivable in itself, in distinction from any of its forms. He then has to derive value from this ground, so that capital is indeed shown to be just a particular form of the universal content. Once the logic of the dialectical theorisation of capital through the forms of exchange is accepted in its proper rigour, though, it becomes obvious that not only does Marx not succeed in deriving value from labour but that any such derivation is impossible. The exchange form as such in no way implies any kind of labour content. Rather, at the beginning of *Capital*, Marx simply assumes the entire economic context, so that the investigation of the exchange system is presented, apparently self-evidently, in terms of the organisation of a given mass of labour. The consequence, disastrous for theory, is that the question of value is then posed as that of the equalisation of labours. Within this context, Marx makes bold claims for his theoretical account of exchange and the value form, purporting to have surpassed not merely classical political economy but Aristotle himself. However, no genetic derivation of value from labour is actually achieved. Instead, Marx's argument relies upon a murky and incoherent notion of 'embodied labour': general human labour is supposedly objectified, or 'crystallised', within the product and it is this mysterious labour substance that then becomes manifest in the abstract form of value through the exchange process.[29] There is in Marx's account no proper derivation of this generality, which somehow already exists within the commodity simply by virtue of the expenditure of labour.[30] The argument thus recedes into ineliminable obscurity precisely at the point where the greatest clarity is required – at the dividing line, where the two paradigms are supposed to come together. The

---

[29] While its rejection as 'Ricardian' has been central to modern value theory, 'embodied labour' is what in fact enables Marx to situate the dialectical form theory within the economistic framework: where value is the form of appearance of a pre-existing labour content, the theory still moves from inner to outer. If the notion of embodied labour is abandoned altogether, therefore, that movement becomes impossible and the basic idea of the theory collapses. Those Marxist value theorists who continue to hold on to some version of embodied labour (for example, Patrick Murray and Riccardo Bellofiore) are thus in a way right – or, at least, more consistent – in being wrong: Marxism cannot do without such a conception.

[30] 'The social unity of labour, its "general character", that which is "common" to all productive functions, is intrinsic to the products of labour. … According to Marx, generality exists "invisibly" in the commodity in the form of an immediate unity between use-value and value. It exists thus as the "ghostlike objectivity of value", in which "all sensuous aspects are eliminated". This unity is, as it were, posited for itself when the products of labour are equalized in the exchange process and when it finally is constituted in the form of money. The entire further exposition in *Capital* rests on this conception of value' (Reichelt 2005, p 42).

breakdown of the theory at this crucial juncture is, in effect, Marx's admission that he is unable to carry the logic of capitalist thought beyond itself. In the same way that classical political economy simply presupposed the objective abstraction of value, and classical epistemology presumed the existence of the mind that cognises the world through concepts, so Marx ultimately has to take the conceptuality of value as given and does not achieve any genetic explanation. Since the form is not developed from the content, the content cannot be taken as underlying the form. In the end, for Marx, as for economic thought generally, the abstract categories of capital remain ideal, transcendent being that is simply given and inexplicable. Indeed, what Marx's argument about value and embodied labour really serves to demonstrate is that the 'materialist', labour and production, paradigm can never attain theoretical consistency because it necessarily depends upon an objective ideality for which it is unable to account and so must simply assume.[31]

Where Marx tries to go beyond classical thought by deriving form from content, he only succeeds in more thoroughly demonstrating the impossibility of the economic problematic to which he was so fervently committed. The same is true of his effort to establish the content in separation from the form through the category of 'social labour'. Marx's idea is that exchange relations follow from production relations. Classical political economy tended to equate capital directly with nature because, so Marx claimed, it could not see the relations of production of capital as one, historically specific, form of the underlying generality of social labour – that is, of the universal relation to things. This is how Marx criticised the reductionism of classical theory and purported to historicise it:

> What distinguishes the Marxian project is the attempt to constitute production as the materializing process of a social relation. Marx attempts to complete the classical theory by establishing the social determination of production as the logical basis for the material determination of commodity exchange.[32]

While this procedure has been widely acclaimed for its supposed debunking of bourgeois naturalism, it is, in truth, spurious. In order to substantiate his conception, Marx has to establish a position between two extremes: on the one hand, because he wants something beyond capital, he cannot follow classical theory in equating capital directly with nature; but on the other, as labour is supposed to be the universal content of which capital is an inessential form, he cannot allow any of the determinations of capital

[31] This is the mysticism of the economic, which only dialectic can dispel.

[32] Levine 1978, p 6.

to enter into the constitution of labour as the social substance. Acceding to either of these alternatives would implicate form and content in each other again and so invalidate both Marx's concept of capital and his idea of critique. Marx therefore tries to outdo the classical conception by interposing a third category, 'social labour', between capital and nature: the economic relations of capital are consequent upon the social relations of production. Labour and production are thus declared to be already social in themselves, prior to the actual sociality of the market. However, in attempting to force together the two sides of the economic problematic in this way, Marx is left with nothing but a vacuous non-concept:

> What, then, accounts for that social determination of production which provides the logical basis for the social determination of the forms of economic interaction? On this question, Marx is effectively silent. Yet silence on this question speaks more loudly than all protestations regarding the social relations of production, the sequence of 'modes of production,' and the material conditions of social life. After a century of Marxian theory, the idea of social production, once shorn of that rich content provided for it by Marx in the specification of *capitalist* production, remains an empty shell. That this conception remains deficient is the result not of a failure of Marx's followers to seek out a concrete content for the idea of social production made independent of its bourgeois 'form,' but of their failure to discover any positive quality which continues to adhere to the idea of labor when its specification to capital is left aside. Yet, only so long as it is possible to remove the 'bourgeois form of labor' without obliterating altogether the idea of labor as a social relation, can the laboring which works for capital be considered a form of labor.[33]

Because generalised exchange is supposed to be grounded in social labour, the determination of the sociality of labour cannot make reference to exchange – labour has to be immediately social as such, so that exchange may be just one particular form of this inherent sociality. But, as David Levine points out, 'it is precisely this *a priori* constitution of labor as a social relation which deprives social labor of any determinable content.'[34] In the absence of exchange, Marx is left without anything that would substantiate labour

33 Levine 1978, pp 7–8 (emphasis in original). Relatedly, Jacques Bidet observes of the question-begging nature of Marx's discourse on socialism, as the immediate and undistorted manifestation of social labour, that 'what disappear without being replaced are the explanatory determinations of socialisation, as Marx expounded these apropos capitalism' (Bidet 2009, p 286).

34 Levine 1978, p 8.

as the general social element and so justify the notion of social labour as the ground of capital. What Marx wants to be the content that undergirds his whole theoretical structure is thus 'devoid of content', nothing more than 'the mere abstract assertion of the sociality of labour'.[35] 'Social labour' and 'relations of production' only in fact arise as categories within the world of generalised exchange, but for Marx to admit that direction of causation would be to contradict the basic logic of his theory. As with embodied labour, in trying to radicalise the economic problematic by establishing the inner world of labour and production as universal content and the outer world of capital as inessential form, Marx can only posit empty pseudo-categories. The conceptual basis of the attempt to go beyond the classical project by wholly separating content from form and deriving the latter from the former lacks all determinacy. The imagined content cannot be substantiated as the ground of the actual forms.

The dialectical theorisation of value entirely negates the two-world logic that undergirds Marx's conception of capital. What the critique of the categories through which Marx tried to surpass classical theory reveals is that not only is it impossible to move theoretically from inner to outer, but that the inner itself cannot be established in its own right at all. That is, the two-world structure, and the representational paradigm that follows from it, is not just theoretically unworkable and bad – it is illusory. Only when it is recognised that Marx is wholly taken in by this illusion, that it expresses the deepest longing of his thought and that his entire theory is constructed around it, is it possible to understand both the enormous suggestive power of his concept of capital and its radical falsity. Economic theory as such is constituted through the two-world idea, the radical separation of form and content, because it is the necessary mode of experience of the economic subject. In its sovereign freedom, that subject understands itself as in primary relation with things. All mediation is then secondary and dependent, the nominalistic product of the agency of Individuals. The second world should thus follow from the first as a simple reflection: the concept is a representation of the object and value is an expression of Individual labour (or, in neoclassical theory, Individual preference). The working out of the metaphysical form of the modern subject culminated, first, in the Kantian reformulation of the reflection problematic around the idea of the transcendental, and then the *Aufhebung* of the monadological condition altogether in the Hegelian dialectic. In lifting the epistemological problematic out of itself, Hegel demonstrated that the Individual's apparently self-evident structure of

[35] Levine 1978, p 8. Levine goes on: 'This indeterminacy is fully exposed when the supposedly social labor is described concretely either as the immediate natural relation of man to nature ("work"), or as the purely subjective relation of individual purposive activity'.

experience is in fact completely internal to the dialectic – it is the way in which the dialectic appears when the division of inside and outside is assumed by the understanding as the necessary ground of experience. In this way, subjective idealism became objective idealism. The Individual cannot be coherently theorised wholly from within its own borders but necessarily refers beyond itself to the infinite conceptuality of the dialectic; correlatively, the unlimitedness of the dialectic does not appear directly but only as mediated through the sharply bounded Individual. The immediacy upon which the two-world, reflection logic is based is already, in itself, thoroughly mediated, while the universal mediation of the dialectic appears as unmediated immediacy, the direct relation to things.

Although he is evidently situated within this theoretical context, Marx does not follow through the logic of reflection to a dialectical theory of capital because he is a fanatic of the Individual. From the beginning, his thought is fixated on a single desire: that the Individual be liberated completely so that it may encompass the entire world, leaving nothing outside. Instead of reflecting upon the division that structures the modern subject's mode of experience, therefore, Marx takes it at face value. The freedom of the Individual is expressed in its primary relation to things. Because that relation comes first, it has for Marx the status of a metaphysical truth: the relation to things, the inner world of labour and production, is the ground of Being. This truth exists in a practical, bodily way. It is manifested through the active and instrumental exertion of the limbs that produces objects of utility, not through the reflective and exploratory effort of the mind that produces concepts. Hence, Marx fetishises labour and loathes mediation. He has a dread fear of the abstract and conceptual, a sneering contempt for thinking and the mind as such.[36] Practical reason is exalted as the origin of all that is real, while theoretical reason is derided as the source only of illusions. In the same way that Marx cannot allow exchange any freedom in relation to production, so he cannot permit thought to be determined by anything other than practice. Consciousness must derive from being.[37] The danger that abstraction represents is that in separating the Individual from the reality of practical activity and interposing itself between subject and object, it splits

[36] 'A question of the head, as always according to Marx, a question of the head, or the cap- and the spirit', observes Jacques Derrida in his reading of the *18th Brumaire* (Derrida 1994, p 139). Derrida's is, of course, the most influential discussion of the rhetoric of ghosts and spectrality, conjuring and exorcism, fear and desire, that pervades Marx's writings in his longing to be done with mediation – with the head – altogether, so that the object may finally be grasped in its purely material immediacy.

[37] Cf. Marshall Sahlin's analysis of Marx's purported 'genealogy of conceptual thought', where his doctrinal practicism drives him into absurdity (Sahlins 1976, pp 139–47; see also Iacono 2016, pp 143–50).

apart the relation to things, distorting what should be direct and transparent.[38] The idea of the fetish-character of the commodity – that the object, which is in-itself obvious and without mystery, is metamorphosed into something uncanny and spectral only when it enters into the exchange process – really bespeaks Marx's enlightened terror at the uncontrollable play of simulacra conjured up by universal exchange. To Marx, for whom the Individual is absolute, mediation always signifies an external and illegitimate limitation on the innate freedom of the subject. Capital, as universal mediation, is therefore both the supreme mystification of the rational relation to things and the ultimate form of despotism, in which Individuals are subordinated to an abstract, conceptual power.

The illogicality that destroys Marx's theory of capital is thus built right into its foundations. The development of the reflection problematic within modern philosophy demonstrated that the Individual and its structure of experience is in fact just the appearance form of the dialectic. However, in his infatuation with the sovereign subject, Marx takes the Individual as ultimate and elevates its primary experience, the direct relation to things, into a metaphysical ground. He then conceives all forms of mediation as alienations of the original immediacy of labour and production. This is the basic absurdity: capital is to be grounded in its own form of appearance. What Marx takes to be altogether outside is in fact wholly within, the first world completely internal to the second. The entire critical theory of capital is constructed on this fundamental incoherence, which is the original source of all of the expositional problems and theoretical aporias that modern value theory has painstakingly revealed. Economic theory as such is back-to-front in that it must attempt to explain capital on the basis of the Individual. By elevating the economic problematic into a metaphysics and philosophy of history, though, Marx drastically magnifies this intrinsic theoretical deformation.[39] The contradictions of economic theory revolve around the division between the first world and the second, between the Individual and the objective system of value. Marx surely had some awareness of this, as his critiques of classical political economy demonstrate, but his solution – splitting content and form apart completely and then relating

38 Marx's fanatical affirmation of the Individual is the source of his extraordinary epistemological naivety regarding so-called use value (Baudrillard 1981, Chapter 7; Agamben 1993, p 48; Derrida 2004, p 188; Bidet 2009, pp 279–81). To his way of thinking, in its properly utilitarian existence the object is transparent and immediate, presenting itself just as it really is, without any subjective addition or mediation; through exchange, however, what is naturally immediate and self-evident is distorted into the indirect and artificial.

39 Or, to put it in a different way, Marx's theory always remains very definitely an economic theory and never properly becomes a theory of capital.

them to each other as the essential to the inessential – only intensifies those contradictions.[40] The assurance that licenses Marx to discount the whole conceptual world of capital as really just so much fantastical misperception arises from his intense belief in the self-evidence of the primary relation to things. Once, however, it is shown that that immediacy is wholly mediated, that the economic is the appearance of the dialectic, then the tables are turned: it is actually Marx's clear-headed, rationalistic materialism that is thoroughly mystified and incapable of comprehending itself. Precisely in the certainty that he has escaped, he is in fact all the more thoroughly entrapped. Marx's favourite term for denouncing the entire sphere of mediation and conceptuality is 'inversion': again and again, in one text after another, with the pounding insistence so characteristic of his rhetorical style when theory slides into dogma, he declares that the universal ground has been 'inverted' into a limited, abstract and alienated form.[41] This charge should really be turned against Marx himself. The entirely conceptual reality of capital is inverted by him into the specious concreteness of the economic paradigm transfigured into metaphysics. The solid ground of labour and production that so infatuates Marx is nothing more than a hallucinatory image cast by the dialectic of value.

The recognition that Marx's theory is altogether back-to-front transforms the meaning of his materialism. The explanatory logic of historical materialism implies a series of theoretical generalities sitting behind the categories particular to any historically specific mode of production and establishing the universal condition of economic life as such.[42] While it was evidently entailed by his concept of capital, Marx, as Jacques Bidet notes, was in fact extremely reluctant to address this issue directly and to set it out with any degree of clarity and systematic thoroughness:

> It is only tangentially that he ever broaches it. This is the case with the labour process in general, which is introduced only in the interest of understanding, by way of antithesis, the process of capitalist production.

---

40 Indeed, there is a sense in which Marx's conception of capital is more profoundly mistaken than any other economic theory precisely because of the extremity of his commitment to the economic. The confusions of classical theory in a way come closer to the truth than the doctrinaire pronouncements of Marx, as it is exactly those equivocations that, when followed through, open out into the dialectical transcendence of the economic problematic. Marx's certainties, by contrast, lead only into the dead-end of the economic made absolute.

41 The trope of an 'inverted world' (*verkehrte Welt*) is drawn from Hegel (Hegel and Schelling 2000, p 283; Hegel 2018, pp 95–7/¶¶157–60)).

42 Respectively, 'the general categories of economics', 'the categories of the labour process in general' and 'the categories of the mode of production in general' (Bidet 2009, p 274).

> And the same goes for the general categories of economics, which are never again presented for their own sake [after the aborted attempt in the 1857 'Introduction' to the *Grundrisse*].[43]

Marx's evident antipathy to explicating this basic ground of his theory in itself suggests the deep illogicality. For the first world, apparently so obvious, so solid and self-evident, is in fact forever elusive and intangible – always tantalisingly there, or so it seems, yet always just out of reach. Marx generally hesitates to come too close, preferring to preserve the illusion by allowing it to shimmer suggestively in the middle distance.[44] When he does try to approach it, though, and take it in his hands, it evaporates. An account of 'labour in general' is offered by Marx only at one point in his argument, 'just before the exposition of surplus-value, and in order to show the difference between capitalist production and production in general'.[45] This passage was worked through three times (in the *Grundrisse*, the *1861–63 Manuscripts*, and Volume I of *Capital*), and in his analysis of the different versions Jacques Bidet precisely demonstrates the logical impossibility by which Marx is confounded as soon as he tries to say anything substantive about the primary material world behind the secondary conceptual world: 'from the *Grundrisse* onwards, Marx experiences a difficulty in formulating an exposition of "labour in general" that does not involve the specific determinations of what *Capital* subsequently calls "abstract labour"'.[46] That is, Marx is unable to present the generalities of economic life, supposedly existent across history beneath all particular systems of mediation, other than through the categories of capital. The attempt to describe the first world, the world behind capital, always finds itself simply repeating capital.

While Bidet approaches this central contradiction in Marx's thought from the direction of social theory, Helmut Reichelt identifies the same problem in Marx's attempt to refunction the philosophical categories of essence and appearance:

> Despite all the differences between Marx's and Feuerbach's conceptions of materialism, they agree on one thing: their attempts to comprehend reality as an inversion, as an inverted form of human or social relations, rests [*sic*] on the assumption that the essence of that reality,

43 Bidet 2009, p 275.

44 'False clarity is only another name for myth. Myth was always obscure and luminous at once. It has always been distinguished by its familiarity and its exemption from the work of concepts' (Horkheimer and Adorno 2002, p xvii).

45 Bidet 2009, p 276.

46 Bidet 2009, p 277.

> the non-inverted unity, can be conceived independently of its form of appearance.[47]

This is the logic of Marx's critique of 'bourgeois' thought generally, that it mistakes the 'inverted' forms of the material-practical essence for the truth. 'How', though, Reichelt asks, 'can this human reality, a reality of human-social reason, be conceived?'[48] What would the essence itself, divested of its distorting forms of appearance, actually look like? In posing the question, Reichelt touches directly upon the deep confusion in Marx that Bidet likewise encountered: whenever he tries to portray the essence as such, in abstraction from its mere appearance as capital, 'Marx is only able to offer a "mirror image" whose central elements are derived from autonomized (*verselbständigte*) social reality, in which social unity exists only in inverted form'.[49] The essence is in fact completely dependent upon the appearance that it is supposed to precede. The first world can be imagined at all only in terms of the second – it is, as it were, an inverted form of the inverted form. Finally, Marshall Sahlins, from yet another perspective, that of cultural anthropology, reaches what is effectively the same insight at the culmination of his discussion of Marx's materialist reason:

> I am making a very large claim: that the species to which Marx's 'species-being' belongs is *Homo economicus*. It was, however, a special variety. Marx's vision of the human condition in the *Paris Manuscripts* seems rather a spiritualized 'market mentality,' combining human needs (of self-realization), natural scarcities (of objective means), and man's progressive liberation from this dismal condition by purposive action – his progressive enrichment through increasingly effective exercise of his appropriative powers and interchange with other men. Even the 'alienation' of the early phases of this career involves that dualist opposition of man and society characteristic of a bourgeois functionalism.[50]

Here, again, is the perception that the general condition, which in Marx's idea should underlie capital, is in fact itself just a version of capital – 'spiritualized', as Sahlins puts it. Always it turns out that what Marx is fascinated by, the

47 Reichelt 2005, p 36.
48 Reichelt 2005, p 35.
49 Reichelt 2005, p 35. Discussing the *1844 Manuscripts*, Reichelt reiterates the point: 'Marx seeks here, too, to describe essence in abstraction from its inverted form of existence. Yet, here too, Marx is only able to develop a mirror image of what emancipated Man, emancipated from his alienated, inverted world, might mean' (Reichelt 2005, p 38).
50 Sahlins 1976, p 161.

idea of a universal, untrammelled condition of the immediate relation to things, cannot be articulated for itself but only as a reflection, or copy, of what it is supposed to precede.

At these moments the truth of Marx's materialism is all but recognised: that it is simply the world of capital in the absence of capital. While Bidet, Reichelt and Sahlins register this at a phenomenal level, it is theoretically explained by the dialectical critique of the economic. Universal mediation presents itself as universal immediacy. What appears to be wholly non-conceptual is completely conceptualised – indeed, it appears as non-conceptual precisely *because* it is completely conceptualised. The condition that is presumed to underlie the abstract forms of value only exists, and can only be articulated, through capital because it is itself nothing but capital as it is immediately apprehended by the sovereign Individual. That the non-conceptual materiality of labour and production is no more than a mirror image of the universal conceptuality of generalised exchange is clearly apparent in the illogicality involved in the construction of the notion of commodity money:

> The commodity-money idea embodies a contradiction which makes itself felt in the derivation of money: first, posit a system of commodity circulation which could only exist and be made intelligible as a monetary economy. Then, remove the money, which is the life-blood of the system. Finally, deduce the function of money from the resulting disabilities in the commodity circulation. This method distorts the theoretical account of the money relation, since it deduces money from artificially induced failings of a monetary economy which has lost its money.[51]

The material immediacy, the Individual in its primary relation to things, is really the completely monetary world with the money removed – capital without capital. This is why the attempt to describe it can only take the form of a mirror image, all the elements of which are drawn from the world of capital. As a fanatic of the Individual, no one is so enthralled by this image, so completely absorbed by the semblance of immediacy that arises from deep within the experience of universal mediation, as Marx. For all his passionate conviction of its truth, however, Marx finds it impossible to say anything substantive about the supposedly primary materiality. As Jacques Bidet recognised, it appears in his work only indirectly, by way of antithesis to capital. Marx's materialism thus demonstrates its own impossibility: it is an illusion of the universal conceptuality that is its condition. This falseness

[51] Levine 1983, p 21. This is, *in nuce*, the difference between dialectic and reflection philosophy.

is in fact already evident in the early writings, the basic idea of which is always the same: the repeated denunciation of the abstract forms of modernity (speculative philosophy, the state, religion, private property and so on) as inversions and alienations of the practical-material activity of Individuals, what Marx designates the '*real*'. The word is emphasised over and over again, as if Marx were determined to compel the immediate, non-conceptual world into existence by sheer force of will. However, as so often, the excess of his rhetoric betrays him: the 'real' is really the unreal. Throughout these texts what is imagined to be most solid and indisputable is in fact never more than a shadow, entirely abstract and without content. Nothing substantive is, or can be, said about the 'real' in its own right. In fact, the only things that are actually *there* are the conceptual forms that Marx holds to be mere mystifications – they are what is really real, and there is no determinacy without them.

The consistent pattern of Marx's thought is thus that the illusion of the material is taken to be real, while the reality of the conceptual is taken to be illusory. The fullest expression of this logic of inversion is the 'materialist conception of history' itself. A universal ground of labour and production, which remains wholly abstract and indeterminate, is posited as the underlying reality of history, and the actual historical forms through which this material substance supposedly manifests itself are held to be no more than transient and inessential. Just as epistemology is the dialectic without the dialectic, and the economic is capital without capital, so the materialist conception of history is Idealism without the Idea, the mirror image of the Hegelian philosophy of history. From within the universal conceptuality of capital, history appears to the Individual as an essentially material process: when the objective Concept is removed, the immediate relation to things, the primacy of the 'forces of production', becomes the ground and the dialectical unfolding of the Concept is naturalised into the inexorable increase of productive capacity.[52] Hence, Marx's conception of history is thoroughly idealist in form – an objective and impersonal subject or 'essence', progress and development through stages, teleology towards an absolute in which the freedom and universality of the human subject are realised – but with a spuriously material content. However, where for Hegel, the progress of spirit is driven by dialectical contradiction, in Marx the class divided relations of production must always be external to the productive forces. Consequently, his theory of history lacks any proper motive force, relying instead on a mysticism of the material in the irresistible, and apparently self-generating and

52 It has long been recognised that historical materialism is really just a radicalisation of the modern socio-economic, conception of history, which originated in the French and Scottish Enlightenments (Pascal 1938; Meek 1967, pp 34–50; Meek 1976; Meek 1977, Chapter 2).

self-expanding, development of the forces of production. As always in Marx, there is no genetic derivation of form from content. Rather, the conceptual is collapsed directly into the material: labour creates value through its mere expenditure and the productive forces engender history spontaneously and autogenously from out of themselves. Just as economic thought presupposes the objective ideality of value, therefore, so the materialist conception of history rests upon the idealist metaphysics of the forces of production.[53]

The material ground from which Marx tries to derive capital is in fact nothing but capital considered 'as if it were dissolved'.[54] The figure that results from this dissolution is always the modern subject, the sovereign Individual, whose experiential form is codified in the epistemological problematic. What is characteristic of Marx is the extremity of his attempt to refashion that problematic through the drastic division of content and form, the elevation of the material to absolute truth, and the derogation of the conceptual as alienation. In this way, Marx sought to realise the deepest dream of the modern subject: to be itself the whole. This is the most imperative desire of his thought – truly a kind of spell by which it is enraptured right from the start and that drives it ever onwards, with monomaniacal intensity, in pursuit of the illusion of the absolutely real. The power of Marx's thought is the power of that illusion in modernity, the almost tangible image that capital projects from within itself of a condition beyond itself, that of the radically emancipated Individual who is identical to the whole. In the *German Ideology*, Marx and Engels famously write that through the capitalist division of labour the Individual is confined to a limited sphere of activity: 'he is a hunter, a fisherman, a shepherd, or a critical critic, and must remain so

[53] '[Marx] attributes a simply absolute potential to the productive energies of human beings and their extension in technology. Even without great interpretative powers it is possible to discern in this the idea of the creative spirit, and ultimately Kant's "original apperception". Thus this vast metaphysical pathos, this speculative pathos about the forces of production, expects that in a manner never properly explained, but one in which something like the metaphysical substantiality of these productive forces is presupposed, the latter would assert themselves victoriously in the conflict between the forces of production and the relations of production. … This metaphysics of the forces of production is reminiscent of the Hegelian World Spirit' (Adorno 2008, p 96). 'When Marx, starting with the 1844 *Economic and Philosophical Manuscripts*, thinks the being of man as praxis, and praxis as the self-production of man, he is after all secularizing the theological idea of the being of creatures as divine operation. After having conceived of being as praxis, if we take God away and put man in his place, we will consequently obtain the result that the essence of man is nothing other than praxis through which he incessantly produces himself' (Agamben 2011a, p 91).

[54] '*Tanquam dissoluta consideretur*': the phrase comes from the 'Preface' to Hobbes' *De Cive*: 'to make a more curious search into the rights of States, and duties of Subjects, it is necessary … they be so considered, as if they were dissolved' (Hobbes 1998, p 32). See Agamben 1998, pp 35–8 and 109.

if he does not want to lose his means of livelihood'.[55] By contrast, in the liberated condition, when the logic of division has been magically spirited away, the Individual is released from any form of limitation: he 'can hunt in the morning, fish in the afternoon, rear cattle in the evening, criticise after dinner ... without ever becoming hunter, fisherman, shepherd or critic'.[56] With the disappearance of capital, the Individual becomes immediately universal – each one is suddenly the entire society in himself. Likewise, in his discussion of the 'fetish-character of the commodity', Marx contrasts the Individual, Robinson Crusoe on his island, with the unrestricted whole, 'the association of free men, working with the means of production held in common'.[57] As Marx conceives it, Robinson apprehends himself as the universality of society, the totality of the social division of labour, in microcosm: 'Despite the diversity of his productive functions, he knows that they are only different forms of activity of one and the same Robinson, hence only different modes of labour'.[58] Correlatively, the association of free producers is nothing but the Individual, Robinson, writ large: 'All the characteristics of Robinson's labour are repeated here, but with the difference that they are social instead of individual'.[59] Just as Robinson was the whole contained within the Individual, therefore, so the imagined free society is the Individual become the whole.[60]

Here the ultimate sense of Marx's concept of capital at last becomes clear: the absolute freedom of the modern Individual, the complete negation by the conscious-intentional subject of any externality, anything at all outside itself, that would constrain or impinge upon its sovereignty.[61] History comes

---

55 Marx and Engels 1968, p 45.

56 Marx and Engels 1968, p 45.

57 Marx 1990, p 171.

58 Marx 1990, p 169. This leads Marx to assert that Robinson's totally monadological condition contains 'all the essential determinants of value' (Marx 1990, p 170), a claim that by itself demonstrates his profoundly undialectical notion of value. There can be no value where there is no exchange.

59 Marx 1990, p 171.

60 Marx's critique of the modern, abstract Individual is thus just as spurious as his purported debunking of classical naturalism, and for the same reason. While he pours scorn on the 'Robinsonades' of classical economic thought, what he objects to is not the figure of the Individual as such but only its supposed limitation to a restricted 'bourgeois' form, because for him the Individual is really the universal.

61 In the properly immanent condition, 'there is *no autonomization* (*Verselbständigung*), that is, there is nothing that abstracts from the individuals, as if it were a thing apart' (Reichelt 2005, p 34 (emphasis in original)). Cf. the claim in the *German Ideology*: 'The reality, which communism is creating, is precisely the true basis for rendering it impossible that anything should exist independently of individuals, insofar as reality is only a product of the preceding intercourse of individuals themselves' (Marx and Engels 1968, p 88). Likewise, Dumont notes that Marx flatly refuses the complex mediation of individual and

to an end when all alienation – all separation and exteriority – has been revoked and the world is wholly internalised to the universal Individual, whose productive activity, its primary relation to things, finally attains immediate self-evidence:

> The point is *the subsuming of the system's nonintentional processes* under the category of the subject's intentional acting. When this act of subsuming is set in *absolute* and *linear* terms, it ceases to be related to the system's historicity and contradictions and becomes a kind of 'egomorphism.' That is to say, it transmutes into the reduction of social relationships – of the relationship with *others* – to the level of the ego and to the way the ego imagines its social supremacy over nature: an ensemble of many egos, who have the same intentions and the same conscience. Finally free of the 'disturbances' of the social system they live in, they can devote themselves to the relationship with nature, within whose practical and inert horizon they can locate the *Other*. Therefore, the systematic and prevailing relationship that comes to the fore is that between many egos and nature, even though this is the consequence of the abolition of the individuals as *others*: the systematicity of unintentional social processes disappears when faced with the fact that the subject's intentional acting has become a delirium of the self. In this way the many egos are, in reality, only one; the individuals are not social because there is only one individual who multiplies himself, as if in magic mirrors. This individual pushes to the limit the bourgeois world's hidden desire: to find oneself alone face to face with the object, face to face with his *own* object, in relation to which the others are either a tool or a disturbance to be eliminated. This desire transcends history in the same way the idea of an absolute degree of intentional action with a zero degree of unintentional processes does. There is no difference between these many egos, which establish a transparent relationship with nature outside history, and President Schreber's delusion regarding the end of the world. Both have eliminated *others* so as to keep the self stable.[62]

This is 'communism' – the world of capital with the entire structure of reflection, all of the separations and divisions that actually constitute the dialectic, removed. The mirror image of universal mediation is total

whole within modernity, simply assuming that they can be made directly identical: 'For Marx, the divorce between the two aspects is merely a pathological social fact. After acknowledging it one should not construe it in thought … but just destroy it' (Dumont 1977, p 125).

62 Iacono 2016, pp 134–5 (emphases in original).

immediacy, the direct unification of subject and object, inside and outside, individual and whole.[63] When capital is imagined as if it were dissolved, the absolute irrationality of the dialectical process of self-valorising value becomes the absolute rationality of the sovereign subject – the market is replaced by the Plan. The glorification of the immediate relation to things, by which the Individual fantasises its own omnipotence, is really the omnipotence of capital in the absence of capital. What Marx's intense identification with the economic paradigm, the very hallmark of his materialism, actually signifies, therefore, is his extreme exaltation of the modern subject. The vision beyond capital of a world of pure, immediate activity – absolute production – is nothing but a delirium of capital.

[63] For this reason, as Roberto Finelli perceives, Marx's attempts to criticise the forms of capitalist modernity on the basis of the 'real' result only in a 'fusional and symbiotic communism' that presumes the 'immediate unity of the individual and the universal' (Finelli 2016, pp 251 and 261).

7

The Concept of Capital: Origins of the Dialectic

Exchange and the subject

In Marx, the phantasmagoria of the economic is not only taken literally but heightened into a metaphysics and philosophy of history. Accordingly, if theory is to dispel this illusion, then Marx's conception of capital has to be rejected in all of its elements. To begin with, capital is not a 'mode of production'. This is so for the simple reason that there are no such things as modes of production. Even before the development of modern value theory, the critique of anthropological Marxism had shown that the supple reality of 'primitive' life is absurdly mangled by being forced into the Procrustean bed of economic materialism.[1] So far from being the necessary and universal foundation of human existence from which all else follows, in these pre-societies production cannot even be identified as a determinate category at all. By the same token, at the opposite end of the historical process, the collapse of 'actually existing Communism' conclusively demonstrated that if there is to be any form of life beyond capital, it will not be reached by beginning from production. Capital cannot be superseded through the reorganisation of social production because 'production' only ever repeats capital in perverted form. Further, not only does it distort the past and foreclose the future, but production also falsifies the present: the revolution in value theory was premised on the perception that the very society that posits production as a universal ground of explanation cannot itself be explained on that basis. With the invalidation of production as a foundational category, the notions of the forces and relations of production also fall away. There is no irreducible material-economic necessity that develops through successive historical forms. Rather, the fundamental relation of capital is the exchange

[1] Baudrillard 1975; Sahlins 1976.

relation and the infinite productivity of the modern world is driven by the endless process of the self-valorisation of value.

The concomitant of the displacement of production by exchange in dialectical theory is the supplanting of labour by value. Capital is not a mode of organisation of social labour but the self-mediated process of the ceaseless expansion of value. The entire metaphysics of labour and the productive subject – which stretches far beyond Marx, across modernity as a whole – expresses the capitalist subject's idea of its own freedom in its primary relation to things, a form of experience that is itself an effect of universal mediation. That is, only within the absolute conceptuality of capital does the subject experience itself as essentially 'labour' at all. Marx's conception of class is thereby also invalidated. If labour is internal to capital, then there is no fundamental schism, around which society would be organised, between those who own the means of production and those who are compelled to work. The idea of history as the history of class struggles and of capital as the latest form of class society, in which those who labour are oppressed by those who do not, is itself entirely capitalistic. In truth, capital cannot be coherently theorised as a system of exploitation.[2] The notion that workers are exploited by capitalists is inseparable from the economic paradigm and so is already internal to capital. It follows from the assumption that the original source of the infinitely complex system of value is the figure of the Individual in direct relation to things, the modern subject 'face to face with his *own* object'. The charge of exploitation is thus based upon a standard of justice – property in the product of one's labour – that is grounded in capital's own appearance form, the economic Individual.[3] Just as the conceptualisation of capital cannot proceed from the Individual as a primary reality, so the normative judgement that labour is exploited by capital is meaningless. Value is not a substance produced by a class of labourers that is unjustly appropriated by a class of capitalists.

As Marx intended them, the categories of the theorisation of capital were to act at the same time as categories of its critique, opening a perspective beyond: from the materialist ground of the economic, capital was to be revealed as a limited and historically specific form of the universal necessity of productive activity. In annulling the primacy of production, dialectical theory disqualifies this critical perspective. Value is not a form of labour and exchange relations are not the consequence of a particular set of relations of

---

2 That the breakdown of his labour theory on the transformation problem negated Marx's idea of exploitation was recognised by Claudio Napoleoni, but without his thereby managing to get to the bottom of what is false in Marx's conception (Napoleoni 1991).

3 Because they are always already internal to capital, and thus unable to comprehend the form problematic of value, critiques that are based on the notion of exploitation can only ever be economistic and distributional, trapped within the false opposition of equality and inequality.

production. It is not the case that in capital the primary productive relations between persons appear indirectly and in 'mystified' form through exchange relations between things. There is, therefore, no such phenomenon as the 'fetish character of the commodity'.[4] The value form does not mystify what would otherwise be self-evident because value is not a representation of labour. The very idea of transparent relations among persons via transparent relations to things is a fantasy of the capitalist subject, for whom society always follows from, and should accord with, the primary productive relation to nature. Marx's theory of fetishism is false because the location outside capital from which he purports to observe 'bourgeois' society and reveal its enthrallment to fetish worship is actually within.[5] This falseness extends beyond the notion of fetishism, through the concept of ideology, and into Marx's idea of history as a whole. The critical status of the theory of capital rested upon its claim to be already in advance of its object, to occupy a position in relation to which capital could be seen to be both theoretically limited and historically transient. Marx thought that 'production' authorised that position beyond. However, the culminating point towards which this conception was supposed to move, and from which Marx claimed to speak in anticipation, communism, is not beyond capital but wholly internal to it, in the same way that absolute transparency of production is a fantastical delusion that arises from within capital, not an immanent reality in excess of it. Although Marx claimed the materialist philosophy of history as the ground and guarantor of his critique, dialectical theory reveals his conception of history, and with it his historicisation of capital, to be entirely false.

Within the field of economic thought, what sets Marx apart and makes him exemplary is that he tries harder than anyone else to overcome the basic metaphysical fracture that constitutes the economic problematic in the first place, the division between the primary material world of labour and production and the secondary conceptual world of exchange. Precisely because he does not accept capital to be the ultimate mode of economic existence, Marx attempts to force the economic problematic beyond itself by eliminating its foundational division between content and form. The

[4] Marx 1990, pp 163–77.

[5] The impossibility of the position of the observer is a central point in Alfonso Iacono's discussion of the problems in Marx's attempt to appropriate the fetish motif from classical liberal thought and use it against it (Iacono 2016, Chapters 4 and 5): 'one would be obliged to suppose that the ideal place of the observer coincides with the very aim of social development: that is to say, a system in which, according to the classical linear theory of progress, everything occurs by means of men's conscious activity. This is, indeed, the case in which the observer cannot be observed since he presumes and professes that he "sees the world as it really is" and denies the necessity of self-observation' (Iacono 2016, p 127).

incoherence and failure of this attempt, which the modern debate on value has at last made fully evident, thus really signifies the incoherence and failure of the economic conception of capital as such. By trying to make the economic idea absolute, Marx only succeeds in invalidating it altogether. As a result, the most basic question about capital is thrown wide open: what is it? The theorisation must start again, right from the very beginning and without any presuppositions. As with the revolution in value theory, the starting point from which this rethinking of the concept of capital is to be developed is exchange. In the economic conception, exchange is assumed to be limited and derivative – it comes from the subject and so, as Marx insists in simply following through the logic, can surely be returned to it – while the subject itself is unlimited and originary. Theory must therefore go *from* the subject *to* exchange. Exactly this conception, which is essential to the self-understanding of the sovereign Individual, is overturned by dialectical theory. What dialectical theory shows is that the original condition, in which the Individual is posited as given and from which exchange should then be derived, always in fact presupposes the universality of generalised exchange: the market should result from the Individual, but the existence of the Individual itself already implies the market as its condition. Because the material ground from which the forms of capital should be derived cannot be established prior to and in separation from the conceptuality of exchange, in economic theory there can be no coherent transition from the subject to the exchange system – there is always an absolute hiatus, an irreducible gap, between the material ground of the economic Individual as primary content and the objective ideality of value as secondary form.[6] If dialectical theory leads out of the contradictions of the economic to an entirely different conception of capital, therefore, then it does so through a fundamental reversal in the logic of theory: exchange does not come from the subject; rather, the subject comes from exchange.

6 Marx realised that classical thought made an illicit leap from individual labour to value, passing straight over the problem of the homogeneity of the economic space, its identity. At the same time, however, he shared the classical conviction that value must come from the Individual, as a representation of its relation to things, a form of labour. He was thus caught within a contradiction, his theory pulled in opposed directions. The result was the arbitrary positing, through reductive abstraction, of universality as immediately embodied within the product of labour: 'Marx saw the condition of [commodities'] quantitative comparison in their reduction to their common characteristic as "coagulations", as "crystallizations" of abstract labour, which the products already possessed before the act of exchange. It seems he neither wanted [to] nor could concede that this positing of unity ensued in the process of the positing of equivalence itself. Conceding this would have questioned his basic materialist position' (Reichelt 2005, p 55).

This was what Adorno intuited – that the self-determining sovereign subject is formed through the objective conceptuality of exchange. There is in Adorno's thought the idea, never fully articulated but towards which it is continually drawn, of a homology between capital and the mind – the recognition that the dialectic of value and the dialectic of the Concept are the same.[7] This perception comes into its own once it is acknowledged that the theorisation of capital must begin from exchange.[8] As value theory has shown, exchange has no content given to it from outside, no 'substance' of labour or utility that it represents in a secondary and derivative way. Rather, it is a strictly logical form of equivalence, in which two objects are posited as being identical. What arises in exchange is thus pure, abstract identity, the Being of Nothing. It is this logic of identity, culminating in universal mediation experienced as unmediated immediacy, that Adorno and Horkheimer attempt to comprehend in *Dialectic of Enlightenment*. Put drastically, the central question of the book could be framed as: How is generalised exchange possible?[9] The first two chapters, in particular, the

---

7 'Adorno talks about an "objective abstraction" in the process of exchange itself, which is "the same as the objectivity of the conceptual moment, irrespective of whether people reflect on this or not"' (Reichelt 2007, p 4, quoting notes taken by Hans-Georg Backhaus from one of Adorno's seminars at Frankfurt in 1962). 'The person who attributes the conceptual to social reality need not fear the accusation of being idealistic. What is implied here is not merely the constitutive conceptuality of the knowing subject but also a conceptuality which holds sway in reality (*Sache*) itself. … The law which determines how the fatality of mankind unfolds itself is the law of exchange. Yet, in turn, this does not represent a simple immediacy but is conceptual' (Adorno et al 1976, pp 79–80; see also Adorno 2017, pp 76–7).

8 In this respect, the dialectical critique of the economic substantiates what remained only an intuition in Adorno: 'How this process of autonomisation [of value in exchange] is to be conceptualised in detail is not explained by Adorno: the central concepts – objective abstraction, inversion, autonomisation, totality, power of the universal over the particular – remain postulates with regard to their concretisation as far as the critique of economics is concerned' (Reichelt 2007, p 6). On Adorno's conception of a critique of political economy, insofar as it can be reconstructed, see Bonefeld and O'Kane 2022 and Braunstein 2023.

9 On the character of the argumentation in *Dialectic of Enlightenment*, see García Düttmann 2000. The kind of argument elaborated in the book reflects the critique of historicism that Adorno and Walter Benjamin developed through the 1930s: 'Instead of telling a story, which would start from some distant and inevitably hypothetical "origin", and then eventually arrive in the twentieth century, the book starts out from where we are now, from the assumptions about concepts and about the world which we habitually deploy. … It sets out to give an account of how we got to these assumptions, but does this by working back from these assumptions themselves. It asks: what must have happened for our thinking to have become what it is?' (Jarvis 1998, p 21). In this respect, *Dialectic of Enlightenment* is akin to what Agamben terms a philosophical archaeology: 'It is clear that the *arché* towards which an archaeology seeks to regress cannot be understood in any way as a given that can be situated either in a chronology (even in a broad category like

'Concept of Enlightenment' and the 'Excursus' on the *Odyssey*, provide a speculative reconstruction of the emergence of identity and the origins of the dialectic by way of what could be termed the 'natural history' of exchange.[10] As such, they can be read as laying the ground for a new concept of capital, understood no longer as an economic phenomenon but as a total system of identity – precisely, in fact, universal exchange.

Prehistory of exchange

Fear

'That thought is guilty, that self-reflection is simply reflection on its own guilt, is the principal idea behind *Dialectic of Enlightenment*. Self-reflection must therefore take the concept of guilt itself as its immediate theme'.[11] If the guilt of thought is its persisting indebtedness to what is not thought, then *Dialectic of Enlightenment* aims to trace the incurring of this burden of guilt back to the subject's constitution of itself as self-identical through its separation from the world.[12] With the division that established identity and set in motion the dialectical process, the subject contracted a debt that still remains in force. In one of the 'Notes and Sketches' appended to the main work, entitled 'Man and Beast', Adorno and Horkheimer consider the limitations of the animal condition as it appears to the reflective consciousness of humans:

> The world of animals is without concepts. There is no word to hold fast the identical in the flux of phenomena, the same genus in the succession of specimens, the same thing in changing situations. Although the possibility of recognition is not absent, identification is restricted to vital patterns. There is nothing in the flux that could be defined as lasting, and yet everything remains one and the same, because there is no fixed knowledge of the past and no clear prospect into the future. The animal responds to its name and has no self, is enclosed in itself, yet exposed, one compulsion is followed by another, no idea

"prehistoric") or even beyond it in an atemporal metastructure. … It is rather a force working in history. … [T]he *arché* is not a given, a substance, or an event but a field of historical currents stretched between anthropogenesis and the present, ultrahistory and history. And as such—that is, insofar as, like anthropogenesis, it is something that is necessarily presupposed as having happened but that cannot be hypostatized into an event in a chronology—it can eventually render historical phenomena intelligible' (Agamben 2011c, pp 10–11; see also Agamben 2022, pp 102–5).

10 Adorno 1985.

11 García Düttmann 2002, p 14.

12 In Agamben's terms, this is 'the guilt that is built up in the link of destiny between *phusis* and *logos*, between life and language' (Agamben 1991, p 90).

> extends beyond it. … For happiness to become substantial, for life to be endowed with death, identifying remembrance is needed, assuaging knowledge, the religious or philosophical idea, in short, the concept.[13]

Unable to determine itself as a subject or the world as an object, to the conceptless animal the ever-changing is the eversame. The inability to raise itself out of its natural condition in order to shape and control its surroundings in freedom makes every animal, 'even the strongest',[14] pathetically vulnerable, always at the mercy of the accidents and contingencies of nature. It is simultaneously trapped within itself and helplessly exposed, closed and open. This vulnerability is what, for Adorno and Horkheimer, drives the human animal, 'so much more ill-equipped than other creatures',[15] to the concept.

In the far distant, prehistoric experience, nature is apprehended as both intensely meaningful, significant even into its finest differences, and also impenetrable and awesome – an enveloping context that is mysterious and marvellous as well as amorphous and terrifying.[16] Before the definitive division of inside and outside, when it is still submerged in the untamed and unknown, the pre-subjective human is permeated throughout its being by the infinite multifariousness of the world. Its thoughts and actions cannot be referred back to the security of a self-contained subjectivity in whose sovereign will they would be grounded, but are instead to be attributed to divine forces, as the manifestations by which natural powers make themselves known.[17] The overwhelming experience of the 'complex concatenation of nature in contrast to its individual link' provokes the primal cry of terror that becomes the name of deity, while the earliest explanatory principle of enlightenment, *mana*, is 'the echo of the real preponderance of nature in the weak psyches of primitive people'.[18] The transcendent and unchanging universal thus exists behind and speaks through the mortal and transient

---

13 Horkheimer and Adorno 2002, p 205.

14 Horkheimer and Adorno 2002, p 205.

15 Adorno 2005b, p 258.

16 The 'ancient terror' from which the continuing force of myth derives 'is no different from the terror that is the first one of all: terror of the world; terror in the face of its mute, deceptive, overwhelming enigma; terror before this place of constant metamorphosis and epiphany, which above all includes our own minds, where we witness without letup the tumult of simulacra' (Calasso 2002, p 266).

17 Myth 'recognizes spirit only as something immersed in nature, a natural power. For it, inward impulses, like outward forces, are living powers of divine or demonic origin' (Horkheimer and Adorno 2002, p 70). Indeed, in the mythological world 'the affirmation of the divine is so imperious, all-pervading, and all-embracing as to minimize and demolish all human responsibility. No one feels guilty, because no one feels himself as the "cause," *aítios*, of what happens' (Calasso 2020, p 350; see also Calasso 1994, pp 93–5).

18 Horkheimer and Adorno 2002, pp 10–11.

particular. This dawning perception of the power of the encompassing generality as the truth of the phenomenal thing foreshadows the much later metaphysical duality of essence and appearance and the modern, rational distinction between object and concept.[19] Myth, and even pre-mythic modes of thought and behaviour – magic, animism and archaic mimesis – are in this way already part of the movement of enlightenment. Still directly reflecting in their content the fragility of the unformed subject in relation to the power of nature, pre-rational modes of thought are attempts to explain the world as a system of force and effect and to develop techniques, in the form of rituals, intended to enable influence over and thus control of natural processes. Underlying Adorno and Horkheimer's account, therefore, is the perception that the pattern of enlightenment has always been the same, stretching in unbroken continuity as far back as the first attempts by humans to free themselves from subjection to nature. Through the long history of its rationalisation, thought has only ever repeated the original fear from which it sprang, continually purifying it and so inscribing it ever deeper.[20]

Equivalence

The perpetual, self-renewing natural order is the essence of the explanation of the world given in myth – timelessness, repetition, enclosure and the impossibility of escape or salvation. All finite things come into being and pass away, but the order as a whole survives, unchanging and indifferent. The identity of the implacable universal is the summation of the blind repetitiveness by which the life of the particular is circumscribed. The world of myth thus constitutes a *Schuldzusammenhang*: forever inadequate to the whole that it cannot grasp, the human subject is guilty a priori, in its mere existence and before it commits any transgression. In the mythic cosmos, which is without transcendence or a horizon of freedom, nothing new or incommensurable may ever come into being: 'the world controlled by *mana*, and even the worlds of Indian and Greek myth, are issueless and eternally the same.'[21] The ordering schema of this context of enclosure is what Adorno and Horkheimer call the 'principle of equivalence'.[22] The cyclical, reiterative character of myth is the product of a relentless mechanism of exchange and equalisation, guilt and atonement, through which every individual thing is subordinated to the process of the whole. In myth, 'all birth is paid for with

19 'The concept, usually defined as the unity of the features of what it subsumes, was rather, from the first, a product of dialectical thinking, in which each thing is what it is only by becoming what it is not' (Horkheimer and Adorno 2002, p 11).

20 'This dialectic remains powerless as long as it emerges from the cry of terror, which is the doubling, the mere tautology of terror itself' (Horkheimer and Adorno 2002, p 11).

21 Horkheimer and Adorno 2002, p 11.

22 Horkheimer and Adorno 2002, p 12.

death, all fortune with misfortune'.[23] The logical necessity of the sequence of cause and effect which binds the system together stems from and endlessly perpetuates the original guilt:

> Mythical inevitability is defined by the equivalence between the curse, the abominable act which expiates it, and the guilt arising from that act, which reproduces the curse. All law in history up to now bears the trace of this pattern. In myth each moment of the cycle pays off the preceding moment and thereby helps to establish the continuity of guilt as law.[24]

Existing as a relentless process of negation, the universal, the One that is always reaffirmed through the principle of equivalence, is a kind of Nothing, an absolute negativity that grinds everything down into identity, rendering what is dissimilar the same. Since it preserves itself through negation, while everything that is merely particular goes under, it is only this sovereign universal that has *being* and truly *is*.[25]

Enlightenment, in Adorno and Horkheimer's argument, results from the internalisation by the subject of the principle of equivalence.[26] Control of nature begins with mimetic imitation – 'the shaman wards off a danger with its likeness. Equivalence is his instrument'[27] – and culminates in the modern

23 Horkheimer and Adorno 2002, p 11.

24 Horkheimer and Adorno 2002, p 16. In *Negative Dialectics*, Adorno ascribes causality to myth, attributing to it the character of 'an archaic juridical relationship of vengeance'. As 'the inheritor of the activating spirit in things', the compulsion of causality reproduces the 'natural-rootedness of humanity' (Adorno 2001b, 'On the Crisis of Causality' and 'Causality as Bane').

25 In this respect, there is a kind of self-dividedness, or negativity, in the relation between the universal and the particular in nature. The logical form of 'life', as Hegel styles it, is thus, to use Agamben's term, a relation of abandonment: the particular is at once included in and excluded from the universal. In Hegel's conception, the self of self-consciousness is then modelled upon this 'original division' or *Urteilung* (Ng 2020).

26 Cf. Hegel's contention in the *Differenzschrift* that, 'the point of transition through which identity constructing itself as nature passes over to identity constructing itself as intelligence, is the internalisation of the light of nature, the lightning stroke of the ideal upon the real' (Hegel 1977a, p 170). Through the internalisation of the universal negation negates itself, and it is this folding back of negation upon itself that initiates the logic of autonomous negation through which the movement of the dialectic proceeds (Henrich 2003, Chapter 21; see also Frank 1989, pp 265–9; Bowman 2013, Chapter 2). Adorno's idea here can be understood as a translation into the terms of his negative philosophy of history of what speculative idealism thought of as intelligence latent within the natural world – that is, nature's immanent striving towards self-reflection, by which it becomes object to itself as subject. As always, the dialectic works from both sides: its purpose is to show not just how the self becomes a world but how the world becomes a self.

27 Horkheimer and Adorno 2002, p 12.

world of generalised exchange – 'bourgeois society is ruled by equivalence'.[28] With the advance of positive knowledge, the substantive contents first of animism and magic, and then of mythic thought, are left behind, but the logic of equivalence runs as the connecting thread through the progress of reason, binding the modern to the archaic. In the successive explanations of being in Western ontology, Adorno and Horkheimer perceive the same inner structure of equivalence and totality hypostatised into ever more abstracted and spiritualised forms. There is thus a direct line of descent from the multiplicity of local spirits and demons in primeval times, which was rationalised into the pantheon of Olympian deities, through pre-Socratic hylozoism, the Platonic forms and Aristotelian metaphysics, down to the mathematisation of the world in modern science and the studied archaism of Heideggerian Being: 'the categories by which Western philosophy defined its timeless order of nature marked out the positions which had once been occupied by Ocnus and Persephone, Ariadne and Nereus.'[29] The identification of the variousness of nature that the concept makes possible consigns the archaic powers to prehistory, but only at the cost of replicating the universal equivalence of myth within the reason that dissolves it. The wider the chasm that separates humans from nature and the deeper the division between subject and object, the greater the power of equivalence and the more thoroughly it is driven into thought:

> The step from chaos to civilization, in which natural conditions exert their power no longer directly but through the consciousness of human beings, changed nothing in the principle of equivalence. Indeed, human beings atoned for this very step by worshipping that to which previously, like all other creatures, they had been merely subjected. Earlier, fetishes had been subject to the law of equivalence. Now equivalence itself becomes a fetish.[30]

Law

For Adorno and Horkheimer, fetishisation of equivalence as worship of the universal is integral to the subject's escape from entrapment in the natural context and its elevation of itself to sovereignty. In the first 'Excursus' of *Dialectic of Enlightenment*, on the *Odyssey*, the wanderings of Odysseus are read as an allegory of the formation of subjectivity through its confrontation

28 Horkheimer and Adorno 2002, p 4.

29 Horkheimer and Adorno 2002, p 3. Hence, as Donald Verene puts it: '*Metaphysics is always myth remembered*' (Verene 2009, p 115 (emphasis in original)).

30 Horkheimer and Adorno 2002, p 12.

with the forces of nature. Adrift on the fluid, unchanging and ever identical sea, Odysseus is repeatedly cast back into the prehistorical world, where he encounters mythical entities from the long-forgotten past. By virtue of its very haphazardness and indirection, the voyage of return to Ithaca has an aspect of conquest about it, as the wild is charted and open seas and strange lands are brought within the bounds of the known. The effect of Odysseus's adventuring, his passage through the disparate world of myth, is that the ancient powers that had 'originally sprung in the face of primal dread'[31] are pushed back to the margins of civilisation as rational order inexorably encroaches upon them: 'the primeval world is secularized as the space he measures out. … The adventurer bestows names on each of these places, and the names give rise to a rational overview of space. … His powerlessness, leaving no part of the sea unknown, aims to undermine the ruling powers.'[32] In this way, the *nostos* enacts a process of dialectical *Entäusserung*. The hero secures his sovereign identity by repeatedly casting himself into circulation, abandoning himself entirely to the elements and losing his ship and all of his companions as he is inexorably reduced to the solitary bare life of the perpetual survivor. He returns to himself by going beyond himself, winning his self-identity by throwing himself away.[33] It is precisely through the contingency of his inadvertent and directionless wanderings, therefore, that Odysseus becomes a systematic and rational self.[34] How, though, is the powerless human able to undermine the ruling powers of the mythical cosmos? When he is cast beyond the bounds of the known world and comes face to face with the prehistoric, what Odysseus confronts is the original image of law:

> The mythical monsters under whose power he falls represent, as it were, petrified contracts and legal claims dating from primeval times. … The fact that it would be impossible to choose any route other than that between Scylla and Charybdis may be interpreted rationalistically

31 Horkheimer and Adorno 2002, p 38.

32 Horkheimer and Adorno 2002, p 38.

33 In this respect, as the exemplary narrative of return, across its span as a whole the *nostos* plays out the dialectical movement of the reversion to self from otherness (Nagy 2006, pp 79–80). Indeed, through the overarching theme of return, the *Odyssey* secularises the traditional motif of the immortalisation, or becoming infinite, of the legendary hero (Nagy 2006, p 84).

34 'The self does not exist simply in rigid antithesis to adventure but takes on its solidity only through this antithesis, and its unity through the very multiplicity which myth in its oneness denies' (Horkheimer and Adorno 2002, p 38). Cf.: 'The process of becoming independent appears not only in the form that capital confronts circulation as an independent abstract exchange value—money—but also in that circulation is simultaneously the process of its becoming independent, that it stems from circulation as something become independent' (Marx and Engels 1987, p 496).

> as the mythical representation of the preponderant power of sea currents over the little ships of ancient times. But translated into the objectifying language of myth, it means that the natural relationship between strength and powerlessness has already taken on the character of a legal relationship. Scylla and Charybdis have a claim on whatever comes between their teeth, just as Circe has a right to metamorphose those who are not immune, or Polyphemus a right to the bodies of his guests.[35]

In the figures of myth, the force of nature becomes the force of law, as power is metamorphosed into right. All who come before the abstract self-sameness of the mythical beings are guilty and must pay the price. That law is the extension of myth through its transformation is why, no matter how rationalised it may become, it always has about it the minatory and forbidding aspect of the archaic. Entangled in this originary legal systematics, Odysseus struggles with a seemingly insoluble dilemma. He can never engage the mythical monsters in direct physical combat because, their power being the power of nature, they cannot be overcome. But nor can he simply find another route past Scylla and Charybdis or the Sirens, for, as expressions of fateful necessity, the claims these ancient powers represent must be satisfied. Within the context of guilt, they can be neither defied nor avoided.

What Odysseus discovers in these situations of extremity is how to fulfil the statute while escaping its penalty – that is, how at once to maintain the principle of equivalence and evade it. His method of self-preservation is cunning, 'the oldest medium of the Enlightenment'.[36] Thus, in the encounter with the Sirens, Odysseus does not attempt to find a different route, nor does he hubristically imagine himself free to listen without succumbing to the lure of their song; instead, 'he cowers [and] the ship takes its preordained, fateful course'.[37] However, through the expediency of having himself bound to the mast while blocking his men's ears with wax, Odysseus succeeds in

---

35 Horkheimer and Adorno 2002, p 45.

36 Cunning, which Adorno termed a 'mythical category' (Hullot-Kentor 2006, p 36), is a central element of dialectic: 'Adorno's project is unthinkable except as a critical transformation of Hegel's doctrine of the ruse [that is, cunning] of reason, which Hegel condensed most succinctly in the *Encyclopedia* when he wrote that "reason is as powerful as it is cunning' (Hullot-Kentor 2006, pp 36–7).

37 Horkheimer and Adorno 2002, p 46. The trick of Odysseus' cunning, therefore, is that he conducts himself towards the mythical powers of nature negatively: he does not attempt to overcome them directly, through the use of force, but indirectly, through his reason. As Hegel says of the dialectical nature of cunning: '[Consider] the honor of cunning against power—to grasp blind power from one side so that it turns against itself ... to make it return into itself as movement, so that it negates itself' (Hegel 1983, p 104).

both complying with the terms of the mythical contract and breaking them. Equivalence is thus violated in the very act by which it is affirmed, the judgement eluded in its acceptance.[38] The law-like demands of the primeval powers have an abstract force, indifferent to the particularity of what comes before them. But they are only the outward embodiment of legality – they have not reflected it into themselves. Adorno and Horkheimer note that the epic holds the primitive Cyclopes in contempt because they have no political life, 'no assemblies for the making of laws, nor any settled customs'.[39] Nor are they able to reason properly, for 'when Homer calls the Cyclops a "lawless-minded monster" he does not mean simply that the Cyclops does not respect the laws of morality but that his thinking itself is lawless, unsystematic, rhapsodic.'[40] Without interiority or self-consciousness, the archaic beings of the prehistoric world are legality in-itself but not for-itself. The figures of myth are thus always figures of repetition – they are identity in an unreflected, external form. Confronted by the powers of prehistory, the strategy of the cunning individual is one of adaptation and immanence: he takes into himself the force of the mythical beings in order to escape them, mastering himself so that he can master the world. Again and again in the course of his adventures, Odysseus applies to himself the abstract power of negation that inheres in the archaic forces of law within whose jurisdiction he comes. The law of his survival is the internalisation of myth as law. By making the rationality of myth his own in this way, Odysseus is able to insert himself into the division between universal and particular that constitutes the natural context precisely as a context of guilt. This is what makes possible the legalistic literalism that recognises and takes advantage of the loophole in the Sirens' contractual claim. In the same manner, through the ruse of the name in Polyphemus's cave, Odysseus breaks the mythical unity of signifier and signified, exploiting the division between word and thing in order to outwit the guileless giant.

Renunciation

Odysseus's successful self-assertion, his fabled capacity to survive thanks to his cunning intelligence, is at the same time self-renunciation. He secures his identity by denying himself – as '*Udeis*', he is both hero and nobody.[41] However, his success comes at a cost. The universal, which is embodied in

---

[38] This is Adorno's transvaluation of dialectical *Aufhebung*. Throughout the movement of negation – the cunning that at once denies and affirms – the subject always stays within that from which it separates itself ever further.

[39] Horkheimer and Adorno 2002, p 51

[40] Horkheimer and Adorno 2002, p 51.

[41] Horkheimer and Adorno 2002, p 47.

the forces of the mythical world, constitutes itself through the negation of the particular, and its internalisation, which makes possible the self-assertion of the subject in the escape from myth, recreates this contradiction within subjectivity. The formation of identity as mimesis of the universal thus demands continual renunciation of the world in its aspect as pre-identical and indeterminate. Odysseus survives where all about him perish because of his capacity to renounce. He turns away from the world, withdrawing from it into himself, in order that he may go out into it and conquer.[42] The ability to withstand the monsters and sorceresses is won through control of the instinctual reactions of nature within. Of the metaphor in Book XX of the *Odyssey*, describing the hero's struggle to contain his rage at the licentiousness that he discovers on returning to Ithaca, Adorno and Horkheimer note:

> The affect is equated with an animal which the human being is subduing … The subject, still split and forced to do violence to nature both within himself and outside, 'punishes' his heart, compelling it to be patient and denying it direct satisfaction in the present for the sake of a more distant future. Beating one's breast later became a gesture of triumph: What the victor really expresses is that the victory is over his own nature. The achievement is accomplished by self-preserving reason.[43]

The stability of the self, which ensures that it can hold itself together where once, bewildered by fear or overcome with desire, it would have given itself up to the unending multiplicity of nature, is achieved through the division of the human subject. By excluding itself from itself, opposing itself as universal to itself as particular, the self becomes self-identical. The internalisation of the universal thus makes possible the formation of the sovereign interior space of subjectivity through which the world 'outside' will henceforth always be mediated. In order to achieve the unity and coherence that permit the channelling of all behaviour through the directive medium of self-consciousness, the self then progressively denies its own pre-logical, pre-conceptual being, repressing the immediacy of the impulses whose free expression, if permitted, would cause the subject to fall back into the

42 'Alone among the Achaean leaders, Odysseus keeps his eyes down. But not out of fear. While his gaze is lowered, Odysseus concentrates his mind, isolates it from all around in a way his companions are not used to doing, weaves a plot, gives shape to a *mēchanḗ*. He is the opposite of the man who is continually caught between the forces, machines and *mēchanaí* of nature and of the gods. To their invisible tangle, Odysseus adds new *mēchanaí*, ones that he has elaborated himself. Now he has the secret, he need not merely submit to it' (Calasso 1994, p 351).

43 Horkheimer and Adorno 2002, p 259.

limitless flux of the indeterminate. Unity and order are thus attained by way of division and negation.[44]

In Adorno and Horkheimer's account, since the constitution of the self replicates the dialectical antithesis of universal and particular, the self's victory over itself is also its own defeat. The subject's rational universality is necessarily restricted because it is predicated upon renunciation. As a result, the survival of the self is continually played out within the ambit of myth. It can set itself apart as an exception, escaping the penalty through the cunning of reason, but it cannot be truly free. The original debt is never actually redeemed but is instead continually deferred.[45] The logic of Odysseus's success is thus that failure is admitted in advance, the superiority of nature submissively acknowledged by the mind that masters it. With self-denial accepted as its governing principle, the struggle against myth compels prudence and realism: 'All bourgeois enlightenment is agreed on the demand for sobriety, respect for facts, a correct appraisal of relative strength. Wishful thinking is banned.'[46] Likewise, fulfilment is renounced because giving oneself up to the world in the self-forgetfulness of pleasure means dissolution of the self through relapse into amorphous nature, and so can only be regarded as delusion or foolishness. Wisdom, in the form of worldly resignation, instead places a ban upon utopia: the present is continually forfeited to the future, happiness forever put off for the sake of security and self-preservation. What makes the *Odyssey* exemplary is that, in the tension between epic and myth,

[44] As Adorno and Horkheimer understand it, the self is the contradictory product of the self-assertion of the subject through self-denial, so that the superiority of nature is acknowledged in its very overthrow. Accordingly, they conceive the formation of the self as taking place through the process of *Verleugnung* – disavowal – that Freud identified as central to the phenomenon of fetishism (Freud 2005). The self itself is thus a fetish, in the sense in which Agamben develops the term from Freud: arising directly upon the division between subject and world, it is the medium of their reciprocal affirmation–negation (Agamben 1993, pp 31–5 and 145–7). It follows that the essential character of the fetish is to be an infinitude that never attains the whole: 'Precisely because the fetish is a negation and the sign of an absence, it is not an unrepeatable unique object; on the contrary, it is something infinitely capable of substitution, without any of its successive incarnations ever succeeding in exhausting the nullity of which it is the symbol' (Agamben 1993, p 33).

[45] 'The principle of law remains untouched by cunning, even if the cunning individual fulfils the mythic statutes and thus destroys them. If we define the universal as the inequality of what renders everything equal, then we can claim that cunning always remains the instrument of a universal that it never endangers' (García Düttmann 2002, p 28).

[46] Horkheimer and Adorno 2002, p 44. Cf. Morgenthau: 'The insight and the wisdom of the statesman gauge accurately the distribution and relative strength of opposing forces and anticipate, however tentatively, the emerging pattern of new constellations. The statesman has no assurance of success in the immediate task and not even the expectation of solving the long-range problem' (Morgenthau 1965, p 221).

as the subject pulls itself away from the timeless archaic world, the narrative dramatises the formation of identity through the elimination of what does not accord with the universal. As the price of progress, Odysseus learns that he must always forego and that, no matter what the world-spanning extent of his universal reason, it will be forever insufficient. Disillusionment and self-limitation are integral to the mature, developed subject:

> [He] can never have the whole, he must always be able to wait, to be patient, to renounce; he may not eat the lotus or the cattle of Hyperion, and when he steers through the narrows he must include in his calculation the loss of the companions snatched from the ship by Scylla. He wriggles through – that is his survival, and all the renown that he gains in his own and others' eyes merely confirms that the honor of heroism is won only by the humbling of the urge to attain entire, universal, undivided happiness.[47]

In applying to himself the abstract universality of the archaic powers of myth, Odysseus negates himself as a pre-identical being and turns himself into the image of the authority to which he was once subject. He evades the punishment of myth, therefore, by himself becoming myth: 'it is implacable nature that he now commands, which triumphs on his return home as the implacable judge, avenging the heritage of the very powers he has escaped.'[48]

Sacrifice

At the heart of Adorno and Horkheimer's account of the formation of identity through renunciation is sacrifice, 'the oldest religious practice of humanity'.[49] As they understand it, the institution of sacrifice already marks an advance in the logic of identity.[50] At the very beginnings of the

---

[47] Horkheimer and Adorno 2002, p 45.

[48] Horkheimer and Adorno 2002, pp 38–9.

[49] Agamben 1991, p 105. In addressing the thematic of sacrifice, Adorno and Horkheimer's purpose should be understood as philosophical, not historical or anthropological. Roberto Calasso observes that 'the whole history of modern philosophy is deeply troubled by sacrifice, by its terrible truth: Hegel's dialectics is a transcription, an adulterated transcription of sacrifice; Schopenhauer is the Western *saṃnyāsin*, the renouncer, and always therefore associated with sacrifice; Abraham is the sacrifice around which Kierkegaard's thought revolves; and Dionysus … is Nietzsche's sacrifice' (Calasso 2018, pp 157–8).

[50] The undivided and pre-subjective world through which Odysseus wanders, in an age before production, is thus also pre-sacrificial: 'Within this non-cultivated space, no sacrifices are made, for here no one is bound by the practice that regulates relations between the gods and human beings and through which, by repeating the division of a ritually sacrificed

process of enlightenment, before it has hardened into a determinate and bounded entity, the human being makes itself like the thing that it fears, attempting to know nature, and so to influence it, by means of magical and animistic practices. Where the emergent subject is still largely within the natural context, therefore, knowledge is based on affinity and takes the form of mimesis:

> The rites of the shaman were directed at the wind, the rain, the snake outside or the demon inside the sick person, not at materials or specimens. The spirit which practiced magic was not single or identical; it changed with the cult masks which represented the multiplicity of spirits. ... The magician imitates demons; to frighten or placate them he makes intimidating or appeasing gestures.[51]

The central perception that shapes Adorno and Horkheimer's account of the prehistory of the dialectic is that identity is originarily apotropaic. It is a mechanism of self-preservation, 'a protective power that repels the uncanny by attracting it and assuming it within itself'.[52] Through mimetic identification with the forces of nature, the human being takes the power of the universal into itself in order to preserve itself. The original division of inside and outside, the *Urteilung*, is thus effected by the process of equivalence. It follows that the practice of sacrifice is premised upon a definite separation of the subject from the encompassing natural context. At the same time, however, the necessity of the offering that is made in sacrifice presupposes the continued superiority of unmastered nature over the still-developing subject. The subject has set itself apart but it cannot yet sustain itself from itself; rather, in its comparative weakness, the interior space of human primacy remains dependent upon the external world, to which it must continue to relate itself in its very separation. In this way, the practice of sacrifice at once divides and unites, marking out the boundary and traversing it at the same time. What is enacted in the sacrificial ritual, therefore, is a delicate negotiation of continuity and discontinuity: the subject pays obeisance and in doing so deepens the separation. Having torn itself out of the unending web of interconnection that binds the natural context together, it must make reparation. It must atone for its guilt by paying back in exchange, forsaking something of itself in order that equivalence may be re-established. However, because

animal, those human beings acknowledge themselves to be mortal eaters of bread' (Hartog 2001, p 30).

51 Horkheimer and Adorno 2002, p 6.

52 Agamben 1993, p 138.

it has irreparably separated itself through the internalising of the universal, it cannot give itself up entire to the powers of nature in the old mimetic manner. Instead, it sacrifices.

The evolution of the practice of sacrifice is thus the unfolding of the logic of division. It is this dialectical character that Adorno and Horkheimer point to when they describe the sacrificial procedure as simultaneously rational and irrational. The cunning of sacrifice is its winning of reason from the encompassing unreason, the extension of the sphere of the subject through its acknowledgement of the power that exceeds it. In this respect, sacrifice is 'a human contrivance intended to control the gods, who are overthrown precisely by the system created to honour them'.[53] Just as mimetic equivalence brought about the primordial separation, so the veneration of the deity in sacrifice in fact serves to advance the autonomy of the subject: 'All sacrificial acts, deliberately planned by humans, deceive the god for whom they are performed: by imposing on him the primacy of human purposes they dissolve away his power'.[54] Poised on the line between inside and outside, no longer entirely within nature but not yet self-grounded, in sacrifice the subject performs a complex double movement of self-assertion through self-denial.

> In the destruction – even only of herbs – the guilt on which culture is established is affirmed: its detachment, its isolation from everything else, insofar as it isolates a thing-victim and expels it. By dedicating the victim to something other than itself, society recognises its dependence upon that from which it has detached itself. And at the same time it holds the outside world at a distance, offering it the victim rather than itself. This is the act of reverence. This is the cunning trick of enlightenment. At first, they are inseparable. The ploy is wrapped in reverence, and it works as a slow corrosive, like the poison (German: *Gift*) in the gift. As a *Gift*-gift.[55]

Sacrifice resulted from the division within the subject and, in being offered up to the divinity beyond, the natural thing is at the same time sacrificed to the universal self within, which communes with the deity through the ritual.[56] The power of the subject is thus continually enhanced by means

53 Horkheimer and Adorno 2002, p 40.

54 Horkheimer and Adorno 2002, p 40. 'By yielding part of the world to the divinity, the sacrificer wants the divinity to give him the rest of the world, and no longer to intervene there with its uncontrollable whim. The sacrifice is also trying to gain the divinity's permission to use the world' (Calasso 2018, p 149).

55 Calasso 2018, p 163.

56 'The identical, enduring self which springs from the conquest of sacrifice is itself the product of a hard, petrified sacrificial ritual in which the human being, by opposing its

of the dedication to that which transcends. In this respect, sacrifice is the *ur*-form of negation. It is the overcoming of the pre-conceptual opacity of nature through the division of the world from itself, fracturing it into the duality of ideal, universal essence, on one side, and material, particular existence, on the other.[57] In the moment of its destruction, the sacrificial object is elevated to the ideal, consecrated to the deity as a 'bearer of the divine substance', and so made identical.[58] The enormous importance of sacrifice in the process of anthropogenesis attests the immense effort that the inscription of the division of inside and outside demanded. Separation from the pre-rational world could only be effected through the laborious exertion of discipline and control that was concentrated into the sacrificial ceremony: the setting apart of the sacred space, the numberless rules and prescriptions, the precise assigning of functions, and the strict procedure in the performance of the ritual, governed by the power of the officiants through whom the dread of death was mediated. For the pre-conceptual thing to be raised to the universal and become intelligible being necessitated its destruction. In the process of sacrifice the world was demonstrated to be nothing in itself: its truth was not to be found in conceptless indetermination but was revealed solely through its apotheosis as immortal essence. By being spiritualised into the concept through sacrifice, the world was, in dialectical terms, *aufgehoben* – at once negated and preserved.

Sacrifice presupposes the recognition of an objective ideality in relation to which it becomes possible to think in terms of equivalence and identity. Through their common mediation to the divine essence that transcends and encompasses them all, one thing becomes the same as, and so can be exchanged for, another. In this respect also, as Adorno and Horkheimer conceive it, the long epoch of sacrifice in the formation of the human subject was transitional between the extremes of primitive magic, on one side, and modern rational exchange, on the other:

consciousness to its natural context, celebrates itself' (Horkheimer and Adorno 2002, p 42). Likewise, in his early work on Kierkegaard, Adorno describes sacrifice as 'the final category of the destruction of the natural', observing that in the 'theology of sacrifice … the individual must "perish" to become "himself"' (Adorno 1989, pp 107–8).

57 If sacrifice inscribes the boundary line, then its essential movement is taking in by casting out, or including by excluding: 'For all the variegated multiplicity of its forms, the practice of sacrifice can be reduced to just two gestures: expulsion (purification) and assimilation (communion). These two gestures have only one element in common: destruction. In each case, the victim is killed or devoured, or abandoned to a certain death' (Calasso 1994, pp 291–2). From the twofold, inside/outside dynamic of sacrifice there derives the dialectical structure of consciousness: 'consciousness *distinguishes* something from itself while at the same it *relates* itself to it' (Hegel 2018, p 55/¶82 (emphases in original)).

58 Horkheimer and Adorno 2002, p 40.

> Magic implies specific representation. What is done to the spear, the hair, the name of the enemy, is also to befall his person; the sacrificial animal is slain in place of the god. The substitution which takes place in sacrifice marks a step toward discursive logic. Even though the hind which was offered up for the daughter, the lamb for the firstborn, necessarily still had qualities of its own, it already represented the genus. It manifested the arbitrariness of the specimen. But the sanctity of the *hic et nunc*, the uniqueness of the chosen victim which coincides with its representative status, distinguishes it radically, makes it non-exchangeable even in the exchange.[59]

In breaking the power of the pre-identical thing, laying open its mystery in blood on the altar, sacrifice detaches the sphere of the conceptual from what, through this division, becomes the material world, separating the potential from the actual. The magical word, tied to its object, becomes the discursive concept, which holds itself apart and from that commanding distance can refer to infinitely many things.[60] Through the progress of sacrifice, therefore, the conceptualisation of the world is relentlessly advanced. Sacrifice both negates the living actuality of the thing, transforming it into a bare existent on one side and an immaterial essence on the other, and at the same time purifies the universal, separating it further and further from the intramundane world and making it ever more abstracted, unified and all-encompassing. Over millennia, what began as the profusion of natural spirits and demons, tied to specific locations, is thus eventually sublimated into the single omnipotent God, entirely separate from the world in His limitless creative power as pure form. Correlatively, the primitive human being is transformed into the universal Individual, made in the image of his God and endowed with the divine gift of reason that sets him above the rest of creation.

As the mechanism of rationalisation, sacrifice thus demythologises itself. This is its irrational aspect. Precisely through sacrifice, it becomes impossible to believe any longer either in the supernatural beings to which obeisance was once paid or in the sacrificial ritual through which the division was mediated. The various historical practices of sacrifice progressively consign themselves to the past, therefore, by way of the very civilising process that they facilitate: 'Demythologization always takes

---

59 Horkheimer and Adorno 2002, p 7.

60 'Sacrificing something that *stands for* something else sets in motion the very machinery of language and algebra, conquering digitality. The deception by which the creature with its throat slit on the altar can be a substitute and not the thing itself provokes an enormous growth in power, such that its extension will cancel out all consciousness of the need for sacrificial giving' (Calasso 2018, p 179 (emphasis in original)).

the form of the irresistible revelation of the futility and superfluity of sacrifices'.[61] The progress of demythologisation is not a movement away from sacrifice, though, but further into it. The evolution of sacrifice is at once the increasing separation of subject and world and the increasing identity of subject and deity. At the culmination of this double movement form and content are definitively split apart, while transcendence collapses altogether into immanence, realising itself by investing itself entirely in the world. In Adorno and Horkheimer's speculative history of the dialectic, the logic of equivalence fulfils itself in capitalist modernity: the universality of rational exchange is the 'secularization of sacrifice'.[62] Considered as an instrument of dialectical negation, sacrifice implies historical movement through the unfolding of the logic of division and the advance of demythologisation. Conversely, in its very form and even before it attains its concept as capital, exchange signifies immanence and stasis, the endless self-reference of the divine essence ceaselessly mediating itself with itself in an eternal present. Generalised exchange is thus the condition of absolute identity that completes the universal history of sacrifice.

Towards a concept of capital

The idea of *Dialectic of Enlightenment* is that the sovereign subject comes into being as a self-identical unity through successive processes of equivalence. The subject does not pre-exist exchange, therefore, as economic theory must assume. Rather, it becomes a subject only through exchange. Or, more precisely, as the most conceptually developed form of equivalence, generalised exchange is the condition of fully achieved subjectivity – the modern subject is a being of exchange. Capital, as the universalisation of exchange, is thus universal subjectivity. Properly speaking, therefore, we *are* capital. Where it momentarily lets go of the dogmas of labour and production and allows itself simply to follow the logic of capital, in the authentically dialectical manner of passively looking on,[63] Marxian value theory has on occasion come close to recognising as much:

> The central axis of bourgeois society is only established with the form of universal, immediate exchangeability. This form is, in a strict

[61] Horkheimer and Adorno 2002, p 42.

[62] Horkheimer and Adorno 2002, p 40. 'Substitution, exchange, value: pivotal elements around which the world we call modern revolves. Their origin lies in sacrificial practices – and in the metaphysics of sacrifice. There is no sacrifice that does not involve exchange; there is no sacrifice that does not acknowledge substitution; there is no sacrifice that does not have a value at its core' (Calasso 2015, p 347).

[63] Hegel 2018, pp 36–7/¶58. See also Houlgate 2022, pp 59–64.

> Hegelian sense, the form of self-consciousness – a consciousness tied to objects, the objectified self of consciousness.[64]

When value theory insists that it is value, not labour, that is the subject of capitalist society, this should be taken literally. Capital can only be coherently theorised as a system of exchange – that is, as a system of identity. Indeed, identity totalises itself as a system precisely when it achieves the form of exchange.[65] Once value is able to return to itself continually in an infinite process of self-valorisation, the subject has succeeded in grounding itself upon itself. It does not look to, or lose itself in, anything outside itself; rather, all externality has become internal, posited by value itself in the course of its own movement. Capital is thus the subject become sovereign, autonomous and self-determining, giving its own laws to itself and sustaining itself from itself. It is the self closed upon itself as wholly self-referential. If the subject derives from exchange and universal exchange is universal subjectivity, then it follows that the first requirement of a concept of capital is that it should not be conceived, in any way, as an economic or social system. All such supposedly general and transhistorical 'material' categories, of which capital would be a particular instance, are already internal to capital, effects of universal mediation. They always depend upon the figure of the Individual as their necessary substratum. It is intrinsic to the concept of capital, by contrast, that it has no such ground, nothing that stands behind it in this way. Rather, capital must be thought solely through the logic of equivalence, as the self-perpetuation of identity achieved through its complete interiorisation of the world.

At the centre of the revolution in the understanding of capital that has been effected by modern value theory is money. In both orthodox economic theory and traditional Marxism, the world is assumed to be economic in-itself: value precedes exchange and money is merely a convenient instrument for resolving the problems of barter. What dialectical theory demonstrates, however, is that money does not simply facilitate an intrinsic exchangeability, externally representing a pre-existing value substance. Rather, it makes objects exchangeable in the first place, actualising value as the universal essence of the commodity. It is money, therefore, that brings the space of value into existence. Again, at its furthest points, the rethinking of value within Marxism has glimpsed some of the far-reaching implications of this theoretical reversal for the meaning of money:

> 'Money is the material, **existing concept**, the form of unity, or the possibility of all things' [Hegel in the *Jenenser Realphilosophie*]. … As

64 Reichelt 2005, p 58.

65 Considered against the scale of human history as a whole, capital in fact follows very quickly upon the consolidation of exchange identity in money.

> an 'existing concept', money is at the same time characterized as the 'existing universal' and he adds 'here value exists as such', and 'money is the real existence of the universal. This universal is not only an external, objective universal but also a subjective universal, a universal of a wholly different sort'. Hegel was not able to develop this thought any further. What is important, however, is that this universal of a 'wholly different sort' is subjective and at the same time objective, and as an objective [*sic*] it is an 'existing universal', that is, totality and abstraction, both at the same time. It is like the 'I' as an existing concept ... But it is like the 'I' not as an 'I' but as a thing.[66]

If the self comes into being through a logic of equivalence, culminating in universal exchange, then money is pure selfhood, literally the essence of subjectivity. In its formation through the ritual of sacrifice the self objectifies itself to itself – it exists as a universal-abstract self-identical 'I' within to the extent that it exists as a universal-abstract medium of identity without. It would be legitimate to speculate, therefore, that the cognitive mind as such is an inherently monetary phenomenon. Like money, its concept is universal mediation: absolute abstraction and infinity, total identity and complete exchangeability. The consolidation of money and the consolidation of personhood, the identity of the self, should thus be thought together, as two sides of a single logical process. As the objectification of mind, money renders the disparate and formless pre-identical world knowable, making it discursive and rationally intelligible. In modernity, it is constitutive of what Kant conceived of as the a priori transcendental subject, the capacity of the self to unify and articulate the sensory manifold as an ordered and coherent object field by referring it to its self-identity. When its concept is developed through dialectical theory, money is revealed both as essential to the process of enlightenment *per se* and as intrinsic to the freedom of the subject. Through money, the subject lifts itself out of amorphous nature and mediates it to itself, organising it as a conceptual totality: the greater the power of money and the more determinate its form, the more extensively the world is mediated to the subject. In this way, money is the embodiment of what Kant called the spontaneity of the subject, the fact that the self is not simply tied, passively, to receptivity but shapes the world actively, in sovereign freedom.[67] When, in capital, the world has been completely monetised, so that money becomes money engendering more money, then only that which is monetarily mediated is conceivable. Within the system of absolute identity, things exist at all, and have validity, only so far as they can be articulated in the discursive language of money.

66 Reichelt 2005, p 52 (emphases in original).

67 Kant 1999, pp 246–7/B132–3.

The development of the identity of the monetary self towards universality works through the progressive negation of the world. The object becomes conceptual only by way of the sacrificial emptying out of its pre-identical being. This is the work of enlightenment in Adorno and Horkheimer's recasting of the dialectic: 'Humans believe themselves free of fear when there is no longer anything unknown. … Nothing is allowed to remain outside, since the mere idea of the "outside" is the real source of fear.'[68] Accordingly, history unfolds as a relentless logic of critique. The substantiality of the pre-identical world is inexorably corroded, disqualified as mythical by the advance of identity, so that in the end there may be nothing in which the subject does not find itself entirely reflected back to itself.[69] The end point of this process is reached in capitalist modernity. For Kant, the 'thing in-itself' is a merely noumenal object, a problematic thought-entity that must be at least thinkable but cannot be known. From the indeterminate sensations transmitted by this next-to-nothing, the subject, by means of the transcendental machinery of its synthetic categorial capacity, manufactures the object as an intelligible commodity. In the self-transcendence of epistemology as dialectic, the reduction of the pre-conceptual thing to a nugatory, liminal value is revealed as the condition for the realisation of the absolute Concept. Only when the world has been evacuated of all substance of its own is it possible for identity to fold back on itself completely and become self-grounded. Indeed, the premise of the absolutisation of identity as capital is the disintegration of the world to such a degree that it is no longer capable of sustaining the subject at all. Infinite, unceasing exchange thus becomes a compulsive necessity: the subject *must* continually produce itself from itself, through the ceaselessly reiterated circuits of the system of capital, because there is nothing substantial and coherent 'outside' for it to refer to anymore. As Adorno and Horkheimer put it, 'the world becomes chaos, and synthesis salvation'.[70] The absolute freedom of the subject thus demands the sacrificial destruction of the world as anything other than the subject. Through the entire dialectical process of enlightenment, all meaning is gradually transferred from the world into the subject, but the subject itself only has one meaning – identity.

The subject's abandonment of the world in sacrifice is at the same time its abandonment of itself as a part of the world. In the formation of identity through the internalisation of the universal, the subject progressively separates itself from itself, the abstract-universal self simultaneously excluding

68 Horkheimer and Adorno 2002, p 11.

69 'For the Enlightenment, anything which cannot be resolved into numbers, and ultimately into one, is illusion. … Unity remains the watchword from Parmenides to Russell. All gods and qualities must be destroyed' (Horkheimer and Adorno 2002, pp 4–5).

70 Horkheimer and Adorno 2002, pp 2–3. In the same way, it is only the rigidified identity of the state that stands between the subject and the formless anarchy of the state of nature.

and spiritualising the natural-material being. Hence the famous claim in *Dialectic of Enlightenment* that 'the history of civilization is the history of the introversion of sacrifice – in other words, the history of renunciation':

> The human being's mastery of itself, on which the self is founded, practically always involves the annihilation of the subject in whose service that mastery is maintained, because the substance which is mastered, suppressed and disintegrated by self-preservation is nothing other than the living entity, of which the achievements of self-preservation can only be defined as functions – in other words, self-preservation destroys the very thing which is to be preserved.[71]

The modern subject is the final outcome of this sacrificial logic of renunciation. Such is the metaphysical meaning of the various separations and divisions that Louis Dumont noted as being essential to the formation of the economic Individual: only once the subject has made itself absolutely sovereign by divesting itself of any involvement with anything beyond itself is all relation mediated by identity. The principle of subjectivity itself therefore implies radical separation and individualisation as its *telos*. This extreme degree of severance is the premise both of the construction of the universality of rational, scientific knowledge in epistemology and of its dialectical self-reflection.[72] The epistemological self of modernity is thus the ultimate product of demythologisation as the process of 'the ontological evacuation of the subject'.[73] In Kantian critique, the possibility of cognition depends upon its transcendental principle, the pure 'I think' of the synthetic unity of apperception, being entirely devoid of any content. Nothing that is not identical may come within its borders. Hence the drastic division between form and content that sits at the base of Kant's architectonic of pure reason. Correlatively, in Kant the self-renunciation of the subject has reached so far that, within the experiential structure of transcendental idealism, '*even the thinking subject is* in inner intuition *a mere appearance to itself*'.[74] The modern subject knows itself

[71] Horkheimer and Adorno 2002, p 43. With its emphasis on renunciation, Adorno's account of sacrifice brings together both its destructive-suppressive aspect and its kenotic aspect, that is, its aspect of self-limitation, self-emptying and withdrawal. On the thematic of sacrifice in post-Kantian continental thought, with particular reference to the kenotic dimension, see Bubbio 2014.

[72] 'The self which, after the methodical extirpation of all natural traces as mythological, was no longer supposed to be either a body or blood or a soul or even a natural ego but was sublimated into a transcendental or logical subject, formed the reference point of reason, the legislating authority of action' (Horkheimer and Adorno 2002, p 22).

[73] Jarvis 2004, p 73.

[74] Kant 1996, p 141 (emphasis in original); cf. Kant 1999, pp 247–9/B153–6.

not as it is but only as it is constructed by itself. In the dialectical opening out of epistemology, this absolute emptiness of the modern subject, its extreme limitation, became the condition of its unlimited plenitude:

> For Kant, thinking is and must be empty of being; for Hegel, it is and must be full of it. Yet this difference about 'thinking' rests on an accord about subjectivity. The fullness which Hegel's 'thinking' has is by no means its own property. It is not something it has by virtue of an inner intuition. Subjectivity 'as such' is 'our entirely empty self, the self without any further content'. On the contrary, its fullness comes only on condition of an absolute relinquishment of the illusion that there are any properties which belong to thinking, of its plunging into externality. That thinking is to be everything requires that it not have any ontological content of its own.[75]

The subject separates itself completely from the world so that it may fill itself completely with the world. The universalisation of the subject, its absorption of the entire world into itself, is thus at the same time its utter self-sacrifice, a process of ontological evacuation that is completed only when it has become nothing but a being of exchange, an 'entirely empty self, the self without any further content'. The modern capitalist subject, the absolutely free, sovereign and self-determining Individual, is totally bare.

Perhaps the most immediately consequential effect of the dialectical theorisation of capital is that it finally breaks the spell of the economic altogether. That the primary, non-conceptual materiality that sits at the base of the economic problematic is always already completely mediated means that the world is not, in fact, economic in itself. Instead, if the material and the conceptual exist in an original identity, reciprocally producing each other through the logic of division, as dialectical theory demonstrates, then the world becomes a place of labour and production to the extent that it becomes a place of exchange-identity.[76] Properly speaking, therefore, there is no such thing as 'economics', as a positive doctrine of the irreducible natural necessity of material production. Rather, economics is a discourse of sacrifice. The system of generalised exchange, which is the precondition of modern economic thought, is the logical outcome of the sacrificial

---

[75] Jarvis 2004, p 75 (the quoted phrase is from Hegel's *Aesthetics* (Hegel 2014, p 891)). For Hegel, 'the highest Idea of the Kantian philosophy is the complete emptiness of subjectivity, or the purity of the infinite concept' (Hegel 1977b, p 96).

[76] As the Biblical story in Genesis 3 has it, the fall into labour and production follows from the separation from nature – the banishment from the Garden of Eden – through the acquisition of self-consciousness, or identity (cf. Hegel 1991, pp 61–3).

process of enlightenment by which the world is made identical.[77] In this way, dialectical theory transforms the very concept of capital. So far from being an economic form, capital is really a total system of identity, or validity, which is constituted through universal exchange. Correlatively, the economic, as the complete reduction of the world to bare materiality, is an effect of the universal conceptuality of capital. It follows from this radical reframing of the concept of capital that the nature and significance of a theory of capital are likewise fundamentally transformed. For what its dialectical concept makes clear is that capital is an essentially spiritual phenomenon – indeed, absolute spirit – which posits the materialism of the economic from out of itself, as that in which it realises itself.

Moreover, if capital is not a mode of production with a dialectical form but actually *is* the dialectic, then it is properly metaphysical.[78] What arises in exchange is, as modern value theory has shown, the Being of Nothing, the presence of an absence that systematically unfolds itself in its immanent universality until it has made itself the whole. It is through this universal absence that the world becomes present, 'there', as an objectified and knowable reality in the first place. Value is thus the essence that underlies all appearances, the animating soul that makes them rationally intelligible. When it attains its concept as capital, value finally realises itself as the Being of all beings, the reason and life of the world, which is always present in its absence, always there but never directly graspable as such. In *Dialectic of Enlightenment*, Adorno and Horkheimer propose that in the pre-Socratic moment and through into classical Greek philosophy myth was rationalised into metaphysics. The subject takes the universal into itself in order to make itself the universal. The self-unfolding process of the dialectic is nothing other than the working out of this mimetic logic of identity, so that the movement of history ultimately describes a circle: from the entirely immanent world of

77 'Human labor, whereby the unity of finite and infinite only comes about to the extent that it is permeated by spirit and wrung out of the action of spirit, is, however, already a more profound sacrifice and an advance beyond the kind of sacrifice that originally appeared merely as the giving up of an immediate finitude. For the sacrifice involved in productive human labor is the *action of spirit* – the effort that, negating particular self-consciousness, holds fast the purpose that dwells within representationally, and brings it forth outwardly, for intuition' (Hegel 2007a, p 357 (emphasis in original)).

78 In the terms of Hegel's critique of Kant, therefore, capital is not a subjective form through which unity is imposed upon a pre-given sensory manifold – that is, an economic form – but is rather the objective form of Being itself, its completed self-realisation through the movement of the dialectic. This perception is already implicit in modern value theory in its idea of a homology between the categories of *Capital* and those of Hegel's *Logic*. The perception is distorted, however, by the continuing desire to translate ontology into economics, rather than to recognise the economic as the appearance form of dialectical ontology.

myth, to the entirely immanent world of capital.[79] Modernity, in which the subject has finally become the whole, thus recreates the *Schuldzusammenhang* of myth – a closed context of guilt, absence of transcendence or an outside, general equivalence and a universal that maintains itself through the blind destruction of the particular. Just as pre-subjective life in the archaic world of myth was everywhere permeated by a multitude of spirits, so the bare existence of the sovereign Individual in the demythologised world of modernity is completely pervaded by the infinite spirit of capital.

[79] The logic of dialectic is simultaneously progress and regression, so that at the end it returns to its beginning, uncovering its own foundation: 'The movement of the *Phenomenology* is only superficially a movement forwards. It is also, much more fundamentally, a movement downwards or backwards or inwards, into that which we have already become, into the innumerable mediations of spirit, the historical slaughter-bench, which has made the apparent natural immediacy of everyday experience possible' (Jarvis 2010, p 162). Or, as Hegel puts it: 'the whole of science is in itself a circle in which the first becomes also the last, and the last also the first' (Hegel 2010, p 49).

8

Sovereignty and Dialectic

So long as capital is thought on the model of representation, it is not possible to grasp the logical relation between the political and the economic. The representational paradigm that is intrinsic to the economic conception of existence silences and hides the dividing line upon which it is based. Since it cannot understand, or even really see, its own foundation, therefore, it necessarily falsifies the relation between the two sides of the division. Once capital has been broken out of the representational paradigm of economic thought altogether, though, and reconceived not as one particular form of material-economic life among others but as a universal system of identity that reduces the world to bare materiality, then the way is opened to return to the problematic of capital and the international and to rethink the relation between the economic space of the world market and the political space of the international states-system. That is, through the dialectical theorisation of capital, it finally becomes possible to grasp the logical relation between value and sovereignty, and so to comprehend the modern world-system as a whole. If, in representation, the division is rendered mute and passive, in dialectic, by contrast, it becomes active and dynamic. The dialectical system of identity, which culminates in universal exchange, works through a logic of inside and outside: value, as pure identity, takes the whole world into itself by emptying itself completely of the world. The two sides are thus implicated in each other, in a single dialectical movement of reciprocal opposition and identity. When it is brought into this theoretical perspective, the concept of sovereignty shows itself to be exactly homologous with the concept of value. The political and the economic thus come together at the logical level in the theory of dialectic.

This dialectical character of sovereignty emerges clearly from Giorgio Agamben's analysis in *Homo Sacer* and its companion volume, *State of Exception*. The staging ground of Agamben's discussion is what he reconstructs as the 'debate' between Walter Benjamin and Carl Schmitt, an intermittent series of positions and counter-positions that ran from Benjamin's 'Critique of Violence' of 1921, through to his 'Theses on the Concept of History' from 1940.[1] In his *Auseinandersetzung* with Benjamin, Schmitt found himself in exactly the opposite position to that which he occupied in his contemporaneous dispute with Hans Kelsen and legal positivism: where, against the pure immanence of the positivists, he insisted on the ineliminable openness of the legal system to its outside, against Benjamin, who sought to transcend the sphere of law entirely, he insisted with equal vehemence on its necessary closure. What makes Schmitt's account of sovereignty paradigmatic for Agamben, and his debate with Benjamin so significant, therefore, is that it concerns precisely the dialectical, inside/outside, dynamic that arises at the borderline, in the 'state of exception'.[2]

Identity and division

Schmitt and the exception

As it is figured in the debate between Schmitt and Benjamin, the state of exception forms a kind of metaphysical crisis point, where the very possibility of the political is at issue. This is why the argument is conducted in terms of the philosophy of history and the relation between myth and law, violence and justice. If its esoteric meaning is what is at stake in the debate with Benjamin, why such metaphysical import should be concentrated into the obscure and marginal space of the state of exception becomes clear only in relation to the exoteric aspect of Schmitt's argument in *Political Theology*, its polemic against liberalism. Schmitt's primal fear was that universal mediation, liberalism's endless discussion, would enervate politics to the point of eliminating it altogether, and so accelerate modern society's descent into nihilistic disintegration and ungovernability.[3] While its terminology and approach varied across his career, Schmitt's theorising

---

1 Benjamin 2021 and 2006.

2 No doubt it is correct to say that 'Agamben's analysis of sovereignty and bare life – and his theory of biopolitics more generally – are probably unthinkable without Schmitt' (Attell 2015, p 157). However, as Sergei Prozorov has pointed out, the significance of Schmitt in the economy of Agamben's thought differs substantially from that of other important influences, such as Benjamin and Heidegger: 'While Schmitt's political thought was certainly *employed* in a variety of ways after *Homo Sacer*, Schmitt was not really *engaged* with as a philosophical interlocutor. Instead, I suggest that the use of Schmitt in Agamben's *oeuvre* has been *paradigmatic* in the rigorous methodological sense that Agamben later developed' (Prozorov 2017, p 87 (emphases in original; on 'paradigms', see Agamben 2009, Chapter 1)). That is, the specific virtue of Schmitt's theory of sovereignty, for Agamben, lay in 'exemplifying the apparatus that he sought to render inoperative' (Agamben 2009, p 88). At the close of the age of the *jus publicum Europaeum*, Schmitt registered with singular perspicacity and force the indistinction of law and violence that would become the universal condition of the globalised world (Agamben 2019b).

3 Schmitt 1988, Chapter 2.

always sought to rescue what he regarded as the authentically political moment of immediate, constitutive power from the corrosive effects of mediation.[4] Thus, in *Political Theology*, against legal positivism, which sought to construct a completely seamless order of legal norms in which the state would be reduced to the technical-formal role of a guarantor that 'should remain in the background as *ultima ratio*',[5] Schmitt insists that the legal system can never be completely closed upon itself because the legal form as such is not self-sufficient.[6] It relies for its fulfilment upon an element external to its own immanent sphere. In their drive to produce a coherent and self-enclosed deductive system of law, however, the positivists simply closed their eyes to the ineliminable question of power implied in the problem of the relation of law to life because, for them, 'everything that contradicts the system is excluded as impure'.[7] As a result, they dismissed the exception as something extra-juridical and irrational. This blindness left them unable to grasp the concept of sovereignty, or to account for the relation between legality and power.[8] What motivates Schmitt's interest in the exception, therefore, is that it takes legal thought to the very limit of its jurisdiction, to the point at which it is confronted with what is not the same as it. In the instant of decision, sovereignty and world come face to face, and the force of law is applied directly to life.[9]

The exception is thus, as Schmitt notes at the outset of his discussion, 'a borderline concept … one pertaining to the outermost sphere'.[10] The decision on the exception carries such metaphysical weight for Schmitt because it is in the encounter with what it cannot comprehend that the regularised interior space in which the legal norm can be applicable finds it

4 When, from the 1940s, Schmitt's thought turned to the geopolitical, this hostility to liberalism and mediation was translated into the mythopoetic terms of the elemental opposition of land and sea, Behemoth and Leviathan (Schmitt 2003 and 2015).

5 Schmitt 2005, p 25.

6 'Every legal thought brings a legal idea which in its purity can never become reality, into another aggregate condition and adds an element that cannot be derived either from the content of the legal idea or from the content of a general positive legal norm that is to be applied' (Schmitt 2005, p 30). Or, as Agamben puts it, Schmitt perceived that 'the application of a norm is in no way contained within the norm and cannot be derived from it' (Agamben 2005a, p 40).

7 Schmitt 2005, p 21.

8 'All tendencies of modern constitutional development point toward eliminating the sovereign in this sense', i.e. as the ultimate point of unity that gives coherence to the legal order as a whole (Schmitt 2005, p 7).

9 *Ausnahmezustand*, 'state of exception', thus 'in German discourse and beyond, became the technical term for defining the "no man's land" between the legal order and the political fact, between law and its suspension' (Agamben 2021, pp 82–3).

10 Schmitt 2005, p 5.

justification and legitimacy. The inner truth of the juridico-political sphere is thus revealed at the extreme, in the crisis of the confrontation with the unknown. In his account, Schmitt articulates this foundational significance of the exception in terms of identity and non-identity:

> The exception is that which cannot be subsumed; it defies general codification, but it simultaneously reveals a specifically juristic element – the decision in absolute purity. The exception appears in its absolute form when a situation in which legal prescriptions can be valid must first be brought about. Every general norm demands a normal, everyday frame of life to which it can be factually applied and which is subjected to its regulations. The norm requires a homogeneous medium. This effective normal situation is not a mere 'superficial presupposition' that a jurist can ignore; that situation belongs precisely to its immanent validity. There exists no norm that is applicable to chaos. For a legal order to make sense, a normal situation must exist, and he is sovereign who definitely decides whether this normal situation actually exists.[11]

The exception is thus located at the foundation of the ordered, 'homogeneous' political-legal space. Only through and against 'that which cannot be subsumed' can the 'normal, everyday frame of life', the domain of juridical rules and regulations, be created. The element of the exception, branded as chaotic and irrational, must therefore be set aside for the self-identical inner space to have validity. No juridico-political order can exist without this separation being made, which is the necessary and indispensable task of the sovereign. The exception, on Schmitt's account, thus has a double function. It is a limit concept in that it marks the borderline of the ordered space of sovereignty, the point beyond which the authority of the sovereign does not reach. But it is also the element that gives life to the sovereign authority, which proves its power through the decision on the exception.

Schmitt's intention in *Political Theology* was to demonstrate the necessary superiority of the sovereign decision to the mere norm of law.[12] The crucial importance of the state of exception for him was that it clearly reveals the ineliminable distinction between the underived and originary authority of

---

[11] Schmitt 2005, p 13.

[12] 'The decision on the exception is a decision in the true sense of the word', he remarks admiringly (Schmitt 2005, p 6). In fact, the true sense of the word lies in the dark zone of sacrifice: 'Sacrifice involves the first uprooting, the first detachment, the original *decisio* (from *caedo*, meaning to kill the sacrificial victim with spilling of blood)' (Calasso 2018, p 146).

sovereignty and the secondary legal order that depends from it. Where the system of law reaches its limit, sovereign power is revealed in all its majesty. This essence of sovereignty, which cannot be reduced to the mediation of law and statute because it is the immediate founding power, is what in his later work Schmitt would term *nomos*:

> *Nomos* comes from *nemein* – a [Greek] word that means both 'to divide' and 'to pasture.' Thus, *nomos* is the immediate form in which the political and social order of a people becomes visible – the initial measure and division of pasture-land, i.e., the land-appropriation as well as the concrete order contained in it and following from it. … *Nomos* is the *measure* by which the land in a particular order is divided and situated; it is also the form of political, social, and religious order determined by this process. Here, measure, order, and form constitute a spatially concrete unity.[13]

Nomos denotes the way in which humans first take hold of the world, producing a stable and objectified order of political life. It is inseparable from the control and settlement of territory, the division and bounding of land, and the determinate and localised 'concrete order' of human life that is thereby established.[14] *Nomos* is thus associated by Schmitt at its root with both universality and delimitation. In *Political Theology* Schmitt outlines, but does not comment upon, the specific contradiction that is thus contained in the concept of *nomos*. The issue of sovereignty within any particular political order ultimately resolves, for Schmitt, into the question, 'who is supposed to have unlimited power?',[15] a question that is made urgent when that order experiences the disintegrative proximity of the exception. He then goes on to state that 'what characterizes an exception is principally unlimited authority, which means the suspension of the entire existing order'.[16] Unlimitedness thus works precisely through the limit and the state of exception. It is the capacity to decide on the exception and draw the border, the line of delimitation and exclusion, that is the defining mark of the 'unlimited authority' of sovereignty. Sovereign *nomos* is universal, therefore, not despite but because of its boundedness.

---

13 Schmitt 2003, p 70 (emphasis in original). See also Schmitt 2015, pp 59–60.

14 Schmitt here attributes to *nomos* 'the orientational character of original words' in its status as a 'fence-word', citing Jost Trier's assertion that 'every *nomos* consists of what is within its own bounds' (Schmitt 2003, pp 74–5).

15 Schmitt 2005, p 10.

16 Schmitt 2005, p 12.

Adorno and the non-identical

In *Political Theology*, Schmitt proposes that 'the metaphysical image that a definite epoch forges of the world has the same structure as what the world immediately understands to be appropriate as a form of its political organization'.[17] It is through the exception that he then tries to re-establish the metaphysical ground of the political. The point of attack against the closed sphere of positivism was found at its very limit, on the borderline: while the existence of the norm implies a regularised space within which it can have application, the norm cannot itself create that space but instead relies upon the founding power of sovereignty. The effort to escape the system of abstract normativity and to re-find 'concrete' life thus forces Schmitt to the boundary line, as the place where the superiority of sovereignty to law, *nomos* to *Gesetz*, is unequivocally demonstrated: only sovereign power, through the decision, is able to draw the line and so bring into being the regularised space within which the norms can be valid. Where Schmitt sought to reconnect the political to its properly metaphysical ground, so, from the other side, Adorno's metacritique of epistemology and his thinking about identity were articulated through a continual legal-political metaphorics – the 'sovereign subject, which dictates laws to nature',[18] 'the sovereignty of the Spirit',[19] the 'formal juridicality of thinking',[20] 'the lawful synthesis through categories',[21] performed by the subject within the 'jurisdiction',[22] of thought, and so on.[23] As always with Adorno, this metaphoricity was intended substantively: conceptual sovereignty and political sovereignty are to be understood as the same.[24] Like Schmitt, although to directly opposite effect, in his meditations on the concept Adorno perceived that identity has its origin in and works through a logic of division and exclusion. Where for Schmitt, though, the decision on the exception is what affirms the unlimited power of the sovereign, for Adorno it is what ultimately entraps the sovereign subject within myth.

The contradiction in the basic structure of the concept around which the whole of Adorno's thought revolved can in fact be stated quite simply.

17 Schmitt 2005, p 46.

18 Adorno 2001b, 'Peephole Metaphysics'.

19 Adorno 2001b, 'Materialism Imageless'.

20 Adorno 2001b, 'Rhetoric'.

21 Adorno 2001b, 'Objectivity of the Antinomy'.

22 Adorno 1982, p 23.

23 A thorough study of Adorno's intensely self-conscious language would show how its various registers – logical-conceptual, legal-juridical, monetary-commercial, and magical-mythical – are all interlaced with and continually echo one another.

24 Or, as Agamben puts it: 'What constitutes man as a thinking animal has its exact counterpart in what constitutes him as a political animal' (Agamben 1998, p 182).

In the first place, as the medium of identity, the concept is indispensable to thought. There simply is no thinking other than by means of concepts because it is only through the universality of the concept that the world can be determined as a rationally knowable objectivity. As Adorno remarked in conceding Kant's claim that the mind is structured so that it is incapable of thinking in the absence of the universality of the concept: 'without concepts, without abstraction, that is, without the mechanism that [Kant] ascribes to universality, thinking is in fact not possible ... we really would be faced with "blind intuition" ... with non-conceptual givens, from which concepts were absent and on which no light could be thrown'.[25] The identity of the concept is thus the foundation of the rational order of thought. From it, thinking develops as method, the coherent and lawful procedure of the *logos*, which is not rhapsodic, does not lose itself in what is alien to it, but remains with itself, secure and self-possessed in all that it encounters. By diligently following the prescribed path of method and the laws of thought, the thinking subject can be sure that it will not go astray, falling into irrationality and contradiction, but will always stay safely within the security of its jurisdiction. Furthermore, thought as method means that, in principle, the same minimum number of logical axioms can be used to grasp everything, bringing order to the multifariousness of the world and making it available for use. The inexorable drive of methodical thinking towards surveyability and completeness gives thought the character of systematics, a thorough-going organisation in which every individual part is co-ordinated with every other to form a totality, Schmitt's 'homogenous medium'. Since the motive force of the concept is to leave nothing outside the circle of identity, the drive towards system is inherent to thought. It is by means of the identifying power of the concept, therefore, that the subject overcomes everything that is given to it as merely heteronomous, absorbing it into its interiority, in order to make itself sovereign and free.

The central perception of Adorno's critique of identity, however, was that for the concept to become sovereign a price had to be paid. Conceptual order and the determinacy of objectivity can be established only through the disqualification of the world: abstraction 'always comes into being through the elimination of qualities, through the reduction of qualitative distinctions to quantitative forms.'[26] For law to grasp life – for the world to be made conceptual – there must, therefore, be an element of loss, or sacrifice. The aspect of things that is truly immeasurable must be set aside for the sake of order; or, in Schmitt's version, what cannot be made homogenous must be abandoned in order for the inner space to achieve rational identity. This is

[25] Adorno 2001a, p 143.
[26] Adorno 2001a, p 173.

the locus of the central term of Adorno's thought, 'the non-identical', by which he sought to denote that which resists incorporation into thought. The non-identical can only be gestured towards in this deliberately inadequate way because it intends what is set aside by, and so is external to, the discursive medium of the concept.[27] The nature of conceptual generality is such that it cannot encompass the pre-identical being of the world but cuts it short in order to shape it to its own immanent order. Through the judgement of identity, therefore, the non-conceptual is 'eliminated from thought, exiled from the latter's home domain.'[28] In this way, for Adorno, the concept re-enacts in rationalised form 'one of the primal images of mythic violence: it amputates the incommensurable'.[29] The contradiction in the structure of the concept is thus that precisely in enabling the subject to know the world, it separates it from it. Indeed, the greater the power of the concept, the further that the order of reason reaches, the more radically subject and world are divided. The concept thus at once reveals and conceals, making present by making absent.

Where Schmitt, in his account of sovereignty, accepted the contradictory combination of the limited and the unlimited without question, for Adorno, by contrast, the inside/outside structure of the concept was *the* central problem of philosophy, which he perceived running like a red thread

[27] There is, in fact, a certain ambiguity in Adorno about what exactly the 'non-identical' denotes. Sometimes it appears to refer to the affinity between the human being and the world while they are still continuous with each other as elements of nature. However, this aspect of things is not so much non-identical as pre-identical, since it is anterior to the structure of identity altogether, that is, prior to the division of inside and outside. Indeed, it is precisely this affinity that must be negated and set aside in order for identity to come into being. At other times, though, it appears to refer to the non-conceptual materiality that, after the division, stands 'outside' the concept and to which it refers. As dialectical theory shows, though, this materiality is in fact internal to the dialectical structure of identity – it is identical precisely in its non-identity.

[28] Adorno 2001b, 'Indissolubility of the Something'.

[29] Horkheimer and Adorno 2002, pp 8–9. Adorno and Horkheimer describe this exclusion of the non-identical as 'the situation for which Kierkegaard praised his Protestant ethic' (Horkheimer and Adorno 2002, p 9). The reference here to Schmitt's 'Protestant theologian' (Schmitt 2005, p 15), who was the subject of Adorno's first, and highly Benjaminian, book (Adorno 1989), is perhaps not incidental. Reading *Dialectic of Enlightenment*, a text in many ways deeply indebted to Benjamin, in relation to the Schmitt–Benjamin debate reveals a number of subterranean ripostes to Schmitt in the work. Indeed, when it is considered from this perspective, Adorno and Horkheimer's 'philosophical fragments' take on the character almost of an addendum to or commentary on the dispute that Agamben reconstructs between Schmitt and Benjamin. (See also, in this context, the section of *Minima Moralia* entitled 'Passing muster' (Adorno 2005d, pp 131–2).)

through the entire history of Western thought.[30] The transition from myth to reason that took place in the pre-Socratic moment marked a decisive stage in the formation of identity, irrevocably setting in place the division between thought and being, method and matter. The trajectory of all philosophy since then has been to try to mediate this division by accounting for the object through the subject ever more thoroughly, so that in the end the subject produces the object completely out of itself. As Adorno saw it, however, this entire ambition of thought is doomed to failure because the mediation of the concept can never repair the division upon which it is founded: 'the advancing *ratio* … has as an advancing mediation ever more ingeniously hidden that break without ever coming to master it'.[31] Philosophies of identity are thus condemned by their own principle. The more unlimited and universal they become, the more limited and particular they are: 'Their inclusiveness *is* the break'.[32] The narrative of this failure is what Adorno found written in the history of epistemology. Theories of knowledge constitute a series of increasingly sophisticated and comprehensive attempts to close the gap by spiritualising the world into conceptuality, with the aim of achieving a final identity. Despite the enormous efforts they make to deduce the world from subjective immanence, though, such systematic conceptual constructions must always, in the end, reinscribe the division that constitutes their founding borderline.

For Adorno, this contradictory structure, by which thought interiorises the world only by shutting itself off from it, gives the lie to the subject's claim to sovereignty, its self-exaltation as possessing, in Schmitt's words, 'unlimited authority'. The drive for mastery progressively undermines itself: the more the subject knows, the less it knows, and the further its sovereign authority reaches, the more it is enclosed within itself.[33] The most insistent term in Adorno's thought for this contradictory inside/outside dynamic, by which the subject entraps itself through its own self-assertation, is *der Bann*:

> With the concept *Bann* Adorno means a dialectical process that begins with an authoritative pronouncement that in some sense draws a

---

[30] The contradictions of philosophies of identity, which must always assume the division, are developed in detail by Adorno in his discussion of Husserlian phenomenology (Adorno 1982), as much as in his more general analyses of Kant and Hegel. However, they extend at least as far back as the difficulties of the mediation of form and matter already evident in Aristotelian metaphysics (see Adorno 2000).

[31] Adorno 1982, p 13.

[32] Adorno 1982, p 13 (emphasis in original).

[33] Accordingly, Adorno read the history of modern, post-Hegelian continental philosophy (Kierkegaard, Bergson, Husserl and Heidegger) as a series of failed *Ausbruchsversuchen* ('outbreak attempts') from the universal immanence of capitalist subjectivity (Gordon 2016).

> boundary within which something is driven out, forbidden, declared taboo, and outside which whatever does not conform to the edict is expelled and left exposed in oblivion. This act of drawing a boundary, of determining what belongs and what is to be excluded, impoverishes and mutilates experience and unwittingly leads to the very opposite of what it intends. The most crucial act of *Bann*, for Adorno, may be just this moment of reversal, in which the one who 'casts' the 'spell', falls victim to it, the authority who makes the pronouncement is compelled to suffer the sentence that has been imposed.[34]

The *Bann* is the sovereign decision that stands at the origin of the dialectic. The order of reason, as much as the order of the law, is constituted by drawing the boundary and expelling whatever does not conform to the unity of identity, abandoning it to oblivion.

The logic of sovereignty

In Schmitt's thinking, the crucial importance of the exception is that it serves to affirm the originary quality of the founding power of *nomos*, which establishes the identity of the 'normal situation' through an untrammelled act of sovereign will. *Nomos* thus sets in motion the fateful cycle of law-making and law-preserving power that Benjamin sought to break through the enigmatic figure of 'divine violence'.[35] In Adorno's thinking, by contrast, the pronouncement by which the sovereign inscribes the borderline establishes the contradictory, inside/outside, structure of the concept and so initiates the dialectical process of identity and non-identity. Where, for Schmitt, its grounding in the concept of *nomos* is intended to invest the sovereign with the authority of antiquity, derived from the originary moment of foundation, in Adorno the relation between the archaic and the contemporary becomes the dialectical entwinement of myth and modernity: sovereign *nomos* is refigured as *der Bann*. This is likewise the sense of Agamben's analysis of the logic of sovereignty, centred on 'bare life', and his deliberate extension of the theme of biopolitics beyond modernity to the history of the political as

[34] Turner 2016, p 208. In his comprehensive discussion of Adorno's use of '*der Bann*', Christopher Turner draws out the complexity of its meaning: 'all five senses of the term—as an authoritarian power, an area over which that power is exerted that relegates what cannot be controlled to a hinterland, the public act of prohibiting or commanding something, the penalty of being excluded, and a spell or curse—found in the *Grimm* are operative in Adorno's concept. … translating it as "spell" or "bane" collapses it into a univocal sense that fails to do justice to Adorno's usage' (Turner 2016, p 207).

[35] Benjamin 2021, p 60.

such. Indeed, Agamben's claim is that, in making biological life its central concern, the modern state:

> does nothing other than bring to light the secret tie uniting power and bare life, thereby reaffirming the bond (derived from a tenacious correspondence between the modern and the archaic which one encounters in the most diverse spheres) between modern power and the most immemorial of the *arcana imperii*.[36]

In this respect, the logic of Agamben's argument in *Homo Sacer* is the same as that of Adorno and Horkheimer's in *Dialectic of Enlightenment*. Just as it is the completion of sovereign space in the wholly politicised world that exposes its genesis in the state of exception, so it is the totalisation of value as capital that reveals the wanderings of Odysseus as the emblematic origin of identity. Indeed, when they are read in relation to Adorno and the dialectical theorisation of capital, the major terms of Agamben's account of sovereignty can all be recognised as transcriptions of the dialectic.[37]

Inclusive exclusion

Agamben notes that Schmitt's theory of the exception implies that in the constitution of political space there can be no simple separation of inside and outside. This is because the most important act of the sovereign, who stands at the apex of the political order and guarantees it, is to decide on the exception, which is situated on the far side of the norms of law. In the liminal space of the state of exception, therefore, the sovereign is simultaneously inside and outside.[38] This double position is what Agamben terms 'the paradox of sovereignty': 'the sovereign, having the legal power to suspend the validity of the law, legally places himself outside the law' so that it may, in fact, be said that 'the law is outside itself.'[39] In acting outside the space of law, but only so as to redraw the line, the sovereign thus shows himself,

---

36 Agamben 1998, p 6.

37 While it has been justly observed that 'there are few thinkers whose concerns coincide with Agamben's so often as Adorno's' (de la Durantaye 2009, p 360), little work has in fact been done on the relation between the two philosophers, perhaps because Agamben himself has always maintained a careful distance from Adorno (see, for example, Agamben 2007, pp 117–37 and Agamben 2005b, pp 35–9). For some preliminary reflections, see Dickinson 2017.

38 'Although he stands outside the normally valid legal system, he nevertheless belongs to it, for it is he who must decide whether the constitution needs to be suspended in its entirety' (Schmitt 2005, p 7).

39 Agamben 1998, p 15.

behind 'the everyday frame of life', to be always still within the non-political world, Schmitt's 'chaos'. If Schmitt's aim is to clarify the relation between the state of exception and juridical order in order to justify the power of sovereign *nomos*, Agamben observes that 'it is a paradoxical articulation, for what must be inscribed within the law is something that is essentially exterior to it, that is, nothing less than the suspension of the juridical order itself.'[40] There is thus no unproblematic division of inside from outside because in founding the ordered interior space sovereignty necessarily remains always involved with the exterior. In the decision on the exception, the sovereign, who is the origin of the juridico-political order as a whole, is as at the same time external to it.

Not only, in the sovereign, is the inside external to itself, but the outside is also inside in its very exclusion. The exception, Agamben argues, is not simply severed from the juridical order as something wholly different but is held in a relation with that order: it is, after all, only an exception by virtue of its non-incorporation, which presupposes relationality. Through the exception, therefore, sovereignty does not just try to confine, or contain, that which is excessive or transgressive. Rather, the exception is the mode by which the unlimited power of sovereignty is constituted:

> Here what is outside is included not simply by means of an interdiction or an internment but rather by means of the suspension of the juridical order's validity – by letting the juridical order, that is, withdraw from the exception and abandon it. The exception does not subtract itself from the rule; rather the rule, suspending itself, gives rise to the exception and, maintaining itself in relation to the exception, first constitutes itself as a rule. The particular 'force' of law consists in this capacity to maintain itself in relation to an exteriority.[41]

That which does not lose itself in the flux but maintains its own inner coherence in the face of everything that confronts it as disturbing and alien is self-identical or infinite, in the Hegelian sense. Although he does not use the term, what is delineated in Agamben's explication of the state of exception is something like the originary movement of abstraction by which the subject withdraws itself from the indeterminate multifariousness of nature, creating the ordered, regularised inner space, governed by laws. Agamben describes the dynamic of the state of exception as 'the capture of life in law',[42] the '*inclusive exclusion*'[43] by which legality at once separates itself

[40] Agamben 2005a, p 33.
[41] Agamben 1998, p 18.
[42] Agamben 1998, p 26.
[43] Agamben 1998, p 21 (emphasis in original).

from and relates itself to the non-legal.[44] Inclusive exclusion is thus simply another way of describing the contradictory structure of the concept that is comprehended in dialectical thought: the interior, abstract space of the concept and the exterior material world are separated from each other through an original division, and at the same time related to each other through that same division in a relation of non-relation.[45] The non-conceptual is thus inside in being outside.[46] Moreover, once this inside/outside logic of division coheres as a permanent and stable structure, it comes to be assumed as what is most proper to human beings, its universal validity presupposed in all cognition: no objective experience is possible other than through it because, since it encompasses both sides of the division, nothing falls outside it. This is the sense of Agamben's numerous analogies of the logic of sovereignty to the self-presuppositional structure of language, the relation of the linguistic to the non-linguistic and of the overall totality of language to concrete instances of language use, *langue* and *parole*.[47] The universal structures of abstraction that make possible human life as something separate from the world thus come into being through the modality of the state of exception.

To Schmitt, the importance of the exception is that it demonstrates the status of sovereign power as superior to law as statute. In drawing out the implications of Schmitt's account, however, Agamben develops a theory of the exception not just as the crisis point at which sovereignty proves its validity but as the form of relation by which the human political space is constituted in the first place: 'What is at issue in the sovereign exception is not so much the control or neutralization of an excess as the creation and definition of the very space in which the juridico-political order can have validity.'[48] *Political Theology*'s interest in the exception lies in how it functions

---

[44] The notion of inclusive exclusion can thus be understood as a refiguration of dialectical identity-in-otherness, or Hegel's speculative perception that the concept 'overgrasps' the object: 'It will be seen in the Logic that this is just what thought and the universal are: that thought is itself and its other, that it overgrasps its other and that nothing escapes it' (Hegel 1991, p 50/§20). Or, as Adorno put it: 'Dialectic reaches the insight that the closed process also includes the non-included. It thus reaches a boundary to knowledge itself' (Adorno 1982, p 39).

[45] Robert Hanna remarks of Hegel's conception of dialectical contradiction: 'In a nutshell, Hegel is saying that when a phenomenon excludes itself by virtue of what it includes, and includes itself by virtue of what it excludes, it is "contradictory" in his sense' (Hanna 1996, p 279).

[46] 'The "ordering of space" that is, according to Schmitt, constitutive of the sovereign *nomos* is therefore not only a "taking of land" (*Landesnahme*) – the determination of a juridical and a territorial ordering (of an *Ordnung* and an *Ortung*) – but above all a "taking of the outside," an exception (*Ausnahme*)' (Agamben 1998, p 19).

[47] See, for example, Agamben 1998, pp 20–1, 25, 30 and 50, and Agamben 2005a, pp 36 and 39–40.

[48] Agamben 1998, p 19.

to reaffirm sovereign power. To that extent, Schmitt, despite taking it to its boundary-concept, continues to presuppose the priority of political order, from within which the exception, however necessary it may be, must always appear as something egregious and threatening. His view of the exception thus remains one from within the inner space of sovereignty. Agamben deposes this perspective in order to reveal the state of exception as a mode of relationality through which the conceptual generality of law comes into being.[49] In setting aside the Schmittian interest in reinscribing the boundary and instead seeking to explore the point of indifference between the legal and the non-legal, Agamben draws discussion of sovereignty away from the assumption ultimately shared by both Schmitt and his legal-positivist antagonists, that of the primacy of the political space of sovereignty. When that assumption, foundational to political thought, is displaced, the inclusive exclusion of the exception is revealed as 'the originary structure in which law refers to life and includes it in itself by suspending it'.[50]

The peculiar mode of relation by which law takes hold of life through the exception is what Agamben (drawing not on Adorno but on Jean-Luc Nancy) calls 'the *ban*'.[51] The fundamental idea of his investigation of the paradox of sovereignty is that '*the originary relation of law to life is not application but Abandonment.* The matchless potentiality of the *nomos, its originary "force of law,"* is that it holds life in its ban by abandoning it.'[52] As 'the originary juridico-political relation',[53] the ban names the paradox of sovereignty: what has been banned, or is held in a relation of ban, is subjected to the force of law in its exclusion – it comes under the law as such – and in this way it is included in the political relation through being banished. In the relation of ban, the very principle of the inside, the sovereign, is outside the legal order and what is outside, that which is banned, is included in the order through its exclusion. The ban thus denotes the contradictory logic of the exception, in which the distinction between inside and outside is both drawn and effaced:

> He who has been banned is not, in fact, simply set outside the law and made indifferent to it but rather *abandoned* by it, that is, exposed and threatened on the threshold in which life and law, outside and inside,

---

[49] 'To refer to something, a rule must both presuppose and yet still establish a relation with what is outside relation (the nonrelational). The relation of exception thus simply expresses the originary formal structure of the juridical relation' (Agamben 1998, p 19).

[50] Agamben 1998, p 28.

[51] 'From the old Germanic term that designates both exclusion from the community and the command and insignia of the sovereign' (Agamben 1998, p 28).

[52] Agamben 1998, p 29 (emphases in original).

[53] Agamben 1998, p 109.

> become indistinguishable. It is literally not possible to say whether the one who has been banned is outside or inside the juridical order.[54]

Agamben's exploration of the paradox of sovereignty delineates the complex topology that arises as a result of the ban structure. In *Dialectic of Enlightenment*, however, Adorno and Horkheimer go further by attempting to account for it. The logic of the state of exception, as Agamben lays it out, works in two directions: on one side, the outside is captured by the inside, so that what is banned is held in a relation of non-relation; on the other, the inside is outside itself because in the moment of the decision on the exception the sovereign must act in a self-authorising way, beyond the reach of the system of legal norms. The borderline space of the state of exception thus implicates both sides in each other precisely as it separates them. In explaining the origin of this dialectical, inside/outside, structure through their account of the formation of subjectivity, Adorno and Horkheimer add a further lay of complexity to Agamben's analysis. The mythical world through which Odysseus journeys is a closed and unchanging order of repetition and necessity, guilt and retribution. In *Dialectic of Enlightenment*, the paradox of sovereignty arises from Odysseus's struggle to liberate himself from this mythic context of guilt: 'Against this Odysseus fights. The self represents rational universality against the inevitability of fate. But as it finds the universal and the inevitable already inextricably entwined, its rationality necessarily takes a restrictive form, that of an exception.'[55] The order of myth is the original order of the law. Odysseus can neither overthrow the powers of nature by force, nor can he simply disregard the rights they claim. Instead, the medium of his escape, cunning, maintains the principle of equivalence in breaching it – he fulfils the statutes of myth in evading them. Through the creation of its own interior space of freedom and self-determination, therefore, the subject does not dissolve the hopeless context of guilt altogether and so truly liberate itself. Rather, because its identity is formed only through the internalisation of the universal experienced in nature, the subject remains within myth in its very escape from it. The order of sovereignty has thus only ever been an exception from the order of myth. In setting himself apart from myth, Odysseus is still held within its ban. At the same time, from the other side, in the moment of decision at the borderline, myth is also outside itself. It withdraws itself, maintaining itself in its sovereignty, by abandoning the subject outside its jurisdiction and yet holding it a relation of non-relation.

---

54 Agamben 1998, pp 28–9 (emphasis in original).

55 Adorno and Horkheimer 2002, p 46. The German original in fact has 'der Ausnahme', 'the exception' (Horkheimer and Adorno 2009, p 66; cf. Adorno and Horkheimer 1992, p 123).

Sovereignty takes the form of inclusive exclusion, therefore, because the sovereign subject is itself an inclusive exclusion from myth.[56]

State of exception

'In laying bare the irreducible link uniting violence and law', Agamben writes in the first 'Threshold' of *Homo Sacer*, 'Benjamin's "Critique of Violence" proves the necessary and, even today, indispensable premise of every inquiry into sovereignty'.[57] The state of exception constitutes the originary political element, or moment, because it reveals that irreducible link – when the system of norms is suspended, the application of law to life is exposed as a relation of violence. Agamben traces the awareness of the 'scandalous unification of the two essentially antithetical principles that the Greeks called *Bia* and *Dikē*, violence and justice',[58] back to its earliest expressions in the Western tradition, beyond the Sophistic opposition of *nomos* and *physis*, in Hesiod, Solon and, above all, Pindar's fragment 169. Bringing together the end of the process with its beginning in this way then enables him to reinterpret the meaning of a fundamental trope of modern political thought, the Hobbesian state of nature.[59] If the political order is founded on the logic of exceptionality, then the state of nature cannot be considered to be an original pre-political condition that is spatially and temporally anterior to the

---

[56] It is for this reason that Odysseus is the exemplary figure of the origin of the dialectic. Robert Hullot-Kentor notes that Adorno's first ideas for the thematics of the 'Excursus' on the *Odyssey* were developed in relation to Oedipus but that he 'ultimately focused this study on Odysseus rather than Oedipus because, while both are classical figures of heroic intellect, Homer stands on the border of Western civilization between history and prehistory in a way that Sophocles does not' (Hullot-Kentor 2006, p 36). That is, in Odysseus the archaic and the modern, myth and enlightenment, come together as in no other: 'Odysseus was the first to have mediation triumph over the immediate, postponement over presence, the twisted mind over straightforwardness. All the character traits that would be assigned over the centuries to the merchant, the foreigner, the Jew, the traveling player were coined by Odysseus in himself. … So, whereas Achilles and Agamemnon stand out in our memories as leftovers of another creation, consumed by catastrophe, Odysseus is still familiar to us, a sort of invisible companion. … Achilles has to be evoked; Odysseus is already at our side, wherever we are, whatever the circumstances' (Calasso 1994, p 366). In this respect, Odysseus constitutes something like a historical origin, in Benjamin's sense of the term (Benjamin 2019, pp 23–6).

[57] Agamben 1998, p 63.

[58] Agamben 1998, p 31.

[59] For discussion, see Prozorov 2009 and Prozorov 2014a, pp 103–7. There is perhaps a certain slippage or instability in Agamben's argument at this point between 'state of exception' and 'state of nature'. He does not explain why, in modernity, the state of nature presents itself as the permanent material ground out of which the ideal space of political order is created.

constitution of the Commonwealth and that is left behind in the transition to properly political life. It is not the case that first there is the state of nature, as the primary condition, and then there is the political community, as a secondary and derived formation, an artificial construction grounded on a pre-conceptual condition. Instead, because identity is formed through the ban, the exteriority of the state of exception is necessarily interior to the order of sovereignty and continues always to exist within it. This virtual condition, the 'being-in-potentiality' of the law,[60] manifests itself when the juridico-political space is considered 'as if it were dissolved', in the moment when, faced with the crisis of the exception, sovereign power suspends the validity of the norms and confronts life immediately.

> The state of exception … is not external to the *nomos* but rather, even in its clear delimitation, included in the *nomos* as a moment that is in every sense fundamental. At its very center, the localization-ordering link thus always already contains its own virtual rupture in the form of a 'suspension of every law'.[61]

The state of nature, which appears as the immediate ground of the mediated juridico-political order, must be understood to be, in fact, its effect. It presupposes the existence of sovereign identity exactly in its suspension. The natural, non-conceptual condition is what appears in the relation of ban, when identity applies in not applying. Like value, therefore, sovereignty does not arise on one side of the line and pass across the division to be represented on the other. Rather, it is situated *in* the division, mediating inside and outside in their reciprocal exclusion and inclusion.

As Agamben reads it, the Pindaric fragment on *nomos basileus* is the earliest formulation of the paradigm of sovereignty, posing the enigma of the dialectical 'conjunction of opposites'.[62] It may well be that nowhere before had the paradoxical unification of *Bia* and *Dikē* that constitutes sovereign subjectivity been expressed with such striking concision. However, in their reconstruction of the origins of the dialectic, Adorno and Horkheimer once again go further. If, by the time of Pindar, sovereignty could be precisely stated as the bringing together of law and violence, in the Homeric epic, through the adventures of Odysseus, the prehistory of this 'antithetical union' is dramatised. The basic theme of the *Odyssey*, structuring its narrative arc, is the crisis of sovereign authority and its re-establishment – Odysseus first hopelessly lost and then triumphantly returned. In the absence of the

[60] Agamben 1998, p 35

[61] Agamben 1998, p 37.

[62] Agamben 1998, p 31.

sovereign, the kingdom of Ithaca exists in a state of suspension: not yet completely disintegrated but without the 'normal situation' that the effective exercise of sovereign power guarantees, and so exposed to the lawlessness of the suitors. While the political space is held in a precarious condition of indistinction, so, correlatively, the *nostos*, the story of the wanderings, is the world of Odysseus *tanquam dissoluta consideretur*. In his enforced circulation beyond the boundaries, where 'the everyday frame of life' and all that is familiar to him have fallen away, Odysseus slips directly out of time, into the archaic, anomic world of mythical monsters and sorceresses. When the localisation and ordering that ground the identical self are placed in suspension, the primeval past suddenly rises up, showing itself not to be past at all but continually active within the present, and revealing itself in all its power as soon as the normal situation ceases to be valid. Historical time does not simply leave the time of myth behind, therefore, but is in dialectical relation with it.

The juxtaposition of different times in the epic narrative – the contemporaneity of Odysseus's mythical wanderings with the stories of Telemachus and Penelope – is thus not just the rationalisation of diverse legends through their incorporation into an overarching unity. More substantively, it is an expression, or function, of the state of emergency. Where the integrity of the subject's identity faces a mortal threat, time is dissolved into space and the state of exception, the moment of the formation of identity in the struggle with myth, irresistibly returns.[63] The spatial and narrative differentiation in the *Odyssey* of the situation within, in Ithaca, and the situation without, on the sea, should thus be understood as representing the two sides of the crisis of sovereignty: the law is in suspension while the sovereign confronts that which is beyond the law. For what Odysseus experiences in his adventures is nothing less than a series of states of exception. Again and again, at the outer margins of the known, he is thrown into extreme situations, states of emergency, that put at issue his very survival and in which, if he is to preserve himself, he must decide.[64]

[63] As Adorno and Horkheimer remark: 'At the Homeric stage, the identity of the self is so much a function of the nonidentical, of dissociated, unarticulated myths, that it must derive itself from them. The element which shapes and organizes individuality internally, time, is still so weak that the unity of the adventures remains an outward one, their sequence being formed by the spatial changes of scene, the succession of sites of local divinities on which the hero is flung by the storm. Whenever, at later historical stages, the self has again experienced such weakness, or narration has presupposed it in the reader, the manner of depicting life has slipped back into the form of successive adventures' (Horkheimer and Adorno 2002, p 39).

[64] 'The exception, which is not codified in the existing legal order, can at best be characterized as a case of extreme peril, a danger to the existence of the state, or the like' (Schmitt 2005, p 6).

Correlatively, though, if sovereign power undergoes its crisis beyond the established boundaries, it is also reasserted in the same movement, winning its strength through the encounter with the pre-identical and the escape from myth. Following Adorno and Horkheimer in reading the *Odyssey* in this way amplifies Agamben's analysis of the state of exception. What Agamben frames as the originary modality of the political, the contradictory inside/outside dynamic through which the space of sovereignty is established, is understood in *Dialectic of Enlightenment* as the critical moment in the constitution of sovereign subjectivity, or of identity as such.

In every case, what is at issue in Odysseus's confrontations with the forces of myth is the border between himself and the prehistoric world, the dividing line that separates the interiority of the subject from boundless and indeterminate nature.[65] As he is driven through the formless and disconnected spaces of the mythic cosmos, Odysseus repeatedly comes into contact with what is truly outside or, perhaps more properly, before – that is, not yet divided by identity – and in doing so experiences the proximity of the dissolving power of nature. His celebrated cunning then consists in his ability to hold himself together and find a way to mark himself off, reinscribing the boundary.[66] Thus in the encounter with the Sirens, who

[65] Accordingly, what above all characterises the world of Odysseus's wanderings is the absence of division: 'In this non-human space ... Odysseus now encounters a radical otherness, where the whole matter of boundaries is brought into question, and the categories separating human beings, beasts and the gods are confused. The space, the reverse of the humanized space from which Odysseus has come, seems to be devoid of cultivation or sociability, isolated and without detectable boundaries' (Hartog 2001, p 24). Because it is undivided, the pre-identical world is also unintegrated and without mediation: 'In this space there is no communication between one being and another. ... There is no proper route between these inaccessible places, no route that links them or that would make it possible simply to move from one to the next ... Just one place after another, without any transition' (Hartog 2001, pp 25–9). Unlike the world of the *Iliad*, therefore, which is characterised above all by war, the Odyssean world of wandering and adventure is truly pre-international. While Odysseus passes over from one space to another, the spaces themselves are not related.

[66] Within the philosophy of history, Odysseus does not simply represent the civilising tendency but actually embodies in himself the dialectical contradictions of separation – he *is* the threshold: 'It is part of the essence of Odysseus that he be the last of the heroes, the one who closes the cycle. Being the last, Odysseus is the closest to the life that will follow, a life never more to close in any cycle. He treads the boundary line. ... And yet, last among the heroes to return, Odysseus is also the one who right up to the end maintains his contact – and what an intimate contact it was – with the primordial powers who appeared in the first phases of the cycle. His wanderings were partly a compendium, a roll call, of all those beings and places that were already growing confused in many a memory, already being removed to the realm of the fabulous. With Odysseus, they are present, powerful and whole for one last time, and in Odysseus they salute the last traveler able to see them with his own eyes and bear witness' (Calasso 1994, p 350).

know everything 'that has ever happened on this fruitful earth', the danger by which Odysseus is threatened is the disintegration of the 'fixed order of time'.[67] This order, which constitutes the 'inner sense' of the subject,[68] is predicated upon spatial separation: 'the tripartite division is intended to liberate the present moment from the power of the past by banishing the latter beyond the absolute boundary of the irrecoverable and placing it, as usable knowledge, in the service of the present'.[69] The song of the Sirens, however, erases the dividing line, dissolving the self-identity that is constituted through the differentiation of the temporal present from what has been and pulling the subject back into the depths of the immemorial past. According to the necessities of the world of myth the Sirens cannot be avoided; Odysseus must confront them. The solution he finds in order to escape their threat is then virtually an allegory of the state of exception. On the one hand, he blocks the ears of his men with wax, cutting them off from the world as it was before identity by making them deaf to the allure of the mythic song. Thus restricted, they are kept safe inside, fixated in the present on their collective labour of rowing with all their might. On the other, Odysseus forcibly delimits himself, physically securing the border that separates him from the primeval world. As the only one who is permitted to remain in contact with pre-identical nature, he has himself bound tightly to the mast so that he may experience the overpowering beauty of the Sirens' song and yet still escape its destructive spell. The blissful pleasure of the undivided world is to be known only longingly, from a distance, and

67 Horkheimer and Adorno 2002, p 25. Lacking any division, the space of the *nostos* is also prehistoric: 'This world, devoid of any true sociability, is immobile. It has no past, no memories. It is a world where nothing is remembered, where no itinerant bard lives, and where all those cast ashore will be wiped out: the lotus is a flower of oblivion, and Circe's drug is a *pharmakon* that effaces all memories of one's homeland' (Hartog 2001, p 28).

68 Kant 1999, pp 178–84/B46–58.

69 Horkheimer and Adorno 2002, p 25. Marking out this border is the function of the prohibition on anachronism that is the foundational principle of the modern understanding of the past as 'history': past and present must be kept strictly apart so that they do not contaminate each other (Fasolt 2004; see also Davenport 2016). François Hartog proposes that in the *Odyssey* the order of time, like the order of the subject, is still in formation (Hartog 2015, pp 41–53). Referring in particular to Odysseus' tears at hearing the blind bard Demodocus sing of the episode of the Trojan horse at Alcinous's banquet, Hartog observes: '[Odysseus] inhabits an intermediary zone in which he is no longer and not yet Odysseus, not yet capable of declaring "I am Odysseus." And what emerges in this gap opened up between alterity and identity is indeed an experience of time. Not, as we have stressed, the anguished experience of finitude, since Odysseus knows he is mortal and would not wish it otherwise. Nor is it an experience of time as flux. Rather, this experience of self-estrangement can be called an encounter with historicity' (Hartog 2015, pp 52–3).

is thereby neutralised and rendered forever unattainable.[70] In the extreme situation, where the human order experiences a threat to its very existence, the sovereign shows himself to be situated on the borderline, simultaneously inside and outside the law.

As *Dialectic of Enlightenment* reads them, the adventures of Odysseus illustrate different dimensions of the formation of sovereign identity that takes place in the state of exception. For the encounter with the Sirens, this is the consolidation of temporal consciousness through the division of the present from the past. In the land of the lotus eaters, what Odysseus and his men are menaced by is not death but loss of will and reversion to passivity and lassitude. Ingestion of the flower dissolves the firmness and resolution of the self-directed subject. From the perspective of civilisation, the danger it therefore represents 'is no other than that of regression to the stage of gathering the fruits of the earth and the sea, older than agriculture, cattle-rearing or even hunting – older, in short, than any production'.[71] The intoxicating taste of the lotus draws the subject back into an earlier form of life, revoking its sovereign command of itself and undoing the objectification of the world. Its effect is thus to negate the primacy of practice, releasing those who eat it from compulsory labour and production and returning them to dependence upon nature through simple subsistence. Faced with this threat of regression, Odysseus's decision exemplifies the dialectic of enlightenment. On the one hand, he is right to reject the life of the lotus eaters, which is in truth only 'an illusion of bliss, a dull aimless vegetating';[72] but on the other, 'in being exerted by rationality, by Odysseus, this right is inevitably drawn into the realm of wrong' because 'his immediate action is one which reasserts domination'.[73] Odysseus denies the power of nature by imperiously cutting himself off from it. He saves himself from the disintegration of identity by re-establishing the force of law, exerting mythic violence against myth in the reassertion of his sovereign authority, as the men who had succumbed to the lotus are dragged back to the ship and placed in irons.

---

70 If Odysseus stands at the origin of the dialectic of identity, something of his predicament can still be discerned, thoroughly demythologised but still unresolved, in Kant's account of the structure of theoretical reason. On the one hand, as Adorno noted (Adorno 2001b, 'Preponderance of the Object'), Kant refused to allow knowledge to seal itself off completely in tautology and stubbornly acknowledged inalienable non-identity in the form of the thing-in-itself, the cause of all appearances. On the other, for the sake of the sovereignty of conceptual order and systematics, he drew the bonds of identity, the permitted limits, so tightly that the pre-identical is rendered virtually powerless and unknowable.

71 Horkheimer and Adorno 2002, p 50.

72 Horkheimer and Adorno 2002, p 49.

73 Horkheimer and Adorno 2002, p 49.

Like the lotus eaters but from a later, 'truly barbaric' stage,[74] the cyclops Polyphemus has no system of rational production but simply takes what the fertile earth gives, trusting in nature to provide.[75] Not only do they not work the land, but the cyclopes, who live solitary and self-sufficient existences, have no political organisation, no objective law-making and no regular and orderly process of intercourse and exchange. As Adorno and Horkheimer comment, 'abundance needs no law, and civilization's accusation of anarchy sounds almost like a denunciation of abundance'.[76] Nor do they respect and pay homage to the Olympian gods, whom they long pre-date, or acknowledge the custom of hospitality to guests.[77] Because he lives in an anarchic pre-political condition, a kind of state of nature, Polyphemus has no identity – he is not a self[78] – and it is this absence that becomes the medium of Odysseus's escape from destruction. Trapped in the Cyclops' cave, Odysseus names himself *Udeis* or 'nobody', suspending his identity in order to preserve it. The savage giant is unable to see through the ruse because, without self-reflection and interiority, he confuses the word for the thing; that is, he cannot conceive of their separation. In the crisis moment of the state of exception, Odysseus thus makes his decision: he bans himself, saving himself by denying himself and preserving his life 'by making himself disappear'.[79] 'Mimicking the amorphous realm'[80] and

---

74 Horkheimer and Adorno 2002, p 50.

75 Since no identical subject yet exists, the archaic world knows no production: 'But every place where the travellers pause presents them with the same disconcerting discovery: nowhere is the land cultivated (even if it happens to produce of its own accord, as in the Golden Age), and even where herd-raising is practised – as among the Cyclopes and the Laestrygonians – it is never accompanied by agriculture. Shepherds they may be, but cultivators they are not (yet)' (Hartog 2001, p 24). 'For Homer, the definition of barbarism coincides with a state in which no systematic agriculture, and therefore no systematic, time-managing organization of work and society, has yet been achieved' (Horkheimer and Adorno 2002, p 50).

76 Horkheimer and Adorno 2002, pp 50–1.

77 Laura Slatkin notes that what is characteristic of all of the mythical beings that Odysseus encounters is that they are either ignorant of or otherwise pervert the foundational proto-international institution of *xeinia*, that is, the reciprocal exchange relationship of 'guest-friendship' through which a form of recognition is established (Slatkin 2006, pp 319, 322–3). *Xenos* denotes a dialectical conjunction of opposites, meaning both 'host' and 'guest'.

78 According to Adorno and Horkheimer, Polyphemus's lack of subjecthood is signified by the cyclops' most distinctive feature: 'the singleness of the eye suggests the nose and mouth, more primitive than the symmetry of eyes and ears without which, and the combining of their dual perceptions, no identification, depth, or objectivity is possible' (Horkheimer and Adorno 2002, p 50).

79 Horkheimer and Adorno 2002, p 46.

80 Horkheimer and Adorno 2002, p 53.

negating himself as 'nobody', he becomes a Being of Nothing, the presence of an absence.[81]

Finally, on the island of Circe, the dissolving power of the amorphous is encountered as the seductive allure of the feminine. 'Circe's signature is ambiguity', a destabilising unboundedness and indefinition that 'is expressed even in her lineage: she is the daughter of Helios and the granddaughter of Oceanus. In her the elements of fire and water are not yet separated, and it is this indeterminacy … which constitutes the essence of promiscuity and the courtesan'.[82] Just as Circe lacks a clearly defined identity, so at the touch of her wand Odysseus' men lose theirs. Unmanned, they revert to the animal form of swine. Armed with the magical herbs given him by Hermes, though, Odysseus is able to take hold of himself in the face of mortal danger and withstand Circe's bewitchment, first threatening her with his sword and then forcing her to conclude a contract in the swearing of the oath, thereby subordinating her more ancient power to the law of the Olympian gods. In this way, he redraws around himself the magic circle of identity that protects him from the extreme peril of disintegration, preserving his sovereign and patriarchal authority by separating himself from nature: 'Circe's power, which subjugates men as her slaves, gives way to her enslavement to the man who, through renunciation, has refused to submit'.[83]

Potentiality

It is this capacity to renounce, attained in the experience of the different states of exception through which he passes, that wins Odysseus his freedom. He survives where his men perish because he is able to restrain himself. In giving himself over to adventure, he learns to hold himself back and to resist the irresistible attraction of the immediate: he does not open Aeolus's bag or moor his ship in the harbour of the Laestrygonians, nor does he taste the lotus flower or eat the cattle of Hyperion. What constitutes Odysseus's identical self as sovereign, therefore, is that it is able not to pass over directly into actuality: it does not lose itself in the world but withholds itself within itself, reserving itself to itself. Just as he survives by denying himself, so Odysseus can act successfully because, unlike the others, he can *not* act.

[81] On the play between negation and cunning, *Outis* and *Metis*, in the episode of the name, see Heller-Roazen 2017, pp 7–11.

[82] Horkheimer and Adorno 2002, pp 54–5.

[83] Horkheimer and Adorno 2002, p 53. Cf., in this context, the incident of Odysseus' fatal silencing of Anticlus, who is unable to master himself and resist when Helen calls beguilingly to the Greek warriors within the Trojan horse (Homer 2014, p 45): 'Of all the heroes Odysseus alone could ignore the sound of his name and coerce the rest to acquiesce in the nonbeing in which he himself was already an adept' (Austin 1972, p 15).

The subject's withdrawal into itself, effected through renunciation and the marking of the boundary, is always predicated, however, on the primacy of the actual. Odysseus' capacity for sovereign self-command is a humble acknowledgement of the superior power of nature. In this regard, as Adorno and Horkheimer read it, the *Odyssey* again illustrates, or gives a narrative form to, what is a 'signal concept'[84] not just of Agamben's account of sovereignty but of his thought as whole, one to which it repeatedly recurs: 'potentiality'.[85]

Agamben moves from the inside/outside structure of the sovereign ban to the metaphysics of potentiality by way of a consideration of an essential couplet of political theory, constituting and constituted power.[86] His argument is that these two modalities of power at once include and exclude each other. The 'free praxis' of constituting power cannot be reduced to constituted power, as the liberal attempt to constrain the founding authority by legal regulation would like. Because it works through the ban structure, though, nor can it be separated from sovereign power, as the radical democratic tradition imagines. It is in this interplay of the limited and the unlimited that the structural analogy between sovereignty and potentiality lies. The central point of Agamben's understanding of potentiality, developed through a distinctive reading of Aristotle,[87] is that 'potentiality is not simply non-Being, simple privation, but rather *the existence of non-Being*, the presence of absence'.[88] What interests Agamben is always this mode of existence of potentiality, the fact that, as Aristotle insisted, potentiality is not merely subordinate to the act but possesses its own autonomy: it is determinate non-Being, the actuality of negation. To have a potentiality, or a faculty, thus means 'to *have* a privation' – or, put differently, to be the Being of Nothing.[89] This is why, for Agamben, potentiality should more properly be thought as 'impotentiality', the ability not to. Potentiality does not exist only in the capacity to do something but, more importantly, in the capacity not to do it,

[84] Attell 2009, p 37.

[85] In his essay 'On Potentiality', Agamben declares that 'I could state the subject of my work as an attempt to understand the meaning of the verb "can" [*potere*]. What do I mean when I say: "I can, I cannot"?' (Agamben 1999d, p 177). Kevin Attell notes that the concept of potentiality constitutes the 'link between Agamben's earlier first-philosophical work and the more explicitly political thought from *Homo Sacer* on' (Attell 2015, p 86). For a discussion of the parallel that Agamben draws between sovereignty and ontology through his account of potentiality, see Brown 2013.

[86] Agamben 1998, pp 39–44.

[87] For discussion, see Attell 2009 and 2015, pp 84–100. Importantly, in his 2015 book Attell provides a translation of and commentary on key passages from the expanded Italian edition of the essay that was published subsequently to the English version, which was itself a translation of a public lecture from 1987.

[88] Agamben 1999d, p 179 (emphasis in original).

[89] Agamben 1999d, p 179 (emphasis in original).

to withhold oneself from the act.[90] The distinctiveness of human potentiality, what makes the human subject universal or unlimited, is this ability to relate to the world through the mode of negation, as impotentiality: 'while fire can only burn, and other living beings are only capable of their own specific potentialities – they are capable only of this or that behavior inscribed into their biological vocation – human beings are the animals capable of their own impotentiality'.[91] Potentiality, as the capacity to reserve oneself to oneself and not immediately to pass over into actuality, is thus an essential aspect of the concepts of freedom and sovereignty: 'To be free is not simply to have the power to do this or that thing, nor is it simply to have the power to refuse to do this or that thing. To be free is … *to be capable of one's own impotentiality*, to be in relation to one's own privation.'[92] Once potentiality is perceived in its full significance as impotentiality, then the relation between potentiality and actuality is changed. When the potential translates itself into the actual it is not simply annulled or lost; instead, the movement from potentiality to actuality is the realisation of impotentiality in actuality.[93] Impotentiality exists within actuality as its proper being. The actual is therefore to be understood as internal to the autonomy of potentiality, as the existence of non-Being. It is the product of the impotential, its giving of itself to itself:

> *If a potentiality to not-be originally belongs to all potentiality, then there is truly potentiality only where the potentiality to not-be does not lag behind actuality but passes fully into it as such.* This does not mean that it disappears in actuality; on the contrary, it *preserves itself* as such in actuality. What is truly potential is thus what has exhausted all its impotentiality in bringing it wholly into the act as such.[94]

Through this reading of potentiality as impotentiality, Agamben develops the structural correspondence between the sovereign ban, 'which applies to the exception in no longer applying', and potentiality, 'which maintains itself in relation to actuality precisely through its ability not to be'.[95] Where, in Adorno and Horkheimer's argument, Odysseus institutes the dialectical

---

90 For a discussion of Hegel's dialectical conception of possibility as the possibility not to be, see Brown 2018 and, more extensively, Brown 2020. For Brown, Hegel's emphasis on the negative side of possibility makes him an important precursor of Agamben's account of potentiality.

91 Agamben 2011b, p 44.

92 Agamben 1999d, pp 182–3 (emphases in original).

93 'The privative negation of "potential not to be" is therefore "potential not to not be"' (Attell 2015, p 96).

94 Agamben 1999d, p 183 (emphases in original).

95 Agamben 1998, p 46.

process by separating himself from the world through the sovereign ban, so the concept of potentiality that Agamben elaborates achieves its fullest realisation in modernity as capital. Value, as the pure abstraction that arises in exchange, is nothing other than the presence of an absence, the real existence of non-Being. In this respect, the prehistory of exchange, sketched in *Dialectic of Enlightenment*, is to be understood as the becoming-potential of the human subject, its withdrawal from the encompassing immediacy of the world through the attainment of the capacity not to be – it can because it can not. The progress of the value form towards the actualisation of its concept is the continual enhancement of this capacity: the more the subject is able to resist the power of the actual, to withdraw itself and so to mediate the immediate, the greater is its potentiality, and the more extensive its freedom as command over the world. The crystallisation of the subject in the money form of value is the consolidation of potentiality as the stabilised and permanently embodied presence of absence, which is able both to reserve itself to itself and to transform itself into a limitless multitude of things. At the end of this logic of development, when value completes itself as capital, the non-Being of potentiality becomes self-grounded and enclosed within its own circle of movement. Capital is thus absolute potentiality. The objective abstraction of value has separated itself completely from the world in order that it may unite itself completely with the world. Self-valorising value is not this or that particular thing but everything *in potentia*: there is nothing that it cannot become, nothing in which it cannot realise itself. Exactly as Agamben specifies, therefore, in the process of capital value as potentiality does not disappear into actuality but preserves itself in it. When value passes into actuality in the never-ending cyclical motion of capital, it only ever does so in order that it may return to itself. Indeed, seen in this perspective, modern value theory's understanding of the self-enclosed movement of the dialectic of capital can be recognised as the realisation of, in Agamben's terms, perfect potentiality. Actuality has become just a moment within the virtual process of capital. It is posited from out of potentiality, when the impotential gives itself to itself.[96]

[96] 'At each stage of the process, in going beyond itself, a given shape of capital is only returning to another of its shapes, and since the whole movement forms a circuit it remains always itself as it traverses every stage of its round; thus capital in its movement attains genuine infinity; its circuit allows it to remain always within its own terms of existence, its divisions are internal moments, its relations are only to other parts of itself, hence its advance is not to something beyond itself but only into itself, bringing forth from itself all its potentialities and displaying them to itself.' (Arthur 2004b, pp 140–1)

Form of law

Sovereignty as absolute potentiality is what Agamben terms 'form of law', a mode of relation that he takes to be illustrated in Kafka's story 'Before the Law'.[97] The mythic force that the protagonist of the story, 'the man from the country', seeks to liberate himself from is the ban: held outside the door of the law, he is subjected not to this or that particular law but to the law as such, in its totality. He cannot pass across the threshold and enter into the law but is instead included in it by being excluded from it. In this way, he is 'delivered over to the potentiality of law because law demands nothing of him and commands nothing of him other than its own openness'.[98] The law thus holds him in its ban and condemns him to guilt – in the situation of inclusive exclusion, he is always in debt, always in relation to something that he cannot fully assume. The extreme situation of abandonment depicted by Kafka is, for Agamben, the limit form of law, its '*being in force without significance (Geltung ohne Bedeutung)*'.[99] In this circumstance, the law no longer has any substantive content. However, it does not therefore disappear or cease to apply. Rather, it remains in effect – indeed, is all the more powerfully in effect – precisely as mere law, entirely empty and without any determinate substance or meaning beyond itself. When the law enters into this extreme situation of absolute openness through its radical emptying out, its complete ontological evacuation, as the sheer 'form of law', it pushes the sovereign ban to its logical limit: the law relates to the world by holding it entirely outside itself and so applies absolutely in being wholly without content, pure nothing.[100]

That the law now exists in this void form was announced for modernity, Agamben suggests, by Kant: 'what Kant calls "the simple form of law" (*die bloße Form des Gesetzes*) in the *Critique of Practical Reason* is in fact a law reduced to the zero point of its significance, which is, nevertheless, in force as such'.[101] Through the strict separation of form and content, the abstract categorial structure of transcendental idealism is rendered completely empty and thus a priori – all content can only be known, or have validity, by being mediated through that structure, but it must come entirely from outside, as a posteriori. For Kant, the possibility of the lawfully ordered objectivity of

[97] For Agamben's understanding of the significance of this text, see also the final section of the essay 'The Messiah and the Sovereign: the Problem of Law in Walter Benjamin' (Agamben 1999c).

[98] Agamben 1998, p 50.

[99] Agamben 1998, p 51 (emphasis in original). The phrase is taken from Gershom Scholem.

[100] 'Kafka's legend presents the pure form in which law affirms itself with the greatest possible force precisely at the point in which it no longer prescribes anything – which is to say, as pure ban' (Agamben 1998, pp 49–50).

[101] Agamben 1998, p 51.

knowledge thus depends upon the transcendental sphere having no empirical content at all. In this sense, the synthetic unity of apperception, the pure 'I think' that is the central principle of the architecture of transcendental idealism, is a 'being in force without significance': it is capable of referring to everything in general because it is itself nothing in particular. Its unlimited universality, as absolute potentiality, is its complete privation, its total absence of content. The radical emptying out of the formal a priori is the basic logic of Kant's account of the necessary organisation of experience in modernity generally – the structure of identity closes itself off as homogeneous and consistent with itself in its complete abstraction. It thus becomes universal mediation by placing all content outside itself. This radical purification of the law makes the ban, and with it the state of exception, the condition of existence in the modern world:

> What, after all, is the structure of the sovereign ban if not that of a law that *is in force* but does not *signify*? Everywhere on earth men live today in the ban of a law and a tradition that are maintained solely as the 'zero point' of their own content, and that include men within the form of a pure relation of abandonment. All societies and all cultures today (it does not matter whether they are democratic or totalitarian, conservative or progressive) have entered into a legitimation crisis in which law … is in force as the pure 'Nothing of Revelation'.[102]

If, according to Agamben, it is Kant who reveals the form of modern experience as a 'being in force without significance' that results from the generalisation of the sovereign ban, then the meaning of this condition only becomes fully apparent when it is understood in relation to the logic of dialectic. At the origin of the dialectic stands the decision that draws the boundary. The subject forms its identity through the relation of ban by which it separates itself from nature – Odysseus and the states of exception encountered in the world of myth. The dialectic, as the process of demythologisation, then unfolds through the working out of the contradictory dynamic of inclusive exclusion that is established by the ban structure: on the one hand, it is the elimination of whatever will not fit the uniformity and abstraction of identity, so that the particular becomes identical to the universal; on the other, it is the concentration of identity into itself, as it purifies itself through the sacrifice of all content. In this way, the development of identity is the relentless advance of incorporation by exclusion.

---

[102] Agamben 1998, p 51 (emphases in original). The phrase 'Nothing of Revelation' is again taken from Scholem.

For the great majority of human history, this process worked through a tripartite structure based upon a double division: outside, inside and beyond. Up to the advent of modernity, most of the world still exceeded the reach of the human subject and thus remained on the far side of the bounds of identity. The borderline line did not yet separate the subject absolutely from the world, and so identity lacked the strength to dissolve the substance of pre-conceptual being completely in order to bring it within. Correlatively, for so long as the space of the subject continued to be in minority to unmastered nature, which retained its substance as something genuinely other, the subject understood itself also as in a relation of obligation to a transcendent power, the deity (or deities) in the other-worldly beyond. In modernity, however, this tripartite structure is collapsed, as the world is reduced to immanence: the outside is brought entirely inside and the beyond comes down to earth.[103] The sacrificial logic of the purification of identity thus results in the Kantian transcendental subject, the completely empty and abstract being of exchange, that recognises no authority outside its own reason and whose experience is structured by the strict separation of form and content. Seen from this perspective, what their dialectical theorisation reveals is that capital and the international are the culmination of the logic of identity as inclusive exclusion: through their self-enclosure, they include the world entirely into themselves by excluding it entirely from themselves. Exchange and the state imply the stabilisation of the sovereign subject as a unified being through the consolidation of identity against non-identity, and when they become totalised as capital and the international, the subject has withdrawn into itself altogether, definitively closing itself off from the world by inscribing an absolute boundary. In thus perfecting its interiority, identity is at last able to be absolute exteriority: once its circuit has closed upon itself, value can throw itself away altogether without ever losing itself because in continually passing into actuality it only ever returns to itself. The infinitude of the modern subject, its unrestricted openness, is thus achieved through radical separation and emptying out. As total inclusion through total exclusion, capital and the international, or value and sovereignty, hold the whole world in their ban. They set themselves completely apart from the world in order that they may be the entire world.

[103] It was this metaphysical transition that was worked out, or enacted, above all in German philosophy between Kant and Hegel (Baur 2011), which is why that philosophy stands at the centre of modern thought. This also perhaps explains the centrality to that philosophy of the thematic of self-consciousness, as the conceptual structure in which both inside and outside, and transcendence and immanence, come together.

Bare life

Inclusive exclusion, state of exception, potentiality, form of law – all of these categories of Agamben's account of the logic of sovereignty reveal their full sense only when they are situated within the logic of dialectic. The same is true of what is perhaps the most celebrated of Agamben's political concepts: bare life. Adopted and adapted from Benjamin's 'Critique of Violence',[104] this is the central term around which Agamben's account of sovereignty comes together. As 'the bearer of the link between violence and law',[105] bare life constitutes the 'hidden point of intersection between the juridico-institutional and the biopolitical models of power'.[106] Within the logic of sovereignty set out in *Homo Sacer*, bare life is the correlate of the exception: if sovereign power establishes itself through the pronouncement of the ban, then the constitution of a 'politically qualified' form of life necessarily involves the expulsion of whatever does not submit to the order and homogeneity of the inside space. Bare life, emblematised for Agamben by the Roman law figure of *homo sacer*, is accordingly life that is disqualified and invalidated through its negative relation to sovereign authority. Excluded from the community but held fast by the force of the ban, it is life that may be killed but not sacrificed. Where for Schmitt the norm lives off the exception, so for Agamben bare life is the 'originary political element':[107] sovereign power exists through the drawing of the boundary, the production of bare life, and the maintenance of the inside/outside relation of inclusive exclusion.

The primary idea of *Homo Sacer* is that not only do the state of exception and bare life stand at the origin of political order, as the negative foundation upon which it rests, but that at the end, in the contemporary world, they become generalised. Indeed, it is this concern with the archaeology of 'life' as a political category in modernity that motivates the recasting of biopolitics and its expansion across the history of sovereignty as a whole. Agamben's claim, clearly drawing upon but also extending Schmitt,[108] is that with the collapse, following World War I, of the distinction upon which the *jus publicum Europaeum* had been based, between the interstate order of Europe and the 'free' space beyond the line, the stability of the division between inside and outside began to dissolve: 'What happened and is still happening before our eyes is that the "juridically empty" space of the state of exception … has transgressed its spatio-temporal boundaries and now, overflowing

[104] For a careful discussion of Agamben's repurposing of Benjamin's *bloßes Leben* as *nuda vita*, see Salzani 2015.

[105] Agamben 1998, p 65.

[106] Agamben 1998, p 6.

[107] Agamben 1998, p 181.

[108] Schmitt 2003.

outside them, is starting to coincide with the normal order'.[109] Where the normal situation increasingly takes on the indeterminate character of the state of exception, belonging to the community and being excluded from it also begin to become indistinct. That is, in the biopolitical condition that was inexorably universalised through the course of the 20th century, everybody tendentially becomes bare life: 'in our age all citizens can be said, in a specific but extremely real sense, to appear virtually as *homines sacri*'.[110] The argument of *Homo Sacer* plays out between these extremes, bringing together the archaic and the modern. However, nowhere in the book does Agamben provide an account of how and why this reversal has come about, or explain the logic of transformation by which the exceptionality of bare life becomes the general condition.

The logic upon which the central idea of *Homo Sacer* relies is, once again, that of dialectic. In the section of the book entitled 'Sovereign Body and Sacred Body', Agamben outlines a structural correspondence between the sovereign and bare life: the former is outside the law in being inside it, while the latter is inside the law in being outside it. Occupying the anomic zone of indistinction between law and life, they are reflections of each other across the borderline. This identification of the two extremes in their division is already, in a way, foreshadowed in the *Odyssey*. At the end of his circulation through the world of myth, having survived each of the states of exception by drawing the boundary and separating himself from nature, Odysseus is finally reduced to bare life: through the unceasing struggle for self-preservation, wresting his identity from the power of the archaic, he has lost all of his men, his ships and everything that he brought back from Troy, and been stripped down to an absolutely naked and abandoned existence,until he is at last washed up on the shore of Scheria. It is only then, only once he has endured his 'path of despair'[111] to the very end and so been completely desolated as nothing more than bare existence, that Odysseus can return to Ithaca and resume his sovereign authority. As Adorno and Horkheimer laconically note, 'the epic already contains the correct theory'.[112] For what the myth of Odysseus emblematises is the working out of the dialectic as the logic of demythologisation. Identity, or politically qualified life, establishes itself through the state of exception and the exclusion of the non-identical, the abandonment beyond the border of bare life. The sovereign space thereby marks itself off from the outside, distinguishing itself as the qualified space of autonomy and order. Once set in process by the contradictory structure of the ban, the dialectic advances through

[109] Agamben 1998, p 38.
[110] Agamben 1998, p 111.
[111] Hegel 2018, p 52/¶78.
[112] Horkheimer and Adorno 2002, p 27.

the movement of inclusive exclusion. At each stage, with every new shape of spirit, identity incorporates more of the world into itself by progressively sacrificing the substantiality of pre-conceptual being and eliminating it as non-identical. The borderline is thus the medium of identity: the more deeply the separation is inscribed, the more the outside is brought inside. At the same time, the subject is able to incorporate objectivity into itself, so that it may always recognise itself in its other, only by cancelling its affinity with the world as it was before division and identity. The power of identification and the extent of its command over the world are correlative to the ontological evacuation of the subject: the subject becomes a political being to the degree that it empties itself out as a pure Being of Nothing.

The outcome of the dialectical process of identity as the sacrificial expulsion of nature is thus the reduction of the subject to nature. This is the meaning of the economic problematic and the foundational political *topos* of the 'state of nature' in modernity. When the corrosive logic of enlightenment has dissolved all affinity to anything beyond its sharply inscribed boundaries, the self-identical subject comes to experience itself as the autonomous Individual existing outside society and in primary relation to things. To the Individual, radically denuded in its complete abstraction, existence is defined by the inescapable economic imperatives of self-preservation and the fundamental ontology of labour and productive activity. From this irreducible natural ground, everything that is more than brute material reality can only be secondary and derivative, false to the extent that it does not directly answer to the rational imperative of survival.[113] The universalisation of bare life is thus the correlate of the universalisation of the economic condition; both are the consequence of the totalisation of identity. So, just as the *Odyssey* in its way foresaw, at the end of the history of its formation, when it has completely separated itself from nature, making itself unconditioned and self-referential,

[113] 'With the development of the division of labor, the abstract dimension of labor makes the field of *survival* shift: since the necessary products can be purchased only at the market and since independent production within the family unit has ceased to exist, survival becomes an *economic* problem. It ceases to be at one with life and becomes a condition that precedes any other activity. … This way of organizing time becomes a *system* within which the imaginary production of identity is governed by survival. The centrality of the topic of survival brings us, from *Robinson Crusoe* up to modern science fiction stories, to the ultimate sense of our way of life. Allowing the crisis to run its full downward course, to the most extreme conditions of survival, imagination makes the bourgeois individual's primary qualities visible, especially his ability to use scarce resources rationally. … But, quite ironically, if survival provides us with the elements we need for seeing our way of life as if in a mirror, it is because our way of life tends to reduce itself to survival' (Iacono 2016, pp 132–3 (emphases in original)). According to Dieter Henrich, 'the basic structure of modern philosophy' is in fact located in the link between self-preservation and self-consciousness (Henrich 1974).

identity reverts to mere nature: the sovereign subject is bare life. Or, to put it differently, the Individual is at once absolutely conceptual and absolutely material. At their furthest point of separation, the two extremes thus come together. Life that has been brought completely inside and made totally identical appears as life that is completely outside and excluded, the bare life of the pre-political Individual in the state of nature.

As Agamben construes it, the ultimate significance of the debate between Carl Schmitt and Walter Benjamin is that in the struggle over the status of the exception the destiny of the political at the conclusion of its historical development is made evident. This is why the debate takes place at the extreme, on the borderline. What is at issue in the state of exception, as the point at which law and life come together, is the operation of what Agamben terms the 'machine' of sovereignty. For Schmitt, the function of the state of exception is to reaffirm the validity of sovereign authority: through rendering them momentarily indistinct by suspending the law, inside and outside are once again to be separated by the decision on the exception. Benjamin, by contrast, tries to bring the rule of mythic law-making power to a close by deranging the mechanism of decision and so invalidating the logic of exceptionality through which sovereignty works. The eighth of the theses 'On the Concept of History' constitutes the decisive entry in the esoteric dossier of the Schmitt–Benjamin debate, according to Agamben, because in it, through the claim that 'the "state of exception" in which we live is the rule', Benjamin signals the advent of the political condition in which decision is unable any more to do what Schmitt would have it do: 'When the exception becomes the rule, the machine can no longer function. In this sense, the undecidability of norm and exception formulated in the eighth thesis puts Schmitt's theory in check. Sovereign decision is no longer capable of performing the task that *Political Theology* assigns to it.'[114] Schmitt thus turns to decision and the exception at precisely the moment when they cease to be able to do what he intends.[115] The inside space of sovereign power can no longer be stabilised through the decision on the exception because, with the culmination of the dialectic through the complete interiorisation of the world and the complete externalisation of the subject, the exception and the normal situation have become indistinct. In totalising itself, sovereignty generalises the ban structure and the relation of exception. It incorporates the entire world into itself by forcing it entirely outside itself: inclusion is exclusion and exclusion is inclusion.

---

[114] Agamben 2005, p 58.

[115] This is the innermost reason for the exhaustion of Schmitt's political thought in the age of the globalisation of capital and the completion of the international space (Galli 2015, Chapter 5; Galli 2010, pp 179–82). The assertion of sovereign authority against mediation fails to see that the two sides of the opposition are in fact inseparable from each other – that absolute sovereignty *is* universal mediation.

Conclusion: Dialectic and the Messianic

In modern thought, the problematics of knowledge (epistemology), the economic (value) and the political (sovereignty) all have the same basic tripartite structure. On one side, there is a non-conceptual material reality that exists in-itself, as primary and underived. On the other, there is a system of mediation through which the given materiality is represented. In the relation between these two sides, which are separate and distinct from each other, the former is the standard against which the latter is to be measured. Truth is then the transparent and undistorted correspondence of the system of mediation to the given materiality. Finally, the crucial third element of the problematic is an Individual – whether as knower, labourer or citizen – who stands between the two sides. In order to be able to judge their relation, and the extent of its truth affordance, this Individual must be able to distinguish itself from each side while nevertheless remaining involved with both. The basic problem with this setup is that, if it is to work, the act of relating must satisfy contradictory requirements: for knowledge to be objective (that is, knowledge *of* something and not merely solipsism), the gap between the system of mediation and the primary materiality must be maintained; but for there to be truth, it must be closed. Unable to resolve this contradiction by simultaneously bringing the two sides together and holding them apart, the problematic breaks down altogether around its central mediating figure of the Individual. The insurmountable difficulty is that while the external standard must be known by the Individual for the comparison to be effected, once it is so known it becomes just another mediated thought-construction and so can no longer serve as an independent standard. The objectivity of knowledge is thus irretrievably lost – nothing can be known as it is 'in-itself', outside the system of mediation – and with it goes truth. The implications of this breakdown are twofold. First, the Individual cannot mediate the division between the conceptual system and the non-conceptual materiality – that is, it cannot coherently inhabit the division of inside and outside. Secondly, since it is constructed around the Individual, with the collapse of its central support, the problematic itself must be completely reformulated.

This is the transition to dialectic. In the movement from Kant to Hegel, philosophical thought sought to eliminate the residual dogmatism of the metaphysical structure of reflection as it was expressed in transcendental idealism – that the three poles of its problematic, the 'thing in-itself', the system of valid knowledge, and the investigating consciousness, are all ultimately taken as given and left uncriticised[1] – in order to make the critique of reason self-consistent. What it realised was that, if it is to be properly justified, the knowing of the investigating consciousness must be of the same character as that of the system of valid knowledge itself:

> In other words, the knowing of true knowing comprising the activity of the transcendental philosopher must have true knowing as its object in the same way that true knowing has its own object. This, however, can only be the case if true knowing is a knowing of true knowing. Then the transcendental knowing of true knowing will have the same relation to its object as does true knowing itself, for what both will have knowledge of is true knowing.[2]

Overcoming the separation between the investigating consciousness and the system of valid knowledge then also eliminates the radical division between thought and the primary materiality. For if the system of mediation is itself a knowing of true knowing, then there is no longer any rigid separation of knowledge and its object: what knowledge knows is not something wholly other than thought (which is in any case impossible) but, rather, itself. Through the working out of its own logic, therefore, the problematic of the modern subject – the Individual and its structure of consciousness – resolves itself into dialectic. The unbridgeable separation of inside and outside becomes the reciprocal production of subject and object, in their simultaneous opposition and identity, through the dialectical logic of division.[3] The idea of truth is thereby transformed, becoming the correspondence of the concept not with a given, non-conceptual materiality but with itself, in the identity of inside and outside. Likewise, in dialectic thought is not criticised from an ungrounded external vantage point but performs its own self-critique through the immanent process of its development. Reconstructing the movement of

1 In 'the epistemology of Kantian critical philosophy … [t]his threefold distinction is simply presupposed, never justified' (Siep 2021, p 64).

2 Winfield 1988, p 70. For a detailed discussion of this move, effected in the most concise way in the 'Introduction' to the *Phenomenology*, by which Hegel transforms the epistemological problematic into the unfolding of the dialectical movement of inside/outside, see Bristow 2012, Chapter 5. For commentary on its significance for Hegel's conception of thought generally, see Verene 2007, Chapter 2.

3 Bowman 2013, Chapter 1.

that 'self-consummating skepticism' is the programme of the *Phenomenology of Spirit*.[4] It is also the real meaning of the historical atlas: at every stage in the evolution of political and economic space, the system of mediation measures inside and outside against each other, recognises their continuing contradiction, and redetermines both in pursuit of identity. What the historical atlas lays out across its pages is thus, in essence, a mapping of the dialectic, as it works itself out into the completed totality of the Concept. In unfolding the logics of political and economic space, it traces the development of the twinned, dialectical, inside/outside structures of value and sovereignty, which culminates in modernity with the world-spanning systems of capital and the international.[5]

Value and sovereignty are thus what Hegel termed infinite concepts, or concepts of reason. As such, they are concepts of the speculative identity of opposites. This is what is meant by their being 'borderline' concepts: they are situated, or arise, *on* the boundary line, at once bringing the two sides together and separating them from each other in an original identity of thought and being. This shared rootedness in the fundamental division from which they both spring is precisely their dialectical quality. The basic inadequacy of the modern social sciences – here, Politics and IR, Economics and IPE – by contrast, is that they can only think of value and sovereignty as finite, non-dialectical concepts, that is, as concepts of simple separation and opposition. As such, they are concepts of what Hegel called abstract identity, or concepts of the understanding. To the understanding, which clings to the security of finitude and limitation, the original identity of thought and being can only appear as incomprehensible. Where it refuses to acknowledge their speculative identity, though, theory is confronted with the impossible task of reconstituting the unity of concept and object after they have already been severed from each other. Since the infinite cannot be grasped through finite concepts, the disciplines of the social sciences can never conceive the modern world-system of capital and the international as a whole.[6] Governed by the division, which must remain unthinkable to them as their foundational presupposition, they are unable to comprehend the unity of political and economic space. Instead, they

---

4 Hegel 2018, p 52/¶78. Scepticism in its authentic form, as Hegel understood it (Hegel 2000; Hegel 1991, pp 130–1/§81), is the negation of all claims of the finite to the infinite. Conceived as 'self-consummating skepticism', therefore, the dialectic is the movement of this negativity through successive forms of finitude up to the Absolute.

5 Indeed, the totality of the modern world-system is *dialectical* precisely because it has two sides which simultaneously include and exclude each other, as both opposed and identical – two 'torn halves of an integral freedom, to which, however, they do not add up'.

6 That the infinite cannot be comprehended in terms of the finite is the basic theme of Hegel's critique of metaphysics, in both its pre-Kantian dogmatic tradition and its Kantian critical reformulation (Bowman 2013).

can only assume the world market and the states-system to be intrinsically separate and discrete spheres that are related to each other only a posteriori, in a merely external way. The enclosure of the modern scientific conception of knowledge within the logic of division and totality, of which it is the immediate consciousness, means that it cannot reflexively understand that logic itself.[7] Rather, the whole that capital and the international together form, as two internally related sides of a single dialectical totality, can only be captured in philosophical terms, through the traditional language of metaphysics, as the Unconditioned or the Absolute.[8]

At the end of the *Phenomenology of Spirit*, once consciousness has passed through all of its successive logical shapes, Hegel finally arrives at what he terms 'Absolute Knowing'. This is the metaphysical condition in which 'spirit has brought to a close the movement of giving shape to itself inasmuch as that movement is burdened with the insurmountable differences of consciousness'.[9] When its long journey of self-discovery reaches its conclusion, the antithetical structure that is definitive of the experience of consciousness – the separation and opposition of subject and outside, or inside and outside – is transcended altogether.[10] At the limit of its unfolding, therefore, the immanent movement of the dialectic comes to a standstill in the absolute identity of immediate opposites, or fully achieved subject–object. This condition of the suspension of oppositions in the perfected identity of the two sides is the properly metaphysical meaning of the completed totality of capital and the international.

In marking the division, the state of exception initiates a double dynamic of inclusion and exclusion: the setting apart of the inside is at the same time a capturing of the outside. Or, in dialectical terms, separation is identity. At the culmination of this movement of inside/outside, the completely mediated world appears as completely unmediated. The very givenness of the original condition is thus, in fact, an effect of universal mediation. When the subject becomes absolute by being radically cut off from the world, it is reduced to the bare, isolated Individual existing before and outside society in immediate relation to things. Correlatively, when the world is wholly internalised by identity, it is emptied out into the indeterminate nowhere of the state of nature and the material necessity of its economic imperative. The movement of the dialectic is thus ultimately circular. At its origin, identity

---

7 Where the understanding is trapped within limits that it cannot comprehend, dialectic, precisely in thinking the division, is the path of freedom.

8 Within the modern world-system, as a totality that has no outside, all relations are ultimately self-relations, 'and to have no relation except to oneself is to be absolute' (Bowman 2013, p 185).

9 Hegel 2018, p 465/¶805.

10 Maker 1981, 1982 and 1994, Chapter 5.

separates the human from nature, raising it out of the animal condition and qualifying its existence as properly rational. At the end, however, it returns the human to nature: the subject of universal mediation is bare life, the Individual concerned above all with self-preservation.[11] In modernity, therefore, when equivalence has become generalised, exteriority no longer exists as a different order of being set apart from qualified life, the animal as opposed to the human. Rather, in the moment at which political and economic space succeed in encompassing the whole world, inside and outside enter into indistinction. Their absolute differentiation is their absolute indifference: inside is outside and outside is inside.

During the entire epoch of sacrifice, so long as the world still largely exceeded the grasp of the subject, the transcendent was experienced as existing beyond the immanence of the intramundane. Through the progress of demythologisation, however, immanence and transcendence are forced further and further apart until, at the extremity of their antithesis, the distance between them collapses and they pass straight into each other. In secular modernity, when sacrifice has become exchange, transcendence thus itself becomes immanent. In the totalised world of capital and the international there is neither any outside nor any beyond. Modernity does not leave the pre-modern logic of transcendence behind, therefore, but is, rather, its completion.[12] Transcendence separates itself from the world in order to identify itself with the world; it incorporates the world into itself by excluding it from itself. When it has separated itself entirely, emptying itself out and expelling the world altogether, it invests itself completely in the world.[13] Conversely, existence is included in transcendence by being excluded from it as a conceptless materiality. When it is wholly included, entirely encompassed by generalised exchange, it is wholly excluded, as the radical immanence and immediacy of the original condition, the political state of nature and its correlative economic necessity. At the limit of their separation, immanence and transcendence thus fuse directly together and become indifferent: absolute transcendence is absolute immanence. Or, to put it in Giorgio Agamben's terms, in modernity life becomes sacred. Within the condition of universal mediation, life is the supreme category of secular immanence because it is the logical bearer of infinite transcendence. The modern subject is at once bare life and sovereign power.

---

11 'The concept which completes itself with the absolute Idea re-establishes the immediate being of the beginning. The absolute Idea is identical to nature' (Hyppolite 1997, p 169).

12 'God's transcendence is at an end. But he is not dead; he has been incorporated into human existence' (Benjamin 2004a, p 289).

13 In this respect, a political map of the contemporary world presents a perfected image of inclusive exclusion: the world has been entirely incorporated into political space by being entirely excluded from it.

The convergence of transcendence and immanence in the sacralisation of existence as such is at the same time the identity of universal and particular through their extreme opposition. On the one hand, the Individual conceives itself to be its own foundation: the categories that define it – sovereignty, autonomy, independence, self-determination, freedom, agency – all bespeak the self-referentiality of subjectivity become immanent to itself. On the other, when the metaphysics of modern subjectivity are thought through to their conclusion, the sovereign Individual is transcended altogether. The dialectical theorisation of value displaces the Individual as the ground of being so that it becomes simply the bearer of the objective system of identity. The modern subject is completely dependent upon its functionality to this system, the development of which proceeds according to its own logic, without any reference to the needs or preferences of Individuals. Precisely in its radical individuation, therefore, the agency of the modern subject, its sovereign capacity for self-directed action, is really the appearance form of the universality of state and capital. Absolute individuation is thus at the same time absolute universalisation. Or, to put it differently, freedom *is* determinism.[14] In this way, once again, modernity recreates the closed context of myth. The emergence of the subject in prehistory took place through the relation with transcendence because only the universal possessed being and could truly act in the world. With the advance of demythologisation, the subject progressively identifies itself with the universal until, in modernity, they become immanent to each other. The dynamic of freedom is thus simultaneously a movement of enclosure: every step towards emancipation is a step into totalisation. Once, in prehistory, at the appointed hour and in the designated space, identification with the universal was enacted through the awful ritual of sacrifice, performed by those invested with the special power of mediation with the deity. When, in modernity, the subject has separated itself altogether, and the transcendent has come down to earth, it no longer sacrifices to the universal by way of prescribed rituals but communes with it ceaselessly through generalised exchange. In the totalised context of guilt, everything is mediation, everywhere is sacred space, every day is feast day, and every act is sacrifice.[15]

Having finally attained its concept as universal mediation, the modern subject encompasses the entire world. It does so, however, not as a global subject but only as an international one. The whole remains fragmented and self-divided, and thus unaware of itself as a whole: 'absolute consciousness, unconscious',

[14] 'The condition of freedom, identity, is immediately at the same time the principle of determinism' (Adorno 2001b, 'Freedom, Determinism, Identity').

[15] Benjamin 2004a; Agamben 2019a.

as Adorno put it.[16] That the dialectic culminates in a whole that is not a whole – that the sum total of presence is only an absence – reveals the truth of its logic. If identity is originarily apotropaic, the subject taking into itself the power that it fears in order to preserve itself from it, then it never actually escapes from the closed context of myth. Rather, its entire development is circumscribed by, and always held within, the condition from which it would be free. The consequence of this inside/outside dynamic is that the unfolding of the dialectic does not follow a linear path, which would finally issue in a self-conscious global subject, but instead works out a movement of reversal, so that at its end it recreates its origin. The subject first formed itself as a subject by mimetically identifying itself with the natural powers to which it had always been in thrall. Through the logic of sacrifice that is thereby set in motion, identity progressively displaces the archaic forces of myth and establishes itself as sovereign. It conquers the world by renouncing it, appropriating it for itself by expelling it from itself. In modernity, when identity has both separated the subject altogether and emptied it out entirely, the dialectical reversal is completed, as the subject itself becomes the universal power by which it is subjected. Myth thus revenges itself in its overthrow, as the subject is caught in the ban of its own identity. This is the meaning of the stringent division of content and form that determines the experiential structure of the modern Individual. The transcendental subject at once includes and excludes the empirical subject; likewise, in the Hegelian conception, it is the Absolute Idea that is free, not the empirical individual.[17] It is only at this limit point, when the world is completely wrapped into the self-movement of identity by being completely banished outside it, that the dialectic finally closes upon itself and becomes self-generating and self-reproducing totality. The dialectical logic that began with the distinction of inside from outside thus culminates in their absolute indistinction: the rigorous subordination of society to the rule of law dissolves it into the state of nature; the generalisation of exchange reduces the subject to the economic condition of mere survival; and the globalisation of sovereignty fragments the intentionality of political reason into the subjectless anarchy of the international.

Through the pages of the historical atlas, from the remotest beginnings right up to the end of the 20th century, as political and economic space gradually extended their reach, what stands out before anything else is the continual extension of the interior realm of the subject through the ever sharper differentiation of the inside from the outside. Once that process has

[16] Adorno 2001b, 'On the Interpretation of the Transcendental'. If self-consciousness follows from the division of inside and outside, then the totality of division, or the Absolute, to which all of the borderlines are internal and so which has no opposite, cannot itself be self-conscious.

[17] Magee 2010, pp 467–9.

completed itself, however, and everywhere has been absorbed into political space, what stands out instead are the borderlines themselves. In this respect, the history of philosophical thought precisely matches the history of political being: through the entire course of its development, what it was always foremost concerned with was the mediation of the world, the capacity of the Concept to resolve the formless and undetermined world into itself and turn it into intelligible objectivity. Once the dynamic of mediation has attained its goal, though, and subject and object have become completely identical through complete separation, it is the division between them, the boundary line itself, that then confronts thinking. This metaphysical situation is the presupposition of Hegel's conception of the culmination of philosophy as the collapse of the oppositional structure of consciousness into the absolute indistinction of inside and outside, which is announced at the end of the *Phenomenology* and that then forms the starting point of the *Logic*.[18] It is also the ultimate sense of the generalisation of the state of exception that is the principal thematic of Agamben's 'Homo Sacer' project.

The encounter with the original division is set out in an almost programmatic way as the determining experience of Agamben's thought in the final section of one of his first books, *Stanzas*.[19] Characteristic of philosophical debates of the 1970s, the ostensible topic of these decisive pages is the semiotic problematic. In this context, what Agamben is concerned with above all is the significance of the Saussurean formulation 'linguistic unity is double', the constitution of the unitary structure of the sign through division: 'Insofar as the duality of thing manifesting and thing manifested is implicit in the sign, it remains something double and fragmented, but insofar as this duality is manifested in the one sign, it is something rather rejoined and united'.[20] What baffled Saussure and ultimately confounds semiotics, as the science of the sign, is the contradictory combination of identity and separation that is inherent to signification as such. For this reason, the problem of the sign can only be comprehended when it is lifted out of semiotics and instead set within its properly metaphysical context:

> The foundation of this ambiguity of signifying resides in the original fracture of presence that is inseparable from the Western experience

[18] Hegel 2010, pp 23–38; Houlgate 2006, Chapter 7.

[19] This 'original division' is Hölderlin's *Urteilung* or 'original judgement': '*Judgement* is, in the highest and strictest sense, the primal separation of the object and the subject that are most intimately united in intellectual intuition, that separation, by which object and subject first become possible, the original division' (Hölderlin 2009, p 231 (emphasis in original)). See also the 'Epilogue' to *The Use of Bodies* for a synoptic statement of this defining problem of Agamben's thought (Agamben 2015, pp 263–79).

[20] Agamben 1993, pp 135–6.

> of being. Because of that fracture, all that comes to presence comes there as to the place of a deferral and an exclusion, in the sense that its manifestation is simultaneously a concealment, and its being present, a lack. This originary co-belonging (*coappartenenza*) of presence and absence, of appearance and concealment was expressed by the Greeks in their intuition of truth as *alétheia* (revelation), and on the experience of this fracture the discourse that we still call with the Greek name 'love of wisdom' is founded. Only because presence is divided and unglued is something like 'signifying' possible; and only because there is at the origin not plenitude but deferral [whether this is taken to mean the opposition of being and appearance, the harmony of opposites, or the ontological difference between being (*Sein*) and an entity (*Seiende*)] is there the need to philosophize.[21]

Signification functions as a relating of form and content, but its secret lies neither on one side of the line, nor on the other, but in the middle, in the dividing line itself, which at once conceals and reveals. The meaning of this line has, however, been 'constantly left in shadow'[22] by the tradition of philosophy, which was founded upon it and so could see only the increasingly perfect union of concept and object that it made possible. When the two sides have come into absolute identity by way of their complete reciprocal exclusion, the relation appears as one of manifestation, in which an external and pre-existent object is brought to expression through its signifier. As with value and sovereignty, though, the insoluble problem of semiotics is that signification cannot be coherently accounted for on the model of representation. Agamben's concern is thus to break open the semiotic problematic altogether by bringing to light what had always been overlooked and obscured, precisely the dividing line itself, the 'barrier resistant to signification'.[23] When the boundary line is understood as instituting a dynamic of presence and absence, inclusion and exclusion, its dialectical essence, as 'a putting together of impossible things',[24] can be recognised. Signification, the hermetic congealing of the relation of form and content around the borderline, then no longer presents itself as the representation in discourse of a given objectivity but is instead revealed to be the demythologised inheritor of a much older mode of speech, the language of prehistory, 'in which the original fracture of presence was alluded to in

---

21 Agamben 1993, p 136.
22 Agamben 1993, p 137.
23 Agamben 1993, p 139. The phrase is drawn from Jacques Lacan (2006, p 415).
24 Agamben 1993, p 139. The phrase comes from Aristotle.

the paradox of a word that approaches its object by keeping it indefinitely at a distance'.[25]

In a series of fundamental texts through the 1980s, which lead up to the 'Homo Sacer' project, Agamben then proceeded to explicate the barrier resistant to signification as 'the place of negativity' – the originary site of negation from which the process of anthropogenesis has always descended.[26] In a way again typical of the philosophical discourse of the time, this metaphysical structure was elaborated largely in relation to the thematic of language, before being translated to the field of the political as the theoretical underpinning of the account of sovereignty. The analysis of, on the one hand, the initiation of the dialectic of consciousness in the conceptual movement of sense-certainty ('taking-the-this'), and, on the other, the existential structure of Dasein ('being-the-there'), demonstrates that in both Hegel and Heidegger the passage from animal sound to human speech, from *phoné* to *logos*, is transected by an essential negativity.[27] The articulation of natural sound as meaningful discourse is achieved only in the encounter with death: through the internalisation of the empty universal, the 'confused voice'[28] of the animal is definitively put aside as the subject steps into the space of identity. The border between inside and outside, the dividing line itself, is thus the place of negativity. As such, it is what, in this context of the metaphysics of language, Agamben refers to as the originary logical dimension of 'Voice' – that is, no longer animal sound but not yet intentional speech. Because it is nothing other than absolute negation, the thoroughgoing mediation of the human subject by the imperative power of death, this Voice, as Hegel and Heidegger again emphatically affirm, is experienced only as silence. It is a Voice that says nothing, that asserts no determinate propositions and issues no commands, but that instead, in simply announcing a pure intention to signify, opens the very space of language and being.[29]

---

25 Agamben 1993, p 138. Just as Adorno and Horkheimer perceive the transition from myth to enlightenment as dialectical, both division and continuity, so Agamben locates the 'dissimulation … of the fracture of presence' (Agamben 1993, p 137) in the mythologeme of Oedipus and the supersession of the Sphinx's oblique and enigmatic mode of speaking by the univocity of enlightened signification.

26 Agamben 1991.

27 Agamben 1991.

28 Agamben 2018, p 18.

29 'The essential relationship between language and death takes place – for metaphysics – in Voice. *Death and Voice have the same negative structure and they are metaphysically inseparable.* To experience death as death signifies, in fact, to experience the removal of the voice and the appearance, *in its place*, of another Voice … which constitutes the originary *negative* foundation of the human word. To experience Voice signifies, on the other hand, to become capable of another death – no longer simply a deceasing, but a person's ownmost

From this foundational division, there derives a double negativity in the experience of being, as it is manifested in the structure of language. In the first place, the fracture of presence sets in motion the apotropaic process of dialectical *Aufhebung*: in being drawn into the space of language, the world is at the same time expelled from it. This movement of simultaneous negation and preservation, casting out and taking in, is what, in the linguistic sphere, Agamben terms the 'structure of the presupposition':[30]

> Human language is necessarily pre-sup-positional and thematizing in the sense that in taking place, it decomposes the thing itself (*to pragma auto*) that is at issue in it and in it alone into a being *about which something is said* and a *poion*, a quality or determination *that is said of it*. To speak of a being, human language supposes and distances what it brings to light, in the very act in which it brings it to light.[31]

The transformation of the world into the material of linguistic reference is a separation and a silencing. The thing that is spoken about in language is itself excluded from language; universal determinations can be predicated of it, but it cannot itself be said.[32] The unsayable, as Agamben repeatedly insists, is therefore not outside and unrelated to language, as some sort of mystical alterity, but is its very presupposition – in becoming sayable, the world becomes unsayable.[33]

---

and insuperable possibility, the possibility of his *freedom*' (Agamben 1991, p 86 (emphases in original)).

30 Agamben 1999h and 2018. In *The Use of Bodies*, the structure of the presupposition is further specified as the 'ontological apparatus' (Agamben 2015, Part II, Chapter I).

31 Agamben 1999h, pp 106–7 (emphases in original).

32 Agamben here quotes Wittgenstein: 'I can only *name* objects. Signs represent them. I can only speak *of* them. I cannot *assert them*. A proposition can only say *how* a thing is, not *what* it is' (Agamben 1999h, p 108 (emphases in original)).

33 The structure of presupposition, or the logic of negation, by which the world is silenced in order to be brought into language, is classically set out by Hegel in the section on 'Sense-Certainty' with which the dialectical movement of the *Phenomenology of Spirit* commences (Hegel 2018, pp 60–8/¶¶90–110; see also Houlgate 2013, pp 40–1). The contradictory combination in modernity of complete sayability and complete unsayability is expressed in the two-world structure that is common to the epistemological, economic and political problematics: on one side, a primary material world that is inaccessible and unknowable as it is in itself, and on the other a secondary system of universal mediation through which the first world is represented. In *Dialectic of Enlightenment*, Adorno and Horkheimer capture the paradox of this basic duality in their observation about Kant: 'The wisdom he imparted is oracular: There is no being in the world that knowledge cannot penetrate, but what can be penetrated by knowledge is not being' (Horkheimer and Adorno 2002, p 19).

Secondly, because it is grounded in negativity and silence, language is subject to an impossibility of self-reference, which in the end condemns it to anonymity. The field of language is divided into two dimensions: names, by which the linguistic nature of the object is established, and discourse, what is said within language. However, not only is it impossible for the object that is named by the name to be said in language, but the intentionality of naming itself cannot be brought into the space of discursivity. The condition that opens language and makes it possible, the negative foundation, may not itself become an object of language. If discourse could speak its own taking place, then the structure of the presupposition that is constitutive of linguistic signification as such would be nullified: 'what is essential is that if I want to say an *intentio*, to name the name, I will no longer be able to distinguish between word and thing, concept and object, the term and its reference'.[34] By the same token, just as there is no name for the name and no word for the word, so, as a result of the split that is intrinsic to it, self-reflection lacks a nominative form – what is most proper to the subject is necessarily marked by laceration and fracture.[35] It follows from the irreducible anonymity of linguistic signification, its grounding in the negativity of division, that there can be no metalanguage, no superordinate language of language that would stand above the anarchic multiplicity of different linguistic spaces and bring them together as a self-conscious whole.[36] The very universality of language – that it has no exteriority, no outside – rests upon the silence and unspeakability of the negative foundation. Everything can be brought within the realm of language, therefore, except language itself.

The spatialising division of inside and outside that transforms the natural thing into an object of language at the same time marks a temporal boundary.[37] In being included in language, as something about which things are said, by being excluded from it, as the unsayable presupposition of discourse, the object is brought into the present by being banished into the past:

[34] Agamben 1999e, p 213.

[35] Agamben 1999f.

[36] Agamben 1999b. As Agamben puts it in the earlier text *Infancy and History*: 'The fact that consciousness has a dialectical structure means that it can never grasp itself as an entirety, but is whole only in the total process of its becoming' (Agamben 2007, p 38).

[37] 'The historical condition of human beings is inseparable from their condition as speaking beings; it is inscribed in the very mode of their access to language, which is originally marked by a fracture' (Agamben 1999b, p 51); 'Precisely because being gives itself in language, but language remains unsaid in what it says and manifests, being destines itself and unveils itself for speakers in an epochal history. The historicizing and chronogenetic power of the λόγος is a function of its presupposing structure and its ontological weakness' (Agamben 2018, p 10).

> The 'what,' *ti*, that was at issue in the name is subsumed into discourse as a *kata tinos*, 'that about which' something is said. They – both the *what* and the *about which* – are therefore the *same thing*, which can be grasped as *to ti ēn einai*, the Being-the-what-that-was. In this logico-temporal process, the Platonic *thing itself* is removed and conserved or, rather, conserved only in being removed: e-liminated.[38]

The sovereign present of being, what *is*, exists only through its negative relation to itself as what is not, what therefore *was*. The object can *be* in language only by having been expelled from language as something already gone – something that has been definitively negated and so become unreachable as non-being. It is through this negative movement of separation, by which the world is divided from itself and abandoned to an irrecoverable past beyond the boundary, that the present is formed as the space of politics, agency and freedom. The becoming present to itself of the subject, its self-identity, is thus simultaneously its becoming historical, its differentiation of itself from itself.

If history as such is the unfolding of this temporalising logic of inclusive exclusion, then in the globalised world of modernity it reaches its end. The absolute self-presence of the modern subject, its status as sovereign, is the result of its radical evacuation, its expulsion of everything from itself across the borderline and into the past. In that moment, therefore, it ceases to be historical. The total historicisation of humanity by way of the complete externalisation of the world is, in fact, its dehistoricisation, its terminal arrest in the stasis of an eternal present, the absolute immanence and self-identity of infinite exchange.[39] At the end of its process, therefore, history is finally confronted with the irreducible ahistoricity of its own foundation. The diachronic aspect of history, its character as movement, change and development, flows from the synchronic condition of spatial division and fracture. When, in modernity, the division becomes absolute, history is unified as an immanent and all-inclusive context. The unlimited extension of the field of history, its subsumption of the entirety of humanity to its single measure, is thus a function of absolute limitation, the totalisation of the world in the self-divided and conflictual form of the international. Just as with language, however, the negative foundation that opens the dimension of historicity in the first place cannot itself be brought within the space of

---

38 Agamben 1999g, p 37 (emphases in original). See also Agamben 2005b, p 100.

39 History comes to an end when the past as such and all tradition are finally overcome as merely given and heteronomous. The sovereignty of the autonomous and self-determining modern subject – that is, its absolute freedom in being self-grounded – thus implies the eversameness of the universal present (Maker 2009, esp. p 25).

history. If it were possible for history to say itself, to speak its own historicity, then the differentiation of past and present that is its essential presupposition would be cancelled. Just as Realism has recognised in IR, therefore, the diachronic-temporal movement of history necessarily depends upon, and is always contained within, the synchronic-spatial condition of division, which is itself without history. For this reason, there can be no universal history founded upon the logic of presupposition. Instead, when the movement of the dialectic has played itself out, time reverts to space and history to myth.

The meaning of the problematic of capital and the international in the philosophy of history is that the logic of the original division of inside and outside has completed itself. At its furthest point, theoretical reflection on the international has managed to recognise at least something of this historical finality. The deepest perception to which it has attained is that, from the perspective of the international, the character of the inside space is irrelevant. In the end, it makes no difference how politics is organised within because there is no possible form of the inside that can escape the negativity of the outside. No matter how it is constituted, simply by virtue of being an 'inside' it is necessarily caught within the fractured space of the international. This extreme perception can be gained only at the end of the process, when there is no more outside to be incorporated, no new shape of the inside to be assumed, and the logic of sovereignty is instead forced up against its limit. However, although it is its essential presupposition, theorisation of the international has only ever encountered that limit as an incomprehensible block. In the same way, economic thought has never managed to become conscious of its own constitutive division. For both, the borderline remains the barrier resistant to signification, the mute and unthought foundation upon which their entire discourses rest.[40] The metaphysical experience that is embodied in the international space of universal exchange is that at the culmination of the dialectic, in the fully globalised world, presence and absence, being and nothing, have become immediately identical. The history of the formation of the subject, which is constituted through sovereignty and value, culminates in the anarchy of the international states-system and the capitalist world market, which are without a subject. Complete politicisation is thus depoliticisation – in finally incorporating the entire world into itself, political being cannot help but lay bare the negativity and absence that lie at its foundation. It is here, on the point of indistinction between absolute subjectivity and absolute subjectlessness, that the problematic of capital and the international is situated.

---

[40] For this reason, there has only ever been international relations theory and no theory of the international, economic theory and no theory of capital.

At the end of its dialectical journey, therefore, thinking comes face to face with the original division, the presupposition of *logos en arkhē*: 'The word that is absolutely in the beginning, that is therefore the absolute presupposition, presupposes nothing if not itself; it has nothing before itself that can explain it or reveal it in turn (*there is no word for the word*)'.[41] This absolute presupposition is, precisely, revelation – the originary word, founded only upon itself and with nothing anterior to it. Through the logic of self-determination that the revelation of the word sets in motion, the world is laid open to sense and intelligibility. However, because the word always presupposes itself in everything that is said, it cannot itself become an object within the space of mediation that it founds. The revelation that is the presupposition of reason is thus inexplicable to it: 'the meaning of revelation is that humans can reveal beings through language but cannot reveal language itself'.[42] In whatever way beings are said, their comprehensibility as such necessarily refers back to the incomprehensible. From this dark ground, the progress of enlightenment unfolds through a contradictory movement of concealment and unconcealment, in which openness itself, what makes the interior space of the subject possible, continually hides, or withdraws itself, in every opening. Through each of the shapes of being, all of the forms of political and economic space whose evolution is set out in the historical atlas, being itself has always remained silent and unspoken.[43] That is why existence in modernity takes the anarchic and subjectless form of the dialectical totality of capital and the international. With the final globalisation of the world, however, the contradiction of the limited and the unlimited has played itself out and the movement has come to an end. In the condition of universal mediation, everything has been revealed except for revelation itself, everything mediated except for mediation as such. The gap that remains between completion and incompletion, the difference between the international and the world, is the absolute anonymity of the subject that is the presupposition of identity. All that is left, therefore, is to resolve the logic of inside/outside, or the structure of the presupposition, by undoing the original division.[44]

---

41 Agamben 1999a, p 41 (emphasis in original).

42 Agamben 1999a, p 40.

43 '*Sayability itself remains unsaid in what is said and in that about which something is said … knowability itself is lost in what is known and in that about which something is known*' (Agamben 1999g, p 33 (emphasis in original)). The necessary precondition of Agamben's perception that the thing itself is not external to language but is the thing in its essential sayability is the dialectical idea of the original identity of thought and being.

44 This is precisely the logic of dialectic: to work through the structure of the presupposition so that it ultimately undoes itself and thought becomes completely presuppositionless (Maker 1990).

In the totalised world, when everywhere has become immediately inside/outside, the only thing that has not been folded into identity, because it is neither inside nor outside, is the division itself. As the dynamic of contradiction comes to a standstill, therefore, issuing in its own arrest, the meaning of the borderline undergoes a dialectical reversal. Without any further movement of inside/outside to ground, it can no longer function as the silent and hidden mechanism of identity. Instead, with the final closure of the space of identity, the sovereign relation is disarticulated and the totality of immanence is set in apposition to its own foundation, which now transcends it. This is the meaning of the central idea of Agamben's thought: the messianic.[45] At the limit of inclusive exclusion, it is in the limit itself that the potentiality of redemption is to be found. So long as thought presupposed its own sovereignty and situated itself within the bounded space of the political, the problematic of capital and the international could not be grasped. Instead, the fractured and divided form of global political space could only be apprehended in the way in which it always has been by IR, as a condition of existence that is, in the end, simply given and impenetrable to thought – the bare fact of anarchy. In the same way, economic theory cannot comprehend capital so long as it presupposes its essential division: from within the divided space of value, the two sides of the economic experience can never be coherently mediated. Only when the borderline is no longer assumed as the silent foundation of identity but is instead brought to expression can the fragmented whole of the modern world-system be grasped. Properly speaking, therefore, international theory and the theory of capital are forms of messianism.

The advent of the messianic signifies that the epoch of the law, the history of the dialectical movement of inside/outside, has completed itself and come to an end.[46] The messianic event, therefore, is not something that is to be indefinitely awaited, forever put off into a future that is always 'to come'. Rather, it has already happened. Agamben is careful to emphasise, however, that the messianic is not to be assimilated to the category of the eschatological or to apocalypse – it is 'not the end of time, but *the time of the end*'.[47] What

[45] Although its major statement is to be found in *The Time that Remains* (published in Italian in 2000 and translated into English in 2005), the messianic had in fact been a leading theme in Agamben's thought right from the beginning, in the essays of the 1970s, as the resolution of the metaphysical knot that binds together history, time and myth (Agamben 2007).

[46] 'The essential character of messianism may well be precisely its particular relation to the law. In Judaism as in Christianity and Shiite Islam, the messianic event above all signifies a crisis and radical transformation of the entire order of the law' (Agamben 1999c, pp 162–3).

[47] Agamben 2005b, p 62 (emphasis in original); see also Agamben 2005b, p 101 and Agamben 2012, pp 5–8.

is specifically messianic is neither the secular world within the borderline, nor the kingdom of God beyond it, but the gap between the end and the end. It is the condition that obtains when the dialectic has indeed reached its conclusion, but without having been fulfilled. The term thus denotes precisely the uni-dual structure of the globalised world, the simultaneity of completion and incompletion.[48] It follows that the fundamental shape of experience in the messianic condition is that of 'no longer … not yet': no longer the history of inside/outside, the logic of which has worked itself out to its extreme and can go no further, but not yet the *plērōma*, not yet the redeemed world as an integral whole.[49] At the end of the dialectic, where inside and outside have passed directly into each other, it is not possible to go back, because everything has already been emptied out, and nor is it possible to go forward, because there is nothing left to go forward into. Instead, as past and present are brought directly together through the absolute separation of the borderline, the movement of historical time is suspended.[50] Poised on the dividing line between history and eternity, the time of the modern world-system is, accordingly, *ho nyn kairos* – the messianic 'time of the now'.[51] Messianism is thus what thinking becomes when, at the end of the dynamic of

---

[48] That the globalised world constitutes a messianic condition of simultaneous completion and incompletion is in fact already incipiently perceptible in Adorno's 'Mediations on Metaphysics', the tentative and exploratory final section of *Negative Dialectics*. The circumstance that shapes Adorno's thought at this furthest extent of his reflections on dialectic is that while the movement of identity has indeed completed itself in totality, it has not thereby been transcended. That is, the dialectic no longer drives forward, through determinate negation, to a new and higher form, but has instead reached a limit that it is unable to surpass through its logic of division – a limit at which it becomes dialectic at a standstill. Thought is thus constrained to an aporetic position in between: it is at the end but the end is not the end.

[49] Agamben 2005b, p 69. The messianic is thus neither transcendence nor immanence but the division itself when the opposites have become identical to each other. It might be said that this is precisely the situation in which Hegel leaves philosophical thought – as both complete and not yet complete – and why Agamben insists that thought has still to reckon fully with the Hegelian legacy and the messianic demand that it announces (Agamben 1999f). If the programme of Hegel's philosophy is expressed in the assertion that, 'the sole interest of Reason is to suspend [the] rigid antitheses' of the understanding (Hegel 1977a, p 90), then the intention of Agamben's thought is to take the dialectic beyond Hegel by resolving the original division altogether. (For some brief considerations on Agamben's relation to Hegel, see Garrison 2017.)

[50] From his citation of the 'paralyzed restlessness' of the Hegelian Absolute onwards (Agamben 1991, p 101), the specific location of Agamben's thought is exactly this in-between space, which is traversed by a 'dialectical tension that reaches its highest manifestation in a state of immobility' (Agamben 2013, p 31).

[51] Agamben 2005b, p 61. The messianic announcement is therefore to be distinguished from prophecy: where the prophetic is orientated to the future, the messianic is concerned with the time of the now.

inclusive exclusion, it finds that it can only be located *in* the original division, *in* the infinitesimal caesura that separates the subject from the world.[52] It is for this reason that, in his explication of it, Agamben emphasises that the messianic is not to be conceived of as another time and another space, a form of existence that would be of essentially the same order as and continuous with, but nevertheless somehow beyond, the time and space of the law. In the fully globalised world, there is no such beyond, nowhere else to go. The messianic is not in any way a further extension of the logic of identity – it does not seek to replace the commandments of the law with a new law and a new set of prescriptions. Rather, by situating itself in the division that is constitutive of the world-system of capital and the international, it activates the tension between completion and incompletion.[53] Through the 'immobile dialectic' of the Pauline *hōs mē* – 'as not' – the fragmented totality, the whole that is not a whole, is set against itself.[54]

The principle of the law is the principle of division, the separation of what belongs from what must be banned, inside from outside.[55] Accordingly, if the messianic is the final reckoning with the order of the law, it must above all mean the resolution, or supersession, of division. From its origin in mimesis and sacrifice, the dialectic inexorably builds itself up through incessant division until, in modernity, it constructs the Absolute as the system of absolute reflection, or infinite division. The completion of the logic of division in the perfected identity of subject and object is in the same moment, however, the generalisation of the state of exception. As it finally subordinates the whole world to itself, the principle of the law is thus invalidated – where inside and outside have been brought into indistinction, no further division is possible. It is at this point in the dialectic, when the order of the law has universalised itself through complete evacuation, as being in force without significance, that the division itself, the placeless place, or *utopia*, upon which the entire structure of identity always rested, begins to signify.[56] It does not do so, however, in the mode of signification

52 'The thought that wants to risk itself in this experience has to resolutely situate itself not only in the gap – or contact – between language [*lingua*] and speech, semiotic and semantic, but also in that between the φωνή and the λόγος' (Agamben 2018, p 28).

53 'The messianic ... does not represent a new and more universal identity but a caesura that passes through every identity' (Agamben 2015, p 274).

54 Agamben 2005b, p 23. 'In pushing each thing towards itself through the *as not*, the messianic does not simply cancel out this figure, but it makes it pass, it prepares its end. This is not another figure or another world: it is the passing of the figure of this world' (Agamben 2005b, pp 24–5 (emphasis in original)).

55 Agamben 2005b, p 47.

56 In this respect, speculative philosophy is literally 'news from nowhere' – that is, from *utopia*, or no-place (Verene 2009, Chapter 4). Indeed, the authentic ground of speculative thought is precisely the borderline, inside/outside, positioning of the state of exception: 'When the

because signification was founded precisely upon the insignificance of the borderline. Instead, it signifies from without identity.

This is the sense, in Agamben's reading, of Paul's messianic deactivation of the divisions of the law. The strategy of a division of the division is, in effect, the opening out, or unveiling, of the borderline, its movement from silence to speech.[57] As such, it is the emergence from oblivion of that which, as neither *ennomos* nor *anomos*, does not exist according to the bivalent, inside/outside, logic of the law, but in the modality of a third term – a division of the division – as what 'is-not'.[58] The mode of being of the division cannot itself be determined by division, and it is this ineliminable excess of the boundary line over the space of identity that the messianic figure of the remnant, invoked by Agamben, denotes. The soteriological character of the remnant, its quality as 'that which properly makes salvation possible',[59] lies in the way in which it exceeds the opposition of universal and particular that was set in place by division and that governs the order of the law. In this respect, the remnant is exactly the messianic in-between, the 'no longer … not yet', that marks the non-identity of the whole with itself – it is 'neither the all, nor a part of the all, but the impossibility of the part and the all to coincide with themselves or with each other'.[60] Just as the division that is marked by the borderline is not a substantive space that is yet to be taken

philosopher takes reflection to its limits – to the point where metaphysics becomes news from nowhere – he or she passes beyond the standpoint of reflection and passes on to the standpoint of speculation. The philosopher has come from a role within experience that is safe and secure as the custodian of all knowledge arranged in a system of the whole, to a paradoxical role of being both within and without experience. This paradoxical role generates vision and as the philosopher attempts to make sense of this vision the speculative sense of reason takes over, that allows the maker of the system to formulate a particular sense of the ultimate. The philosopher is now on the ascent to the absolute – to say in the final moments of the system what in principle cannot be said' (Verene 2009, p 42). In his recollections, set out in the essay 'Amorbach', of the happiness he experienced in playing as child in the small strip between the border posts of two German *Länder*, an area that 'belonged to neither state' and was therefore 'free', Adorno intuitively recognises this no-place that is the site of speculation: 'the country they enclosed, and which, playing by myself, I occupied, was a no man's land. Later, during the war, that phrase was used for the devastated space between the two fronts. It is, however, a faithful translation of the Greek – Aristophanic – word that I understood better the less I knew it: utopia' (Adorno 2023, p 17).

57 Agamben 2005b, pp 49–53.

58 Agamben 1999c, p 168. 'From an epistemological point of view', Paul's division of the division, 'consists in cutting the polarized Jew/non-Jew partition so that one could move on to a logic of an intuitionist sort, or better yet, a logic like that of Nicholas of Cusa in his *De non aliud*, in which the A/non-A opposition admits a third term which then takes on the form of a double negation: non non-A' (Agamben 2005b, pp 50–1).

59 Agamben 2005b, p 56.

60 Agamben 2005b, p 55.

within but an infinitesimal non-coincidence that is impossible to subsume because it is the condition of interiority as such, so the remnant is not a numerical portion continuous with the space of identity but the quality that the subject assumes when, its sovereign identity having been rendered inoperative in the messianic now, it is set against itself.

If temporal consciousness originates in division, then the messianic suspension of division effects a transformation not only of space but also of time. At the end of the dialectical process, the separated dimensions of time come together in absolute identity: the past is opened up and encompassed whole, while the future is collapsed into the unending self-sameness of the endless present. Since the completed time of capital and the international has no global subject, though, it is not yet fulfilled time. Instead, the realisation of the absolute present in the infinite division of the Absolute is, in the same instant, the deactivation of the logic of time. Once time has made itself identical to the world by separating itself from it completely as a perfectly abstract, homogenous and universal medium, there is nothing further to be divided. History comes to an end, therefore, in the generalisation of the state of exception, as the division through which time was first established emerges from muteness and obscurity. Just as with the remnant that results from dividing the division, what Agamben explicates as messianic time is thus the silent foundation no longer serving to ground the movement of identity but instead rendered inoperative so that it may come to speech. Accordingly, messianic time does not coincide completely either with the secular chronological time that is within the logic of division, nor with the *plērōma*, the fullness of eternity that would be beyond it; nor is it a third aeon, a transitional time or delay, between this world and the world to come. It is, instead, a space of negativity, 'a caesura which, in its dividing the division between the two times, introduces a remainder [*resto*] into it that exceeds the division'.[61] For this reason, in the same way that the division itself is not conceivable within the bivalent logic that it initiates, so messianic time cannot be grasped in the linear, spatialised terms of the chronological time of inside/outside – the division from which time flows is necessarily unthinkable through the form of representation that it founds. Messianic time is, rather, chronological time set against its own foundation:

> It is something like a time within time – not ulterior but interior – which only measures my disconnection with regard to it, my being out of synch and in noncoincidence with regard to my representation of time, but precisely because of this, allows for the possibility of my achieving and taking hold of it. We may now propose our first

[61] Agamben 2005b, p 64.

> definition of messianic time: messianic time is *the time that time takes to come to an end*, or, more precisely, the time we take to bring to an end, to achieve our representation of time. This is not the line of chronological time (which was representable but unthinkable), nor the instant of its end (which was just as unthinkable); nor is it a segment cut from chronological time; rather, it is operational time pressing within the chronological time, working and transforming it from within; it is the time we need to make time end: *the time that is left us* [*il tempo che ci resta*].[62]

Within this perspective, the *parousia*, the all-in-all, is to be understood not as a second messianic event but as the resolution of the tension between completion and incompletion, between *kairos* and *chronos*, which 'are coextensive but cannot be added together'.[63]

The idea of the dialectic is the mediation of immediacy. The subject separates itself from the world, forming itself as a subject through identification with the universal, so that it may be everywhere at home in the world. It risks the hazards of its long dialectical journey, embracing errancy as the way of truth, through the desire to escape subjection to the all-encompassing immanence of the blind process of nature. The logic of enlightenment is thus universal mediation: thought will accept nothing that is simply given, nothing that is merely presupposed; nor will it allow anything to remain undiscovered and unexplained. When the subject has succeeded in making itself universal it is both completely at home in the world, as the totality of political and economic space, and completely expelled from it, as bare life caught in the ban of its own identity. At its end, therefore, when the logic of contradiction has played itself out, the dialectic comes back to its beginning, to the division – the cut – that initiated the process of mediation in the first place and through which it always subsequently unfolded. In the Absolute of capital and the international, the subject thus stands immediately before its own originary anarchy, its being absolutely without foundation. For Agamben, this threshold forms the horizon within which modern thought remains enclosed.[64] By simply reaffirming the negative foundation as its necessary presupposition, contemporary philosophy renounces its proper vocation:

---

62 Agamben 2005b, pp 67–8 (emphases in original).

63 Agamben 2005b, p 70.

64 'Here the limitations of all critiques of metaphysics are made evident; they hope to surpass the horizon of metaphysics by radicalizing the problem of negativity and ungroundedness, as if a pure and simple repetition of its *fundamental* problem could lead to a surpassing of metaphysics' (Agamben 1991, p 85 (emphasis in original)).

> But does such a thought not obscure precisely what should be the philosophical task par excellence, that is, the elimination and 'absolution' of presuppositions? Was philosophy not perhaps the discourse that wanted to free itself of all presuppositions? ... Is philosophy not concerned precisely with comprehending the incomprehensible?[65]

The meaning of the messianic is that thought no longer tolerates its final presupposition, which is the division itself. Where everything has been mediated, so that the outside has been brought completely inside and the inside abandoned completely outside, all that remains as given and immediate to thought is mediation as such. The subject, whose essence is mediation, is still unmediated to itself.[66] Thought, however, is universal in its very concept – as absolute negativity, it accepts no limits. It will not abide, therefore, the darkness that lies at its origin, the hidden and silent foundation of division. Instead, if it is to fulfil its concept, thought must mediate even its own immediacy. Only then can it be genuinely free and self-determining.[67]

The line that divides inside from outside is at once myth and enlightenment: it both liberates the subject from nature, promising something more, and confines it to nature, enclosing it within the eversame. This is why the dialectic originates in division, why the dialectic *is* the division. In

---

65 Agamben 1999a, p 45. The motivating intention of dialectic is to be absolutely presuppositionless thought. Like Hegel, therefore, although to different effect, Agamben refuses the capitulation of thought before the unknowable, the supposed radical alterity of the absolutely Other (Hyppolite 1997, Part 1, Chapter 1). Rather, the meaning of revelation is that that which completely reveals the world – language, the Concept, God – must itself be completely revealed in the world, so that it becomes fully known (O'Regan 1994, Part 1).

66 Hence Agamben insists that the origin and the end can only be understood when they are thought together: 'In our tradition, a metaphysical concept, which takes as its prime focus a moment of foundation and origin, coexists with a messianic concept, which focuses on a moment of fulfilment. What is essentially messianic and *historic* is the idea that fulfilment is possible by retrieving and revoking foundation, by coming to terms with it' (Agamben 2005b, pp 103–4 (emphasis in original); see also Agamben 2020). Origin and end must come together if thought is to be released from the dynamic that they enclose.

67 This is how Agamben seeks to take thought beyond the limits of the Hegelian rendition of dialectic. As Donald Verene notes, in Hegel's conception the dialectic culminates in absolute identity through absolute division: 'Wisdom or absolute knowing is the final realization by consciousness that the double *Ansich* forever remains double. Its two moments, no matter in what particular form, what particular content they occur, are divided by an absolute gap, a beyond that is not outside consciousness but within consciousness itself, and that is the abiding condition of experience' (Verene 2007, pp 97–8).

Agamben's conception of the messianic, at the culmination of the logic of identity, in the fully globalised condition of universal mediation, when the dynamic of inside/outside has been suspended and the silent foundation comes to speech, the two moments of the division that were compounded in the dialectic begin to come apart from each other: the promissory aspect of the Concept separates itself from the legislative aspect.[68] The mediation of the immediacy of mediation is, in this way, the *katargēsis*, or *Aufhebung*, of the division itself through its disentanglement from law. As the final reckoning with the order of the law, the advent of the messianic thus signifies the dissolution of the jurisdiction of myth. Through 'the definitive elimination of the sacrificial mythologeme', the world is divested of its objectivity and the human being, likewise, of its subject-character, absolving it at last of its immemorial guilt.[69] Indeed, if the subject became a subject only by taking into itself the power of the negative, then the messianic really is the overcoming of death – that is, redemption.[70] Liberation from myth, though, is at the same time reconciliation with myth: where identity trapped the subject within nature by dividing it from it, the messianic frees the subject from nature by undoing the division. Messianism is thus the true and proper form of dialectical thought at the end of the dialectic. It is what speculative metaphysics becomes when the dialectic returns, at the last, to its origin and thinks the division itself. Messianism does not abrogate the movement of the dialectic; rather, the dialectic fulfils itself by transgressing itself. Through the force of its own logic, it annuls the negative foundation, releases itself from itself and transcends into its opposite – into everything that has been sacrificed and abandoned.[71] At the end of history, in the messianic time of the now, the subject steps through the division, out of the totality of the Concept, and into the world as a whole.

---

68 Agamben 2005b, pp 88–99 and 113–24. 'In this light, messianism appears as a struggle, within the law, whereby the element of the pact and constituent power leans toward setting itself against and emancipating itself from the element of the *entolē*, the norm in the strict sense' (Agamben 2005b, pp 118–19).

69 Agamben 1991, p 106. The messianic is thus also the profane – that is, the definitive elimination of the sacred, through which the speculative identity of thought and being is finally dissolved into an integral freedom (Agamben 2015, Chapter 9).

70 'The motif of forcing the gates of hell, of abolishing death, is the innermost cell of all antimythological thought' (Horkheimer and Adorno 2002, p 60).

71 'Non-identity is secretly the telos of the identification' (Adorno 2001b, 'Self-reflection of Thought'); 'The Messiah is the *telos* of the law' (Romans 10:4; Agamben 2005b, p 98).

References

Adorno T.W., *Against Epistemology: A Metacritique. Studies in Husserl and the Phenomenological Antinomies* (MIT Press, 1982).
Adorno T.W., 'The Idea of Natural-History', *Telos*, 57 (1985), pp 111–24.
Adorno T.W., *Kierkegaard: Construction of the Aesthetic* (University of Minnesota Press, 1989).
Adorno T.W., *Hegel: Three Studies* (MIT Press, 1993).
Adorno T.W., *Metaphysics: Concept and Problems*, ed. R. Tiedemann (Polity Press, 2000).
Adorno T.W., *Kant's Critique of Pure Reason*, ed. R. Tiedemann (Polity Press, 2001a).
Adorno T.W., *Negative Dialectics* (2001b): http://members.efn.org/~dredmond/ndtrans.html
Adorno T.W., 'Progress', *Critical Models: Interventions and Catchwords* (Columbia University Press, 2005a), pp 143–60.
Adorno T.W., 'On Subject and Object', *Critical Models: Interventions and Catchwords* (Columbia University Press, 2005b), pp 245–58.
Adorno T.W., 'Why Still Philosophy', *Critical Models: Interventions and Catchwords* (Columbia University Press, 2005c), pp 5–17.
Adorno T.W., *Minima Moralia: Reflections from Damaged Life* (Verso, 2005d).
Adorno T.W., *History and Freedom: Lectures 1964–1965*, ed. R. Tiedemann (Polity Press, 2006).
Adorno T.W., *Lectures on Negative Dialectics*, ed. R. Tiedemann (Polity Press, 2008).
Adorno T.W., *An Introduction to Dialectics*, ed. C. Ziermann (Polity Press, 2017).
Adorno T.W., 'Amorbach', *Without Model* (Seagull Books, 2023), pp 13–21.
Adorno T.W., Albert H., Dahrendorf R., et al: *The Positivist Dispute in German Sociology* (Heinemann, 1976).
Adorno T.W. and Benjamin W., *The Complete Correspondence 1928–1940*, ed. H. Lonitz (Polity Press, 1999).
Adorno T.W. and Horkheimer M., 'Odysseus or Myth and Enlightenment', *New German Critique*, 56 (Spring–Summer 1992), pp 109–41.

Agamben G., *Language and Death: The Place of Negativity* (University of Minnesota Press, 1991).

Agamben G., *Stanzas: Word and Phantasm in Western Culture* (University of Minnesota Press, 1993).

Agamben G., *Idea of Prose* (SUNY Press, 1995).

Agamben G., *Homo Sacer: Sovereign Power and Bare Life* (Stanford University Press, 1998).

Agamben G., 'The Idea of Language', *Potentialities: Collected Essays in Philosophy*, ed. D. Heller-Roazen (Stanford University Press, 1999a), pp 39–47.

Agamben G., 'Language and History: Linguistic and Historical Categories in Benjamin's Thought', *Potentialities: Collected Essays in Philosophy*, ed. D. Heller-Roazen (Stanford University Press, 1999b), pp 48–61.

Agamben G., 'The Messiah and the Sovereign: The Problem of Law in Walter Benjamin', *Potentialities: Collected Essays in Philosophy*, ed. D. Heller-Roazen (Stanford University Press, 1999c), pp 160–74.

Agamben G., 'On Potentiality', *Potentialities: Collected Essays in Philosophy*, ed. D. Heller-Roazen (Stanford University Press, 1999d), pp 177–84.

Agamben G., '*Pardes*: The Writing of Potentiality', *Potentialities: Collected Essays in Philosophy*, ed. D. Heller-Roazen (Stanford University Press, 1999e), pp 205–19.

Agamben G., '**Se*: Hegel's Absolute and Heidegger's *Ereignis*', *Potentialities: Collected Essays in Philosophy*, ed. D. Heller-Roazen (Stanford University Press, 1999f), pp 116–37.

Agamben G., 'The Thing Itself', *Potentialities: Collected Essays in Philosophy*, ed. D. Heller-Roazen (Stanford University Press, 1999g), pp 27–38.

Agamben G., 'Tradition of the Immemorial', *Potentialities: Collected Essays in Philosophy*, ed. D. Heller-Roazen (Stanford University Press, 1999h), pp 104–15.

Agamben G., 'Form-of-Life', *Means Without Ends: Notes on Politics* (University of Minnesota Press, 2000), pp 3–14.

Agamben G., *State of Exception* (University of Chicago Press, 2005a).

Agamben G., *The Time That Remains: A Commentary on the Letter to the Romans* (Stanford University Press, 2005b).

Agamben G., *Infancy and History: On the Destruction of Experience* (Verso, 2007).

Agamben G., *The Signature of All Things* (Zone Books, 2009).

Agamben G., *The Kingdom and the Glory: For a Theological Genealogy of Economy and Government* (Stanford University Press, 2011a).

Agamben G., *Nudities* (Stanford University Press, 2011b).

Agamben G., *The Sacrament of Language: An Archaeology of the Oath* (Polity Press, 2011c).

Agamben G., *The Church and the Kingdom* (Seagull Books, 2012).

Agamben G., *Nymphs* (Seagull Books, 2013).

Agamben G., *The Use of Bodies* (Stanford University Press, 2015).
Agamben G., *What is Philosophy?* (Stanford University Press, 2018).
Agamben G., 'Capitalism as Religion', *Creation and Anarchy: The Work of Art and the Religion of Capitalism* (Stanford University Press, 2019a), pp 66–77.
Agamben G., 'A Jurist Confronting Himself: Carl Schmitt's Jurisprudential Thought', *The Oxford Handbook of Carl Schmitt*, ed. J. Meierhenrich and O. Simons (Oxford University Press, 2019b), pp 457–70.
Agamben G., *The Kingdom and the Garden* (Seagull Books, 2020).
Agamben G., *Where are We Now? The Epidemic as Politics* (Eris, 2021).
Agamben G., *Studiolo* (Seagull Books, 2022).
Agamben G., *The Unrealizable: Towards a Politics of Ontology* (Seagull Books, 2025).
Albritton R. and Simoulidis J. (eds), *New Dialectics and Political Economy* (Palgrave Macmillan, 2003).
Allison H.E., *Kant's Transcendental Idealism: An Interpretation and Defense* (Yale University Press, 2004).
Althusser L., 'The Crisis of Marxism', *Marxism Today* (July 1978), pp 215–27.
Althusser L., *For Marx* (Verso, 2005).
Althusser L., *Reading Capital* (Verso, 2015).
Anievas A. (ed.), *Marxism and World Politics: Contesting Global Capitalism* (Routledge, 2010).
Anievas A. and Nişancıoğlu K., *How the West came to Rule: The Geopolitical Origins of Capitalism* (Pluto Press, 2015).
Aristotle, *Politics* (Hackett, 1998).
Aron R., *Peace & War: A Theory of International Relations* (Transaction Publishers, 2009).
Arrighi G., *The Long Twentieth Century: Money, Power, and the Origins of Our Times* (Verso, 1994).
Arthur C.J., 'Dialectic of the Value-Form', *Value: The Representation of Labour in Capitalism*, ed. D. Elson (CSE Books, 1979), pp 67–81.
Arthur C.J., *Dialectics of Labour: Marx and his Relation to Hegel* (Basil Blackwell, 1986).
Arthur C.J., 'Against the Logical-Historical Method: Dialectical Derivation versus Linear Logic', *New Investigations of Marx's Method*, ed. F. Moseley and M. Campbell (Humanities Press, 1997), pp 9–37.
Arthur C.J., 'Engels, Logic and History', *Marxian Economics: A Reappraisal. Essays on Volume III of Capital – Volume 1: Method, Value and Money*, ed. R. Bellofiore (Macmillan, 1998), pp 3–15.
Arthur C.J., 'The Hegel–Marx Connection', *Historical Materialism*, 11/1 (2003), pp 179–83.
Arthur C.J., 'Money and the Form of Value', *The Constitution of Capital: Essays on Volume 1 of Capital*, ed. R. Bellofiore and N. Taylor (Palgrave Macmillan, 2004a), pp 35–62.

Arthur C.J., *The New Dialectic and Marx's Capital* (Brill, 2004b).
Arthur C.J., 'The Concept of Money', *Radical Philosophy*, 134 (2005a), pp 31–40.
Arthur C.J., 'Reply to Critics', *Historical Materialism*, 13/2 (2005b), pp 189–221.
Arthur C.J., 'Value and Money', *Marx's Theory of Money: Modern Appraisals*, ed. F. Moseley (Palgrave Macmillan, 2005c), pp 111–23.
Arthur C.J., 'Money and Exchange', *Capital & Class*, 90 (Autumn 2006), pp 7–35.
Arthur C.J., 'With What must the Critique of Capital Begin?', *Revista Opinião Filosófica*, 7/1 (2016), pp 64–87.
Arthur C.J., *The Spectre of Capital: Idea and Reality* (Brill, 2022).
Arthur C.J. and Reuten G. (eds), *The Circulation of Capital: Essays on Volume Two of Marx's Capital* (Palgrave Macmillan, 1998).
Attell K., 'Potentiality, Actuality, Constituent Power', *diacritics*, 39/3 (2009), pp 35–53.
Attell K., *Giorgio Agamben: Beyond the Threshold of Deconstruction* (Fordham University Press, 2015).
Austin N., 'Name Magic in the "Odyssey"', *California Studies in Classical Antiquity*, 5 (1972), pp 1–19.
Backhaus H.-G., 'On the Dialectics of the Value-Form', *Thesis Eleven*, 1/1 (1980), pp 94–120.
Backhaus H.-G., 'Between Philosophy and Science: Marxian Social Economy as Critical Theory', *Open Marxism, Volume 1: Dialectics and History*, ed. W. Bonefeld, R. Gunn and K. Psychopedis (Pluto Press, 1992), pp 54–92.
Backhaus H.-G., 'Some Aspects of Marx's Concept of Critique in the Context of his Economic-Philosophical Theory', *Human Dignity: Social Autonomy and the Critique of Capitalism*, ed. W. Bonefeld and K. Psychopedis (Ashgate, 2005), pp 13–30.
Banaji J., 'From the Commodity to Capital: Hegel's Dialectic in Marx's *Capital*', *Value: the Representation of Labour in Capitalism*, ed. D. Elson (CSE Books, 1979), pp 14–45.
Baudrillard J., *The Mirror of Production* (Telos Press, 1975).
Baudrillard J., *For a Critique of the Political Economy of the Sign* (Telos Press, 1981).
Baur M., 'From Kant's Highest Good to Hegel's Absolute Knowing', *A Companion to Hegel*, ed. S. Houlgate and M. Baur (Wiley-Blackwell, 2011), pp 452–73.
Beiser F.C., *German Idealism: The Struggle against Subjectivism* (Harvard University Press, 2002).
Bellofiore R. and Fineschi R. (eds), *Re-Reading Marx: New Perspectives after the Critical Edition* (Palgrave Macmillan, 2009).

Bellofiore R. and Redolfi Riva T., 'The *Neue Marx-Lektüre*: Putting the Critique of Political Economy back into the Critique of Society', *Radical Philosophy*, 189 (2015), pp 24–36.
Bellofiore R. and Redolfi Riva T., 'Hans-Georg Backhaus: The Critique of Premonetary Theories of Value and the Perverted Forms of Economic Reality', *The SAGE Handbook of Frankfurt School Critical Theory*, ed. B. Best, W. Bonefeld and C. O'Kane (Sage, 2018), pp 386–401.
Bellofiore R., Starosta G. and Thomas P.D. (eds), *In Marx's Laboratory: Critical Interpretations of the Grundrisse* (Haymarket, 2014).
Bellofiore R. and Taylor N. (eds), *The Constitution of Capital: Essays on Volume 1 of Marx's Capital* (Palgrave Macmillan, 2004).
Bellofiore R. and Wolf F.O., 'Taking up the Challenge of Living Labour: A "Backwards-Looking Reconstruction" of Recent Italian Debates on Marx's Theory of the Capitalist Mode of Production', *The Unfinished System of Karl Marx: Critically Reading Capital as a Challenge for our Times*, ed. J. Dellheim and F.O. Wolf (Macmillan, 2018), pp 31–90.
Benjamin W., 'Capitalism as Religion', *Selected Writings, Volume 1: 1913–1926*, ed. M. Bullock and M.W. Jennings (Harvard University Press, 2004a), pp 288–91.
Benjamin W., 'Fate and Character', *Selected Writings, Volume 1: 1913–1926*, ed. M. Bullock and M.W. Jennings (Harvard University Press, 2004b), pp 201–6.
Benjamin W., 'On Language as such and the Language of Man', *Selected Writings, Volume 1: 1913–1926*, ed. M. Bullock and M.W. Jennings (Harvard University Press, 2004c), pp 62–74.
Benjamin W., 'On the Concept of History', *Selected Writings, Volume 4: 1938–1940*, ed. H. Eiland and M.W. Jennings (Harvard University Press, 2006), pp 389–400.
Benjamin W., *Towards the Critique of Violence: A Critical Edition*, ed. P. Fenves and J. Ng (Stanford University Press, 2021).
Berki R.N., 'On Marxian Thought and the Problem of International Relations', *World Politics*, 24/1 (1971), pp 80–105.
Bidet J., 'The Dialectician's Interpretation of *Capital*', *Historical Materialism*, 13/2 (2005), pp 121–46.
Bidet J., *Exploring Marx's Capital: Philosophical, Economic, and Political Dimensions* (Haymarket, 2009).
Bobbio N., 'Marxism and International Relations', *Which Socialism? Marxism, Socialism and Democracy* (University of Minnesota Press, 1987), pp 197–212.
Böhm-Bawerk E., *Karl Marx and the Close of His System* (Wolff, 1949).
Bonefeld W., 'Abstract Labour: Against its Nature and on its Time', *Capital & Class*, 34/2 (2010), pp 257–76.
Bonefeld W., *Critical Theory and the Critique of Political Economy: On Subversion and Negative Reason* (Bloomsbury, 2014).

Bonefeld W. and O'Kane C. (eds), *Adorno and Marx: Negative Dialectics and the Critique of Political Economy* (Bloomsbury, 2022).
Booth K., 'International Politics: The Inconvenient Truth', *Realism and World Politics*, ed. K. Booth (Routledge, 2011), pp 325–42.
Bowman B., *Hegel and the Metaphysics of Absolute Negativity* (Cambridge University Press, 2013).
Braunstein D., *Adorno's Critique of Political Economy* (Brill, 2023).
Brenner R., 'The Origins of Capitalist Development: A Critique of Neo-Smithian Marxism', *New Left Review*, I/104 (July/Aug, 1977), pp 25–92.
Bristow W.F., *Hegel and the Transformation of Philosophical Critique* (Oxford University Press, 2012).
Brown N., 'The Modality of Sovereignty: Agamben and the *Aporia* of Primacy in Aristotle's *Metaphysics* Theta', *Mosaic*, 46/1 (2013), pp 169–82.
Brown N., 'Indeterminacy, Modality, Dialectics: Hegel on the Possibility *Not to Be*', *The Significance of Indeterminacy: Perspectives from Asian and Continental Philosophy*, ed. R.H. Scott and G.S. Moss (Routledge, 2018), pp 104–23.
Brown N., *Hegel on Possibility: Dialectics, Contradiction, and Modality* (Bloomsbury, 2020).
Bubbio P.D., *Sacrifice in the Post-Kantian Tradition: Perspectivism, Intersubjectivity, and Recognition* (SUNY Press, 2014).
Bull H. and Watson A., *The Expansion of International Society* (Clarendon Press, 1984).
Burns T. and Fraser I. (eds), *The Hegel–Marx Connection* (Macmillan, 2000).
Calasso R., *The Marriage of Cadmus and Harmony* (Vintage, 1994).
Calasso R., 'The Terror of Fables', *The Forty-Nine Steps* (Pimlico, 2002), pp 259–66.
Calasso R., *Ardor* (Penguin, 2015).
Calasso R., *The Ruin of Kasch* (Penguin, 2018).
Calasso R., *The Celestial Hunter* (Allen Lane, 2020).
Callinicos A., 'Does Capitalism need the State System?', *Cambridge Review of International Affairs*, 20/4 (2007), pp 533–49.
Callinicos A., 'How to Solve the Many-State Problem: A Reply to the Debate', *Cambridge Review of International Affairs*, 22/1 (2009a), pp 89–105.
Callinicos A., *Imperialism and Global Political Economy* (Polity Press, 2009b).
Callinicos A. and Rosenberg J.P., 'Uneven and Combined Development: The Social-Relational Substratum of "the International"? An Exchange of Letters', *Cambridge Review of International Affairs*, 21/1 (2008), pp 77–112.
Cambridge Review of International Affairs, 20/4 (2007).
Campbell M. and Reuten G. (eds), *The Culmination of Capital: Essays on Volume III of Marx's Capital* (Palgrave Macmillan, 2002).
Caravale G.A., 'Marx's Views on Ricardo – A Critical Evaluation', *Marx and Modern Economic Analysis, Volume II: The Future of Capitalism and the History of Thought*, ed. G.A. Caravale (Edward Elgar, 1991), pp 168–207.

Carr E.H., *The Twenty Years' Crisis, 1919–1939: An Introduction to the Study of International Relations* (Palgrave Macmillan, 2001).
Chase-Dunn C., 'Interstate System and Capitalist World-Economy: One Logic or Two?', *International Studies Quarterly*, 25/1 (1981), pp 19–42.
Chibber V., 'Capital Outbound', *New Left Review*, II/36 (2005), pp 151–8.
Cohen G.A., *Karl Marx's Theory of History: A Defence* (Clarendon, 1978).
Colletti L., *From Rousseau to Lenin: Studies in Ideology and Society* (NLB, 1972).
Cutler A., Hindess B., Hirst P. and Hussein A., *Marx's 'Capital' and Capitalism Today*, vol 1 (Routledge and Kegan Paul, 1977a).
Cutler A., Hindess B., Hirst P. and Hussein A., *Marx's 'Capital' and Capitalism Today*, vol 2 (Routledge and Kegan Paul, 1977b).
Davenport A., 'The International and the Limits of History', *Review of International Studies*, 42/2 (2016), pp 247–65.
Davenport A., 'Multiplicity: Anarchy in the Mirror of Sociology', *Globalizations*, 17/3 (2020), 532–45.
Davis A.A., *Hegel on Pseudo-Philosophy: Reading the Preface to the 'Phenomenology of Spirit'* (Bloomsbury, 2023).
Day R.B. and Gaido D.F. (eds), *Responses to Marx's Capital: From Rudolf Hilferding to Isaak Illich Rubin* (Haymarket Books, 2017).
De Angelis M., 'Beyond the Technological and the Social Paradigms: A Political Reading of Abstract Labour as the Substance of Value', *Capital & Class*, 57 (1995), pp 107–34.
de Boer K., 'Hegel's Account of the Present: An Open-Ended History', *Hegel and History*, ed. W. Dudley (SUNY Press, 2009), pp 51–67.
de Boer K., *On Hegel: The Sway of the Negative* (Palgrave Macmillan, 2010).
de Boer K., *Kant's Reform of Metaphysics: The Critique of Pure Reason Reconsidered* (Cambridge University Press, 2022).
de la Durantaye L., *Giorgio Agamben: A Critical Introduction* (Stanford University Press, 2009).
Derrida J., *Specters of Marx: The State of the Debt, the Work of Mourning and the New International* (Routledge, 2004).
Descartes R., *The Philosophical Writings of Descartes, Volume I* (Cambridge University Press, 1985).
de Vroey M., 'Value, Production, and Exchange', *The Value Controversy*, ed. I. Steedman (Verso, 1981), pp 173–201.
de Vroey M., 'On the Obsolescence of the Marxian Theory of Value: A Critical Review', *Capital & Class*, 6/2 (Summer 1982), pp 34–59.
Dickinson C., 'Theodor W. Adorno', *Agamben's Philosophical Lineage* (Edinburgh University Press, 2017), pp 219–29.
Dobb M., *On Economic Theory and Socialism: Collected Papers* (Routledge & Kegan Paul, 1955).
Dobb M., *Theories of Value and Distribution since Adam Smith: Ideology and Economic Theory* (Cambridge University Press, 1973).

Dumont L., *From Mandeville to Marx: The Genesis and Triumph of Economic Ideology* (University of Chicago Press, 1977).

Dunne T. and Reus-Smit C. (eds), *The Globalization of International Society* (Oxford University Press, 2017).

Elbe I., 'Helmut Reichelt and the New Reading of Marx', *The SAGE Handbook of Frankfurt School Critical Theory*, ed. B. Best, W. Bonefeld and C. O'Kane (Sage, 2018), pp 367–85.

Eldred M., *Critique of Competitive Freedom and the Bourgeois-Democratic State: Outline of a Form-Analytic Extension of Marx's Completed System* (CreateSpace Independent Publishing, 2015).

Eldred M. and Hanlon M., 'Reconstructing Value-Form Analysis', *Capital & Class*, 13 (Spring 1981), pp 24–60.

Eldred M., Hanlon M., Kleiber L. and Roth M., 'Reconstructing Value-Form Analysis 1: The Analysis of Commodities and Money', *Thesis Eleven*, 4/1 (1982), pp 170–88.

Eldred M., Hanlon M., Kleiber L. and Roth M., 'Reconstructing Value-Form Analysis 2: The Analysis of the Capital – Wage-Labour Relation', *Thesis Eleven*, 7/1 (1983), pp 87–111.

Elson D. (ed.), *Value: The Representation of Labour in Capitalism* (CSE Books, 1979).

Elster J., *Making Sense of Marx* (Cambridge University Press, 1985).

Elster J., *An Introduction to Karl Marx* (Cambridge University Press, 1986).

Fasolt C., *The Limits of History* (University of Chicago Press, 2004).

Fine B. and Harris L., 'Controversial Issues in Marxist Economic Theory', *Socialist Register* (1976), pp 141–78.

Fine B. (ed.), *The Value Dimension: Marx versus Ricardo and Sraffa* (Routledge & Kegan Paul, 1986).

Finelli R., 'Some Thoughts on the Modern in the Works of Smith, Hegel, and Marx', *Rethinking Marxism*, 2/2 (1989), pp 111–31.

Finelli R., *A Failed Parricide: Hegel and the Young Marx* (Brill, 2016).

Fineschi R., 'Dialectic of the Commodity and its Exposition: The German Debate in the 1970s – A Personal Overview', *Re-Reading Marx: New Perspectives after the Critical Edition*, ed. R. Bellofiore and R. Fineschi (Palgrave Macmillan, 2009), pp 50–70.

Förster E., *The Twenty-Five Years of Philosophy: A Systematic Reconstruction* (Harvard University Press, 2012).

Frank M., *What is Neostructuralism?* (University of Minnesota Press, 1989).

Freud S., *The Unconscious* (Penguin, 2005).

Furner J., 'Marx's Critique of Samuel Bailey', *Historical Materialism*, 12/2 (2004), pp 89–110.

Gadamer H.-G., *Hegel's Dialectic: Five Hermeneutical Studies* (Yale University Press, 1976).

Galli C., *Political Spaces and Global War*, ed. A. Sitze (University of Minnesota Press, 2010).
Galli C., *Janus's Gaze: Essays on Carl Schmitt* (Duke University Press, 2015).
García Düttmann A., 'Thinking as Gesture: A Note on *Dialectic of Enlightenment*', *New German Critique*, no. 81 (2000), pp 143–52.
García Düttmann A., *The Memory of Thought: An Essay on Heidegger and Adorno* (Continuum, 2002).
Garrison A., 'Hegel', *Agamben's Philosophical Lineage*, ed. A. Kotsko and C. Salzani (Edinburgh University Press, 2017), pp 138–45.
Germer C., 'The Commodity Nature of Money in Marx's Theory', *Marx's Theory of Money: Modern Appraisals*, ed. F. Moseley (Palgrave Macmillan, 2005), pp 21–35.
Gilpin R., *War and Change in World Politics* (Cambridge University Press, 1981).
Gordon P.E., *Adorno and Existence* (Harvard University Press, 2016).
Halliday F., 'A Necessary Encounter: Historical Materialism and International Relations', *Rethinking International Relations* (Macmillan, 1994), pp 47–73.
Hanna R., 'From an Ontological Point of View: Hegel's Critique of the Common Logic', *The Hegel Myths and Legends*, ed. J. Stewart (Northwestern University Press, 1996), pp 252–81.
Hardt M. and Negri A., *Empire* (Harvard University Press, 2000).
Hardt M. and Negri A., *Multitude: War and Democracy in the Age of Empire* (Penguin, 2006).
Hardt M. and Negri A., 'Empire, Twenty Years on', *New Left Review*, II/120 (Nov–Dec 2019), pp 67–92.
Harrelson K.J., *The Ontological Argument from Descartes to Hegel* (New York: Humanity Press, 2009).
Harris H.S., *Hegel's Development: Toward the Sunlight 1770–1801* (Oxford University Press, 1972).
Harris H.S., *Hegel's Development: Night Thoughts (Jena 1801–1806)* (Oxford University Press, 1983).
Hartog F., *Memories of Odysseus: Frontier Tales from Ancient Greece* (University of Chicago Press, 2001).
Hartog F., *Regimes of Historicity: Presentism and Experiences of Time* (Columbia University Press, 2015).
Harvey D., *The New Imperialism* (Oxford University Press, 2003).
Harvey D., *A Companion to Marx's Capital* (Verso, 2010).
Hegel G.W.F., *The Difference between Fichte's and Schelling's System of Philosophy*, ed. H.S. Harris and W. Cerf (SUNY Press, 1977a).
Hegel G.W.F., *Faith and Knowledge*, ed. W. Cerf and H.S. Harris (SUNY Press, 1977b).
Hegel G.W.F., *Hegel and the Human Spirit: A Translation of the Jena Lectures on the Philosophy of Spirit (1805–6) with Commentary*, ed. L. Rauch (Wayne State University Press, 1983).

Hegel G.W.F., *The Encyclopaedia Logic*, ed. T.F. Geraets, W.A. Suchting and H.S. Harris (Hackett, 1991).

Hegel G.W.F., 'On the Relationship of Skepticism to Philosophy, Exposition of its Different Modifications and Comparison of the Latest Form with the Ancient One', *Between Kant and Hegel: Texts in the Development of Post-Kantian Idealism*, ed. G. di Giovanni and H.S. Harris (Hackett, 2000), pp 311–62.

Hegel G.W.F., *Lectures on the Philosophy of Religion. Volume 1: Introduction and the Concept of Religion*, ed. P. Hodgson (Oxford University Press, 2007a).

Hegel G.W.F., *Lectures on the Philosophy of Religion. Volume 2: Determinate Religion*, ed. P. Hodgson (Oxford University Press, 2007b).

Hegel G.W.F., *Lectures on the History of Philosophy 1825–6. Volume III: Medieval and Modern Philosophy*, ed. R.F. Brown (Oxford University Press, 2009).

Hegel G.W.F., *The Science of Logic*, ed. G. di Giovanni (Cambridge University Press, 2010).

Hegel G.W.F., *Hegel's Aesthetics: Lectures on Fine Art, Volume II* (Clarendon Press, 2014).

Hegel G.W.F., *Phenomenology of Spirit*, ed. T. Pinkard (Cambridge University Press, 2018).

Hegel G.W.F., *Lectures on the Philosophy of World History. Volume 1: Manuscripts of the Introduction and the Lectures of 1822–3*, ed. R.F. Brown and P.C. Hodgson (Oxford University Press, 2019).

Hegel G.W.F. and Schelling F.W.J., 'On the Essence of Philosophical Criticism Generally, and its Relationship to the Present State of Philosophy', *Between Kant and Hegel: Texts in the Development of Post-Kantian Idealism*, ed. G. di Giovanni and H.S. Harris (Hackett, 2000), pp 272–91.

Heinrich M., 'Reconstruction or Deconstruction? Methodological Controversies about Value and Capital, and New Insights from the Critical Edition', *Re-Reading Marx: New Perspectives after the Critical Edition*, ed. R. Bellofiore and R. Fineschi (Palgrave Macmillan, 2009), pp 71–98.

Heinrich M., *An Introduction to the Three Volumes of Karl Marx's Capital* (Monthly Review Press, 2012).

Heinrich M., *How to Read Marx's Capital: Commentary and Explanations on the Beginning Chapters* (Monthly Review Press, 2021).

Heller-Roazen D., *No One's Ways: An Essay on Infinite Naming* (Zone Books, 2017).

Henrich D., 'The Basic Structure of Modern Philosophy', *Cultural Hermeneutics*, 2 (1974), pp 1–18.

Henrich D., *The Course of Remembrance and Other Essays on Hölderlin*, ed. E. Förster (Stanford University Press, 1997).

Henrich D., *Between Kant and Hegel: Lectures on German Idealism* (Harvard University Press, 2003).

Herz J., *Political Realism and Political Idealism* (University of Chicago Press, 1951).

Himmelweit S. and Mohun S., 'The Anomalies of Capital', *Capital & Class*, 6 (Autumn 1978), pp 67–105.

Hindess B. and Hirst P., *Mode of Production and Social Formation: An Auto-Critique of Pre-Capitalist Modes of Production* (Macmillan, 1977).

Hobbes T., *De Cive: The English Version*, ed. H. Warrender (Clarendon Press, 1998).

Hobbes T., *Human Nature and De Corpore Politico*, ed. J.C.A. Gaskin (Oxford University Press, 2008a).

Hobbes T., *Leviathan*, ed. N. Malcolm (Oxford University Press, 2008b).

Hodgson G., *Capitalism, Value and Exploitation: A Radical Theory* (Martin Robertson, 1982).

Hodgson P.C., 'Hegel's Proofs of the Existence of God', *A Companion to Hegel*, ed. S. Houlgate and M. Bauer (Wiley-Blackwell, 2011), pp 414–30.

Hoff J., *Marx Worldwide: On the Development of the International Discourse of Marxism since 1965* (Haymarket Books, 2017).

Hoffmann S.H., 'International Relations: The Long Road to Theory', *World Politics*, 11/3 (1959), pp 346–77.

Hölderlin F., 'Being Judgement Possibility', *Essays and Letters*, ed. J. Adler and C. Louth (Penguin, 2009), pp 231–2.

Homer, *The Odyssey* (Paul Dry Books, 2014).

Horkheimer M. and Adorno T.W., *Dialectic of Enlightenment: Philosophical Fragments*, ed. G. Schmid Noerr (Stanford University Press, 2002).

Horkheimer M. and Adorno T.W., *Dialektik der Aufklärung. Philosophische Fragmente* (Fischer Verlag, 2009).

Houlgate S., *The Opening of Hegel's Logic* (Purdue University Press, 2006).

Houlgate S., *Hegel's Phenomenology of Spirit* (Bloomsbury, 2013).

Houlgate S., *Hegel on Being, Vol. 1: Quality and the Birth of Quantity in Hegel's Science of Logic* (Bloomsbury, 2022).

Hullot-Kentor R., *Things Beyond Resemblance: Collected Essays on Theodor W. Adorno* (Columbia University Press, 2006).

Hume D., *A Treatise of Human Nature*, ed. E.C. Mossner (Penguin, 1985).

Hyppolite J., *Logic and Existence* (SUNY Press, 1997).

Iacono A., *The History and Theory of Fetishism* (Palgrave Macmillan, 2016).

Iacono A., *The Bourgeois and the Savage: A Marxian Critique of the Image of the Isolated Individual in Defoe, Turgot and Smith* (Palgrave Macmillan, 2020).

International Journal of Political Economy, 27/2 (Summer 1997).

International Journal of Political Economy, 28/3 (Fall 1998).

Jarvis S., *Adorno: A Critical Introduction* (Polity Press, 1998).

Jarvis S., 'What is Speculative Thinking?', *Revue Internationale de Philosophie*, 227/1 (2004), pp 69–83.

Jarvis S., 'Spirit Medium: On Hegel's *Phenomenology*', *Cambridge Literary Review*, 1/2 (2010), pp 157–69.

Kant I., *Practical Philosophy*, ed. M.J. Gregor (Cambridge University Press, 1996).

Kant I., *Critique of Pure Reason*, ed. P. Guyer and A.W. Wood (Cambridge University Press, 1999).

Kant I., 'On the Form and Principles of the Sensible and the Intelligible World [Inaugural Dissertation]', *Theoretical Philosophy, 1755–1770*, ed. D. Walford and R. Meerbote (Cambridge University Press, 2007), pp 373–416.

Kant I., 'Idea for a Universal History with a Cosmopolitan Aim', *Anthropology, History, and Education*, ed. G. Zöller and R.B. Louden (Cambridge University Press, 2009), pp 108–120.

Kicillof A. and Starosta G., 'On Materiality and Social Form: A Political Critique of Rubin's Value-Form Theory', *Historical Materialism*, 15/3 (2007), pp 9–43.

Kirk G.S., Raven J.E. and Schofield M., *The Presocratic Philosophers* (Cambridge University Press, 2007).

Lacan J., 'The Instance of the Letter in the Unconscious', *Écrits* (Norton, 2006), pp 412–41.

Lacher H., *Beyond Globalization: Capitalism, Territoriality and the International Relations of Modernity* (Routledge, 2006).

Lebow R.N., *The Tragic Vision of Politics: Ethics, Interests, and Orders* (Cambridge University Press, 2003).

Levine D.P., *Economic Studies: Contributions to the Critique of Economic Theory* (Routledge & Kegan Paul, 1977).

Levine D.P., *Economic Theory, Volume One: The Elementary Relations of Economic Life* (Routledge & Kegan Paul, 1978).

Levine D.P., *Economic Theory, Volume Two: The System of Economic Relations as a Whole* (Routledge & Kegan Paul, 1981).

Levine D.P., 'Two Options for the Theory of Money', *Social Concept*, 1 (1983), pp 20–29.

Levine D.P., 'The Structure of Marx's Argument in *Capital*', *Marxian Economics: A Reappraisal. Volume 1: Essays on Volume 3 of Capital – Method, Value and Money*, ed. R. Bellofiore (Macmillan Press, 1998a), pp 16–28.

Levine D.P., *Subjectivity in Political Economy: Essays on Wanting and Choosing* (Routledge, 1998b).

Linklater A., 'World History and International Relations', *International Relations*, 21/3 (2007), pp 355–9.

Lippi M., *Value and Naturalism in Marx* (NLB, 1979).

Little R., *The Balance of Power in International Relations: Metaphors, Myths, and Models* (Cambridge University Press, 2007).

Locke J., *An Essay Concerning Human Understanding* (Penguin, 2004).

Magee G.A., *Hegel and the Hermetic Tradition* (Cornell University Press, 2008a).

Magee G.A., 'Hegel and Mysticism', *Hegel and Nineteenth-Century Philosophy*, ed. F.C. Beiser (Cambridge University Press, 2008b), pp 253–80.
Magee G.A., 'Quietism in German Mysticism and Philosophy', *Common Knowledge*, 16/3 (2010), pp 457–53.
Maker W., 'Hegel's *Phenomenology* as Introduction to Science', *Clio*, 10/4 (1981), pp 381–97.
Maker W., 'Does Hegel have a "Dialectical Method"?', *Southern Journal of Philosophy*, 20/1 (1982), pp 75–96.
Maker W., 'Beginning', *Essays in Hegel's Logic*, ed. G. di Giovanni (SUNY Press, 1990), pp 27–43.
Maker W., *Philosophy without Foundations: Rethinking Hegel* (SUNY Press, 1994).
Maker W., 'The End of History and the Nihilism of Becoming', *Hegel and History*, ed. W. Dudley (SUNY Press, 2009), pp 15–34.
Marx K., *Grundrisse: Foundations of the Critique of Political Economy* (Penguin, 1973).
Marx K., *Value: Studies by Karl Marx*, ed. A. Dragstedt (New Park Publications, 1976).
Marx K., *Capital, Volume 1* (Penguin, 1990).
Marx K., *Capital, Volume 3* (Penguin, 1991).
Marx K., *Capital, Volume 2* (Penguin, 1992).
Marx K., *Marx's Economic Manuscript of 1864–1865*, ed. F. Moseley (Haymarket, 2017).
Marx K. and Engels F., *The German Ideology*, ed. S. Ryazanskaya (Progress Publishers, 1968).
Marx K. and Engels F., *Collected Works, Volume 16* (Lawrence & Wishart, 1980).
Marx K. and Engels F., *Collected Works, Volume 29* (Lawrence & Wishart, 1987).
Marx K. and Engels F., *Collected Works, Volume 43* (Lawrence & Wishart, 1988).
McNulty J., *Hegel's Logic and Metaphysics* (Cambridge University Press, 2023).
Meaney M.E., *Capital as Organic Unity: The Role of Hegel's Science of Logic in Marx's Grundrisse* (Kluwer, 2002).
Mearsheimer J.J., *The Tragedy of Great Power Politics* (Norton, 2014).
Meek R., *Economics and Ideology and Other Essays* (Chapman and Hall, 1967).
Meek R., *Studies in the Labour Theory of Value* (Lawrence & Wishart, 1973).
Meek R., *Social Science and the Ignoble Savage* (Cambridge University Press, 1976).
Meek R., *Smith, Marx, & After* (Chapman & Hall, 1977).
Meikle S., *Essentialism in the Thought of Karl Marx* (Duckworth, 1985).
Milios J., Dimoulis D. and Economakis G., *Karl Marx and the Classics: An Essay on Value, Crises and the Capitalist Mode of Production* (Ashgate, 2002).
Mohun S. (ed.), *Debates in Value Theory* (Macmillan, 1994).
Morgenthau H.J., *Scientific Man vs. Power Politics* (University of Chicago Press, 1965).

Morgenthau H.J., *Truth and Power: Essays of a Decade, 1960–70* (Pall Mall Press, 1970).

Morgenthau H.J., *Politics among Nations: The Struggle for Power and Peace* (McGraw-Hill, 2006).

Morgenthau H.J. and Thompson K.W., *The Principles and Problems of International Politics: Selected Readings* (Knopf, 1950).

Morton A.D., 'Waiting for Gramsci: State Formation, Passive Revolution and the International', *Millenium: Journal of International Studies*, 35/3 (2007), pp 597–621.

Moseley F. (ed.), *Marx's Method in Capital: A Reexamination* (Humanities Press, 1993).

Moseley, F. (ed.), *Marx's Theory of Money: Modern Appraisals* (Palgrave Macmillan, 2005).

Moseley F., *Money and Totality: A Macro-Monetary Interpretation of Marx's Logic in Capital and the End of the 'Transformation Problem'* (Haymarket, 2016).

Moseley F. and Campbell M. (eds), *New Investigations of Marx's Method* (Humanities Press, 1997).

Moseley F. and Smith T. (eds), *Marx's Capital and Hegel's Logic: A Reexamination* (Haymarket, 2015).

Moss G.S., *Hegel's Foundation Free Metaphysics: The Logic of Singularity* (Routledge, 2022).

Murray P., *Marx's Theory of Scientific Knowledge* (Humanities Press, 1988).

Murray P., 'Marx's "Truly Social" Labour Theory of Value: Part I, Abstract Labour in Marxian Value Theory', *Historical Materialism*, 6/1 (2000a), pp 27–66.

Murray P., 'Marx's "Truly Social" Labour Theory of Value: Part II, How is Labour that is under the Sway of Capital *actually* Abstract?', *Historical Materialism*, 7/1 (2000b), pp 99–136.

Murray P., 'The New Giant's Staircase', *Historical Materialism*, 13/2 (2005), pp 61–83.

Murray P., 'In Defence of the "Third Thing Argument": A Reply to James Furner's "Marx's Critique of Samuel Bailey"', *Historical Materialism*, 14/2 (2006), pp 149–68.

Murray P., *The Mismeasure of Wealth: Essays on Marx and Social Form* (Haymarket, 2017).

Nagy G., 'The Epic Hero', *A Companion to Ancient Epic*, ed. J.M. Foley (Blackwell, 2006), pp 71–89.

Napoleoni C., 'Value and Exploitation: Marx's Economic Theory and Beyond', *Marx and Modern Economic Analysis, Volume 1: Values, Prices and Exploitation*, ed. G.A. Caravale (Edward Elgar, 1991), pp 222–38.

Ng K., *Hegel's Concept of Life: Self-Consciousness, Freedom, Logic* (Oxford University Press, 2020).

Nuzzo A., 'System and History', *The Bloomsbury Companion to Hegel*, ed. A. de Laurentiis and J. Edwards (Bloomsbury, 2013), pp 209–14.

O'Connor B., *Adorno's Negative Dialectic: Philosophy and the Possibility of Critical Rationality* (MIT Press, 2005).
Oliva A., Oliva A. and Novara I., *Marx and Contemporary Critical Theory: The Philosophy of Real Abstraction* (Palgrave Macmillan, 2020).
O'Regan C., *The Heterodox Hegel* (SUNY Press, 1994).
Orléan A., *The Empire of Value: A New Foundation for Economics* (MIT Press, 2014).
Overy R., *Times Complete History of the World* (Times Books, 2015).
Pascal R., 'Property and Society: The Scottish Historical School of the Eighteenth Century', *The Modern Quarterly*, 2 (1938), pp 167–79.
Pilling G., 'The Law of Value in Ricardo and Marx', *Economy and Society*, 1/3 (1972), pp 281–307.
Pilling G., *Marx's Capital: Philosophy and Political Economy* (Routledge & Kegan Paul, 1980).
Pitts F.H., *Critiquing Capitalism Today: New Ways to Read Marx* (Palgrave Macmillan, 2018).
Postone M., *Time, Labor, and Social Domination* (Cambridge University Press, 2003).
Prozorov S., 'The Appropriation of Abandonment: Giorgio Agamben on the State of Nature and the Political', *Continental Philosophy Review*, 42 (2009), pp 327–53.
Prozorov S., *Agamben and Politics: A Critical Introduction* (Edinburgh University Press, 2014a).
Prozorov S., *Ontology and World Politics: Void Universalism I* (Routledge, 2014b).
Prozorov S., *Theory of the Political Subject: Void Universalism II* (Routledge, 2014c).
Prozorov S., 'Carl Schmitt', *Agamben's Philosophical Lineage*, ed. A. Kotsko and C. Salzani (Edinburgh University Press, 2017), pp 87–98.
Ravenhill J. (ed.), *Global Political Economy* (Oxford University Press, 2020).
Redding P., *Continental Idealism: Leibniz to Nietzsche* (Routledge, 2009).
Reichelt H., 'From the Frankfurt School to Value-Form Analysis', *Thesis Eleven*, 4/1 (1982), pp 166–9.
Reichelt H., 'Some Notes on Jacques Bidet's Structuralist Interpretation of Marx', *Common Sense*, 13 (1993), pp 68–75.
Reichelt H., 'Why did Marx Conceal his Dialectical Method?', *Open Marxism, Volume 3: Emancipating Marx*, ed. W. Bonefeld, R. Gunn, J. Holloway and K. Psychopedis (Pluto Press, 1995), pp 40–83.
Reichelt H., 'Social Reality as Appearance: Some Notes on Marx's Conception of Reality', *Human Dignity: Social Autonomy and the Critique of Capitalism*, ed. W. Bonefeld and K. Psychopedis (Ashgate, 2005), pp 31–68.
Reichelt H., 'Marx's Critique of Economic Categories: Reflections on the Problem of Validity in the Dialectical Method of Presentation in *Capital*', *Historical Materialism*, 15/4 (2007), pp 3–52.

Reuten G., 'The Difficult Labor of a Theory of Social Value: Metaphors and Systematic Dialectics at the Beginning of Marx's *Capital*', *Marx's Method in Capital: a Reexamination*, ed. F. Moseley (Humanities Press, 1993), pp 89–114.
Reuten G., 'The Source versus Measure Obstacle in Value Theory', *Rivista di Politica Economica*, 4–5 (1999), pp 87–115.
Reuten G., 'The Interconnection of Systematic Dialectics and Historical Materialism', *Historical Materialism*, 7/1 (2000), pp 137–65.
Reuten G., *The Unity of the Capitalist Economy and State: A Systematic-Dialectical Exposition of the Capitalist System* (Brill, 2019).
Reuten G. and Williams M., *Value-Form and the State: The Tendencies of Accumulation and the Determination of Economic Policy in Capitalist Society* (Routledge, 1989).
Robinson W.I., *A Theory of Global Capitalism: Production, Class, and State in a Transnational World* (Johns Hopkins University Press, 2004).
Robles-Báez M.L., 'On Marx's Dialectic of the Genesis of the Money Form', *International Journal of Political Economy*, 27/3 (1997), pp 35–64.
Roemer J., *Analytical Foundations of Marxian Economic Theory* (Cambridge University Press, 1981).
Roemer J., *Analytical Marxism* (Cambridge University Press, 1986).
Rosdolsky R., *The Making of Marx's 'Capital'* (Pluto Press, 1989).
Rosenberg J.P., 'Basic Problems in the Theory of Uneven and Combined Development. Part II: Unevenness and Political Multiplicity', *Cambridge Review of International Affairs*, 23/1 (2010), pp 165–89.
Rosenberg J.P., 'International Relations in the Prison of Political Science', *International Relations*, 30/2 (2016a), pp 127–53.
Rosenberg J.P., 'Uneven and Combined Development: "The International" in Theory and History', *Historical Sociology and World History: Uneven and Combined Development over the Longue Durée*, ed. A. Anievas and K. Matin (Rowman & Littlefield, 2016b), pp 17–30.
Rubin I.I., *Essays on Marx's Theory of Value* (Black Rose Books, 1973).
Sahlins M., *Culture and Practical Reason* (University of Chicago Press, 1976).
Salzani C., 'From Benjamin's *bloßes Leben* to Agamben's *Nuda Vita*: a Genealogy', *Towards the Critique of Violence: Walter Benjamin and Giorgio Agamben*, ed. B. Moran and C. Salzani (Bloomsbury, 2015), pp 109–24.
Schmidt B.C., 'On the History and Historiography of International Relations', *Handbook of International Relations*, ed. W. Carlsnaes, T. Risse and B.A. Simmons (Sage, 2013), pp 3–28.
Schmitt C., *The Crisis of Parliamentary Democracy* (MIT Press, 1988).
Schmitt C., *The Nomos of the Earth in the International Law of Jus Publicum Europaeum* (Telos Press, 2003).
Schmitt C., *Political Theology: Four Chapters on the Concept of Sovereignty* (University of Chicago Press, 2005).

Schmitt C., *Land and Sea: A World-Historical Meditation*, ed. R.A. Berman and S.G. Zeitlin (Telos Press, 2015).

Sedgwick S., 'Hegel's Critique of Kant: An Overview', *A Companion to Kant*, ed. G. Bird (Blackwell, 2006), pp 473–85.

Sedgwick S., *Hegel's Critique of Kant: From Dichotomy to Identity* (Oxford University Press, 2012).

Sekine T., *The Dialectic of Capital: A Study of the Inner Logic of Capitalism – Volume 1* (Haymarket Books, 2021a).

Sekine T., *The Dialectic of Capital: A Study of the Inner Logic of Capitalism – Volume 2* (Haymarket Books, 2021b).

Shaikh A., 'The Poverty of Algebra', *The Value Controversy*, ed. I. Steedman (Verso, 1981), pp 266–300.

Siep L., *Hegel's Phenomenology of Spirit* (Cambridge University Press, 2021).

Slatkin L.M., 'Homer's *Odyssey*', *A Companion to Ancient Epic*, ed. J.M. Foley (Blackwell, 2006), pp 315–29.

Smith A., *The Wealth of Nations: Books I–III*, ed. A. Skinner (Penguin, 1999).

Smith T., *The Logic of Marx's Capital: Replies to Hegelian Criticisms* (SUNY Press, 1990).

Smith T., 'Value Theory and Dialectics', *Science & Society*, 62/3 (1998), pp 460–70.

Smith T., 'The Relevance of Systematic Dialectics to Marxian Thought: A Reply to Rosenthal', *Historical Materialism*, 4/1 (1999), pp 215–40.

Smith T., 'Hegel: Mystic Dunce or Important Predecessor? A Reply to John Rosenthal', *Historical Materialism*, 10/2 (2002), pp 191–205.

Smith T., 'On the Homology Thesis', *Historical Materialism*, 11/1 (2003), pp 185–94.

Sohn-Rethel A., *Intellectual and Manual Labour: A Critique of Epistemology* (Macmillan, 1978).

Steedman I., *Marx after Sraffa* (NLB, 1977).

Steedman, I. (ed.), *The Value Controversy* (Verso, 1981).

Steedman I., 'The Transformation Problem Again', *Debates in Value Theory*, ed. S. Mohun (Macmillan, 1994), pp 75–81.

Stern R., 'Hegel's Idealism', *The Cambridge Companion to Hegel and Nineteenth-Century Philosophy*, ed F.C. Beiser (Cambridge University Press, 2008), pp 135–73.

Sweezy P., *The Theory of Capitalist Development* (Dennis Dobson, 1946).

Sweezy P., *Socialism* (McGraw-Hill, 1949).

Taylor N., 'Reconstructing Marx on Money and the Measurement of Value', *The Constitution of Capital: Essays on Volume 1 of Marx's Capital*, ed. R. Bellofiore and N. Taylor (Palgrave Macmillan, 2004), pp 88–116.

ten Brink T., *Global Political Economy and the Modern State System* (Haymarket, 2015).

Turner C., 'Under Adorno's Spell: *Bann* as Fundamental Concept rather than mere Metaphor', *New German Critique*, 43/3 (2016), pp 203–22.
Verene D.P., *Hegel's Absolute: An Introduction to Reading the Phenomenology of Spirit* (SUNY Press, 2007).
Verene D.P., *Speculative Philosophy* (Lexington Books, 2009).
Walker R.B.J., *Inside/Outside: International Relations as Political Theory* (Cambridge University Press, 1993).
Walker R.B.J., 'On the Immanence/Imminence of Empire', *Millennium: Journal of International Studies*, 31/2 (2002), pp 337–45.
Walker R.B.J., *After the Globe, before the World* (Routledge, 2010).
Walker R.B.J., *Out of Line: Essays on the Politics of Boundaries and the Limits of Modern Politics* (Routledge, 2016).
Waltz K.N., *Theory of International Politics* (McGraw-Hill, 1979).
Waltz K.N., 'The Emerging Structure of International Politics', *International Security*, 18/2 (1993), pp 44–79.
Waltz K.N., 'Structural Realism after the Cold War', *International Security*, 25/1 (2000), pp 5–41.
Waltz K.N., *Man, the State, and War* (Columbia University Press, 2001).
Waltz K.N., 'International Structure, National Force, and the Balance of World Power', *Realism and International Politics* (Routledge, 2008), pp 137–51.
Watson A., *The Evolution of International Society* (Routledge, 1992).
Wight M., 'The Balance of Power', *Diplomatic Investigations: Essays on the Theory of International Relations*, ed. H. Butterfield and M. Wight (George Allen & Unwin, 1966a), pp 149–75.
Wight M., 'Why is there no International Theory?', *Diplomatic Investigations: Essays on the Theory of International Relations*, ed. H. Butterfield and M. Wight (George Allen & Unwin, 1966b), pp 17–34.
Wight M., *International Theory: The Three Traditions* (Leicester University Press, 1991).
Willaschek M., *Kant on the Sources of Metaphysics* (Cambridge University Press, 2018).
Williams M., 'Why Marx neither has nor needs a Commodity Theory of Money', *Review of Political Economy*, 12/4 (2000), pp 435–51.
Winfield R.D., *Reason and Justice* (SUNY Press, 1988).
Winfield R.D., 'The Method of Hegel's *Science of Logic*', *Essays on Hegel's Logic*, ed. G. di Giovanni (SUNY Press, 1990), pp 45–58.
Winfield R.D., 'The Logic of Marx's *Capital*', *Freedom and Modernity* (SUNY Press, 1991), pp 169–202.
Winfield R.D., *Rethinking Capital* (Palgrave Macmillan, 2016).
Wolfers A., *Discord and Collaboration: Essays on International Politics* (Johns Hopkins University Press, 1965).

Wood E.M., 'The Separation of the Economic and the Political in Capitalism', *New Left Review*, I/127 (May–June 1981), pp 66–95.
Wood E.M., *Empire of Capital* (Verso, 2003).
Wood E.M., 'Logics of Power: A Conversation with David Harvey', *Historical Materialism*, 14/4 (2006), pp 9–34.

Index

References to footnotes show both the page number and the note number (14n37).